MW00804430

NORTH KOREAN HUMAN RIGHTS

The evidentiary weight of North Korean defectors' testimony depicting crimes against humanity has drawn considerable interest from the international community in recent years. Despite the attention to North Korean human rights, what remains unexamined is the rise of the transnational advocacy network, which drew attention to the issue in the first place. Andrew Yeo and Danielle Chubb explore the "hard case" that is North Korea and challenge existing conceptions of transnational human rights networks, how they operate, and why they provoke a response from even the most recalcitrant regimes. In this volume, leading experts and activists assemble original data from multiple sources in various languages, including North Korean sources, and adopt a range of sophisticated methodologies to provide valuable insight into the politics, strategies, and policy objectives of North Korean human rights activism.

Andrew Yeo is Associate Professor of Politics and Director of Asian Studies at The Catholic University of America in Washington DC. He is the author of *Activists, Alliances, and Anti-US Base Protests* and coeditor of *Living in an Age of Mistrust: An Interdisciplinary Study of Declining Trust and How to Get it Back*. He received his PhD in Government from Cornell University.

Danielle Chubb is Senior Lecturer in International Relations and a member of the POLIS research network at Deakin University in Victoria, Australia. She is the author of *Contentious Activism and Inter-Korean Relations*. Before arriving at Deakin in 2012, she worked as a Research Fellow at Pacific Forum CSIS in Honolulu, and completed her PhD in International Relations at The Australian National University.

North Korean Human Rights

ACTIVISTS AND NETWORKS

Edited by

ANDREW YEO

The Catholic University of America

DANIELLE CHUBB

Deakin University, Victoria

CAMBRIDGE
UNIVERSITY PRESS

CAMBRIDGE
UNIVERSITY PRESS

University Printing House, Cambridge CB2 8BS, United Kingdom

One Liberty Plaza, 20th Floor, New York, NY 10006, USA

477 Williamstown Road, Port Melbourne, VIC 3207, Australia

314–321, 3rd Floor, Plot 3, Splendor Forum, Jasola District Centre, New Delhi – 110025, India

79 Anson Road, #06–04/06, Singapore 079906

Cambridge University Press is part of the University of Cambridge.

It furthers the University's mission by disseminating knowledge in the pursuit of education, learning, and research at the highest international levels of excellence.

www.cambridge.org
Information on this title: www.cambridge.org/9781108425490
DOI: 10.1017/9781108589543

© Andrew Yeo and Danielle Chubb 2018

First published 2018

Printed in the United States of America by Sheridan Books, Inc.

A catalogue record for this publication is available from the British Library.

Library of Congress Cataloging-in-Publication Data
NAMES: Yeo, Andrew, 1978– editor. | Chubb, Danielle L., editor.
TITLE: North Korean human rights : activists and networks / edited by Andrew I. Yeo, The Catholic University of America and Danielle Chubb, Deakin University, Victoria.
DESCRIPTION: New York : Cambridge University Press, [2018] | Includes bibliographical references and index.
IDENTIFIERS: LCCN 2018009834 | ISBN 9781108425490 (alk. paper)
SUBJECTS: LCSH: Human rights – Korea (North) | Human rights – Korea (North) – International cooperation. | Human rights workers – Korea (North)
CLASSIFICATION: LCC JC599.K7 N68 2018 | DDC 323.09513–dc23
LC record available at https://lccn.loc.gov/2018009834

ISBN 978-1-108-42549-0 Hardback

For our children, Joshua and Joyce, and
Jarrah and Karri

Contents

Figures

Tables

Notes on Contributors

Celeste L. Arrington is Korea Foundation Assistant Professor of Political Science and International Affairs at the George Washington University. She specializes in comparative politics, with a focus on law and social movements, the media, policymaking processes, transnational activism, historical justice, and the Koreas and Japan. She is the author of *Accidental Activists: Victim Movements and Government Accountability in Japan and South Korea* (2016). She has been a fellow at Princeton's Law and Public Affairs Program, the Institute for Advanced Study, and Harvard's Program on US–Japan Relations. She received her PhD from the University of California, Berkeley.

Jieun Baek is a PhD candidate in Public Policy at the University of Oxford. Previously, she was a research fellow at the Belfer Center for Science and International Affairs at Harvard University where she wrote *North Korea's Hidden Revolution: How the Information Underground is Transforming a Closed Society* (2016). Baek also worked at Google, where, among other roles, she served as Google Ideas' North Korea expert. She received both her BA and MPP from Harvard University.

Danielle Chubb is Senior Lecturer in International Relations and a member of the POLIS research network at Deakin University in Victoria, Australia. She is the author of *Contentious Activism and Inter-Korean Relations* (2014), which examines the historical evolution of South Korean discourse over the issues of human rights, democracy, and unification. Danielle received her PhD from The Australian National University.

Sandra Fahy is an Associate Professor of Anthropology in the Faculty of Liberal Arts at Sophia University, Tokyo, Japan. She is the author of *Marching through Suffering: Loss and Survival in North Korea* (2015), among other publications. Her forthcoming book is titled *Without Parallel: Our Style Human Rights and North Korea*. She received her PhD in

Anthropology from the School of Oriental and African Studies at the University of London, and her MA in Interdisciplinary Anthropology, History, and Literature from York University.

Patricia Goedde is Associate Professor at Sungkyunkwan University, School of Law, in Seoul, Korea. She has published in journals including *Human Rights Quarterly*, *Fordham International Law Journal*, *Clinical Law Review*, and *Korea Observer* on topics related to human rights in North Korea, the North Korean legal system, public interest law clinics, refugee advocacy, and due process rights for detainees. Goedde also serves on the board of directors for the Korea Human Rights Foundation. She received her PhD and JD from the University of Washington School of Law, and is a licensed attorney of the Washington State Bar Association.

Joanna Hosaniak is Deputy Director of Citizens' Alliance for North Korean Human Rights (NKHR) in Seoul, where she has worked since 2004, and Lecturer at the Underwood College, Yonsei University. Hosaniak led international advocacy to establish the UN Commission of Inquiry for the Democratic People's Republic of Korea (DPRK) and the UN Panel of Experts on Accountability for the DPRK. Born in Warsaw, Poland, Hosaniak received her MA in Korean Studies from Warsaw University and her PhD in International Studies from Sogang University, South Korea, where she studied the issue of addressing past crimes in the former communist countries in Europe.

Rajiv Narayan is Director of Policy at the International Commission Against the Death Penalty, and Senior Consultant Adviser at the Rafto Foundation. Prior to that, he worked for 13 years at Amnesty International, researching and reporting extensively on North Korea, South Korea, and Japan. He was also a visiting professor at the Graduate School of International Studies at Yonsei University in Seoul, South Korea. He received his PhD from the University of London.

Jacob Reidhead is a PhD candidate in Sociology and Korea Studies at Stanford University. His research models informal political organization in South Korea and studies the coevolution of these political networks alongside domestic debates on North Korea policy. In 2008, he was a Food Monitor for aid being sent to North Korea for Mercy Corps. He has an MA in Sociology from the University of Washington, an MS in Statistics from The Ohio State University, and a BS in Mathematics from Arizona State University.

Jay Song is Senior Lecturer at the Asia Institute of the University of Melbourne, Australia, and Global Ethics Fellow of the Carnegie Council for

Ethics in International Affairs in New York. Prior to her current positions, she was the Director of Migration and Border Policy at the Lowy Institute (Sydney) and Assistant Professor of Political Science at Singapore Management University. She is the author of *Human Rights Discourse in North Korea: Post-Colonial, Marxist and Confucian Perspectives* (2010). She received her PhD in Politics and International Studies from the University of Cambridge.

Andrew Yeo is Associate Professor of Politics, Director of Asian Studies, and a Fellow at the Institute for Policy Research and Catholic Studies at The Catholic University of America in Washington DC. He is the author of *Activists, Alliances, and Anti-US Base Protests* (2011) and coeditor of *Living in an Age of Mistrust: An Interdisciplinary Study of Declining Trust and How to Get it Back* (2017). His research interests include international relations theory, East Asian regionalism, the formation of beliefs and worldviews, civil society and social movements, and Korean politics. Yeo received his PhD in Government from Cornell University and his BA with distinction in Psychology and International Studies from Northwestern University.

Foreword

These things shall be: a loftier race
Than e'er the world hath known shall rise
With flame of freedom in their souls
And light of knowledge in their eyes

At about the time that I was taught to sing the above hymn at school, written by John Addington Symonds,[1] I received from my teacher a copy of the newly adopted *Universal Declaration of Human Rights* (UDHR).[2] It had been brought into effect at a meeting of the recently created General Assembly of the United Nations. In the chair at the time was Dr. H. V. Evatt, the chief Australian delegate. He had been a judge but when war came he resigned, entered politics, and became a leading minister in the government of Australia. He was elected the third president of the UN General Assembly. He had played an important role in the negotiations that led to the adoption of the UN Charter in 1945. He was one of the Charter Generation. Presiding in the General Assembly on December 10, 1948, he declared the UDHR adopted. He said it was a "Magna Carta" of the new age.

Hymns were not normally sung in Australian public schools. However, Addington's hymn was approved as sufficiently secular because it contained few references to God. Its sentiments were particularly attractive to the Charter Generation.

The Charter Generation was inspired by feelings of idealism. Those feelings grew out of the terrible state of the world in 1945. The huge loss of human life, the destruction of cities and economies, the disclosure of the Holocaust, and the widespread crimes against humanity instilled a commitment to

---

[1] J. A. Symonds (1840–93) "These Things Shall Be" (1891). See https://hymnary.org/text/these_things_shall_be_a_loftier_race.
[2] UN General Assembly A(iii) of December 10, 1948 (UDHR).

xv

building a better world. Likewise, the detonation of nuclear weapons over Hiroshima and Nagasaki, Japan, in August 1945, with unprecedented loss of life and suffering, propelled the United Nations with a great sense of urgency. The mushroom cloud, caused by the detonation of the nuclear weapons, burned an eidetic image into our minds. Unless the world could respond to the challenges, and build a better global order, the dangers and the continuation of conflict and further crimes against humanity seemed likely to become the terminal heritage of humankind.

It was in this atmosphere that the United Nations Charter[3] was adopted. Originally, it was intended to include a bill of universal rights. However, the drafters ran out of time. A drafting committee was thus created to do the drafting. That committee was chaired by Eleanor Roosevelt, widow of the wartime president of the United States of America. It included many important scholars, including René Cassin (France) and P. C. Chang (China). The senior officer of its secretariat was John Humphrey of Canada. I came to know Professor Humphrey in the 1980s when we both served in the International Commission of Jurists in Geneva. It was he who wrote the first version of the UDHR, including the stirring words of the first article:[4]

> All human beings are born free and equal in dignity and rights. They are endowed with reason and conscience and should act towards one another in a spirit of brotherhood.

In the world of the Charter Generation, where ideals were mixed with practical necessities, universal human rights definitely had a vital place. Human rights were listed among the first preambular objectives of the United Nations Organisation. They became one of the pillars upon which the Organisation was to be based. The Charter Generation envisaged peace and security that would be guarded and upheld by the Security Council. They accepted special voting rights for the designated great powers.[5] Following the successful prosecution of the War by the Allies, it was expected that those powers would act responsibly and protectively, as a result of from their special position and extra powers. They would help to protect the world from endless involvement in destructive wars.

According to this view, the General Assembly, where all nations had equal voting rights, would reflect the wisdom and broad directions of humanity, expressed by the nation states. Those states would themselves recognize that the UN Charter was established in the name of the "Peoples of the United

---

[3]   UN Charter, June 26, 1945, 59 STAT. 1031; TS 993, entered into force October 24, 1945.
[4]   UDHR, Art 1.   [5]   UN Charter Art 27.3 ("veto" provision).

Nations."[6] The UDHR specifically envisaged the treaty law that was later to evolve, converting the language of the UDHR into binding legal requirements. It was expected that the nations would faithfully fulfill these obligations. Special procedures were developed and the Human Rights Council (HRC) evolved from the Human Rights Commission. By procedures designed for the scrutiny of state conduct, including by the later developed system of Universal Periodic Review (UPR), it was hoped that every nation would be subjected to regular, neutral, and expert scrutiny. Their conduct would be measured against the established standards of the United Nations.

The Charter Generation certainly envisaged that nation states, at home, would foster knowledge of, and commitment to, universal human rights. They would do so through the participation of active civil society organizations, both national and international, and by free exchange of knowledge and opinions resulting from enhanced travel, dialogue, broadcasting, and other media. When the world was concerned about the state of human rights for peace and security, the United Nations could be relied on to intervene prudently. Blue helmets would guard transitional or dangerous circumstances. The nonproliferation of nuclear weapons would be upheld by international law. And the International Court of Justice would lay down requirements for peace, security, and justice, including by the destruction of nuclear armaments and the prohibition on the use, or threat of use, of such weapons.[7]

These were some of the ideals that, it was hoped, would protect the world against the repetition of war crimes, genocide, and crimes against humanity. Such crimes, along with damage to the environment, unyielding poverty, and other dangers, would threaten the very survival of the human species if they were not addressed. The Charter Generation believed that the world would embrace a new legal order:

> Nation with nation, land with land
> Unarmed shall live with comrades free.
> In every heart and brain shall throb
> The pulse of one fraternity

Sadly, although much has been achieved, the dreams that accompanied the Charter have not been attained. During and after the Cold War, the special voting rights of the great powers were misused. The Security Council was logjammed and often incapable of enforcing peace with justice. The General

---

[6] UN Charter begins, "We the Peoples of the United Nations . . . ."
[7] International Court of Justice, Advisory Opinion on the Legality of the Threat or Use of Nuclear Weapons (1996) 2 ICJ 2.

Assembly became too frequently bogged down in global and regional geopolitics. The Human Rights Commission, and then the HRC, on many occasions fell victim to regionalism, and often radically different notions of the meaning of human rights and how to attain them.

While many civil society organizations – both national and international – arose and worked with the HRC and its officeholders, some were opposed to a global consensus on human rights. Some saw the UDHR, treaty law, and the HRC itself as Western inventions enforcing Western values. Specifically, some rejected steps that would try to render accountable the perpetrators of international crimes. In many countries, national and international civil society organizations faced hostile retaliation from their own states. Ordinary citizens would often fail to express, or even hear, voices raised to condemn violations of human rights and to demand redress. While international human rights bodies have sprung up and played a most useful role in stimulating, supporting, implementing, and enforcing the United Nations human rights machinery, often that machinery has been fragmented. Commonly, it has been poorly funded. Sometimes it is targeted by hostile laws designed to undermine such operations. Occasionally, such bodies are in conflict with each other, because of different values, distinctive methodologies, or mutual jealously.

Yet many civil society organizations, both national and international, are dedicated to universal human rights. They share a common objective to end crimes against humanity and human rights abuses and to render those responsible answerable for such wrongs. They aim to progress from mere condemnation to active accountability. But all too often this presents an impossible challenge. The consequent failures and weaknesses have imperiled still further the dreams of the Charter Generation.

This book seeks to place under scrutiny a particular case: human rights in the Democratic People's Republic of Korea (North Korea). It seeks to examine the work of national and international civil society organizations. It chronicles the people who have escaped from great wrongs and shared their stories. It describes the United Nations agencies and institutions in order to extract practical and theoretical lessons presented by the case of North Korea. Inevitably, that case offers lessons both for the states themselves and for the global community.

The editors and authors of this book are too young to have been members of the Charter Generation. Nevertheless, they reveal themselves, for the most part, as practical and worldly enough to accept the importance of international human rights doctrine. They understand and accept the grave departures shown to exist in North Korea. They see the need for the international community to be more successful in tackling the established instances of human rights violations than it has been in the past.

On March 21, 2013, at its 22nd session, the HRC established a Commission of Inquiry on Human Rights in DPRK (COI). There was no call for a vote on the proposal. This was the only time that this has occurred in the creation of such a COI.[8] On May 7, 2013, I was appointed to chair the COI. I joined Marzuki Darusman of Indonesia, the Special Rapporteur on DPRK, who under the HRC resolution, was ex officio a member. Sonja Biserko of Serbia, an expert on crimes against humanity and genocide, was the third member. In accordance with our mandate, the COI resolved to adopt a novel, transparent, and technologically friendly methodology.[9] The COI report was produced within the timeframe set by the HRC. It was presented to that body on February 7, 2014.

Denied cooperation with or admission to North Korea, the COI had to rely on the testimony of escapees who had fled to the Republic of Korea (South Korea). Most of them gave their testimony openly, in public. Filmed images of such evidence was uploaded to the Internet. There is a great deal of attention given in this book to the evidence of these "defectors" concerning conditions in North Korea. As explained, there have been occasional cases of false or exaggerated testimony. This had led to criticisms of the testimony as a whole.[10] However, given the refusal of North Korea to cooperate and the fearsome punishments imposed on suspected enemies of the state within North Korea, the use of such escapee testimony was unavoidable and indeed essential.

Criticism by North Korea of the COI's witnesses was to be expected. However, the so-called scholarly criticism strikes me as mostly unpersuasive. The testimony before the COI is available on the Internet for the whole world to see and evaluate. Having sat through hours of this testimony, as it was given, I believe that it was overwhelmingly truthful and convincing. The picture disclosed is shocking. The human rights abuses that are revealed need to be addressed urgently.[11]

The impediments that North Korea placed in the way of gathering reliable and accurate evidence of its wrongdoings were partly physical (limitations on movement within and out of the country). But they were also partly

[8] C. Henderson (ed.) *Commissions of Inquiry: Problems and Prospects* (Oxford/Bloomsbury: Hart Publishing, 2017), xi.

[9] A/HRC/25/crp.1.

[10] Jay Song, "Unreliable Witnesses: The Challenge of Separating Truth from Fiction When It Comes to North Korea," available at www.policyforum.net/unreliable-witnesses/.

[11] G. J. Evans, *The Responsibility to Protect – Ending Mass Atrocity Crimes Once and for All.* Washington DC: Brookings Institution Press, 2008.

technological (the deprivation of telephone, postal, or other telecommunications; the absence of radio, television, film, and other media). And they were also partly psychological (a number of escapee witnesses described saturation propaganda, and many spoke of the overwhelming pressures imposed by one-sided information, adulatory of the regime). The report was powerful and convincing. The proof of the pudding lies in the very strong votes that followed in the HRC, the General Assembly, and even, when it was placed on the agenda by a procedural resolution, the Security Council.[12]

Until recently, I did not know of the effort that went into the initial adoption of the HRC resolution, creating the COI. That effort naturally engaged key member states of the United Nations, in both the HRC and the General Assembly. However, a number of important member states did not, at first, support the creation of a COI. Most significantly, South Korea and Japan, two crucial players, were opposed. It was only the indefatigable work of international civil society organizations, mostly based in Geneva, which pursued the idea relentlessly, that won success. I pay tribute to the efforts of many of the nongovernmental actors, including especially one of the chapter authors of this book, Joanna Hosaniak of Citizens' Alliance for North Korean Human Rights (NKHR) based in Seoul (see Chapter 6).[13] The way civil society secured a COI that would speak to the world of great wrongs is an exciting story showing the intelligent and effective interaction between governmental and nongovernmental players.

Some of the writers in this book raise what they see as the "core challenge" arising from the modalities of UN human rights procedures (including COI reports). They suggest that the procedures commonly undermine the practical attainment of improvements in the human rights landscape of a country such as North Korea. If a country is totalitarian in its government and controls strictly any access to witnesses and places of oppression, why would it ever agree to submit voluntarily to accountability for proved wrongs? Does such a process (whether in the International Criminal Court, a special tribunal, or anywhere else) not threaten the very continuance of the regime in the country concerned? Would they ever agree to this? Why would they not resist it and obstruct it?

Still, noncooperation does not exempt humanity from the obligation to investigate, record, reveal, and prosecute crimes against humanity and human

---

[12] M. D. Kirby "United Nations Report on North Korea and the Security Council: Interface of Security and Human Rights" (2015) 89 *Australian Law Journal*, 714.

[13] M. D. Kirby "North Korea and the Madonna of Czestochowa" in *The University of Notre Dame Australia Law Review*, 19, 2017: 1–13.

rights violations as can be proved to the requisite standard of proof.[14] The COI having received a mandate from UN HRC, we did not enjoy the luxury of ignoring the testimony or declining to provide its report. As an appeal to history and as a record for the later establishment of truth, UN mandate-holders are obliged to do their best. They must not be deflected. They should not gild the lily in the hope that a "soft" report might gain a tiny measure of improvement. In accordance with the UN Charter, each of the goals of the Organisation has to be pursued at the same time – peace and security, but also human rights. The national and transnational civil society organizations described in this book are bound to develop a professional expertise in seemingly paradoxical thinking and in contradictory strategies.

There is now considerable objective evidence that the publication of the COI report on North Korea did in fact produce some important changes within that country. The improvements may be seen in the moves by North Korea to participate, for the first time, in the procedures of Universal Periodic Review in the HRC.[15] Yet it goes further than this. This year the international community obtained a rare insight into the thinking of the upper echelons of North Korean's officialdom. Their Deputy Ambassador in London, Thae Yong-ho, disappeared from his post and turned up in Seoul. His subsequent interviews are all the more powerful because they are understated. In a 2017 talk for the Center for Strategic and International Studies in Washington DC, he advocated insistence on human rights and security in North Korea while at the same time urging an increase in dialogue between the two Koreas. His perspective appears close, in some respects, to that of the newly elected president of the Republic of Korea, Moon Jae-in. Several of the contributions to this book help to enlighten non-Koreans about the internal political dis-agreements within South Korea concerning the best way to make progress in dealings with the North and in achieving improvements on the ground. This is enlightenment of great value.

The United Nations is imperfect because it is a human institution. The COI on North Korea was also, no doubt, flawed in particular ways. Had there been more time for the preparation of its report, it might have been a little different. Whether, as some authors in this book have suggested, the report took North Korea to a different level on the "spiral" theory or the "boomerang" theory, by which human rights processes are theorized, the

---

[14] The standard of proof adopted by the COI is explained in the COI report A/HRC/25/crp.1 at 15–17, paras 63–78.
[15] Sun-young Choi, et al., *The UN Universal Periodic Review and the DPRK: Monitoring of North Korea's Implementation of Recommendations*, Database Center for North Korean Human Rights (NKDB), Seoul, 2017.

world is a better place for the disclosures that the COI presented to the HRC and the world. The openness of the COI procedures would have been much less effective if there had been no national and transnational organizations to energize, follow-up, and insist upon the scrutiny of human rights abuses and to demand accountability for the wrongs.

I congratulate the civil society organizations described in this book. They have made the United Nations' human rights enterprise more useful and practical than it would otherwise have been. I acknowledge the criticisms ventured and the questions asked in this book. They are essential to continuing the task envisaged by the aspirations of the UN Charter. It is important to have the range of perspectives collected in this book – not only for the case of North Korea, but for all other countries facing serious human rights challenges. However, North Korea is a very special case. This is partly because of its recent developments in the technology of nuclear weapons and in the creation of sophisticated missiles that could deliver those weapons over great distances. Unless the world responds effectively to the peril that is presented by North Korea, the dangers to human survival are great. But if the perils on the part of North Korea are not resolved, larger dangers will surely present before too long from other countries. And unless the crimes against humanity and other human rights abuses found by the COI in North Korea are not addressed effectively, peace and security on the Korean peninsula cannot be assured.

Just as the UN Charter envisaged, universal human rights, peace and security, and international justice are intimately intertwined. That is why the COI report on North Korea remains highly relevant to the world today. It is why the transnational organizations described in this book remain crucial for finding the solutions – and for questioning those adherents to the idealism of the Charter who presume to offer some of the ways forward.

The Hon. Michael Kirby AC CMG*
Sydney, Australia
December 10, 2017

---

* Chair of the United Nations Human Rights Council's Commission of Inquiry on Human Rights Violations in the Democratic People's Republic of Korea (2013–14); Justice of the High Court of Australia (1996–2009); President of the International Commission of Jurists (1995–98).

Preface and Acknowledgments

The grave situation of North Korean human rights has drawn significant attention from activists and policymakers around the world. Numerous NGO reports, journalistic accounts, and personal narratives of defectors have helped shape our understanding of the human rights situation in this closed society. Perhaps for these reasons, then, the scholarly literature on North Korean human rights has remained relatively thin. The weight of evidence chronicling human rights abuses is already extensive, and the closed nature of the country also poses additional barriers for scholars seeking to conduct original and reliable research on North Korea.

Nevertheless, we expect scholarship on North Korean human rights to grow. In particular, the rising number of North Korean defectors in the past two decades has opened a small window through which to peer into North Korea. Specifically, defectors' insights and testimonies have enabled researchers to systematically collect information pertaining to human rights abuses and assess the prospects for social and political change in North Korea.

While the role of defectors has been heralded as a positive development for both North Korean human rights advocacy and scholarship, as social scientists we must still critically examine the evidence we collect and how it is collected, and then weigh it against potentially confounding or contradictory information. Doing so provides a level of assurance that we retain some degree of objectivity in our analysis and are not simply confirming our own biases. To that end, a special issue of *Critical Asian Studies* on North Korean human rights, led by Christine Hong and Hazel Smith, has pushed scholars to think much more critically about North Korean human rights while advancing alternative perspectives which together challenge, if not undermine, the dominant narrative of human rights. Although we disagree with some of their findings (which we address in the Conclusion to this volume), we acknowledge their work upfront to highlight scholarly debate in the inquiry of North Korean human rights, even as facts on the ground – gross human rights violations taking place in North Korea – remain undeniable. With the exception of the North Korean regime, very few people will deny that such abuses exist. As we argue in our book, however, what one does with those facts, how they are interpreted, and how one responds to the knowledge of human rights violations is politically contested.

This book is fundamentally about the politics of North Korean human rights and the advocacy networks which have advanced this issue domestically and internationally. We do not focus on North Korean human rights in and of themselves – which, as discussed above, have been well-documented by NGOs, activists, and defectors (and in a forthcoming book, Without Parallel: North Korea's "Our Style" Human Rights by our close collaborator Sandra Fahy) – but rather on the North Korean human rights transnational advocacy network. As such, the primary actors in our book are the activists, NGOs, states, lawmakers, and intergovernmental institutions which comprise the network. Our book is aimed at revealing different coalitions and cleavages within domestic and transnational networks, as well as the relationship between human rights actors and the North Korean regime. Unique to this network is the role of North Korean defectors who, in the absence of civil society inside North Korea, provide valuable information about rights abuses and lend greater credibility to the transnational advocacy movement. As such, in addition to studying North Korean human rights movements, this book seeks to expand our theoretical understanding of transnational advocacy networks, including their efficacy and limits.

Beyond scholarship, this book is a reflection of transnational friendships. It came to fruition out of our overlapping scholarly and personal interests in North Korea. Two other friends, Sandra Fahy and Jay Song, have been close collaborators with us on this project from its inception. Although their names do not appear on the book cover, their influence, particularly as it pertains to the inclusion of discourse and human rights, is apparent throughout the volume.

Our project originated out of a conversation in November 2014 between one of the editors (Andrew) and Jay Song about the need to explore network ties between North Korean human rights defectors, activists, and NGOs. The conversation continued online as the two then roped in Danielle and Sandra to discuss how one might understand the emergence and trajectory of North Korean human rights advocacy by way of examining the evolution of human rights discourse. During dozens of email conversations and Skype conference calls connecting us across four different time zones (Washington, Singapore, Tokyo, and Melbourne), the four of us developed a research grant proposal in early 2015, with Andrew and Danielle as coprincipal investigators. The group was awarded a two-year research grant from the Korea Foundation in April 2015.

This project was a major commitment in terms of time, resources, and energy, and we (Andrew and Danielle, speaking now as coeditors of this volume) would not have pulled through were it not for our close collaboration and friendship. As with any coedited project, it helped to share the burden of writing, editing, event planning, and chasing up contributors. Sitting at opposite sides of the International Date Line, we literally worked on this project around the clock, with Danielle signing off at night just as Andrew started for the day. We were also fortunate in that our intellectual approaches to the study of transnational advocacy movements aligned fairly closely, thus avoiding the potential for sharp intellectual disagreements. Beyond the practical and intellectual rewards of coediting, however, what made this collaboration truly special was the understanding and transparency we shared and the encouragement we offered to one other in our perpetual struggle to obtain the optimal work–life balance in our respective lives. It is a true blessing to join forces with a collaborator who values productivity, but who also understands the great importance of family.

Needless to say, the successful completion of this multiyear project required the support of a much wider network beyond the two of us. We are grateful to the Korea Foundation, and, in particular, the efforts of Ms. Seayoun Lee, who remained a strong advocate of this project from the start to its finish. Frankly, this project would not have become a reality without her guidance and representation on our behalf, and the generous financial support from the Korea Foundation which followed.

Despite the close camaraderie developed over the past several years, it is hard to believe that we (the volume editors) have met in person only twice in our lives. Although in the digital age much work can be conducted via cyberspace (at this point, we have exchanged thousands of emails and chat messages, communicating almost daily over the past six months), it still cannot replace the value of direct interaction. We therefore benefited immensely from two meetings held at different stages of the project, allowing us and our contributors to present draft papers and circulate ideas. In June 2015, we organized a closed, two-day workshop in Melbourne, Australia, hosted by the Alfred Deakin Research Institute for Citizenship and Globalisation (ADI) at Deakin University. The workshop, held in the depths of a Melbourne winter, would not have been possible without the terrific administrative support we received from ADI. We extend our gratitude especially to Cayla Edwards, for her ongoing support and advice, as well as ADI director

Fethi Mansouri, who opened our workshop and has been supportive of this endeavor since its inception. Thanks also to Jo Collins, whose able administrative support ensured, among other things, that all our participants caught the right flights at the right times. We are grateful to have had the able research assistance, during the workshop, of Julia Richardson, whose notetaking was enhanced by her knowledge of transnational activism. Moreover, we are particularly thankful to our external discussants, David Hundt, Roland Bleiker, and Leonid Petrov, who took time out of their busy schedules to read our papers, attend the workshop, and provide feedback and advice on the project in its early days. Beyond the workshop, extra research assistance was provided by Michael Hatherell, who wrangled with the Issue Crawler software to help with developing intranetwork maps for this project, which form the core of the analysis in Chapter 8.

In October 2016, we held a much larger public conference in Washington DC, hosted by the Institute for Policy Research and Catholic Studies (IPR) at The Catholic University of America, to disseminate our findings and facilitate a broader policy discussion on North Korean human rights activism. The next day, we held a closed, internal workshop with only our paper contributors to provide/solicit feedback on draft papers and move forward with plans toward book publication. We are grateful to all those who served and provided useful feedback in their capacity as panel chair, discussant, and/or roundtable participant at our Washington conference. This group includes Jennifer Hadden, Tsveta Petrova, Celeste L. Arrington, Victor Cha, Roberta Cohen, Kathy Moon, Greg Scarlatoiu, Frank Jannuzi, and Marcus Noland. We want to especially thank Stephan Haggard, who not only delivered the keynote address at the conference, but, as a true mentor among junior colleagues, stopped by our book workshop the following morning to listen in and provide invaluable advice on putting together a coedited volume. We extend our deep thanks to the staff at IPR, including Woinishet Negash, Lydia Andrews, and Dan Petri, who worked closely with Andrew behind the scenes for months to plan and execute our international conference. The numerous compliments we received regarding our conference reflect their hard work. Accolades also go to Nicholas Hamisevicz, who assisted with conference logistics, but, more importantly, provided research support and transcribed notes during the conference and book workshop. Likewise, Allison Kim, an undergraduate student at Georgetown University at the time, proved to be a truly amazing and highly capable research assistant. During her two-year tenure, she observed protests, compiled data, and learned new software to analyze qualitative data. Ralph Albano, Associate Provost for Research, and John Schmidt, in the office of sponsored accounting, offered their guidance in managing our grant budget. Thank you!

We thank each of our contributors not only for their chapter contributions and commitment to our project, but also for sharing their important insights with the entire group. In addition to these authors, we recognize Mikyoung Kim, who participated in our Melbourne and Washington DC workshops, and Young Hoon Song, who joined our conversation in Melbourne. Over the past two years, our conversations and correspondences with all of our contributors, both individually and collectively, have deepened our understanding of North Korean human rights advocacy, discourse, and transnational activism. Our project would not have achieved the high standard we strived toward without their expert knowledge, input, cooperation and, most importantly, enthusiasm. This has been an outstanding team to work with, and we can only hope that all our future collaborations are as cheerful, supportive, and positive as this one. As inexperienced editors, we were probably more demanding and "hands-on" than one might anticipate for an edited volume project, so thank you for your forbearance. Nevertheless, we hope this has been as rewarding an experience for our contributors as it was for us. We certainly appreciate the good humor of our contributors during the intensive editorial process.

Several friends read and commented on different parts of the manuscript. We thank Phillip Ayoub, Jennifer Hadden (again), and our contributors Sandra Fahy and Patricia Goedde for giving us feedback and encouragement. At an earlier stage, Hyung-Gu Lynn also provided invaluable advice about building internal coherence among chapters. We also received excellent suggestions from two anonymous reviewers, which helped us frame our introductory chapter (Chapter 1) and sharpen the book's focus on transnational advocacy.

Helping us reach the finish line have been the fantastic team at Cambridge University Press, especially our editor, John Berger in the New York office, and on the production side, Matt Sweeney and Mathivathini Mareesan. Back in Melbourne, we thank Martine Hawkes for her superb editorial support, and again extend thanks to the Alfred Deakin Institute for supporting the production of the final product. In South Korea, we are grateful to Su Min Ahn for granting us permission to use her powerful artwork for our book cover design, and thank Greg Samborski for providing us the photograph of the image.

We would be remiss not to take a moment to thank the many activists who not only dedicate much of their personal and professional lives to the cause of North Korean human rights, but who have also talked to us about their work many times over the past decade. Here, especially, we want to acknowledge

Greg Scarlatoiu, Roberta Cohen, Suzanne Scholte, Henry Song, and Joanna Hosaniak for the time they have taken to provide us with insights about the work they do through their respective organizations. This has taken many forms: conversations, emails, research interviews, and supporting our participant–observer attendance at events or meetings.

Finally, but very importantly, we thank our families, who chugged along with us for several years on this project. Our spouses will probably remember us being, at times, aloof, distracted, or absent. Our little ones (four children under the age of five, between us) will probably have early memories of us typing away in front of our computers in a major effort to meet deadlines. We hope one day our children will recognize the importance of this sort of research, which is bigger than any one of us. Andrew would like to thank Joshua and Joyce for being as patient as one might expect for any child under the age of five, and trying very hard not to interrupt Daddy during his work time. The two of you are my joy. None of this could have been accomplished, of course without Yoon's moral support and prayers behind the scenes. Danielle also thanks her two little ones, Jarrah and Karri, who somehow never complained when Mummy had to go to work on the weekend, or sometimes couldn't be home to tuck them into bed. And to the wonderful Bret, whose cheery patience and support has made it all possible.

Washington DC and Melbourne, Australia
September 2017

Note on Transliteration

Throughout this book we employ the Revised Romanization system of transliteration, except in cases where words or names have their own divergent, widely used spelling, such as Seoul or Kim Jong Un. For transliteration of Japanese text in Chapter 4, we use the modified Hepburn system with macrons for long vowels. For commonly referenced words or names the conventional spelling is used.

Abbreviations

AI	Amnesty International
APPG	All-Party Parliamentary Group on North Korea
CEDAW	Convention on the Elimination of Discrimination Against Women
COI	Commission of Inquiry on Human Rights
COMJAN	Investigation Commission on Missing Japanese Probably Related to North Korea
CPR	Civil and political rights
CR	Congressional record
CSIS	Center for Strategic and International Studies
CSOs	Civil society organizations
CSW	Christian Solidarity Worldwide
DFF	Defense Forum Foundation
DPRK	Democratic People's Republic of Korea
DUP	Democratic United Party
EAHRNK	European Alliance for Human Rights in North Korea
ESCR	Economic, social, and cultural rights
EU	European Union
EUFreeNK	Free North Korean Association in EU
FA	Swedish, Danish, Norwegian, and Icelandic football associations
FIFA	Fédération Internationale de Football Association
FNKR	FreeNK Radio
HRC	UN Human Rights Council
HRNK	Committee for Human Rights in North Korea
HRW	Human Rights Watch
HRWF	Human Rights Without Frontiers
ICC	International criminal court

ICNK	International Coalition to Stop Crimes Against Humanity in North Korea
IGOs	Intergovernmental organizations
ILO	International labor organization
INGOs	International nongovernmental organizations
JFBA	Japan Federation of Bar Association
KCNA	Korean Central News Agency
LDA	Latent Dirichlet Analysis
LFNKR	Life Funds for North Korean Refugees
LiNK	Liberty in North Korea
NED	National Endowment for Democracy
NGOs	Nongovernmental organizations
NKAHRA	North Korean Abductions and Human Rights Act
NKDB	Database Center for North Korean Human Rights
NKFC	North Korea Freedom Coalition
NKFW	North Korea Freedom Week
NKHR	Citizens' Alliance for North Korean Human Rights (also: Citizen's Alliance)
NKIS	North Korea Intellectuals Solidarity
NKnet	Network for North Korean Democracy and Human Rights
OHCHR	Office of the United Nations High Commissioner for Human Rights
PvdA	Dutch Labor Party
ROK	Republic of Korea
UN	United Nations
UNGA	UN General Assembly
UNSC	UN Security Council
UPP	United Progressive Party
UPR	Universal periodic review

Adaptive Activism
Transnational Advocacy Networks and the Case of North Korea

Danielle Chubb and Andrew Yeo

The international community must accept its responsibility to protect the people of the Democratic People's Republic of Korea from crimes against humanity, because the Government of the Democratic People's Republic of Korea has manifestly failed to do so.

Report of the Commission of Inquiry on Human Rights in the Democratic People's Republic of Korea[1]

On March 21, 2013, the United Nations Human Rights Council established the Commission of Inquiry on Human Rights in the Democratic People's Republic of Korea (DPRK). The UN Commission of Inquiry on Human Rights (COI) was tasked to investigate "the systematic, widespread and grave violations of human rights in the DPRK, with a view to ensuring full accountability."[2] One year later, the COI released its report. In a powerful statement, the Chair of the Commission declared that "the gravity, scale, duration and nature of the unspeakable atrocities committed in the country reveal a totalitarian state that does not have any parallel in the contemporary world."[3] The report found that these human rights violations "arise from policies at the highest level of the State" and amount to "ongoing crimes

---

[1]   UN Human Rights Council 2014, sect. V.
[2]   These findings include, but are not limited to: violations of the freedoms of thought, expression, and religion (where the state claims "an absolute monopoly over information and total control of organized social life"); violations of the right to food, stemming largely from discrimination, state restrictions on food aid delivery, and prioritization of resources toward military spending even in times of mass starvation; and arbitrary detention, torture, and execution, with people found guilty of political crimes "disappeared" into political prison camps where "the inmate population has been gradually eliminated through deliberate starvation, forced labor, executions, torture, rape and the denial of reproductive rights." For the complete findings, see UN Human Rights Council 2014.
[3]   UN Human Rights Council 2014.

against humanity … which our generation must tackle urgently and collectively."[4]

The COI's report, released in March 2014, marked an important juncture for North Korean human rights advocacy and represented the culmination of years of dedicated transnational advocacy on behalf of North Korean human rights. The most immediate effect of the COI report was the profile it gave the issue of North Korean human rights. Once a subject relegated to the sidelines and considered secondary to the important statecraft of security and nuclear diplomacy, the human rights situation in North Korea was broadcast to the world. There is now little doubt remaining as to the legitimacy of the claim that horrific violations take place inside the country on a daily basis.

While much has been revealed about human rights in North Korea, far less has been said about the advocacy networks that drew attention to the issue and helped bring about the COI in the first place. The COI report, which for the first time documented the full litany of human rights abuses carried out by the North Korean regime against its own people, was made possible on the back of decades of advocacy and research undertaken by a global network of dedicated human rights actors. The success these nonstate actors have had in raising this issue at the highest level of the United Nations (UN) is surprising because it has occurred without direct access to the North Korean state. As we discuss in this chapter, current scholarly models of how transnational activism works assume the existence of at least some local opposition movements working inside the country. Yet the North Korea case suggests that this is not, in fact, a necessary scope condition. Moving forward, current research into human rights change also points to the conclusion that local actors are necessary for lasting human rights change, but assumes that change is top down (that is, that change happens when states are responsive to international and domestic pressure). Yet despite the absence of domestic actors, North Korean human rights activists continue to pursue better outcomes in North Korea, and not always in the "top down" way we might expect. These observations thus raise two questions which animate this opening chapter, and indeed the other contributions in this volume. First, how does a transnational advocacy network emerge to push for change in a highly repressive context where there is no domestic opposition? And second, by what pathways might transnational activists create change in such contexts?

This volume turns the spotlight onto the work of those actors who have worked tirelessly to expose the human rights situation in North Korea. Human rights actors within the North Korean transnational advocacy network include

---

[4] Kirby 2014.

domestic and international nongovernmental organizations (NGOs), intergovernmental organizations (IGOs), government agencies, legislative bodies, foundations, think-tanks, churches and other religious organizations, journalists, scholars, students, and concerned citizens. The network therefore comprises individuals as well as organizations and coalition movements, which "form links across actors in civil societies, states, and international organizations, [multiplying] the channels of access to the international system."[5] Table 1.1 provides a small sample of actors within the North Korean human rights network.[6]

In this chapter, we explore the ways in which the case of North Korean human rights activism both confirms and challenges existing scholarship on transnational human rights activism, and the role advocacy networks play in the diffusion of human rights norms, discourse, and practice. In particular, we draw attention to the weaknesses with current models of human rights change and examine how state and nonstate actors challenge highly repressive regimes by investigating the quintessential "hard case" of North Korea. We proceed by first offering a brief review of existing models of transnational advocacy networks and human rights change and review their applicability to the task of understanding North Korean human rights advocacy. We then extrapolate three variables that we argue are critical to understanding the emergence and evolution of North Korean human rights activism: discourse, network dynamics, and defectors. Finally, we turn our attention to human rights outcomes, exploring the different mechanisms of change that link activism to outcomes. We conclude by recapping our theoretical aims and outlining what is to follow in the remaining chapters of this volume.

TRANSNATIONAL ADVOCACY NETWORKS, DOMESTIC OPPOSITION, AND THE CASE OF NORTH KOREA

Since the late 1990s, a large body of scholarship has explored the role played by transnational advocacy networks in world politics.[7] Taken as a whole, this literature has been instrumental in documenting the ways in which nonstate actors have transformed outcomes on the world stage by wielding significant moral and ideational power. In bringing about new normative frameworks, as

---

[5] Keck and Sikkink 1998, 1.

[6] Table 1.1 only represents organizations working specifically on "human rights issues," defined in terms of civil and political rights. When using a broader definition to include social and economic rights, other contributors also consider that humanitarian organizations fall under the scope of human rights. For example, see Chapter 2 by Reidhead.

[7] See, for example, Keck and Sikkink 1998; Khagram, Riker, and Sikkink 2002; Della Porta and Tarrow 2005; Busby 2010; Hadden 2015; Risse, Ropp, and Sikkink 1999; 2013.

TABLE 1.1. *Sample of North Korean human rights organizational actors by country*

Actor	Country
Free NK Radio	South Korea (defector-led)
North Korea Freedom Coalition	USA
The Committee for Human Rights in North Korea (HRNK)	USA
North Korea Intellectuals Solidarity	South Korea (defector-led)
PSCORE (People for Successful Corean Reunification)	South Korea
Liberty in North Korea (LiNK)	USA
Helping Hands Korea	South Korea
Justice for North Korea	South Korea
Life Funds for North Korean Refugees	Japan
The Council for Human Rights in North Korea (Canada)	Canada
North Korea Strategy Center	South Korea (defector-led)
Citizens' Alliance for North Korean Human Rights	South Korea
Network for North Korean Democracy and Human Rights	South Korea
Database Center for North Korean Human Rights	South Korea
European Alliance for Human Rights in North Korea	United Kingdom
All-Party Parliamentary Group on North Korea	United Kingdom
International Coalition to Stop Crimes Against Humanity in North Korea	South Korea / Transnational
Amnesty International	United Kingdom (Global)
Human Rights Watch	
United Nations Human Rights Council	United Nations (Global)
National Endowment for Democracy	USA
Radio Free Asia	USA

well as compelling adherence (behavioral changes) to international human rights norms, the outcomes achieved by the principled actors that make up these advocacy networks have been heralded as evidence that neither states nor nonstate actors simply act out of strategically determined self-interest, but that ideas and values matter in world politics.[8]

---

[8]   These conceptual claims can be found in the work of scholars from the same period. See, for example, Katzenstein, Keohane and Krasner 1998; Price and Tannenwald 1996.

Keck and Sikkink's *Activists Beyond Borders* is often taken as the launching point for any discussion on transnational advocacy networks.[9] Although the idea of "networks" is what draws many scholars to Keck and Sikkink's seminal work, their emphasis on "advocacy" is also of great relevance to the contributions in this volume. As Keck and Sikkink state, "advocacy captures what is unique about these transnational networks: they are organized to promote causes, principled ideas, and norms, and they involve individuals advocating policy changes that cannot be easily linked to a rationalist understanding of their 'interests.'"[10] Thus, the authors expose how transnational advocacy networks strategically wield resources and influence to transcend their material disadvantage vis-à-vis states and shift prevailing "structures of power and meaning."[11]

Perhaps Keck and Sikkink's most influential contribution to the study of transnational advocacy networks is the "boomerang pattern" of information flow and international pressure directed against a rights-violating regime. When opportunities between the state and domestic actors are blocked, and local activists and NGOs are thus unable to place direct pressure on their own governments, they reach out to international allies for support. These allies – be they international NGOs (INGOs), UN groups, other states, single-issue rights organizations, or individual actors – then work to raise global awareness and apply political leverage and outside pressure against the repressive, rights-violating state.[12] Beyond the boomerang pattern, Risse and Sikkink present a more dynamic "spiral model" of human rights change.[13] This model, which we discuss in more detail in this chapter's final section on compliance issues, seeks to understand the broader processes of normative diffusion. Like the boomerang pattern, the spiral model places domestic activists at its center.[14]

On the surface, certain aspects of the boomerang pattern do bear out in the North Korean case, even in the absence of local dissident voices. Transnational advocacy networks have played a critical role in raising awareness, advocating, and lobbying on behalf of North Koreans who remain mostly powerless against a totalitarian state. As contributors to this volume describe (see chapters by Yeo [3], Arrington [4], Narayan [5], Hosaniak [6], and Chubb [8]), the North Korean human rights network has gained the support of significant actors, including the UN and the European Union

---

[9]   Keck and Sikkink 1998. We use other terms, including transnational movement, transnational advocacy group, or international campaign in reference to North Korean human rights activism. However, our thinking on activism in this volume resonates most closely with the transnational advocacy network concept.
[10]   Keck and Sikkink 1998, 8–9.   [11]   Keck and Sikkink 1998, 23–5. See also Price 2003, 583.
[12]   Keck and Sikkink 1998, 12–13.   [13]   Risse and Sikkink 1999.   [14]   Risse and Sikkink 1999, 5.

(EU); powerful states, such as the United States; and major NGOs, such as Human Rights Watch and Amnesty International.

While some aspects of North Korean human rights activism appear to conform to existing models of transnational networks and human rights change, other attributes of the North Korean case suggest it is an outlier. First, no civil society or domestic opposition exists in North Korea.[15] Both the boomerang pattern and the spiral model take domestic (or local) civil society as their starting points for transnational advocacy and human rights change. Yet even without local advocates, the North Korean human rights campaign has still achieved some success. How did this happen, and what does this tell us about the limitations of existing theory? To what degree do the models described above help us understand the North Korean human rights case? A core assumption is that a transnational network is activated (or at least enabled) by local actors providing vital information and legitimacy to actors outside the state. Domestic actors provide first-hand accounts and information about human rights violations. They alert transnational actors to the existence of abuse or strengthen and establish existing concerns. This, in turn, bolsters the legitimacy of the claims of the transnational network, rendering their advocacy more effective.[16] In what ways, then, is the North Korean human rights case an outlier, requiring a modification of these models for highly repressive contexts, where it is difficult to gain verifiable information about human rights abuses and where local populations can neither challenge their own governments nor interact directly with the outside world?

Given that the dominant frameworks for human rights advocacy presuppose that local human rights activists (that is, grassroots movements inside the repressive state) play a legitimating role at the earliest stages of the model, how do we then account for the widespread acceptance of the claims made by North Korean human rights activists in the absence of any such locally based dissident actors? The argument that networks create a "transnational structure" for challenging norm-violating regimes from below and above, and "empower and legitimate"[17] the claims of local activists against their own repressive regimes, appears less relevant in the North Korean context in the absence of any localized North Korean civil society. Yet, despite their absence, the transnational campaign has experienced impressive mobilizing capacity

---

[15] While there are reports of North Koreans who privately criticize or speak ill of the regime, there is no evidence of mobilization or sustained collective action in North Korea. See also Joo 2014; Armstrong 2003; Tudor and Pearson 2015.

[16] Risse and Sikkink 1999, 20.   [17] Risse and Sikkink 1999, 5.

and a series of significant legislative outcomes at the domestic and international levels.

Second, and related to the above, the level of repression in North Korea is virtually unparalleled in the contemporary world.[18] While other studies examine the validity of the spiral model in highly repressive contexts, very few of them address a state like North Korea where the local population remains completely isolated from the outside world.[19] Schwarz goes so far as to argue that in repressive, totalitarian settings where citizens are not granted political rights, there is little value to be gained from using models of human rights change: "the analysis of totalitarian regimes seems to offer little benefit since by definition little or no respect for human rights can be expected."[20] As Jetschke and Liese discuss in their review of the original spiral model, in cases of severe repression, authoritarian governments have proven successful in limiting the opening of domestic opportunity structures and preventing the strengthening of networks between domestic and transnational civil society.[21] As such, this is a quintessential "hard case" test of the spiral model.

In the wake of severe repression and the absence of any visible civil society, the evidence offered by contributors to this volume, and outlined further in this chapter's next section, reveals that the North Korean defector-activist community serves as a conduit for local opposition, even if it does not directly challenge the regime from within. It is through their work with North Korean defectors that transnational activists have managed to build a convincing case. As Hosaniak discusses in Chapter 6, the decision of the UN High Commissioner for Human Rights, an important gatekeeper of human rights legitimacy, to take up the claims of the North Korean human rights movement came about as a direct result of the High Commissioner's meeting with former North Korean political prisoners.

In short, existing theoretical frameworks do help illustrate the trajectory of North Korean human rights advocacy today and the degree to which activists have been effective in both gaining international attention for their issue and promoting change. However, the North Korean case also reveals important theoretical and empirical limitations to our current understanding of how transnational human rights actors secure legitimacy in cases where the rights-

---

[18] Freedom House, which evaluates the degree of civil and political liberties of each country globally, has placed North Korea in its "worst of the worst" category for 44 consecutive years. In 2017, only Syria scored lower than North Korea. See Shim 2017.

[19] Such studies include Saudi Arabia. See Alhargan 2012; Fleay 2006; Stachursky 2013. Jetschke and Liese provide a more comprehensive list and a discussion of case studies that have adopted the spiral model. See Jetschke and Liese 2013, 28–31.

[20] Schwarz 2004, 205.   [21] Jetschke and Liese 2013, 30.

violating actor is a closed, totalitarian state which has successfully sealed off its domestic population from the rest of the world.

DISCOURSE, NETWORK DYNAMICS, AND DEFECTORS

Three variables are central to the application of our conceptual model of change, and each of these helps shed further light on important elements of the North Korean human rights advocacy network. A deeper understanding of discourse, network dynamics, and defector voices helps elucidate how transnational human rights networks emerge and seek to bring about change in the context of a "hard case" authoritarian state such as North Korea.

Discourse

A central claim of this volume is that activists' interpretations of their normative commitments – as reflected in their discursive frames – carry consequences for advocacy movements in terms of strategies, agendas, and outcomes. The chapters in this volume, therefore, focus on the discourse of North Korean human rights actors. By discourse, we mean the words, language, statements, and debates which appear in speech or text form from nonstate and state actors. Discursive frames refer to the ideas, principles, and norms that inform discourses.[22] This focus enables us to examine the dynamics of the network, including its fragmented nature, at both the domestic and transnational level. It also allows us to better understand the role that defector voices have played in the evolution of the movement.

To casual observers, principled actors within the North Korean human rights advocacy network appear aligned to a common cause: ending human rights abuses in North Korea. While this assumption is true at a basic level, it belies the diversity of activists involved in the movement and fails to take into account the politicized nature of discourse over North Korean human rights. Network activists advocating on behalf of North Korean human rights fall across a broad political spectrum and pursue diverse outcomes ranging from bringing about human rights-compliant behavior in the repressive state to provoking regime change or collapse. By exploring the varieties of discursive frames that activists deploy, as well as the relationship between such discursive frames, transnational mobilization, and human rights advocacy outcomes, the

---

[22] We assume that these are context-specific and, across this volume, vary with respect to domestic or transnational settings. The importance of context has been recognized in work on ideas and discourse and is further explored in Chapter 3. See also Schmidt 2008.

chapters in this volume are able to assess with greater rigor several important issues surrounding North Korean human rights advocacy. These include: network membership and the different coalitions and cleavages that emerge within and between domestic and transnational networks; the ways in which different human rights actors define and interpret their normative commitments, and how this has led to a high degree of contestation within the movement; the range of policy pathways and strategies promoted by diverse actors vying for prominence within the network; and, finally, the variation in state responses to North Korean human rights activism, including that of North Korea, over time and in different national settings.[23]

How activists and policy officials talk about North Korean human rights is often embedded in different domestic political contexts. As such, one is able to follow the evolution of North Korean human rights activism and the rise of transnational advocacy networks by tracing different discursive debates concerning human rights across time and geographic space and piecing them together. Through discourse, we uncover how the issue of North Korean human rights has been contested, debated, and politicized by state and nonstate actors alike. For instance, in Chapter 3, Yeo examines how the unfolding of human rights debates in US foreign policy strongly influenced the direction of North Korean human rights activism and the security framing of human rights in the United States. This contrasts with North Korean human rights activism in Japan and the centrality of the abductee issue in that country's discourse, as argued by Arrington in Chapter 4.[24] A comparison of North Korean human rights activism and discourse across different national contexts thus highlights the multifaceted nature of human rights advocacy across different polities.

The extent to which we find domestic differences in North Korean human rights discourse leads to additional questions regarding the type of discourse which emerges when activism shifts scale from the domestic to the transnational realm. Do domestic advocacy groups adopt the language of the broader transnational advocacy network, ultimately aligning or transforming existing frames into a global frame by embracing the language of universal rights, accountability, and compliance?[25] Or do they manage to insert their own particular domestic agenda into the broader transnational human rights frame, thus influencing the agenda of North Korean human rights at the

---

[23] On examining how rights movements emerge, contest, and frame their activist claims in multilevel environments, see Ayoub and Chetaille 2017.

[24] North Korean agents systematically kidnapped Japanese citizens during the 1970s and 1980s.

[25] On the transposition from domestic to global frames, see Tarrow 2005, 63. See also Benford and Snow 2000; Della Porta 2007; Rothman and Oliver 2002; Yeo 2009.

global level? Perhaps human rights actors simply wear two hats, employing a domestically tailored frame and advocacy strategy in their home country on the one hand, while uniting with global activists, NGOs, and IGOs and adopting their movement frame when targeting North Korea at the UN on the other.[26] Such issues are taken up in Chapters 6, 7, and 8, where the contributors explore the transnational dimensions of North Korean human rights activism.

Network Dynamics

Scholarship on transnational movements and agenda-setting has helped bring greater nuance to our understanding of network dynamics.[27] While existing models of human rights change do recognize that transnational advocacy networks are inherently conflictual, scholars have long believed that networks provide the communicative environment in which participants can be expected to "mutually transform."[28] Keck and Sikkink, for example, see "frame disputes" among human rights activists as a powerful source of normative change within networks.[29] Frame disputes certainly stimulate change within networks in the North Korean human rights case, but they do so often in the absence of any sort of mutual transformation. How, then, are issues defined and agendas, strategies, and policy goals agreed upon? In the case of North Korea, which is characterized by the *absence* of a local civil society with which to consult on key issues around strategy and policy direction, these frame disputes are rendered even more complex. What action will best bring about positive change for the North Korean people, ensuring their dignity and improving their lives? Throughout this volume, network dynamics are closely linked to discursive contestation. There is thus a close relationship between these two variables. But by separating them, we are able to more clearly identify the agential and structural forces at play when it comes to normative contestation.

In the absence of any definitive voices from inside the country answering questions such as these, it is unsurprising that there is a great deal of disagreement between "human rights" and "humanitarianism" advocates as noted by Reidhead in Chapter 2.[30] But beyond this, human rights activists find themselves at odds over questions such as what the frame defining their advocacy

[26] Tarrow 2005, 42–5.
[27] On the role of network dynamics in agenda-setting, see Bob 2005; Hertel 2006; Carpenter 2014.
[28] Keck and Sikkink 1999, 100; Keck and Sikkink 1998, 214.   [29] Keck and Sikkink 1999, 92.
[30] See also Yeo 2014.

should be. While the COI seemed to come firmly down on the side of "accountability" and pursuing greater compliance with international law (see Goedde, Chapter 7), voices within the movement that see the North Korean regime as incapable of change, and instead advocate the pursuit of justice through policies of isolation, coercion, and change, have also played a significant role in bringing the movement to where it is today (see Chapter 3 by Yeo and Chapter 8 by Chubb). We explore both sides of this human rights narrative – and all the "sides" in between – in the chapters of this book, as these are debates that vary from country to country, and are then amplified at the transnational level.

The multivalent (a term used by Arrington in Chapter 4) nature of North Korean human rights discourse is indicative of network dynamics. Scholars including Carpenter, Bob, and Hertel argue that "network dynamics" are a key variable when it comes to issue-creation at the international level.[31] One of the most striking characteristics of the North Korean human rights movement – an observation carried in each one of this volume's contributions – is the high degree of normative contestation regarding movement principles and strategy among groups and individuals.[32] As discussed earlier, this is a fractured movement, dealing with divisive issues around how to prioritize rights, pursue desirable policy pathways, and appropriate advocacy strategies and tactics. If discourse helps us uncover these differences, a focus on network dynamics helps us understand the role such normative contestation plays in determining movement agendas, strategies, and outcomes.

The chapters in this volume reveal that normative contestation has a powerful effect on network outcomes at the level of agenda-setting. The COI – a key moment in the movement's history – has been celebrated by a diverse set of actors across the North Korean human rights movement. It represents, as Bob predicts, an "amalgam" of competing interpretations

[31] Bob and Carpenter argue that the more powerful players within a given network play an outsized, and sometimes problematic, role when it comes to shaping interpretations of human rights. In contrast, Hertel's work paints a more complicated picture, one in which normative contestation can affect both norm evolution and policy outcomes, with less powerful actors capable of bringing about incremental normative change, despite their lower profile. See Bob 2005; Carpenter 2014; Hertel 2006.

[32] This is a form of normative contestation, by which we specifically refer to behavioral norms. While the content of human rights norms is not contested (activists agree over the "rightness" of human rights), we do find contestation over behavioral norms. We assume that this contestation is generated by different principles regarding human rights action against North Korea (how to best act so as to be doing good). In this volume, references to "normative contestation" should be construed as referring to disputes over behavioral norms which may present as a manifestation of differing normative agendas. For an in-depth discussion of the differences between normative beliefs and behavioral norms, see Crawford 2002, 86–98.

regarding how to affect human rights change inside North Korea.[33] Based on these insights, in Chapter 8 Chubb examines the incorporation of a wide range of movement goals, some of them seemingly inchoate, in the COI's report. Goedde, in Chapter 7, also speaks to network dynamics as she considers the implications of these competing normative and legal agendas for bringing about behavioral change in North Korea.

A key question for scholars of transnational activism is whether actors ultimately resolve normative contestation to make progress toward their stated goals and agenda. The chapters in this book interrogate closely the various ways in which normative contestation plays out among diverse actors within the North Korean human rights network. In the volume's Conclusion, however, we argue that normative contestation has not been an insurmountable barrier to achieving major international exposure and legitimacy. As the North Korean case demonstrates, human rights actors are simultaneously value-driven *and* highly strategic. Hence, they are extremely adaptive, capable of coordinating with coalition partners on elements of the campaign which accord with their personal agendas and values. However, when necessary, they also work separately to further their own agenda, whether that be naming-and-shaming the regime, launching balloons with anti-North Korea leaflets across the demilitarized zone from South Korea to North Korea, facilitating information campaigns across the North Korean border, or seeking a more bureaucratic approach to addressing human rights issues through the utilization of transnational legal mechanisms.

Defector Voices

A final key element in understanding North Korean human rights activism is the role of North Korean defectors in the human rights advocacy network. These actors have played an increasing and instrumental role in the struggle for North Korean human rights. Among the nearly 30,000 defectors who have left North Korea and resettled elsewhere, a handful have organized to bear witness and raise national and international awareness of ongoing human rights abuses in their country of origin. These defectors have directly experienced oppression in the North Korean system, and in many cases are victims of or witnesses to state violence.

In the absence of an active local civil society movement inside North Korea, the inclusion of defector voices in the North Korean human rights campaign has been both transformative and controversial. These voices

---

[33] Bob 2009, 29.

formed the core evidence sustaining the COI's recommendation of referral to the International Criminal Court. The testimonies (both on and off the record) of these survivors and witnesses were crucial in the face of the refusal of the North Korean government to allow the COI entry into North Korea. Many of these testimonies took the form of public hearings, which Commissioner Kirby argued was a decision made in the belief that it "permits the international community to assess the witnesses and to make their own assessments as to whether they are telling the truth."[34] At the same time, critics have challenged the veracity of defector accounts, recommending caution when relying on testimonies which cannot always be independently corroborated.[35] This point was accentuated when the North Korean government revealed inconsistencies in celebrity defector-activist Shin Dong Hyuk's account of his life inside the gulags, with Shin eventually admitting to fabricating portions of his memoir.[36]

This volume documents the ways in which North Korean human rights advocates have incorporated defectors' voices into their campaign to add legitimacy and credibility to their movement and to support the claim that North Korea exists as one of the world's worst human rights violators. Conversely, outside support – whether in the form of funding from institutions such as the National Endowment for Democracy or through network resources from major human rights NGOs and UN organizations which amplify defectors voices – is crucial to the survival of these defector organizations. In this sense, none of the actors in the network are local in the truest sense, and, instead, all of them act as "rooted cosmopolitans," mobilizing on behalf of issues and actors outside their places of origin and building social networks to inhabit a transnational space.[37] They have what Della Porta and Tarrow call "multiple belongings and flexible identities."[38] Yet defectors also fall outside this definition. Unlike their fellow transnational activists, defector-activists never truly return to their origins, and they are at the same time both external and domestic actors. They are, in Tarrow's formulation, truly "detached individuals," and necessarily transnational citizens.[39]

Ties between defectors and the broader advocacy network are mutually beneficial, but as with all NGO dynamics, they also carry potential principle–agent problems in which defector groups become co-opted and

---

[34] McDonald 2014.
[35] Jolley 2014. For a scholarly critique of the role of defectors in the North Korean human rights movement, see Hong 2013; Song and Hong 2014.
[36] Harden 2012. For other issues regarding defector accounts, see Song 2015.
[37] Tarrow 2005, 40–3.   [38] Della Porta and Tarrow 2005, 238.   [39] Tarrow 2005, 43.

beholden to the agenda of larger organizations.[40] Generally speaking, the participation of the diaspora or exiled dissident communities in human rights campaigns is not unusual.[41] However, North Korea may be one of the few cases – if not the only case – where no organized activism exists inside the regime-violating state. North Korean defectors, therefore, play a unique role in the transnational advocacy campaign.

FROM DENIAL TO COMMITMENT AND BEYOND

The spiral model outlines a five-stage process describing how repressive regimes gradually shift their behavior from that of a human rights norms violator to that of a norms-compliant actor.[42] Beginning with a *repression* stage, a norm-violating state such as North Korea may express *denial* when first confronted by transnational advocacy networks with accusations of human rights violations. As pressure mounts from without and within, the regime may offer *tactical concessions* resulting in minor policy shifts or rhetorical commitments. For instance, the regime may release a few political prisoners, permit greater political movement, or offer statements indicating its support for international human rights. In this context, domestic actors are mobilized and protected by growing transnational linkages. Over time, a regime may grant human rights *prescriptive status*, further validating the claims of domestic actors. States begin to change domestic laws in line with human rights norms, ratify international human rights conventions and treaties, and, more generally, incorporate human rights norms and practices within domestic institutions and legal frameworks. The creation of the new political space that enables these changes is the direct result either of significant policy change on the part of the state or of regime change. The final phase is *rule-consistent behavior* resulting in a behavioral change compliant with international human rights.

The authors are clear that the spiral model does not assume a linear trajectory toward human rights change. States may revert back to abusive

---

[40] On the principle–agent problem with NGOs, see Cooley and Ron 2002. For more critical views, see Song and Hong's study, which argues that the National Endowment for Democracy's "'human rights' work is part of a much larger strategy of destabilizing the North Korean government in line with US interventionist aims against its foes." As the authors write, "Central to the NED-financed second culture of 'North Korea' has been a relatively small handful of North Korean defectors, mostly based in South Korea, whose deputatization by US power to speak on behalf of a 'democratized' North Korea, as signaled by their ready reception on Capitol Hill, represents a deterritorializing thrust against actual North Korean state authority." Song and Hong 2014, 41.

[41] Some examples include Iran, Cuba, and China.   [42] Risse and Sikkink 1999, 19–33.

behavior. Some regimes may appear to be stuck in a particular phase or in-between phases (such as denial and tactical concessions) for a long period. Or states may be operating in multiple phases simultaneously, which appears to be true in the case of North Korea.[43] More recent work by the same authors in *The Persistent Power of Human Rights* recognizes some of the limitations of the original model.[44] As contributors to *Persistent Power* note, the model fails in its capacity to understand why human rights change does not occur in the worst cases, since "few states with a previous record of gross and systematic human rights violations have transgressed through stages four and five of the model."[45] More than a decade after the publication of the spiral model, its authors thus shift their focus to these latter phases – the move from commitment to compliance – and seek to identify the scope conditions that determine whether or not human rights change will occur.[46] *Persistent Power's* focus on the model's latter stages is justified. While the model's understanding of the earlier stages of human rights change are largely borne out in the empirical research that has since emerged, the latter stages require further specification.

The spiral model helps evaluate where North Korea currently stands in regards to its evolution in human rights thinking. It also serves as a barometer for examining the efficacy of advocacy networks to date in changing human rights behavior. Slight shifts in North Korean behavior, however minimal, do correspond to the early stages of the spiral model. Although the North Korean regime remains recalcitrant – often in a state of denial, as highlighted by Sandra Fahy in Chapter 10 – naming-and-shaming and ongoing international pressure also seems to have resulted in tactical concessions. As a signatory of six international human rights conventions,[47] the regime has "felt obliged at different times to report to the UN" changes it has made in its domestic laws.[48] Examples include limited reforms on laws pertaining to children and

---

43 As such, the model should be taken as an ideal-type heuristic for thinking about human rights change, not a specific plan of action for any particular advocacy movement.
44 Risse, Ropp, and Sikkink 2013.
45 Jetschke and Liese 2013, 37. Stages four and five refer to prescriptive status and rule-consistent behavior.
46 Risse and Ropp 2013, 5, 16–22.
47 These include the International Covenant on Civil and Political Rights; the International Covenant on Economic, Social and Cultural Rights; the Convention of the Elimination of All Forms of Discrimination Against Women; the Convention on the Rights of the Child, Convention on the Rights of Persons with Disabilities; and the Optional Protocol to the Convention on the Rights of the Child on the sale of children, child prostitution, and child pornography.
48 Cohen 2012.

people with disabilities, as well as revisions to its Criminal Code and Criminal Procedures Code shortening pretrial detention and restricting night time interrogations.[49] In December 2016, North Korea ratified the UN Convention on the Rights of Persons with Disabilities, a treaty it had signed in 2013, and in May 2017 facilitated a visit to the country by the UN's Special Rapporteur on the rights of persons with disabilities.[50] North Korea is far from norms-compliant, but the evidence presented in this volume suggests that ongoing international pressure has at least prodded the regime to make concessions at the margin as outlined in the spiral model, even as it continues to deny human rights abuses and repress its people.

Consistent with Risse, Ropp, and Sikkink's own reflection and criticism of the spiral model, much of the work of the North Korean human rights advocacy network is confined to the early stages of human rights change, even as transnational actors continue to seek ways to bring more fundamental change to North Korea. For example, the COI report relies on international law mechanisms bringing about human rights change by drawing North Korea closer into the international community. This approach, however, is itself rife with contradiction. Can threats of bringing those responsible for North Korean abuses to account be reconciled with other recommendations within the COI report, which argue that human rights change in North Korea relies on greater engagement with the state and its people? As Goedde discusses in detail in Chapter 7, this is the core challenge the UN faces in its efforts to bring about change in North Korea.

Outside these efforts, regime destabilizing strategies have a great deal of prominence among some network members. While regime type is considered as a scope condition in the models (the more democratic a state is, the more likely change will occur), few studies have investigated the degree to which destabilization of an authoritarian regime might be adopted as a human rights tactic.[51] Human rights and international relations scholars have paid increasing attention to issues of compliance – that is, the degree to which states actually adhere to human rights norms. This is particularly true of the spiral model and its emphasis on the behavior and actions of the offending state. However, a focus on regime accountability and compliance as an observable indicator of change unintentionally biases our understanding of transnational advocacy networks and the strategies they use to promote change. Beyond

---

[49] UN Human Rights Council 2009.
[50] McDonald 2016; United Nations Office of the High Commissioner for Human Rights 2017.
[51] Exceptions include scholars who examine the ways in which states use human rights as a political tool of domination, or as pretext for interventions and regime change. See Bricmont 2006; Perugini and Gordon 2015.

legal measures and policy shifts, less frequently observed are the bottom-up mechanisms of change pursued by transnational advocacy networks which eschew issues of compliance and accountability. Frustrated with the slow pace of change, some activists in the North Korean human rights movement have pushed for a more direct, interventionist approach to human rights advocacy. Jieun Baek's contribution in Chapter 11 is particularly thought-provoking in this regard, as she unveils activist strategies to deliver information about the outside world directly to ordinary North Koreans to undermine the regime's legitimacy. The North Korean case, therefore, sheds light on alternative strategies to human rights change that may be specific to activism targeted at totalitarian societies.

The last ten years have seen a proliferation of both quantitative and qualitative studies of human rights change.[52] Importantly, many of these focus on international law mechanisms. What we learn from these studies about the potential for human rights change in "hard case" authoritarian contexts such as North Korea, where there is no evident popular mobilization, does not bode well for the next stages of the North Korean human rights movement. Indeed, North Korea seems stuck in a loop between stages of denial and tactical concessions. Additionally, empirical research into human rights change in such contexts suggests that further change without local support is unlikely. As discussed earlier, the spiral model of human rights change relies on domestic support. Risse and Ropp go so far as to suggest that democratic governance seems to be a prerequisite for human rights change.[53] Without institutions of accountability, the social mechanisms central to effective activism – naming-and-shaming, persuasion and learning, and legal enforcement – are absent. Simply put, autocratic regimes cannot be "[shamed] into compliance."[54] As Davis, Murdie, and Steinmetz argue, the importance of an educated public explains the resources human rights organizations put into human rights education: "domestic support is critical in limiting how the state can respond to human rights criticism."[55] Hafner-Burton, in her systematic survey of human rights change, contends that participation in the international human rights legal system only leads to greater human rights protection in contexts where institutions for accountability exist domestically. Furthermore, she argues that once initial progress has been made on the international stage, localization of the transnational movement is essential for bringing about substantive change.[56] The question is whether the North

---

[52] Hafner-Burton and Ron 2009. [53] Risse and Ropp 2013, 16–17.
[54] Risse and Ropp 2013, 17. [55] Davis, Murdie, and Steinmetz 2012, 209.
[56] Hafner-Burton 2013, 155–9.

Korean human rights network – as fragmented as it is, and lacking a domestic support base – can still bring about meaningful human rights change inside North Korea.

In defense of international law mechanisms, Simmons marshals evidence suggesting that formal treaty commitments do seem to impel governments toward better human rights practice as the signing of such treaties generally signals serious intent.[57] Is this the case for North Korea? In her examination of North Korea's behavior at the UN, Hosaniak, in Chapter 6 of this volume, argues that rather than signaling a serious commitment toward human rights, North Korea's accession to these treaties were politically motivated – North Korea desired greater inclusion in the international community at the time of signing, especially vis-à-vis South Korea – and the government likely did not appreciate that it would be brought to account on these commitments. In fact, in an effort to avoid referral to the International Criminal Court, Naryan in Chapter 5 reveals that North Korean diplomats met with the UN Special Rapporteur and traveled to Europe to meet with the EU Special Representative on Human Rights. Indeed, Simmons' arguments regarding the value of treaty commitment revolve around the value of this action to affect domestic politics in fluid settings. North Korea is, decisively, not a fluid environment and, as Simmons herself notes, in settings such as stable auto-cracies, the likelihood of political mobilization to demand compliance is unlikely if such demands are seen as a challenge to the regime's governance structures.[58]

North Korean human rights activism has achieved unlikely success to date. Can it continue to defy expectations and achieve meaningful change on behalf of the North Korean people? Baek in Chapter 11 and Goedde in Chapter 7 suggest two alternative but complementary paths moving forward. Baek examines attempts by human rights activists to infiltrate the North Korean government's information blockade, arguing that these direct action efforts have the potential to meet what seems to be a growing desire, on the part of the North Korean people, to learn more about the outside world and North Korea's place within it. Goedde suggests that the international legal approach should be more attuned to contextual variables, arguing that reframing the human rights narrative at the UN to better incorporate North Korean understandings of rights and obligations could go a long way toward resolving the existing tension between accountability and engagement. Goedde links reframing efforts to "direct" information campaigns, suggesting that a greater appreciation of how North Koreans think and talk about rights

---

[57] Simmons 2009, 4.   [58] Simmons 2009, 15.

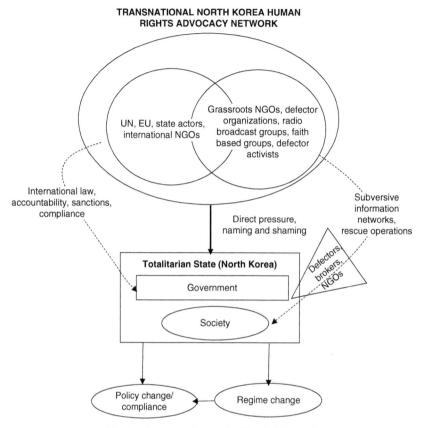

FIGURE 1.1 Mechanisms for change in North Korean human rights

could lead to the development of more effective information packages aimed at local people, arming North Korean human rights activists with a much more potent human rights weapon.

The two-pronged approach to transnational advocacy enabled by the coexistence of different cleavages within the North Korean human rights network reflects the realities observed by contributors to this volume: that competing approaches to human rights activism can complement each other. This lends itself to a modified understanding of the boomerang and spiral models when adapted to highly repressive states. Figure 1.1 illustrates this dynamic.

Building on the boomerang and spiral models for understanding North Korean human rights activism, the transnational advocacy network targets the repressive state, naming and shaming the rights-violating regime and calling for accountability. However, in the absence of domestic partners, some actors, particularly IGOs such as the UN or major INGOs, are more inclined to rely heavily on legal mechanisms, emphasizing accountability and compliance and threatening sanctions. In this top-down approach to human rights advocacy, the regime becomes the primary focal point. There is an expectation or hope that the rights-violating government might implement reforms leading to gradual policy shifts and an eventual transformation in human rights.

Other human rights actors, more often at the grassroots end, take a more subversive, "hands-on" approach, directing their advocacy toward society at large. Such actors place little faith in recalcitrant regimes such as North Korea that they will make any meaningful human rights change in the future. They therefore direct their energies in promoting defections and cultivating information networks in the hopes of undermining the legitimacy of the regime and its grip over the people. In the North Korean case, this has included activists sending information about the outside world in the form of news broadcasts, South Korean dramas, Western movies, and through market activity and exchange. Defectors and the NGOs which support them, as well as agents outside of the human rights network such as profit-motivated brokers, corrupt border guards, and rent-seeking local officials, serve as an important conduit in ensuring the flow of information between human rights actors and ordinary North Koreans. In the absence of North Korean civil society, the advocacy network is essentially cultivating their own local allies, thus sowing the seeds for domestic dissent. If change cannot occur from the top, it might as well come from below.

It is important to note that these alternative pathways to change are promoted in tandem by the broader North Korean human rights advocacy network. Different factions within the network have thus far been willing to work together, and organizations central to the network, such as the Committee for Human Rights in North Korea, have tended to straddle, and thus bridge, different groups. Our research cannot yet tell us whether either of these approaches might prove effective. The likelihood of change in such a repressive context seems low given what we know about how human rights change occurs. However, the capacity North Korean human rights activists have shown for adaptation and coordination in the face of a highly fragmented movement has worked to the advantage of the movement so far.

CONCLUSION AND CHAPTER OUTLINE

As demonstrated by our contributors, and contrary to existing transnational advocacy models, the presence of a local civil society may not, in fact, be a necessary condition for the creation of a powerful advocacy movement or the acquisition of international attention and legitimacy. The strategic acumen shown by a number of key actors across the political spectrum has enabled the development of defector voices alongside the cooperation of international legal bodies. While the role that defectors play in the movement is not without controversy – a matter addressed by Jay Song in Chapter 9 – North Korean human rights activism is unlikely to be where it is today were it not for the inclusion of defectors' discourses. We do not see our argument, or the case of North Korean human rights activism, necessarily undermining the explanatory value of either the boomerang or spiral models. Rather, the inclusion of the North Korean case within the existing body of scholarship on transnational human rights advocacy increases our knowledge of how nonstate actors might seek to overcome the structural hurdles placed in their paths by powerful authoritarian states.

The North Korean human rights movement has not developed as a cohesive whole, and thus lends itself to an edited volume of this kind. Activists in South Korea, Japan, the United States, and Europe come to the issue of North Korean human rights from diverse historical, political, and ideological perspectives. In each chapter, country and regional experts consider the evolution of the movement in a variety of domestic and transnational settings. To understand the movement, we believe it is first important to disaggregate it and consider it in its parts before viewing the movement as a whole.

Methodologically, our contributors raise the bar for scholarship on North Korea and transnational advocacy networks, employing a variety of analytical tools (including computer-assisted content analysis, discourse analysis, Internet hyperlink analysis, network analysis, and case study methods) to shed new light on North Korean human rights activism. Several chapters present new empirical data to indicate why North Korean human rights activism has evolved along its current trajectory and how this has shaped movement and policy outcomes to date. All contributors rely on primary sources, first-hand accounts, and/or original language sources. Several authors have systematically compiled and analyzed large amounts of textual data from media accounts, official statements, and NGO and government reports for this project.

Following this opening chapter, Part I explores North Korean human rights activism and discourse within different national contexts. We begin with the South Korean context: Reidhead, in Chapter 2, delves into the complex political terrain that North Korean human rights activists must traverse. In Seoul, the issue of human rights in North Korea is closely intertwined with questions of reunification, and has its roots deep in South Korea's own authoritarian past where the country's domestic civil society movement originates. Against this backdrop, then, human rights activists from both the progressive and the conservative end of the political spectrum must vie for legitimacy. Reidhead conducts a large corpus analysis of media content in South Korean newspapers to trace North Korean human rights discourse and the rising dominance of groups oriented toward civil and political rights in South Korea.

In Chapter 3, Yeo finds some parallels with Reidhead's analysis in his study of North Korean human rights activism in the United States. As Yeo explains, North Korean human rights activism cannot escape its historical precedents. The issue of North Korean human rights is deeply embedded in a Cold War normative framework, shaped by human rights discourse that dates back to foreign policy debates from the 1970s. As such, North Korean human rights advocacy in the United States tends to adopt a stronger security emphasis than elsewhere through the adoption of a human rights–security nexus framing.

While North Korean human rights discourse and advocacy in the United States and South Korea is shaped by a complex and historically normative framework, Japanese discourse has been more narrowly focused on the abduction of Japanese nationals by Pyongyang in the 1970s and 1980s. In Chapter 4, Arrington investigates how and why the abductions issue has become so inextricably linked to the North Korean human rights issue by scrutinizing the groups and individuals engaged in normative contestation about the framing of the abductions issue as a human rights one. She finds that while the dualism of North Korean human rights discourse in Japan has at times complicated Japanese participation and integration into the North Korean human rights transnational advocacy network, rendering the abductions as a North Korean human rights problem has also advanced the human rights discourse, both inside Japan and transnationally.

In Chapter 5, Narayan, a former Amnesty researcher based in London, discusses North Korean human rights discourse and activism in the European context. Naryan explores the relationships between European civil society organizations and the formal institutional channels in Europe under which North Korean human rights advocacy unfolds. How North Korean human rights advocacy operates in Europe is somewhat unique given the EU's active role in promoting North Korean human rights, both through direct talks with North Korea and through multilateral channels, and due to the fact that several European states maintain formal diplomatic ties with North Korea.

In Part II, the volume transitions from domestic to transnational perspectives. The three chapters in this section consider how actors – coming to the issue from diverse backgrounds and national contexts – seek to develop coherent transnational networks to address the North Korean human rights issue. Here, our focus of analysis shifts to the politics of agenda-setting. Rather than focusing on discursive frame development, the authors spend time unraveling the factors which affect normative contestation within networks: discursive frames, network dynamics, and power relations. In the domestic arena, contentious discursive frames are shaped by norms and ideas specific to each context. In the transnational arena, normative contestation between activists has led to a diverse set of agenda-setting outcomes. The authors in this section discuss some of the consequences of the transnationalization of an issue as highly politicized as North Korean human rights. Hosaniak commences this section in Chapter 6 by offering a practitioner's perspective. Hosaniak's organization – Citizens' Alliance for North Korean Human Rights – is the oldest North Korean human rights NGO and has undergone profound normative, discursive, and political shifts over the course of its 20-year history. Her chapter traces the trajectory of this activism, highlighting the interaction between political context, strategy choice, and networking tactics, with a particular focus on the strategies that led to the establishment of the COI.[59]

Following Hosaniak's activist-oriented narrative of the path toward the COI, Goedde in Chapter 7 uncovers the mechanics and micro-processes of this type of transnational legal mobilization. She looks specifically at the reaction of North Korea to the accountability paradigm and argues that this approach has periodically led to retrenchment rather than progress. Given the logical outcome of the legal accountability approach – termination of the North Korean regime – she argues that a greater focus on engaging North Korean actors on issues around transnational legal norms will lead to more productive and effective outcomes for the movement. Finally, in Chapter 8, Chubb pulls together the findings of the previous chapters on domestic and transnational mobilization by looking specifically at network dynamics and considering the ramifications for theory. This chapter asks how and why the normative and discursive contours of activist networks shift over time and examines what the implications of this have been for campaign outcomes.

In Part III of the volume, we bring North Korean voices back into the conversation. In Chapter 9, Song explores the role that defector-activists have played in affecting the discursive trajectory of the North Korean human rights campaign. While previous chapters touch on the important role that defector

---

[59] Joanna Hosaniak is also a human rights scholar, whose research explores questions of transitional justice in postcommunist states. In this volume, however, Hosaniak's observations are based largely on her lengthy experience as a North Korean human rights strategist and activist. She is currently the Deputy Director General of Citizens' Alliance for North Korean Human Rights.

voices have played in a range of contexts, Song conducts a network analysis around five high-profile defector-activists to provide a critical analysis of the substantive role that defector voices have played in the evolution of the North Korean human rights movement.

Complementing Song's chapter, the next empirical chapter shifts from the voice of human rights victims to that of the perpetrator. This, of course, is the North Korean state, the object and target of the transnational advocacy movement. In Chapter 10, Fahy wades through thousands of pages of texts of the North Korean newspaper *Rodong Sinmun* to systematically examine North Korean responses to accusations of human rights abuse and the findings of the COI in particular. Contrary to popular belief that the regime simply dismisses the validity of such international forums out of hand, Fahy's discursive analysis of North Korean official responses demonstrates the regime's level of engagement with the issues and their efforts to deflect human rights accusations through different means, including the creation of an "ersatz civil society."

Finally, in Chapter 11, Baek begins to explore the possibility of change within North Korea and the role transnational advocacy networks play in promoting greater information flows about the outside world into North Korea. Baek draws particular attention to the idea of information networks and draws out the mechanisms in which activists and defectors penetrate (or bypass) the state to reach out to ordinary North Koreans by disseminating information through USBs, leaflets, DVDs, radio broadcasts, or through market activity between North Korea and China.

In the volume's concluding chapter, Yeo and Chubb come back to the book's central questions: how can we understand the evolution of the North Korean human rights advocacy network and what does this mean for grappling better with the question of human rights change in "hard case" authoritarian states? The North Korean human rights movement is a deeply fractured one that has nonetheless achieved some remarkable milestones. By peering inside and taking its component subnetworks apart at the domestic level, the political and moral motivations of actors and their agendas become evident. This further advances our understanding of how principled actors bring about change in contentious settings. The wall separating North Korea and its people from the outside world has long seemed an insurmountable one, yet thanks to the relentless efforts of the diverse network of individuals working on the issue of North Korean human rights around the globe, cracks are starting to show.

As the contributors to this volume reveal, the focus on accountability mechanisms central to the COI report is not shared by all North Korean human rights activist groups, with some groups preferring more subversive methods of addressing human rights change. While the COI report's findings have been embraced by activists across the movement's spectrum, the lack of a central cohesive message at the core of the North Korean human rights network may prove significant in the next phase of the campaign. Having set the international agenda for North Korean human rights, attention will necessarily shift to questions of human rights change on the ground. The reluctance of some actors in the human rights movement to achieve change through the frame of accountability, preferring instead to take a more direct, interventionist approach, is likely to persist. Whether these cleavages facilitate or hinder human rights change remains to be seen.

REFERENCES

Alhargan, Raed A. 2012. The Impact of the UN Human Rights System and Human Rights INGOs on the Saudi Government with Special Reference to the Spiral Model. *The International Journal of Human Rights* 16 (4): 598–623.

Armstrong, Charles K. 2003. *Korean Society Civil Society, Democracy, and the State*. London: Routledge.

Ayoub, Phillip M., and Agnès Chetaille. 2017. Movement/Countermovement Interaction and Instrumental Framing in a Multi-Level World: Rooting Polish Lesbian and Gay Activism. *Social Movement Studies*: 1–17. DOI 10.1080/14742837.2017.1338941.

Benford, Robert D., and David A. Snow. 2000. Framing Processes and Social Movements: An Overview and Assessment. *Annual Review of Sociology* 26 (1): 611–39.

Bob, Clifford. 2005. *The Marketing of Rebellion Insurgents, Media, and International Activism*. Cambridge: Cambridge University Press.

Bob, Clifford. 2009. New Human Rights Issues: Understanding Their Contentious Rise. *Colombia Internacional* 69: 14–35.

Bricmont, Jean. 2006. *Humanitarian Imperialism: Using Human Rights to Sell War*. Translated by Diana Johnstone. New York: Monthly Review Press.

Busby, Joshua W. 2010. *Moral Movements and Foreign Policy*. New York: Cambridge University Press.

Carpenter, R. Charli. 2014. *Lost Causes: Agenda Vetting in Global Issue Networks and the Shaping of Human Security*. Ithaca: Cornell University Press.

Cohen, Roberta. 2012. Human Rights Progress In North Korea: Is It Possible? *38 North*, March 20. 38north.org/2012/03/rcohen032012/.

Cooley, Alexander, and James Ron. 2002. The NGO Scramble: Organizational Insecurity and the Political Economy of Transnational Action. *International Security* 27 (1): 5–39.

Crawford, Neta. 2002. *Argument and Change in World Politics: Ethics, Decolonization, and Humanitarian Intervention*. Cambridge: Cambridge University Press.

Davis, David R., Amanda Murdie, and Coty Garnett Steinmetz. 2012. "Makers and Shapers": Human Rights INGOs and Public Opinion. *Human Rights Quarterly* 27 (1): 199–224.

Della Porta, Donatella, ed. 2007. *The Global Justice Movement: Cross National and Transnational Perspectives*. London: Paradigm Publishers.

Della Porta, Donatella, and Sidney G. Tarrow. 2005. *Transnational Protest and Global Activism*. Lanham: Rowman & Littlefield.

Fleay, Caroline. 2006. Human Rights, Transnational Actors and the Chinese Government: Another Look at the Spiral Model. *Journal of Global Ethics* 2 (1): 43–65.

Hadden, Jennifer. 2015. *Networks in Contention: The Divisive Politics of Climate Change*. New York: Cambridge University Press.

Hafner-Burton, Emilie. 2013. *Making Human Rights a Reality*. Princeton: Princeton University Press.

Hafner-Burton, Emilie M., and James Ron. 2009 Seeing Double: Human Rights Impact through Qualitative and Quantitative Eyes. *World Politics* 61 (2): 360–401.

Harden, Blaine. 2012. *Escape from Camp 14: One Man's Remarkable Odyssey from North Korea to Freedom in the West*. New York: Viking Adult.

Hertel, Shareen. 2006. *Unexpected Power: Conflict and Change Among Transnational Activists*. Ithaca: Cornell University Press.

Hong, Christine. 2013. The Mirror of North Korean Human Rights. *Critical Asian Studies* 45 (4): 561–92.

Jetschke, Anja, and Andrea Liese. 2013. The Power of Human Rights a Decade After: From Euphoria to Contestation? In *The Persistent Power of Human Rights: From Commitment to Compliance*, edited by Thomas Risse, Stephen Ropp, and Kathryn Sikkink, 26–42. Cambridge: Cambridge University Press.

Jolley, Mary Ann. 2014. The Strange Tale of Yeonmi Park. *The Diplomat*, December 10. thediplomat.com/2014/12/the-strange-tale-of-yeonmi-park/.

Joo, Hyung-min. 2014. Hidden Transcripts in Marketplaces: Politicized Discourses in the North Korean Shadow Economy. *Pacific Review* 27 (1): 49–71.

Katzenstein, Peter J., Robert O. Keohane, and Stephen D. Krasner. 1998. International Organization and the Study of World Politics. *International Organization* 52 (4): 645–85.

Keck, Margaret, and Kathryn Sikkink. 1998. *Activists Beyond Borders: Advocacy Networks in International Politics*. Ithaca: Cornell University Press.

Keck, Margaret, and Kathryn Sikkink. 1999. Transnational Advocacy Networks in International and Regional Politics. *International Social Science Journal* 51 (159): 89–101.

Khagram, Sanjeev, James Riker, and Kathryn Sikkink, eds. 2002. *Restructuring World Politics: Transnational.Social Movements, Networks and Norms*. Minnesota: University of Minnesota Press.

Kirby, Michael. 2014. *Statement by Michael Kirby, Chair of the Commission of Inquiry on Human Rights in the Democratic People's Republic of Korea to the 25th Session of the Human Rights Council*. Geneva, March 17.

MacDonald, Hamish. 2014. Public Inquiry into N. Korean Rights Violations Nears End. *NK News*, February 4.

MacDonald, Hamish. 2016. North Korea to Ratify Disability Convention: State Media. *NK News*, November 25.

Perugini, Nicola, and Neve Gordon. 2015. *The Human Right to Dominate*. New York: Oxford University Press.

Price, Richard. 2003. Transnational Civil Society and Advocacy in World Politics. *World Politics* 55 (4): 579–606.

Price, Richard, and Nina Tannenwald. 1996. Norms and Deterrence: The Nuclear and Chemical Weapons Taboo. In *The Culture of National Security: Norms and Identity in World Politics*, edited by Peter J. Katzenstein, 114–52. New York: Columbia University Press.

Risse, Thomas, and Stephen Ropp. 2013. Introduction and Overview. In *The Persistent Power of Human Rights: From Commitment to Compliance*, edited by Thomas Risse, Stephen Ropp, and Kathryn Sikkink, 3–25. New York: Cambridge University Press.

Risse, Thomas, Stephen Ropp, and Kathryn Sikkink, eds. 1999. *The Power of Human Rights: International Norms and Domestic Change*. Cambridge: Cambridge University Press.

Risse, Thomas, Stephen Ropp, and Kathryn Sikkink. 2013. *The Persistent Power of Human Rights from Commitment to Compliance*. Cambridge: Cambridge University Press.

Risse, Thomas, and Kathryn Sikkink. 1999. The Socialization of Human Rights Norms into Domestic Practices. In *The Power of Human Rights: International Norms and Domestic Change*, edited by Thomas Risse, Stephen Ropp, and Kathryn Sikkink, 1–38. Cambridge: Cambridge University Press.

Rothman, Franklin, and Pamela Oliver. 2002. From Local to Global: The Anti-Dam Movement in Southern Brazil, 1979–1992. In *Globalization and Resistance: Transnational Dimensions of Social Movements*, edited by Jackie Smith and Hank Johnston, 115–32. Lanham: Rowman & Littlefield.

Schmidt, Vivien A. 2008. Discursive Institutionalism: The Explanatory Power of Ideas and Discourse. *Annual Review of Political Science* 11 (1): 303–26.

Schwarz, Rolf. 2004. The Paradox of Sovereignty, Regime Type and Human Rights Compliance. *The International Journal of Human Rights* 8 (2): 199–215.

Shim, Elizabeth. 2017. North Korea Rated "Worst of the Worst" for Violations of Rights, Liberties. *United Press International*, February 1.

Simmons, Beth A. 2009. *Mobilizing for Human Rights: International Law in Domestic Politics*. New York: Cambridge University Press.

Stachursky, Benjamin. 2013. *The Promise and Perils of Transnationalization: NGO Activism and the Socialization of Women's Human Rights in Egypt and Iran*. Abingdon: Routledge.

Song, Dae Hun, and Christine Hong. 2014. "Toward The Day After": National Endowment for Democracy and North Korean Regime Change. *Critical Asian Studies* 46 (1): 39–64.

Song, Jay. 2015. Unreliable Witnesses: The Challenge of Separating Truth from Fiction When It Comes to North Korea. *Asia Policy Forum*, August 2.

Tarrow, Sidney G. 2005. *The New Transnational Activism*. New York: Cambridge University Press.

Tudor, Daniel, and James Pearson. 2015. *North Korea Confidential Private Markets, Fashion Trends, Prison Camps, Dissenters and Defectors*. North Clarendon: Tuttle Publishing.

UN Human Rights Council. 2009. Report of the Special Rapporteur on the Situation of Human Rights in the Democratic People's Republic of Korea, Vitit Muntarbhorn. A/HRC/10/18. February 24.

UN Human Rights Council. 2014. *Report of the Commission of Inquiry on Human Rights in the Democratic People's Republic of Korea*. A/HRC/25/63. February 7.

Yeo, Andrew. 2009. Not in Anyone's Backyard: The Emergence and Identity of a Transnational Anti-Base Network. *International Studies Quarterly* 53 (3): 571–94.

Yeo, Andrew. 2014. Alleviating Misery: The Politics of North Korean Human Rights in US Foreign Policy. *North Korean Review* 10 (2): 71–87.

PART I

DOMESTIC DISCOURSE AND ACTIVISM

A Prisoner's Dilemma of Movement Nationalization
North Korean Human Rights in South Korea, 1990–2016

Jacob Reidhead

TWO ARGUMENTS AND TWO FRAMEWORKS

Over the last quarter century, North Korean human rights have become a central element of South Korean political culture. The North Korean human rights movement in South Korea began in the early 1990s with humanitarian aid and economic engagement following the North Korean famine.[1] These activities prioritized rights associated with economic, social, and cultural rights (ESCR). However, from the late 1990s a conservative-leaning parallel movement arose, drawing attention to public executions, gulags, and the suppression of freedom of civil and political rights (CPR).[2] These conservative and progressive camps coexisted for a brief period, but by the late 2000s South Korea's conservative North Korean human rights movement became dominant both in terms of media discourse and the field of civil society organizations. This chapter makes two arguments regarding the evolution of South Korea's North Korean human rights movement during this pivotal period.

First, South Korea's conservative and progressive camps engaged in a kind of Prisoner's Dilemma over whether or not to establish ties between civil society organizations and national governments, particularly the governments of South Korea and the United States, or to maintain independence between civil society and the state. For each camp, nationalizing their respective movement would ensure its competitiveness, but would come at the cost of politicizing it as well. This chapter argues that both camps had the opportunity to nationalize; the conservative camp opted to nationalize, and the progressive camp did not. The joint outcome of these two decisions was the decline of the progressive movement and the survival, albeit with extreme politicization, of the conservative movement.

---

[1] Good Friends 2003.   [2]   Kang and Rigoulot 2005; Hawk 2010; Kim, MK 2012.

Second, as South Korea's conservative North Korean human rights movement became subsumed by national politics, discourse shifted from debates over ESCR and CPR to core disagreements in South Korean partisan politics: security, democracy, and unification.[3] From a partisan perspective, the problem of North Korean human rights is inextricably linked to the problem of inducing political change in North Korea. The progressive position is that efforts to induce change in North Korea should be limited to cooperative, nonadversarial engagement. By contrast, conservatives favor inducing change by any means possible – cooperative or adversarial. This chapter argues that as the ESCR agenda was first spearheaded by South Korean progressives, and the rise of CPR paralleled the entrance of conservative movement actors, movement discourse initially reflected a split along an ESCR–CPR axis. However, as the conservative movement nationalized and the process of politicization unfolded, movement ideologies became less divided by the type of human rights, ESCR versus CPR, and more divided by conservatives' and progressives' respective strategies for inducing change in North Korea, namely engagement-and-isolation versus engagement-only.

The next section introduces two frameworks from the sociology of culture: one for cultural production, and the other for identity-boundary production. These frameworks are useful for conceptualizing the relationship between actor networks (social structure) and the boundaries of identity (semantic structure). However, these frameworks rarely formalize the dynamics of culture and identity production in contexts of conflict and strategic decision making. This deficiency is addressed by integrating into these sociological frameworks the game theoretic framework mentioned earlier: the Prisoner's Dilemma of movement nationalization. Together, these frameworks help explain how strategic interactions among major actors in South Korea's North Korean human rights movement directly altered the competitiveness of the conservative and progressive movements, and how the resultant changes in actor networks politicized and reshaped the boundaries of movement identities.

Production of Culture and Identity Boundaries

Research into cultural production systems has shown that the competitiveness of cultural products varies according to the structure of production networks and the position of producers within those networks. Foundational frameworks from this perspective include cultural industry systems,

---

[3] Chubb 2014.

collaborative networks in art production, cultural fields, and media studies of the flow of symbolic goods from creators to gatekeepers to publics.[4] More recent work in this vein has focused on the production of culture in settings of competition and conflict.[5] Collins' study of the social organization of philosophical schools highlights a number of findings useful for predicting the success of ideologies competing in a political market. First, leaders of successful movements often connect to high-status peers. Second, reputational contagion benefits all members in a rising identity group (e.g., "halo" or "Matthew" effects). Third, positive network externalities often accelerate the concentration of movements, both spatially and temporally.

These three effects can be seen differentially in the case of South Korea's progressive and conservative NGOs. First, progressive NGOs forfeited their dominant position by failing to build ties with INGOs and South Korea's progressive camp, particularly during a decade of progressive administrations when these ties would have been most beneficial to the movement. By contrast, South Korea's conservative NGOs greatly improved their position by linking to INGOs, South Korea's conservative politicians, and Western governments. Second, the rise of the conservative discourse in South Korean mainstream media benefited conservative NGOs as more domestic and international funding became available for CPR activities. Third, North Korea's growing notoriety during this period decreased political support for humanitarian aid and economic engagement and increased support for economic sanctions, legal action, and military countermeasures. These general attitudes constituted positive network externalities for the CPR activities of conservative NGOs and accelerated the spatial and temporal concentration of the CPR approach to North Korean human rights.

However, cultural products are not static goods, and network maneuvers effected to increase the competitiveness of cultural products can also elicit changes in the content of those products. Theories of identity-boundary production study how changes in networks alter the content and nature of group identities. Two concepts – duality and category-networks – illustrate the relationship between social networks and cultural symbols. Duality is the property of actors and symbols to define and be defined by the other when linked.[6] Category-networks are structures reflecting duality at a higher level of organization. Dense networks of actors are often identified by a symbolic group; reciprocally, this symbolic group derives its identity from this network of actors. Empirical examples of the duality between networks and political

---

[4]   Peterson and Berger 1971; Hirsch 1972; Becker 1982; Bourdieu 1983.
[5]   Caves 2002; Burt 2004; Collins 2009.   [6]   Breiger 1974; White 2008 [1965].

identities illustrate how status networks and partisan identities coevolved during the English Civil War, and how youth activists and protest strategies coevolved in the lead up to the 1992 impeachment of the president of Brazil.[7]

The differential coevolution of South Korea's progressive and conservative NGOs with their respective rhetoric can be observed in South Korean news media from 1990 to 2016. As conservative NGOs forged ties with South Korea's conservative politicians and foreign governments, the CPR discourse flourished, but also adopted an increasingly political slant. By the early 2010s, South Korea's conservative administrations and the US government co-opted most conservative NGOs by becoming their most powerful allies and primary sources of funding. The North Korean human rights discourse in South Korean media, reflecting this radical shift in network composition, became almost entirely preoccupied with South Korean and international politics. By contrast, as progressive NGOs retreated from the field of North Korean human rights, the ESCR discourse waned. Deprived of ties to progressive NGOs and devoid of original ESCR content, South Korea's progressive politicians became even more hyperpolitical and reactionary. They criticized conservatives and the CPR approach, but failed to make any constructive contributions to the movement.

Prisoner's Dilemma of Movement Nationalization

These frameworks of cultural production and identity-boundary production provide useful language for narrating the evolution of South Korea's North Korean human rights movement, but do not offer causal predictions, or explain why the outcome that occurred was more likely than other possible outcomes. However, it is possible to integrate into these schemas the predictive game theoretic framework introduced in Figure 2.1.

Collins' second and third points – reputation contagion and positive network externalities – lie beyond the scope of strategic decision making; however, his first point of whether movements connect to high-status peers, namely national governments, is precisely the strategic choice conservatives and progressives faced in the early 2000s. In terms of a Prisoner's Dilemma, one camp's decision to nationalize is akin to defecting and ensures that the camp will not suffer extinction in the event the other camp also decides to nationalize.

While nationalizing protects a camp from experiencing the worst possible outcome, it also comes at a cost. The duality of a tie between human rights

---

[7] Bearman 1993; Mische 2008.

Faction A \ B	Not nationalize	Nationalize
Not nationalize	A,A	B,C
Nationalize	C,B	D,D

Payoffs
A = Not politicized, equally competitive; B = Not politicized, extinct
C = Politicized, dominant; D = Politicized, equally competitive
Utility
C > A > D > B

FIGURE 2.1 Prisoner's Dilemma of movement nationalization

organizations and the state simultaneously casts the state as an advocate of human rights, but also casts human rights organizations as political instruments or extensions of the state. At the higher level of organization, the character of category-networks anticipates that as more political entities join a civil society movement, the resulting cluster of organizations will assume an increasingly political identity. Circumscribing these cultural production schemas within the game theoretical framework of a Prisoner's Dilemma not only narrates the strategic cultural production choices faced by South Korea's conservative and progressive North Korean human rights movements in the early 2000s, but also predicts the paradoxical effect on movement identity, namely politicization.

In addition, the game theoretical framework identifies historical counterfactuals. These include scenarios where both movements nationalized, neither movement nationalized, or where progressives nationalized, but conservatives did not. These counterfactuals offer a conceptual basis for evaluating the prudence of past decisions – conservatives to nationalize and progressives to not nationalize – and imagine how each camp might want to adjust its strategy in the future.

The ideal outcome, in terms of competitiveness and discourse integrity, is the outcome (A, A), where each movement survives, and neither movement politicizes. Outcome (A, A) is a *Pareto optimal* solution to the Prisoner's Dilemma, dominating (D, D) and not being dominated by (C, B) or (B, C). However, it is also an unstable outcome because neither side can trust his opponent not to politicize. In fact, politicizing is a strictly dominant strategy for both players. If Faction B chooses to *not politicize*, then Faction A opts to *politicize* to become the dominant movement. If Faction B chooses to *politicize*, then Faction A again chooses to *politicize* rather than risk the possibility of going extinct. Thus, *politicizing* is a strictly dominant strategy for both sides, and the outcome (D, D), where both sides *politicize*, is the unique Nash Equilibrium for this game. From this perspective, the observed outcome of South Korea's North Korean human rights movement is a nonequilibrium solution. The progressive movement rejected nationalization while the conservative movement embraced it. As a result, the progressive movement paid the ultimate price in competitiveness, whereas the conservative movement, in exchange for becoming politicized, came to monopolize the field. Retrospectively, the progressive movement's choice not to politicize appears to have been a strategic error. Given the choice to politicize or not, competing movements in a polarized political environment eschew politicization at the risk of going extinct.

As with any instrument of theory, this game theoretic framework is a heuristic and not necessarily a true reflection of reality. A single iteration of a Prisoner's Dilemma reduces the myriad of actors and interactions in the field of North Korean human rights to a narrow set of outcomes for a narrow set of actors. Applied to a series of historic events, this framework is at best a stylized metaphor illustrating macro-level movement dynamics over an era, rather than a literal, one-shot strategic showdown between two rational actors. Even if we indulge the stylized application of a simple game to a complex social movement, the arguments deduced in this case only hold if we believe that all four pairs of strategies were possible and would have led to the outcomes claimed in the game's specification.

Perhaps the least likely counterfactual is the scenario where the progressive movement nationalized, and the conservative movement did not. Reflecting on two decades of nuclear tests, economic sanctions, defector testimonies, and UN resolutions, it may be difficult to imagine the conservative constituency refraining from politicizing the movement. This scenario may be difficult to imagine now given the present predicament, but is entirely conceivable considering the state of affairs in the late 1990s. During this period, a nuclear North Korea seemed far off, and the international community was rallying to respond to the North Korean famine, and not to condemn the regime for CPR abuses. Had progressive NGOs aligned with South Korea's sympathetic progressive administrations and Western allies to coordinate a Sunshine offensive, then the pro-CPR camp may have attempted to nationalize, or not. Had both camps nationalized, it is possible to imagine both persisting to the present day; had conservatives not nationalized, it is equally possible to imagine engagement yielding favorable political change in North Korea and the CPR agenda fading from the movement. At the very least, framing North Korean human-rights-movement nationalization as a Prisoner's Dilemma compels us to consider and debate these counterfactuals. At most, it provides an analytic summary of movement trajectories leading up to the historic 2014 UN Resolution on North Korean human rights and explains the current state of the movement in South Korea.

Empirical support for this chapter is divided into structural and media analyses. Three structural analyses are offered. First, South Korea's North Korean human rights actor network is illustrated over four different time periods. Second, the North Korean human rights discourse in South Korean news media is periodized based on its semantic structure. The periodization of the discourse is shown to align almost perfectly with the periodization of the actor network, indicating a tight relationship between actors and discourse in the process of cultural production. Third, a time-series of the North Korean human rights discourse in South Korean media reveals four key events in discourse history. These occur in 2005, 2008, 2012, and 2014. Media analyses of these four events illustrate this chapter's main argument in greater detail.

The 2005 event depicts the creation of linkages between conservative NGOs, INGOs, and South Korea's conservative polity. The 2008 event depicts the linkage of the South Korean conservative polity to the US government and the consolidation of a conservative, pro-CPR clique in South Korea. The 2012 event demonstrates the demise of the progressive movement and the reactionary stance of South Korean progressive politicians to the dominant conservative clique. The 2014 event illustrates how far removed the conservative discourse became from original movement philosophies and strategies, and the extent to which it re-centered on South Korean and international politics. The conclusion revisits the cultural and identity-boundary production frameworks, circumscribed within a Prisoner's Dilemma of movement nationalization. The framework is used to evaluate past strategies and contemplate possible future strategies for reviving a progressive North Korean human rights movement in South Korea, and/or de-politicizing the current conservative movement.

STRUCTURAL ANALYSES

Periodization of Movement by Actor Network

The two components involved in cultural and boundary production are cultural producers and cultural products. The networks of actors linked to South Korea's North Korean human rights movement depict what

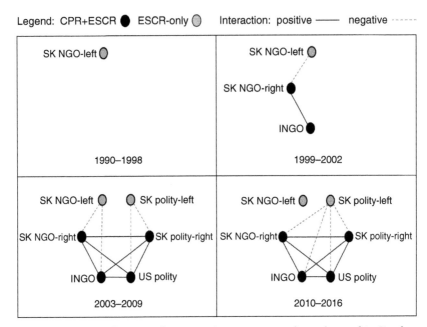

FIGURE 2.2 North Korean human rights actor network, as observed in South
Korean news media, 1990–2016

interactions between which actors resulted in the production of movement
discourse. Figure 2.2 sketches four block models of the North Korean human
rights actor network, as observed in the South Korean news media, between
1990 and 2016. A block model is a network where nodes do not represent
individual entities, but rather categories or classes of individuals and
organizations.

The most prominent actors in the early years of the movement in South
Korea are progressive civic organizations. Kyungyon Moon's history of North
Korean human rights organizations in South Korea from the early 1990s until
2013 offers a comprehensive summary of these movement actors to date.[8]
Moon confirms that the progressive and conservative cleavage in the space
of civil society organizations was further reified as the field became increasingly populated by political entities. The South Korean polity's role in shaping
the North Korean human rights movement has been analyzed with respect to
formal sanctions and policies.[9] This chapter asserts that following the
nationalization of the movement, the South Korean conservative and

---

[8] Moon 2014.   [9] Bae and Moon 2014; Suh 2014.

progressive polities did not merely influence, but rather eclipsed NGOs as the dominant mouthpieces of movement discourse in the mainstream media. These four categories of actors are depicted in Figure 2.2, and their respective roles in discourse production are illustrated by the media analyses that follow.

Supporting actors exerting a weak voice but strong indirect influence in South Korea's North Korean human rights movement are international human rights organizations and the US polity.[10] Figure 2.2 introduces both categories of actors into the respective periods where their interaction with domestic actors began to influence North Korean human rights discourse in South Korea. The ties in these network sketches are not derived from quantitative network data but are compiled from Moon's (2014) history of movement organizations and the media analyses which follow. Periodization of the network into four eras is inspired by Moon's history. The first era, 1990–8, was characterized by the aid and development efforts of South Korea's progressive organizations. The second era, 1999–2002, marked the nascence of conservative organizations, aided by and in cooperation with INGOs. The third era, 2003–9, reflects the period of politicization during which enter South Korean political camps and the US government. During this period, a clique consolidated between conservative organizations, INGOs, the US polity, and South Korean conservatives. By contrast, progressive organizations and South Korean progressives failed to establish strong positive connections between themselves or with international actors. The fourth era, 2010–16, reveals the consolidation of progressive opposition to the conservative, pro-CPR clique and the complete excision of progressive organizations from the movement network. The following analysis of discourse structure reveals how remarkably these changes in the cultural production network of movement actors align with the changes observed in the cultural product that is South Korea's North Korean human rights discourse.

Periodization of Movement by Discourse Network

The dendrogram in Figure 2.3 depicts a clustering of discourse years according to the similarity of each year's discourse structure. The discourse structure was modeled by assembling a corpus of more than 30,000 South Korean national daily newspaper articles published between 1990 and 2016 containing the words *bukhan ingwon* (North Korean human rights).

Articles were drawn from the KINDS and *Chosun Ilbo* databases.[11] These two databases account for nearly all South Korean national dailies, with the

---

[10]　See Chapter 8 by Chubb and Chapter 2 by Yeo in this volume.
[11]　BigKinds 2016; *Chosun Media* n.d.

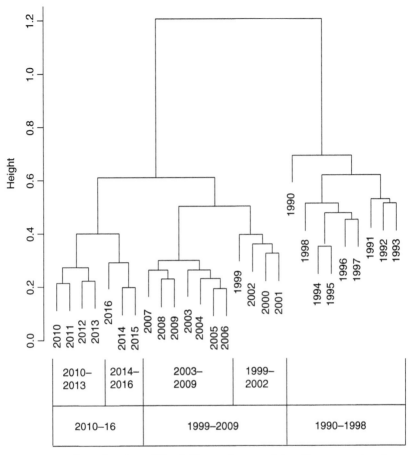

FIGURE 2.3 Periodization of North Korean human rights discourse network as
observed in South Korean news media, 1990–2016

exception of *Donga Ilbo* and *JoongAng Ilbo*. Latent Dirichlet Analysis was
performed in order to extract approximately 1,500 latent topics from the media
corpus. Latent topics can appear in multiple media articles, and each media
article can contain more than one latent topic. This analysis interprets each
latent topic as a semantic node in the discourse. The co-occurrence of two latent
topics in a news article is interpreted as a semantic linkage between those nodes.
These semantic linkages occur at a point in time indicated by the date of the
article. Discourse structure can be represented as a semantic network with latent
topics as nodes and pairwise co-occurrences of latent topics as edges. This
network is longitudinal since nodes and edges can appear and disappear in
corpus articles over time.

A clustering algorithm, applied to pairwise distances, arranged annual network slices in Figure 2.3. Semantic network slices were constructed for each year of the North Korean human rights discourse from 1990 to 2016. The dendrogram reveals that the greatest difference in semantic structure over this period occurs between the period before and after 1999. The period after 1999 is characterized by two major splits: 1999–2009 and 2010–16. The 1999–2009 period may be further divided into the subperiods 1999–2002 and 2003–9. Similarly, 2010–16 was divided into the subperiods 2010–13 and 2014–16.

The quantitative periodization of North Korean human rights discourse as observed in South Korean national dailies aligns almost perfectly with Moon's qualitative periodization of movement actors over the same period, reflecting the strong correlation between cultural producers and products. Moon's analysis began in 1995, and he identifies 1995–9 as the period of *Brotherly Love and Humanitarianism*. This period is characterized by the activities of progressive NGOs pursuing the ESCR approach. Moon labeled the years 2000–3 as *The Development of the Human Rights Agenda*. It was during this period that the CPR approach emerged among conservative NGOs. The years 2004–7 Moon identified as *ESCR vs. CPR*, referring to the contention between progressive and conservative NGOs and their respective approaches. From 2007 to 2012, identity boundaries were politicized, and progressive NGOs largely withdrew from the field in a period Moon labeled *Norm Transition and the Dominance of CPR Perspectives*. Moon's analysis ended with 2013 and was published in 2014, so the period 2014–16 falls outside the scope of his analysis.[12]

Time-Series of Movement Articles in National Print Media

A time-series of article counts of South Korea's conservative and progressive papers of record is a first-order approximation of the volume of public discourse over time. The time-series in Figure 2.4 was extracted from the corpus described earlier. *Chosun Ilbo* is the most widely distributed conservative daily in South Korea, and *Hankyoreh* the most widely distributed progressive daily.

Article counts are low throughout the 1990s, in part because progressive organizations framed their humanitarian activities during this period as the right to life (*saengjon kwon*) or the right to food, and not North Korean human rights (*bukhan inkwon*). Counts of North Korean human rights-related articles gradually begin to increase around 1999 with the emergence of conservative

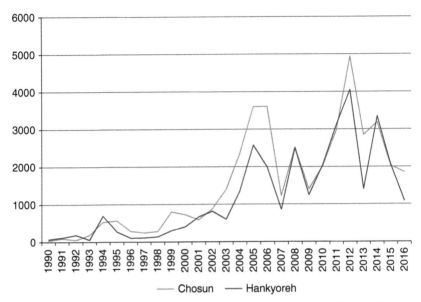

FIGURE 2.4 North Korean human rights news article counts in *Chosun Ilbo* and
Hankyoreh, 1990–2016

organizations. However, even though the two movements were competing and
rapidly expanding during the early 2000s, article counts remain relatively low,
reflecting the low degree of movement politicization during this period.

Figure 2.4 reveals that the volume of print media articles referencing North
Korean human rights rose sharply in 2005 and peaked four times in one
decade: 2005, 2008, 2012, and 2014. The 2005 peak occurred during the period
where the ESCR and CPR approaches were still highly contested. The 2008
and 2012 peaks occur in a period where national human rights norms were
shifting toward a conservative, pro-CPR perspective. The 2014 peak lies outside the scope of Moon's analysis, but should offer a glimpse of the field during
a period in which the conservative perspective had become fully dominant.
One of the most interesting features of these later episodes is the persistence of
progressive media, essentially paralleling conservative article counts, even
after progressive NGOs had declined and were no longer active in the
movement. The following media analysis offers an insight into the changing
content and structure of South Korea's North Korean human rights discourse
during these most dynamic periods. The media analysis also sheds light on the
changing actor networks underlying discourse production and the shifting
boundaries of movement identities.

MEDIA ANALYSIS OF FOUR EPISODES

2005: Consolidation of the Conservative Clique

The 2005–6 plateau of media coverage corresponds to a sequence of events spanning November to December 2005. Round five of the Six Party Talks on North Korean denuclearization was held in Beijing from November 9 to 11. Coming into these talks, the United States and Japan had planned to push forward a joint resolution, possibly adding North Korean human rights to denuclearization as a condition of normalizing relations with North Korea. China and the Roh Moo Hyun administration in South Korea opposed this move as unrealistic as it would present a major roadblock to negotiations.

Shortly after the Six Party Talks, President George W. Bush met with Roh in Gyeongju on November 17 for their fifth bilateral summit. As with the Six Party Talks, North Korean human rights were also on the agenda for this meeting, but Bush's desire that South Korea elevate North Korean human rights on par with the nuclear issue was not reciprocated by the South Korean president. In the joint press conference following their summit, the two emphasized their common commitment to a peaceful resolution of the nuclear crisis on the peninsula, but the issue of North Korean human rights was conspicuously omitted.

This rift was echoed the same day in New York when South Korea abstained from a UN General Assembly vote on an EU-sponsored resolution condemning North Korean human rights. The resolution passed (84 yes, 22 no, 62 abstain), but South Korea's abstention reinforced the China–Korea and US–Japan split among the Six Party Talk participants over the issue of North Korean human rights.

November's chain of diplomatic summits was followed by a sequence of civil society conferences. On November 30, the Sarangbang Group for Human Rights cohosted a conference with member organizations of People's Solidarity for Social Progress, a South Korean alliance of progressive NGOs. As the one-day conference concluded, the organizations released a joint statement blasting the November 17 UN resolution on North Korean human rights as hijacking the cause of human rights to justify the right's true objective of regime change.[13]

Days later, this progressive rebuke of the UN resolution was eclipsed by an event-filled North Korea Human Rights Week (December 5–11), which centered around World Human Rights Day on December 10. Planned by NKnet, the Committee for the Democratization of North Korea, and other

[13] *Hankyoreh* 2005; Lee and Lee 2005.

South Korean conservative North Korean human rights organizations, the week's activities included an international workshop on North Korean human rights, photo exhibition, concert, candlelight march, and various other events. In contrast with the progressives' modest domestic conference, the December 8–10 international North Korean human rights workshop spanned three days. It was held at the luxurious Shilla Seoul hotel and attended by North Korean human rights experts from dozens of domestic and international organizations. Key international participants at the Seoul workshop included Amnesty International, Human Rights Watch, Defense Foundation Forum President Susan Scholte, the US Special Envoy for Human Rights in North Korea Jay Lefkowitz, and the US Ambassador to South Korea Alexander Vershbow. Domestic participants included the Committee for the Democratization for North Korea; South Korea's new-right Liberty Union; former DPRK Workers' Party Secretary and defector Hwang Jang Yop; Grand National party leader Park Geun Hye; more than forty domestic civil society organizations; and a number of North Korean defectors who were invited to provide testimony of North Korean human rights abuses.

This workshop would be the second of three such workshops. The first had been hosted by Freedom House in Washington DC earlier that July, and a third was planned for Europe in March 2006. During the conference, Ambassador Lefkowitz announced that the money set aside by the United States' 2004 North Korean Human Rights Act would be used to help North Korean defectors promote North Korean human rights. Other conference participants called for a wide spectrum of measures, including legal sanctions, reporting, referring Kim Jong Il to the International Court, and regime change. As the workshop concluded, an eight-point document was drafted, nicknamed "the Seoul Declaration." The declaration laid out human rights reform mandates for the North Korean government, demanded the South Korean government take a proactive interest in North Korean human rights, and called on the international community to extend a hand to North Korea while also expanding the international network for North Korean human rights.[14]

2005: Analysis and Discussion

Amid the flurry of diplomatic and civil society activities occurring over this brief few weeks, South Korean media ascertained three differences in the

---

[14]   Lee and Jo 2005; Lee and Lee 2005.

positions of the progressive and conservative camps. The first point of disagreement was over which rights to emphasize. The progressive approach had emphasized aid and development-centered engagement, as embodied in the Sunshine Policy. This strategy was practical, the progressive media argued, because it had directly responded to the humanitarian crisis of the North Korean famine with food aid and fertilizer and promised to do the same for the ongoing refugee crisis.[15] Conservative media criticized inattention of the CPR as "the darkness in the Sunshine Policy," arguing that a "peace without human rights is a fake peace."[16] Moderate progressives took a less dichotomous view and agreed that a constructive discussion about North Korean human rights was needed.[17] Key among these were progressive Christian churches, which simultaneously supported humanitarian aid and CPR such as religious freedom.[18]

The second point of disagreement was over the ordering and timing of North Korean human rights advocacy. Throughout the Six Party Talks, the Roh administration had insisted that North Korean human rights not be raised in parallel with denuclearization as a condition for normalizing relations with the United States, but rather in sequence after denuclearization had been achieved. In the words of Unification Minister Chung, "solving the North Korea nuclear issue is the short-cut to solving the North Korean human rights issue."[19] At the December 10 workshop, Ambassador Lefkowitz countered this view, retorting that there was never a wrong time to address the suppression of human rights.[20] Conservative views were split on this point. The far right agreed with Lefkowitz that North Korean human rights ought to be raised alongside denuclearization, whereas moderate conservatives agreed with Roh that the government should not let the UN resolution interfere with the Six Party Talks.[21]

The third point of disagreement was the debate over which actors should be engaged in North Korean human rights advocacy. At the December 1 meeting, progressive civil society organizations advised against politicizing humanitarian aid, and especially opposed national governments assuming a leadership role in human rights activism.[22] The Roh administration shared this view and opted not to send representatives to either the December 1 or December 10 workshops. In addition to national governments, progressive critics felt that INGO involvement had also become overly politicized and was counterproductive to the practical advancement of North Korean human rights. Conservative media, on the other hand, criticized progressive organizations

---

[15] Lee and Jo 2005; Lee, GS 2005.   [16] Choe, US 2005; Eom 2005.   [17] Go 2005.
[18] Eom 2005.   [19] Kim, YR 2005.   [20] Lee, JH 2005.   [21] Go 2005.   [22] Yu 2005.

and the Roh administration for downplaying CPR. Conservative media countered that sheltering the North Korean regime from criticism would only prolong restoration of rights to the people of North Korea. The Roh administration, and specifically Roh himself, were criticized for being inconsistent on human rights and demonstrating weak leadership. For example, the president's decision to abstain from the UN resolution on North Korean human rights seemed at odds with his earlier support of a 2003 UN resolution on human rights in Myanmar.[23] If the international community was willing to come together to address North Korean human rights, conservatives argued, then South Korean society, and especially its government, needed to play a larger role.[24]

November and December 2005 were a watershed moment for CPR advocacy in South Korea's North Korean human rights movement. The actor network, primarily the pro-CPR camp, was quickly becoming populated by political entities. Conservative media observed that a shift to the right had begun among former student activists, current student groups, North Korean defectors, and members of the international activist community.[25] With the 2004 passage of a North Korean human rights bill in the US Congress, CPR had become a mainstay of the United States' North Korea policy. The December 10 workshop reflected a conscious, strategic decision by these actors to form the conservative pro-CPR clique depicted in Figure 2.2 (2003–9).

By contrast, progressive NGOs had, by choice, formed almost no ties with INGOs or South Korea's progressive polity. Progressive media desperately called on think tanks and civil society organizations to expand the liberal discourse beyond the walls of Korea's ivory towers.[26] However, progressive NGOs' narrow view of movement ownership and the Roh administration's disassociation with North Korean human rights forestalled expansion of the progressive actor network.

2008: Bush–Lee Summit

The 2008 peak of media coverage corresponds to a single event: the US–ROK Summit between Bush and President Lee Myung Bak in Seoul on August 6, 2008. Major items on the summit agenda included the US–ROK Status of Forces Agreement, a bilateral free trade agreement, and North Korean human rights. All three items reflected considerable shifts in the political landscape

---

[23] Bukhangwa 2005; *Chosun Ilbo* 2005. [24] Kim, JH 2005. [25] Choe, BM 2005.
[26] Ahn 2005.

since Bush's summit with Roh in November 2005. Throughout Roh's presidency, his administration had opposed raising the issue of North Korean human rights for fear it would undercut negotiations on denuclearization and obstruct humanitarian and development engagement. This shift in political winds now presented an opportunity for Bush to elevate North Korean human rights, alongside denuclearization, as an equally important prerequisite for normalizing the US–DPRK relationship.[27]

During the summit, Lee capitulated to Bush's North Korean human rights agenda. In exchange for Lee's commitment to raise North Korean human rights as a joint condition for normalization of relations with the North, Bush agreed to support Lee's priority of continuing nonmilitary economic assistance and moving toward a mutually beneficial unification.[28] The United States had wanted to include even stronger language in the joint statement, but South Korea requested a lighter tone. In the end, the language called for "a desire that the human rights situation in North Korea be improved."[29] Both leaders emphasized that North Korea's attempt to engage bilaterally with the United States while cutting out South Korea was not an acceptable strategy and that the United States would remain firm in its relationship with the South.

2008: *Analysis and Discussion*

Conservative responses to the Bush–Lee summit were split. Some conservative politicians and media felt that human rights was a core value in the US–ROK relationship, and that siding with Bush would signal South Korea's commitment to the alliance.[30] These adherents were even more confident of this position when it was reported that presidential candidate Barack Obama planned to adopt Bush's North Korea policy in an upcoming speech at the Democratic National Convention.[31] Moderate conservatives, paralleling the concerns of progressives in 2005, urged caution in elevating North Korean human rights to the level of state and presidential politics. They noted that raising the profile of North Korean human rights was going to put a strain on North–South relations, complicate negotiations over denuclearization, and create uneasiness in South Korean markets.[32] While hardliners argued that denuclearization and North Korean human rights could and ought to be addressed at the same time, moderate conservatives and investors felt that perhaps it was better for the United States and South Korea to address denuclearization and human rights sequentially rather than simultaneously.[33]

[27] Yeom and Kim 2008.   [28] Jeong 2008.   [29] Kim, YS 2008.   [30] Kim, TH 2008.
[31] Lee 2008.   [32] Yeom and Kim 2008; Joo 2008; Yun 2008.   [33] Yun 2008.

The official response of the progressive Minju party echoed the president's concerns about North–South relations and expressed support for the joint statement.[34] Unofficial progressive responses voiced strong disapproval of the United States using South Korea to forward its own agenda. Critics argued that South Korea's North Korea policy was beginning to resemble the neoconservative policies of the first Bush term.[35] Progressive commentators were especially critical of Lee's role in this process: Lee's claim that addressing North Korean human rights as a constructive step toward unification was disingenuous as it unilaterally raised the bar to normalization and betrayed the spirit of the 6.15 and 10.4 Joint Declarations. It was important to continuously address North Korean human rights, progressives clarified, but South Korea should not support the political machinations of US hardliners to obstruct the normalization of US–DPRK relations.[36]

The Bush–Lee summit marked the first instance of executive coordination on North Korean human rights between the governments of the United States and South Korea. It also highlights the oft-forgotten fact that despite being a conservative, Lee had initially been reluctant to politicize North Korean human rights. From the onset of his administration, Lee had adopted the basic tenets of the Sunshine Policy, including nonmilitary food assistance to and economic engagement with North Korea. Lee's acceptance of Bush's proposal symbolized a resetting of the South Korean government's North Korean human rights agenda from its former emphasis on engagement to a multipronged strategy of engagement and isolation.

This new relationship between South Korea's conservative polity and the US government was also the final tie needed to consolidate the conservative pro-CPR clique depicted in Figure 2.2 (2003–2009). Primary actors in the 2005 episode had been ambassadors to the UN, US ambassadors and special envoys, INGOs, and South Korea's domestic NGOs. Now that North Korean human rights had formally entered the sphere of South Korean national politics, it would increasingly be politicians and not civil society organizations who dominated the media spotlight as well as the structure and content of the North Korean human rights discourse.

2012: Progressive Controversy

The next media peak occurred in June 2012 and corresponded to controversial comments made by progressive legislators Im Su Gyeong and Lee Hae Chan of the Democratic United Party (DUP). The controversy sparked by these

---

[34] Seoul Kyungje 2008.   [35] Bak 2008.   [36] *Hankyoreh* 2008.

comments was fueled by several incendiary factors. First, the eighteenth presidential election was scheduled for December 2012, and partisan tensions were at a peak. Second, the progressive camp had recently come under fire when on May 4 politicians from the far-left United Progressive Party (UPP) alleged that members of their party had engaged in election fraud in the nineteenth National Assembly Election held on April 2012. Third, on June 4, Saenuri Assemblyman Yun Sang Hyeon proposed a new North Korean human rights bill in the National Assembly.[37] Each of these factors heightened partisan posturing and predisposed politicians toward the partisan conflict that followed.

On June 1, Assemblywoman Im engaged in a verbal altercation with Joseph Baek, a North Korean defector and Executive Officer of the Young Defectors' Alliance for North Korean Human Rights. Baek had recognized the Assemblywoman as a star of the South Korean student movement once praised in North Korea for her controversial, televised visit in 1989. The two took photographs and exchanged a few pleasantries. Im, upon realizing that Baek was a defector and leader of a conservative North Korean human rights organization, instructed restaurant staff to delete the photos from Baek's camera. A heated exchange ensued during which Im accused Baek and other young defectors of being ignorant about North Korean human rights. Im also berated conservative Assemblyman and activist Ha Tae Won, not present at the incident, as a "turncoat bastard." Ha, a legislator for the conservative Saenuri party, had once been a colleague of Im's in the 1980s student democracy movement before crossing over to the conservative camp in the late 1990s.

Amid the controversy stirred up by Im's remarks, and on the same day that Yun's North Korean human rights bill was introduced in the National Assembly, DUP Assemblyman Lee stated in a radio interview that the proposed bill was diplomatically crude and impertinent. He argued that it was ridiculous that South Korea did not recognize North Korea as a country, considering that it had been admitted to the UN and had engaged in political negotiations with the United States. Lastly, he argued that North Korean human rights was something that the North Korean state needed to address on its own, perhaps with input from North Korean human rights organizations such as Amnesty International, but free of interference from South Korea and other nations.[38]

In the media fluster that ensued, Im quickly issued an apology, emphasizing that she and Assemblyman Ha were doing the same work of helping North

[37] Kim, SH 2012.   [38] Han 2012.

Korean defectors adapt to life in South Korea, but in different ways.[39] By contrast, Assemblyman Lee responded by doubling down. In the days following these incidents, Assemblyman Lee was asked multiple times about his and Im's remarks. He branded conservative opposition to his criticism of the North Korean human rights bill as McCarthyism and expressed frustration that the media was more interested in covering these so-called controversies than his pending candidacy for DUP party chair.[40]

2012: *Analysis and Discussion*

Conservative retorts to Assemblypersons Im and Lee were immediately voiced by Ha and leaders of the defector community. Ha acknowledged Im's apology to him personally, but noted that she had not actually apologized to the defector community or acknowledged the work they were engaged in.[41] On June 5, several North Korean defector- and Saenuri-affiliated organizations held a rally on the lawn of the National Assembly to protest Im's outburst.[42] Defector and Chair of the Free North Korea Movement Alliance, Park Sang Hak, leveled an especially bitter rebuke, stating that in spite of "having drunk from the waters of liberty," Im was "more *jongbuk* [a pro-North follower] than those who had drunk of the waters of the Taedong River."[43] Conservative commentaries quickly extended critiques of the two controversial politicians to accusations that the DUP, the UPP, and the entire left were "pro-North."[44] The most combative critics sardonically asked why the left was unable to escape these pro-North controversies and called for the pro-North politicians to resign.[45] Media analysts noted that North Korea policy and North Korean human rights had become a major point of conflict between progressives and conservatives, and predicted that this would only increase in the run-up to the December 2012 presidential election.[46]

Centrist progressives responded by deflecting attention away from the DUP and toward the UPP and North Korea. DUP politician Moon Jae-in apologized to defectors on behalf of Im and acknowledged that North Korean human rights was a global concern.[47] DUP chair Park attempted to offload the "pro-North" controversy on the UPP and blamed them for creating divisions among the opposition parties.[48] Progressive dailies adopted the latter strategy and further criticized the far-left UPP in order to divert negative

---

[39] Im 2014.   [40] Kim, GH 2012.   [41] Go, EB 2012.   [42] Lee, DH 2012.
[43] Kim, HW 2012.   [44] Kim, JH 2012.   [45] Go 2012.
[46] Mun and Lee 2012; Ahn and Gang 2012.   [47] Yu 2012.   [48] Go, GB 2012.

attention away from center-left politicians and policies.[49] The conservative Saenuri Party had had their fun with the "pro-North" conflict, *Hankyoreh* editorials admonished, but now it was time to move on.[50]

Noncentrist progressives, rather than de-escalate the controversy, followed Lee's lead and launched their own counteroffensive. The language of "pro-North," these progressives warned, was classic red-baiting and McCarthyism. Not all conservatives, they noted, supported this revival of authoritarian-era tactics. They pointed to a division on the right between moderate conservatives, who felt that Saenuri was overreacting, and the "New Right" faction, whom they believed was spearheading the "pro-North" witch-hunt in order to build support for presidential candidate Park Geun Hye.[51] Conservatives countered that it was the left that was overreacting with cries of McCarthyism. Just as the political left had pointed out fissures among conservatives, the political right pointed to fissures among progressives between the DUP and UPP, as well as within the DUP itself.[52]

The June 2012 episode illustrates the extent to which the progressive's strategic choice to not nationalize in years past had altered progressive competitiveness and discourse structure (see Figure 2.3). Without a steady upstream supply of novel rhetoric, progressive politicians' constructive promotion of engagement-oriented ESCR devolved into reactionary criticism of politicized CPR and partisan politics.[53] Ironically, this decision not to nationalize in order to avoid politicization ultimately resulted in hyperpoliticizing those progressive politicians who remained engaged in South Korea's North Korean human rights discourse. The right responded by denouncing "pro-North" elements on the left, and soon the controversy became embroiled in the partisan politics of the upcoming presidential election.[54]

2014: UN Resolution and South Korean North Korean Human Rights Bill

The 2014 peak of media coverage corresponds to the diplomatic run-up, passage, and aftermath of a North Korean human rights resolution in the UN General Assembly and South Korea's fourth attempt to pass a North Korean human rights bill. The tenth of its kind since 2005, the annual passage of a North Korean human rights resolution in the UN had become routine by 2014. However, controversy was ignited on November 6 when EU member states introduced a version of the North Korean human rights resolution recommending that North Korean leaders deemed responsible for human

---

[49] Jo 2012; Kim, GS 2012.   [50] Hankyoreh 2012.   [51] Lee and Gang 2012.
[52] Kim, HW 2012.   [53] *Chosun Ilbo* 2012; Jeon 2012.   [54] Kim, EP 2012; Kim, HO 2012.

rights violations be referred to the International Criminal Court (ICC).[55] A flurry of diplomatic activity ensued. The Chinese ambassador to the United States announced China's opposition to ICC referral.[56] On November 11, US Special Envoy for North Korean human rights Robert King and UN Special Rapporteur for North Korean human rights Marzuki Darusman visited Seoul to consolidate support for the resolution. There they met with South Korean government officials and prominent North Korean human rights activists and organizations.[57] The vote was held on November 19 and the EU version passed 111 to 19 with 55 abstentions, with South Korea voting to pass.[58]

A few days after the UN vote, on November 22, the Foreign Affairs and Unification Committee of South Korea's National Assembly announced that two North Korean human rights bills would be discussed in committee between November 24 and 27.[59] The purpose of the discussion was to attempt to merge two versions of the North Korean human rights bill, one sponsored by each of the two major parties.[60] Both bills agreed that North Korea needed to be responsive to the international community's call to address North Korean human rights. A major difference between the two versions was the conservative party's proposal to fund defector organizations and North Korean human rights organizations.[61] Discussion of the bills continued up until the final day of the legislative session, but in the end no compromise was made and the bill died at the end of the session. It would be two years – not until March 3, 2016 – before South Korea would pass a North Korean human rights bill.

2014: Analysis and Discussion

In the days prior to the UN resolution, South Korean conservative media chronicled diplomatic developments as they unfurled, but offered scant additional commentary. By contrast, progressive commentary reflected undiminished disapproval of the politicization of North Korean human rights. Even if the resolution passed, progressives noted, any actual referral of North Korean leadership to the ICC required the approval of the UN Security Council, an unlikely scenario given the assurance of China and Russia's veto. This fact was well known by nations supporting the resolution, progressives reasoned, and was further evidence that the entire exercise was disingenuous, pure political

---

[55] Jeong 2014. [56] Son 2014; Kim, EM 2014. [57] Won 2014. [58] *Kyunghyang Shinmun* 2014. [59] Gangwondomin Ilbo 2014. [60] Chosun Ilbo 2014. [61] Ahn 2014.

theater, and would only induce North Korea to future retreat from the international community.[62]

All of these objections notwithstanding, the progressive media acknowledged that support for the UN resolution in South Korea was nearly universal, on both the left and the right. Although moderate progressives may have disagreed with the resolution's proposed implementation, they no longer argued against the parallel pursuit of CPR alongside other objectives. The political left's reluctant acceptance of the right's accelerated timing for the CPR agenda was a shift, progressive media admitted, from the "peace and denuclearization first, human rights later" position of the Sunshine Policy era.[63] Defensive editorials clarified that the change in the left's position had not been due to a collective conversion or heedless drift of ideals, but had instead been coerced by external factors. One such article keenly observed that international cooperation between activists, governments, and NGOs had galvanized support for a conservative version of North Korean human rights in the West, leaving little ideological ground for pro-engagement advocates to stand on.[64] This response reflected a partial awareness by progressives that the dominance of the conservative movement and resulting shift in progressive identity boundaries was due in part to conservatives' strategic networking and nationalization.

If progressive support for the UN resolution was half-hearted and with reservations, conservative media relished the international community's condemnation of North Korea and attempted to funnel this legitimating momentum into the passage of the North Korean human rights bill in South Korea's National Assembly. Optimists saw the bill as an opportunity to make actual progress on North Korean human rights.[65] Senior politicians such as Saenuri party leader Kim Mu Seong complained that the inability of the right and left to agree on a North Korean human rights bill was embarrassing.[66] If South Korea was willing to support the UN resolution, but then didn't pass a similar bill at home, it signaled to the international community that South Korea wasn't truly committed to North Korean human rights.[67]

By 2014, the CPR approach to North Korean human rights had achieved widespread legitimacy in the international community, compelling even South Korean progressives to abandon their categorical opposition to the approach. The domination of the conservative movement was due in large part to the strategic choice conservative NGOs made to nationalize their movement by linking to domestic and foreign political actors. However, the

---

[62] Im 2014; Bak 2014; *Hankyoreh* 2014.   [63] Jeong 2014.   [64] Kyunghyang Shinmun 2014.
[65] Chosun Ilbo 2014.   [66] Lee 2014.   [67] Oh and Bang 2014.

consolidation of the conservative clique around these political entities had ironically marginalized the conservative NGOs within their own movement (see Figure 2.2 [2003–2009]). Wholesale politicization of the conservative clique repositioned movement identity and discourse away from civil society debates about human rights advocacy and toward elite political debates over partisan legislation and bureaucratic procedure.

CONCLUSION

The coevolution of the North Korean human rights actor network and discourse structure in South Korea from 2005 to 2014 reveals the two-way relationship between the cultural production of discourse by actors and identity-boundary production among actors by discourse. The actor network was radically restructured by the consistent, strategic decisions of South Korea's progressive and conservative NGOs to form, or abstain from forming, ties with political entities. Restructuring the relationships between discourse producers substantially altered cultural production of North Korean human rights discourse, re-positioning it around the needs and interests of the more dominant actors in the network. Reciprocally, this shift in discourse production changed the roles and identities of network actors. Civil society organizations, which had previously constituted the core of the movement, were now relegated to the margins, either completely excised from the network in the case of progressive NGOs or co-opted by domestic and international political actors in the case of pro-conservative NGOs. South Korean progressives who once played a passive role on the sidelines of the North Korean human rights movement become reactionary and hyperpoliticized as discourse departed from the CPR versus ESCR axis and instead aligned with partisan views of how to induce political change in North Korea.

Keeping in mind these dynamics, as well as the principles illustrated by the Prisoner's Dilemma of movement politicization in a partisan environment, it is possible to conceive a strategy for reviving progressives' pro-engagement, anti-isolation viewpoint and restoring balance to the formerly robust North Korean human rights debate in South Korean civil society. The history of North Korean human rights in South Korea demonstrates that without a critical mass of supporting civil society organizations, a revival of the progressive movement by the South Korean progressive polity alone is highly unlikely. Equally unlikely is an independent resurgence of progressive NGOs without nationalization, which is to say the political sponsorship by a South Korean polity sympathetic to the progressive philosophy. Accordingly, a revival of the pro-engagement, anti-isolation approach would most likely require sustained coordination over several years between progressive NGOs and a pro-ESCR administration.

Considering the overwhelming consensus for the CPR approach to North Korean human rights in the international community, a marginalized, re-emerging progressive paradigm is also not likely to succeed if it ignores CPR as it did in the past. The single greatest challenge to progressive civil society organizations, which already have a coherent ESCR framework for addressing human rights, is the adoption of strategies addressing CPR that also remain consistent with the progressive values of pro-engagement and non-isolation.

Assuming progressive civil society organizations are willing to proactively re-engage in the North Korean human rights movement, it is equally urgent that the South Korean government extends support to these organizations. As tensions rise over security on the Korean peninsula, it remains to be seen whether current and future administrations will deem it strategically expedient and politically feasible to reintegrate this dormant spectrum of civil society organizations in pursuit of a comprehensive approach to human rights, socio-economic and political, for the people of North Korea.

REFERENCES

Ahn, Bo Ram. 2014. Daebuk ppira bangjibeop-bukhaningwonbeop chungdol [North Korean Propaganda Flyer Prevention and North Korean Human Rights Laws Collide]. *Maeil Kyungje*, November 6.

Ahn, Hong Uk and Byeong Han Gang. 2012. Yeogwon "heonjeong pagoejadeul" inyeom chonggongse . . . yagwon "akjil maekasijeum" bangyeok [Ruling Party Launches Offensive on "Constitutional Destroyers"; Opposition Retort "Malicious McCarthyism"]. *Kyunghyang Shinmun*, June 7.

Ahn, Su Chan. 2005. Jinboyeo, daehang bakkeuro nagara . . . jinbojeongchiyeonguso songnyeontoronhoe [Progressives, Come Down out of the Ivory Tower . . . Year-end Forum of the Progressive Political Research Institute]. *Hankyoreh*, December 14.

Bae, Jong Yun and Chung In Moon. 2014. South Korea's Engagement Policy: Revisiting a Human Rights Policy. *Critical Asian Studies* 46 (1): 15–38.

Bak, Hyeon. 2014. Gukjehyeongsajaepanso hoebu eoryeouldeut [ICC Referral will Likely be Difficult]. *Hankyoreh*, November 19.

Bak, Seon Won. 2008. Bijeongsangjeogin MBui jeongsangoegyo [MB's Unusual Summit Diplomacy]. *Kyunghyang Shinmun*, August 8.

Bearman, Peter S. 1993. *Relations into Rhetorics: Local Elite Social Structure in Norfolk, England, 1540–1640.* New Brunswick: Rutgers University Press.

Becker, Howard S. 1982. *Art Worlds.* Berkeley: University of California Press.

BigKinds. 2016. *Korea Press Foundation,* 15 June. www.kinds.co.kr.

Bourdieu, Pierre. 1983. The Field of Cultural Production, or: The Economic World Reversed. *Poetics* 12 (4–5): 311–56.

Breiger, Ronald L. 1974. The Duality of Persons and Groups. *Social Forces* 53 (2): 181–90.

Burt, Ronald S. 2004. Structural Holes and Good Ideas. *American Journal of Sociology* 110 (2): 349–99.

Caves, Richard E. 2002. *Creative Industries: Contracts Between Art and Commerce*. Cambridge, MA: Harvard University Press.

Choe, Byeong Muk. 2005. Seoulseo bukhaningwongukjedaehoe junbi jiphaengwiwon "segyega hamkke ingwon oechimyeon bukhando gyeolgugen dallajil geos" [Organizing Committee Member for the International Conference on North Korean Human Rights in Seoul "Even if the world declares human rights with one voice, ultimately nothing will change in NK"]. *Chosun Ilbo*, December 3.

Choe, U Seok. 2005. Bukan ingwon, haetbyeotjeongchaeng sogui amheuk [North Korean Human Rights, the Darkness within the Sunshine Policy]. *Chosun Ilbo*, December 15.

Chosun Ilbo. 2005. Bukhangwa miyanmaui ingwoneul boneun daehanmingugui nun [Human Rights in North Korea and Myanmar, from the ROK's perspective]. *Chosun Ilbo*, November 18.

Chosun Ilbo. 2012. Buk ingwon undongga Kim Yeong Hwan ssiwa I Seok Gi jinbodang uiwon [North Korean Human Rights Activists and Progressive Party Assemblymen Kim Yeong Hwan and I Seok Gi]. *Chosun Ilbo*, July 22.

Chosun Ilbo. 2014. Yeoya, bukingwonbeop habui mot hamyeon buk hyeopbage gulbokhan kkol doenda [Ruling and Opposition Parties, Failure to Agree on North Korean Human Rights is Succumbing to the North's threat]. *Chosun Ilbo*, November 24.

Chosun Media, n.d. search.chosun.com.

Chubb, Danielle L. 2014. *Contentious Activism and Inter-Korean Relations*. New York: Columbia University Press.

Collins, Randall. 2009. *The Sociology of Philosophies*. Cambridge, MA: Harvard University Press.

Eom, Gi Yeong. 2005. Hangichong – KNCC daerip [Hangichong-KNCC "conflict"]. *Kukmin Ilbo*, December 12.

Gangwondomin Ilbo. 2014. Gukhoe, buk ingwonbeop jejeong nonui bongyeokhwa [National Assembly, Debate Grows over Vote on North Korean Human Rights Law]. *Gangwondomin Ilbo*, November 22.

Go, Eun Bit. 2012. Ha Taegyeong #Im Sugyeong ijung peullei malgo jinsim eorin sagwahaeya# [We Need a Sincere Apology from Ha Tae Gyeong and Im Su Gyeong, not Double Talk]. *Maeil Kyungje*, June 4.

Go, Gwang Bon. 2012. Minjudangeuro beonjineun jongbuk nonran [Pro-North Controversy Spreads to the Democratic Party]. *Seoul Kyungje*, June 4.

Go, Seung Uk. 2005. Bukhaningwongukjedaehoe hugi [Epilogue of the International Conference on North Korean Human Rights]. *Kukmin Ilbo*, December 14.

Good Friends. 2003. *Alternative NGO report on the Committee on Economic, Social and Cultural Rights of the Second Periodic Report of Democratic People's Republic of Korea*, November.

Haggard, Stephan and Marcus Noland. 2007. *Famine in North Korea: Markets, Aid, and Reform*. New York: Columbia University Press.

Han, Seok Hui. 2012, "Bukan ingwonbeom nonuineun gukgagan oegyojeong gyeollye" ... I Haechan bareon pamun ["Debating the North Korean Human Rights Law is Diplomatically Bad Manners Between Countries" ... I Hae Chan's Statement makes Ripples]. *Herald Kyungje*, June 4.

Hankyoreh. 2005. Saengsanjeogeuro baljeonsikyeoya hal bukhan ingwon nonui [North Korean Human Rights Debate Must be Advanced in a Productive Way]. *Hankyoreh*, November 30.

Hankyoreh. 2008. Nambung gwangyekkaji miguge gidaeneun imyeongbang jeongbu [Lee Myung Bak Government Leans on America even for the North–South Relationship]. *Hankyoreh*, August 6.

Hankyoreh. 2012. Saenuridang, 'jongbung nonjaeng jeulgigi' kkeunnael ttaedo dwaetda [Saenuri Party, it's Also Time to Stop "reveling in the Pro-North controversy"]. *Hankyoreh*, June 6.

Hankyoreh. 2014. Bongyeokhwahan 'daebuk ingwon apbak'gwa uriui yeokhal [Our Expanded Role in "applying human rights pressure to the North"]. *Hankyoreh*, November 19.

Hawk, David. 2010. *Pursuing Peace while Advancing Rights: The United States Approach to North Korea*. Washington DC: US-Korea Institute at SAIS.

Hawk, David. 2012. *The Hidden Gulag: The Lives and Voices of "Those Who are Sent to the Mountains."* Washington DC: US Committee for Human Rights in North Korea.

Herald Kyungje. 2012. Gaegyeo yokseolmakmal siin ... gongsiksagwa [Im Su Gyeong's Official Apology Admits Profane Outburst and Explains "Traitor XX, was aimed at the assemblyman"]. June 3.

Hirsch, Paul M. 1972. Processing Fads and Fashions: An Organization-Set Analysis of Cultural Industry Systems. *American Journal of Sociology* 77 (4) 639–59.

Im, A Yeong. 2014. Nambuk bundane daehae saenggakji anhgo buk ingwoneman jipjunghaneun geon munje [Focusing only on North Korean Human Rights and not Thinking about the North–South Division is a Problem]. *Kyunghyang Shinmun*, November 30.

Jeon, Won Chaek. 2012. Jinboneun nuguwa ssauneunga [Who are Progressives Fighting With?]. *Kyunghyang Shinmun*, June 12.

Jeong, Cheol Sun. 2014. Yuen·Mi ingwonteuksa isttara banghan [UN, US Envoys for Human Rights Visit Korea in Succession]. *Munhwa Ilbo*, November 4.

Jeong, Jin Yeong. 2008. Hanmi jeongsanghoedami namgin sukje [Homework Remaining from the Korea-America Summit]. *Hanguk Ilbo*, August 7.

Jeong, Tae Il. 2014. Ya "nambukhwahaega bukingwon haebeop" [Opposition Party " North–South reconciliation is the key to North Korean human rights"]. *Herald Kyungje*, November 19.

Jeong, Yu Seon. 2014. Sasilsang Kim Jeongeun gyeonyang ... gusokryeogeun eopsjiman bukhan gukjemudae gorip gipeojyeo [No Real Power to Detain Kim Jong Un, but North Korea's Isolation Deepens on the International Stage]. *Kookje Shinmun*, November 19.

Jo, Hye Jeong. 2012. "Bukane daehan aejeonggwaing" "toehaengjeong jeongpajuui" bipan [Criticism of "North Korea love fest" and "Degenerate political parallelism"]. *Hankyoreh*, June 11.

Joo, Yong Jung. 2008. Bugingwon jeongmyeon georon [Discussion about North Korean Human Rights Front and Center]. *Chosun Ilbo*, August 7.

Kang, Chol-hwan, and Pierre Rigoulot. 2005. *The Aquariums of Pyongyang: Ten Years in the North Korean Gulag*. New York: Basic Books.

Kim, Eun Mi. 2014. Yuen 'buk ingwongyeoruian chaetaek' ... jeongbu hwanyeong·miguk jiji [UN "adopts human rights resolution on the North"; Government Welcomes, United States Supports]. *Maeil Kyungje*, November 19.

Kim, Eun Pyo. 2012. Yeoyaneun jigeum 'jongbukjeonjaeng' [Ruling and Opposition Parties now in "Pro-North War"]. *Maeil Kyungje*, June 5.

Kim, Geun Sik. 2012. Jongbukgwa haetbyeoteun byeolgae [Pro-North and Sunshine Policy are Separate]. *Kyunghyang Shinmun*, June 11.

Kim, Gyeong Hwa. 2012. Saengbangsong dojung imsugyeong georonhaja jeonhwa kkeuneun beoreong I Haechan ["Abrupt I Hae Chan" Hangs up During Live Interview When Im Su Gygeong is Mentioned]. *Chosun Ilbo*, June 6.

Kim, Hae Young. 2014. Stifled Growth and Added Suffering: Tensions Inherent in Sanctions Policies Against North Korea. *Critical Asian Studies* 46 (1): 91–112.

Kim, Hyeong O. 2012. 'Jongbuk nonran'e gathyeo beorin daehanminguk [ROK caught up in the "Pro-North controversy"]. *Maeil Kyungje*, June 6.

Kim, Hyeong Won. 2012a. Jayuui mul masigodo daedonggang mureul masin saramboda deo jongbok [Despite Drinking the Water of Liberty, more Pro-North than those who Drank from the Daedong River]. *Chosun Ilbo*, June 5.

Kim, Hyeong Won. 2012b. Gukminui haprijeok uimun maekasijeumeuro gonggyeok [Attacking Citizen's Rational Concerns with McCarthyism]. *Chosun Ilbo*, June 8.

Kim, Jae Hyeon. 2012. Bosudanche, Im Sugyeong-I Haechan-Choe Jaeseong uiwon gobal [Conservative Organizations Accuse Lawmakers Im Su Gyeong, I Hae Chan, Choe Jae Seong]. *Herald Kyungje*, June 11 June.

Kim, Jeong Hun. 2005. Yusehui gongdong daehoejang "minganchawonseo jegi ... jeongbudo jeokgeukjeogigil" [Joint Session Chair Yu Se Hui "Raising the civilian dimension, the government ought to be more proactive"]. *Chosun Ilbo*, December 6.

Kim, Mi Kyoung. 2012. *Securitization of Human Rights: North Korean Refugees in East Asia*. Santa Barbara: Praeger.

Kim, Si Hyeon. 2012. Du beon musandoen bukaningwonbeom tto barui [Another Motion Raised for the Twice Unsuccessful North Korean Human Rights Law]. *Chosun Ilbo*, June 4.

Kim, Tae Hyeon. 2008. Bugingwoneul 'geumgi'eseo pureonael ttae [It's Time we Disentangle North Korean Human Rights from Taboo]. *Chosun Ilbo*, August 9.

Kim, Yeong Rae. 2005. Jeongtongil naenyeoncho dangbokgwi [Unification minister Jeong "Early next year the party will make a comeback"]. *Financial News*, December 7.

Kim, Yeong Seok. 2008. Buk ingwonmunje wae gongronhwa ... Mi jaguk yeoronuisik ganghan yocheong [Why make a Public Issue of the North Korean Human Rights Problem? America Strongly Demands Awareness of Domestic Public Opinion]. *Kukmin Ilbo*, August 6.

Kukmin Ilbo. 2005. Bugingwon chamsang, jeongbu nuneman an boina [The Misery of North Korean Human Rights, Visible to all but the Government?]. November 18.

Kukmin Ilbo. 2012. Minjudang, daeyeogongseboda banseongi meonjeoda [Democratic Party, Reflect First Before Launching an Offensive Against the Ruling Party]. June 6.

Kyunghyang Shinmun. 2014. Jeongbu "yuen gyeoruian, bukhan ingwon gukjesahoe uryeo banyeong" [Government "UN resolution reflects concerns international community's concerns over North Korean human rights"]. *Kyunghyang Shinmun*, November 19.

Lee, Dong Hun. 2012. Saenuri-talbukjadanche "Im Sugyeong mangmal" jipjungpohwa talbukja jeonchee daehan modok [Saenuri and Defector Organizations Concentrate on "Im Su Gyeong outburst"; An Insult to all NK Defectors]. *Hanguk Ilbo*, June 5.

Lee, Gil Dong. 2014. Kim Museong "bukhaningwonbeop gukhoegyeryu gukjejeogeuro bukkeureoun il" [Kim Mu Seong "Parliamentary mooring of the North Korean human rights law an international embarrassment"]. *Herald Kyungje*, November 20.

Lee, Gye Seong. 2005. Bukhan ingwongaeseoneul wonhandamyeon [If we Truly want North Korean Human Rights to Improve]. *Hanguk Ilbo*, December 2.

Lee, Ha Won. 2008. Miminjudang "daebung jikjeoboegyo" myeongsi [US Democratic Party Elucidates "direct diplomacy with the North"]. *Chosun Ilbo*, August 12.

Lee, Je Hun. 2005. Bukhaningwon gukjedaehoe [International Conference on North Korean Human Rights]. *Hankyoreh*, December 10.

Lee, Je Hun and Yong In Lee. 2005. "Bukhan ingwon" jinbo-bosudanche gakgak nonuimadang maryeon ["North Korean human rights" Provides a Venue of Debate for Progressive and Conservative Organizations]. *Hankyoreh*, November 30.

Lee, Ji Seon and Byeon Han Gang. 2012. Bosu naebuseodo "saenuri, gwadohan inyeomgongse" saekkkallon yeokpung uryeo [Even Conservatives Concerned about "Saenuri, excessive ideological assault," Backlash against Partisan Rancor]. *Kyunghyang Shinmun*, June 12.

Lee, Yong In and Gi Won Jo. 2005a. Bukhaningwon gukjedaehoe gaemak [Opening Ceremony of the International Conference on North Korean Human Rights]. *Hankyoreh*, December 9.

Lee, Yong In and Gi Won Jo. 2005b. Bukhaningwon gukjedaehoe [International Conference on North Korean Human Rights]. *Hankyoreh*, December 10.

Mische, Ann. 2008. *Partisan Publics: Communication and Contention across Brazilian Youth Activist Networks*. Princeton: Princeton University Press.

Moon, Kyung Yon. 2014. South Korean Civil Society Organizations, Human Rights Norms, and North Korea. *Critical Asian Studies* 46 (1) 65–89.

Mun, Su In and Ga Yun I. 2012. Gyeongjewigi dagaoneunde ... yeoya inyeomgongbangman [With an Economic Crisis Looming, Progressive and Ruling Parties Lock Horns over Ideology]. *Maeil Kyungje*, June 6.

Oh, Nam Seok and Seung Bae Bang. 2014. Gukhoeseon bukingwonbeop 10nyeonjjae jejari [National Assembly's North Korean Human Rights Law Standstill in its Tenth Year]. *Munhwa Ilbo*, November 19.

Peterson, Richard A. and David G. Berger. 1971. Entrepreneurship in Organizations: Evidence from the Popular Music Industry. *Administrative Science Quarterly* 16 (1) 97–106.

Seoul Kyungje. 2008. Hanmi jeongsanghoedam jeongchigwon baneung [Korea America Summit] Reaction from the Political Community]. August 6.

Seoul Kyungje. 2014. Bukhan ingwon siljiljeok haegyeolchaegeun mueosinga [What are Practical Solutions to North Korean Human Rights?]. November 26.

Son, Je Min. 2014. Jung "bukhaningwon ICC hoebue bandae" ilbu bidongmaenggukdeuldo dongjo [China "opposes North Korean human rights ICC referral" and some Non-alliance Countries Concur]. *Kyunghyang Shinmun*, November 6.

Song, Dae Han and Christine Hong. 2014. Toward "The Day After" National Endowment for Democracy and North Korean Regime Change. *Critical Asian Studies* 46 (1): 39–64.

Suh, Bo Hyuk. 2014. The Militarization of Korean Human Rights: A Peninsular Perspective. *Critical Asian Studies* 46 (1): 3–14.

White, Harrison C. 2008 [1965]. Notes on the Constituents of Social Structure. Soc. Rel. 10–Spring '65. *Sociologica* 2 (1): 1–15.

Won, Ho Yeon. 2014. Robert King teuksa 11il banghan ... daruseuman teukbyeolbogogwangwa hamkke 'daebuk ingwon apbak' [Special Envoy Robert King Visits Korea on the 11th ... Along with Special Rapporteur Darusman "Pressures the North on HR"]. *Herald Kyungje*, November 11.

Yeom, Yeong Nam and Gwang Sun Kim. 2008. Hanmi jeongsanghoedam/bungmi FTA bijun hyeomnyeong hwaeum [Korea-America Summit / Cooperative Chords Struck on North Korean Nukes and Free Trade Agreement Ratification]. *Hanguk Ilbo*, August 7.

Yu, Bong Seok. 2005. Rho daetongryeong, "bukhan hanbeon danyeoosijyo" [President Rho, "Why don't you visit North Korea?"]. *Maeil Kyungje*, December 9.

Yu, Tae Yeong. 2012. Mun Jaein "bukdo ingwon jeungjin noryeokaeya" [Moon Jae In "The North also needs to take steps to advance human rights"]. *Segye Ilbo*, June 5.

Yun, Yeong Gwan. 2008. Hanmidongmaengui segyehwa geurigo bukanui ingwon [Globalization of the US–ROK Alliance, and North Korean Human Rights]. *Chosun Ilbo*, August 7.

3

North Korean Human Rights Discourse and Advocacy in the United States

Andrew Yeo

The United States is often at the forefront of condemning the human rights record of totalitarian regimes. Since the early 2000s, human rights advocates in the United States have remained especially vocal in denouncing rights abuses in North Korea and the denial of basic freedoms under the rule of an oppressive dictator. The significant attention raised by advocacy networks in the United States and abroad has sealed North Korea's status as one of the worst human rights offenders in the contemporary era. This understanding of North Korea has become nearly axiomatic for US policymakers.

This chapter investigates the emergence and trajectory of North Korean human rights advocacy in the United States, paying particular attention to shifts in human rights discourse. When did North Korean human rights first emerge as an issue in the United States, and how did it evolve? Why did North Korean human rights initially gravitate toward civil and political rather than social and economic rights? What does North Korean human rights discourse in the United States tell us about the interaction between state and nonstate actors, as well as network ties between US-based human rights actors and the broader transnational advocacy movement?

Although attention naturally gravitates toward the role of defectors, NGOs, and civil society groups in building the North Korean human rights campaign, this chapter acknowledges the important role the US government played in shaping North Korean human rights advocacy and discourse in the United States. State actors are not necessarily the driving force behind the North Korean human rights agenda. However, the findings in this chapter suggest that a preexisting discursive structure articulated within US foreign policy circles shaped the early trajectory and present boundaries of North Korean human rights advocacy in the United States. More concretely, North Korean human rights and the emphasis on civil and political rights in the United States traces its lineage to earlier foreign policy debates in the 1970s and 1980s, which framed human rights within a Cold War, anticommunist framework. Additionally, the fixation on North Korea's nuclear program within the US Congress and the White House has led to the more recent framing of North Korean human rights as a security issue in the United States.

This chapter is organized as follows. The first section provides theoretical grounding by briefly exploring the relationship between state and nonstate actors in advocacy movements as well as the concept of discursive structure. The second section provides empirical data profiling the trajectory and content of North Korean human rights discourse in the United States. The third section fleshes out the emergence, direction, and structure of the advocacy movement by way of examining discourse and discursive shifts and noting when and how the US government exercises influence. The fourth section concludes with a discussion of the current trajectory of human rights advocacy.

THEORETICAL GROUNDING

State and Nonstate Actors

The literature on transnational advocacy networks and transnational activism abounds with stories in which the weak upend the strong.[1] Students of transnational activism highlight how "weak" nonstate actors exercise ideational power (in the form of norms, ideas, and discourse) to overcome more powerful states in the international system. For instance, in their seminal work *Activists Beyond Borders*, Keck and Sikkink demonstrate how domestic activists connect with transnational actors to apply outside pressure against repressive and recalcitrant states.[2] Tarrow's research on transnational contention treats activists as the central protagonists, even as they link with states and institutions in transnational coalitions.[3] Although transnational advocacy networks may certainly include state actors, states either tend to lurk in the background playing second fiddle to a band of nonstate actors or they exist as the direct target of transnational advocacy networks.

Research and reports on North Korean human rights advocacy also emphasize the role of nonstate actors. For instance, earlier scholarship on the legal mobilization of North Korean human rights highlights the importance of nonstate actors and smaller NGOs, in addition to the role of the UN and government agencies.[4] In the United States, human rights NGOs, policy think-tanks, Korean–American church groups, and refugee and defector

[1] Keck and Sikkink 1998, 1; Carpenter 2011; Bob 2005; Shipper 2013.
[2] Keck and Sikkink 1998, 13.   [3] Tarrow 2005, 5.   [4] Goedde 2010.

organizations have all contributed to North Korean human rights discourse. Two nonstate actors have played a particularly instrumental role: the Committee for Human Rights in North Korea (HRNK), and the Defense Forum Foundation (DFF).[5] HRNK raises awareness through its expert reporting on topics including prison camps, refugees, and the *songbun* class system in North Korea. HRNK also draws attention from national and international political figures through the personal network ties of its board members. If HRNK is closely connected with the policy and academic community, DFF operates more as a grassroots organization. DFF was particularly instrumental in the early stages of the North Korean human rights movement; it launched the North Korea Freedom Coalition (NKFC) in 2003, an umbrella group of approximately 70 organizations today.[6] Through its reporting, advocacy, and naming-and-shaming strategies, both HRNK and DFF have helped create what some see as the dominant narrative on North Korean human rights.[7]

If activists and civil society actors are major players in the human rights campaign, then by extension they should shape prevailing discourses. Indeed, nonstate actors, as important discursive agents, shape the norms and beliefs of the advocacy network. The indispensable role of defectors, NGOs, and other civil society groups in advancing North Korean human rights is not disputed here. However, this chapter shifts the focus to the role of the state and its relationship with civil society actors in (re)producing North Korean human rights discourse. Advocacy networks do shape the North Korean human rights policy agenda. However, in the United States, the discourse adopted by activists is itself embedded within a broader discursive structure forged by state actors.

Discursive Opportunity Structure

What is discourse, and what role does it play in understanding the nature and scope of North Korean human rights in the United States? Borrowing from Schmidt's work on discursive institutionalism, discourse refers to an "interactive process of conveying ideas" and comes in two forms.[8] The first is *coordinative discourse*, which revolves around "individuals and groups at the center of policy construction who are involved in the creation, elaboration, and justification of policy and programmatic ideas."[9] The second is *communicative discourse* between political actors and the public. It takes place in the broader political sphere and consists of individuals and groups "involved in the

---

[5] Goedde 2010, 537.   [6] See NKFC, webpage: www.nkfreedom.org/.   [7] Hong 2013, 45.
[8] Schmidt 2008, 303.   [9] Schmidt 2008, 310.

presentation, deliberation, and legitimation of political ideas to the general public."[10] When coordinative discourse precedes communicative discourse on a particular policy issue, the relative role of policymakers in shaping discourse regarding said policy issue is likely enhanced.[11]

The concept of discursive opportunity structure is particularly helpful in understanding the early context of North Korean human rights discourse and its alignment with broader debates regarding human rights in US foreign policy. Sociologists define discursive opportunity structure as "institutionally anchored ways of thinking that provide a gradient of relative political acceptability to specific packages of ideas."[12] In the context of human rights discourse in the United States, "rights" language has predominantly focused on civil and political rights (i.e., freedom of speech, religion, and due process; protection against cruel and unusual punishment, and so on). The discursive structure of human rights in the United States (i.e., coordinated discourse), shaped in part by policy actors, thus influences which frames, narratives, and discourse will be adopted and communicated by other North Korean human rights advocates (i.e., communicative discourse). In short, how NGOs, defectors, and transnational activists construct North Korean human rights discourse is often influenced by existing discursive structures on human rights as articulated in the formal policy sphere.

The timing and sequence of North Korean human rights discourse, particularly at its origin, is especially important. One might credibly argue that the origins of North Korean human rights discourse in the United States began with defector testimonies in the late 1990s. These accounts were documented and reported by NGOs, which, in turn, were reported by the US State Department and then broadcast to the general public via the media. Yet even when North Korean human rights abuses are reported by defectors and activists, the existing policy environment influences how abuses are perceived, interpreted, and broadcast – and whether this leads to greater mobilization.[13]

Certainly, effective mobilization requires movement capacity and creativity on the part of activists. However, to draw policymakers into their campaign, North Korean human rights discourse must also comport with the beliefs of key political actors and movement gatekeepers.[14] Conversely, policymakers and political leaders will align with advocacy movements if it helps them promote their own policy agenda – whether related to human rights or not.

---

[10]   Schmidt 2008, 310.
[11]   Schmidt (2008) assumes that coordinative discourse occurs among policy elites, but as Chubb (Chapter 8 of this volume) argues, activists may also operate near the center of policy construction as they articulate and negotiate the normative agenda with policy elites.
[12]   Ferree 2003, 306.   [13]   Meyer and Minkoff 2004.   [14]   Carpenter 2011, 100.

TRACKING NORTH KOREAN HUMAN RIGHTS DISCOURSE
IN THE UNITED STATES

The North Korean human rights advocacy network in the United States is constituted by grassroots NGOs, international human rights organizations, Korean–American churches, North Korean defectors, government institutions including Congress and the State Department, quasi-governmental institutions and think-tanks such as the National Endowment for Democracy (NED) and the Center for Strategic and International Studies (CSIS), and other organizations which provide a platform for North Korean human rights issues.[15] To track the rise of North Korean human rights discourse in the United States, I conducted a newspaper content analysis of all articles on North Korean human rights from 1985 (when the first article appeared) to 2015, in three major US papers with significant international coverage: the *New York Times*, the *Wall Street Journal*, and the *Washington Post*. The distribution of news stories serves as a proxy for measuring the trajectory of public discourse in the United States.

Furthermore, to understand the general content and tone of North Korean human rights discourse in the United States, I analyzed the words used by state and nonstate actors to report on North Korean human rights abuses. For state actors, this includes content analysis of the US State Department human rights reports on the DPRK from 1988 to 2014, and statements from the floor of the US House and Senate retrieved from the *Congressional Record (CR)* from 1996 to 2015.[16] For nonstate actors, I examine reports published by HRNK and the North Korea Freedom Week (NKFW) agendas distributed by the NKFC.[17] In the following section, I present a historical narrative of North Korean human rights advocacy tracing the events germane to the evolution of North Korean human rights discourse and advocacy. I focus on important historical critical junctures relevant to human rights discourse in US foreign policy generally, and North Korean human rights in particular, to understand how state actors influence North Korean human rights discourse and the direction of US-based advocacy groups. This narrative is based on interviews with NGO activists, former and US government officials, Congressional

---

[15] Moon 2008, 267; Hong 2013.

[16] The State Department first published its human reports on North Korea in 1979. I selected 1988 as a starting point due to limitations in obtaining digital files of reports readable in ATLAS.ti for earlier years. For Congressional records, 1996 is the earliest year in which North Korean human rights is discussed as an issue in its own right.

[17] For a partial list of NKFW agendas, see www.nkfreedom.org/Events/NKFC-Sponsored-Events .aspx.

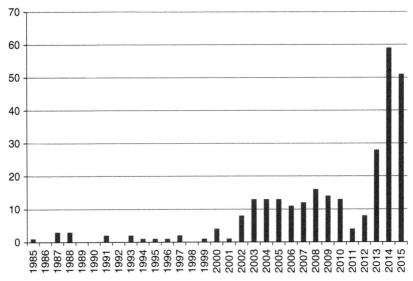

FIGURE 3.1 Articles referring to North Korean human rights in the *New York Times*, *Wall Street Journal*, and *Washington Post*

staffers, and human rights policy experts deeply invested in North Korean human rights, as well as my own participant observation of dozens of North Korean human rights events since 2008.

Media Coverage

North Korean human rights have received significant publicity in the United States over the past decade. But when did North Korean human rights first enter the American public consciousness? A search for all news articles on North Korean human rights in the *New York Times*, the *Wall Street Journal*, *and* the *Washington Post* presents a profile of how North Korean human rights as an issue has developed over time in the United States. Figure 3.1 aggregates the news stories from all three newspapers.

Figure 3.1 represents a rough approximation of the growth in North Korean human rights discourse in the US public sphere. It corroborates arguments from North Korean human rights groups that information (and discussion) on North Korean human rights remained limited until the late 1990s. The rising number of North Korean defectors from the late 1990s onward helped catalyze greater discussion and a growing advocacy movement in the United States, as attested by the steady number of news stories on North Korean human rights

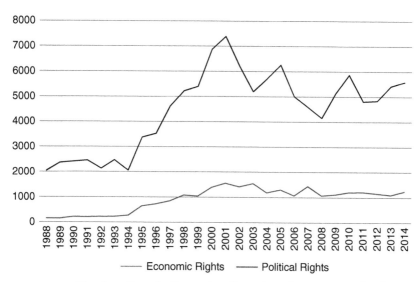

FIGURE 3.2 Number of words allocated to discussion of economic and political rights in US State Department human right reports on North Korea

appearing between 2003 and 2010. The number of news articles increased dramatically from 2013 to 2015 with a peak number of 58 articles published in 2014. This sudden increase can be attributed to the launch of the COI in 2013, and the high-profile campaign pursued by the North Korean human rights advocacy network following the release of the COI final report.

Content and Tone of Discourse

The content of North Korean human rights discourse in the United States overwhelmingly focuses on political-civil rights. This bias was consistent in reports from state and nonstate actors. In Figure 3.2, I present a content analysis of the State Department's annual human rights reports to evaluate the percentage of content devoted to economic or political issues.[18]

When coverage of economic rights is analyzed as a percentage of coverage on political rights, after 1995, economic rights generally reflect only 20 percent of what is devoted to coverage of political rights in any given year.

[18] I highlight State Department reports for several reasons: the method of reporting is consistent and systematic; sections of the report already include headings distinguishing between political and economic issues; the tone remains neutral and even. See US State Department, Country Reports on Human Rights Practices for 2015, Overview and Acknowledgements, www .state.gov/j/drl/rls/hrrpt/humanrightsreport/#wrapper.

State Department reports reflected a neutral tone and were thus less helpful for capturing additional nuances. To capture the tone of North Korean human rights discourse, therefore, I examined statements from Congressional leaders. In particular, I wanted to capture whether North Korean human rights discourse suggested a belligerent, neutral, or empathetic tone when discussing North Korean human rights. Belligerence implies greater attention to the North Korean regime as the object of speech/discourse, whereas empathy suggests an emphasis on the North Korean people as the object of discourse. Statements reporting factual information rather than normative judgment were interpreted as neutral.

A search in the CR produced 66 different entries involving at least one paragraph worth of discussion on North Korean human rights from 1996 to 2015 on the House or Senate floor. This amounted to 124 speech acts provided by individual speakers.[19] I coded the "tone" of the text using first the specific CR entry and then the individual speaker/speech act as the unit of analysis. The tone of the text was coded on a 7-point scale from +3 to –3, signifying greater belligerence and greater empathy, respectively. Although I expected a sharp increase in bellicosity in the early 2000s followed by a decrease in belligerent discourse from the latter 2000s, my analysis of the CR did not detect any noticeable trends or patterns beyond the fact that a slight majority of entries (35 out of 66) were coded in the belligerent tone category, and that Republicans were on average more belligerent than Democrats in their tone (+1.39 for Republicans and +0.36 for Democrats).[20] When describing the North Korean regime in reference to human rights, the five most repeated words included horrifying/horrible (34), totalitarian (25), repressive (16), terrible (10), and evil (7). A few other descriptors attached to the "belligerent" coding included ruthless, tyrannical, rogue, abnormal, butcher, thugs, and vicious. Contrary to popular assumptions that US policymakers supported regime change, there were few if any statements directly supporting such policies. Speakers discussed their desire for change in North Korea, but this usually implied reforms rather than outright regime change.[21] It also differed from some civil society groups, particularly NKFC, which unabashedly resorted to regime-change rhetoric during its rallies.

---

[19] One entry might include statements from multiple speakers.

[20] Tone tended to correlate more closely with individual speakers rather than time period. For instance, the language and words used by speakers such as Sam Brownback, Ed Royce, Frank Wolf, Chris Smith, and Joe Pitts were consistently stronger than the words of Joe Biden, Jim Leach, and Charles Rangel – all of whom were coded making statements in multiple entries.

[21] For instance, Senator Brownback also stated, "the North Korean regime itself must begin to change itself and join the rest of the world in giving hope and freedom to its people." United States Congress 2002.

Finally, in Congress, based on discussions in the CR, North Korean human rights was not wrapped with the religious overtones I anticipated given the assumed outsized role Korean–Americans churches and evangelical Christians (and, to a lesser extent, Jewish groups) played in North Korean human rights advocacy.[22] Religious references such as God, prayer, sin, and compassion only appeared 9 times in the 66 entries.

Although I did not conduct a content analysis of NGO reports and documents, a review of NKFC's annual agenda for North Korea Freedom Week (NKFW) and participant observation by the author at this event in 2009 and 2015 suggests similarities in discourse, particularly the focus on political rights, prison camps, and defectors' issues.[23] In 2016, NKFC chose the theme "Preparing for Regime Collapse and Peaceful Unification" for NKFW. The tenor of discussion at NKFC events included the use of strong, at times inflammatory language toward the regime, while vividly recounting North Korean atrocities (and Chinese complicity) and great suffering among the people.[24] Naming-and-shaming the regime was typical during demonstrations outside Congress and the Chinese Embassy.

Turning to HRNK, a cursory reading of the 26 reports published between 2003 and 2015 suggests a focus on civil and political rights issues. Of these, 12 reported on North Korean political prisons, with David Hawk's *Hidden Gulag* series becoming the most widely recognized study.[25] This contrasts with reports published by INGOs such as Amnesty International and Human Rights Watch (HRW) whose reports cover a more diverse range of human rights issues, covering social and economic issues such as health care.[26]

Different pieces of evidence from content/discourse analysis may convey different facets of North Korean human rights discourse. However, it is clear from this analysis that North Korean human rights discourse in the United States privileges political rights, despite continued violations pertaining to economic and social rights. Voices that advocate taking a human security approach (addressing issues such as food shortages, malnutrition, and health

---

[22] Some officials stated that Korean–Americans, and Korean–American churches in particular, played a major role in North Korean human rights legislation. However, one Korean–American mobilizer who attempted to build a larger Korean–American political movement behind North Korean human rights believes that the lack of unity among Korean–Americans and Korean–American churches on North Korean human rights issues resulted in an underwhelming response. Author's interview with former Freedom House director, Washington DC, November 3, 2015.

[23] See NKFC webpage: www.nkfreedom.org/Events/NKFC-Sponsored-Events.aspx.

[24] The 2015 NKFW events appeared oriented toward fund-raising for defector organizations as much as North Korean human rights advocacy.

[25] Hawk 2003.   [26] See Amnesty International 2010; Human Rights Watch 2006.

care) are few and represent a recent addition to the mainstream North Korean human rights discourse.[27] Finally, discussion on North Korean human rights tends to evoke particular images of the regime, with the tone of discourse ranging from neutral to hardline.

A NARRATIVE OF NORTH KOREAN HUMAN RIGHTS DISCOURSE AND ADVOCACY IN THE UNITED STATES

The preceding section presented a basic profile of North Korean human rights discourse in the United States. However, the evidence does not address how the advocacy network has evolved, or the relationship between state and nonstate actors in shaping human rights discourse in the United States. To address this, I provide a historical narrative of the evolution of North Korean human rights discourse and advocacy. Although North Korean human rights discourse did not gain significant attention in the United States until the late 1990s, debates among US foreign policy elites in the late 1970s and early 1980s played a critical role in establishing the early foundations and tenor of North Korean human rights advocacy. The focus on North Korea's nuclear threat within US foreign policy circles, and the growing transnational network favoring accountability through the COI, also influenced North Korean human rights advocacy in the United States. I begin by describing the political context behind human rights in US foreign policy and demonstrate how such debates shaped the discourse of both state and nonstate actors.

Debating Human Rights in US Foreign Policy

Despite the centrality of individual rights in the US Constitution, human rights in US foreign policy did not receive serious attention until the 1970s.[28] Initiated by a series of hearings on human rights from the House Subcommittee on International Organizations and Movements in 1973, Congress prodded the Nixon and Ford Administrations to establish several mechanisms to formally address human rights issues abroad. Most notably, Congress mandated the creation of a new State Department bureau to promote human rights in 1976.[29] The hearings, spearheaded by Congressman Donald Fraser, were also instrumental in the broadening of the policymaking process to include human rights NGOs.[30] As historian William Schmidli

---

[27] UN Human Rights Council 2014; Yeo 2014.   [28] Forsythe 1990, 439; Cohen 1979, 218.
[29] Cohen 1979, 221.   [30] Schmidli 2011, 348.

argues, the Fraser hearings "reflected a remarkable degree of coordination with the close-knit community of nongovernmental human rights advocates, providing a government-sanctioned venue for NGOs to recommend hearings as well as witnesses to give testimony."[31]

The debate and vision of human rights spanned the political spectrum during the late 1970s, arguably a period of fluidity in US foreign policy in the aftermath of the Vietnam War.[32] From the liberal left, what has been called a "comprehensive articulation of human rights," encompassing social and economic as well as civil and political rights, emerged from leading voices such as Representative Fraser and Senator Ted Kennedy.[33] These liberal advocates for human rights were willing to examine US foreign policy and human rights beyond the lens of a Cold War framework.

In contrast, two different conservative factions promoted an approach to human rights closely linking strategic interests to human rights. First, the rise of neoconservatives, a group of disaffected liberals defined by their staunch anticommunist position, rallied around human rights to criticize the Soviet Union. Leading the charge in Congress was Representative Henry "Scoop" Jackson, who took advantage of human rights provisions in the Helsinki Accords to derail détente.[34] The second group were right-wing Republicans who traditionally carried a hardline position against communist governments. Setting aside their political differences, the two groups promoted an aggressive anticommunist foreign policy founded on "military strength and moral certitude."[35]

Although President Jimmy Carter (1976–80) significantly raised the profile of human rights in foreign policy, his exit after one term paved the way for a brand of rights informed by the ideas of neoconservatives and the Republican right in the 1970s.[36] Initially attempting to downgrade human rights at the State Department, the Reagan administration reversed course and leaked an internal State Department memo calling for a renewed commitment to human rights in US foreign policy.[37] President Reagan appointed Elliot Abrams as assistant secretary of the Bureau of Human Rights, and Jeanne Kirkpatrick as the UN Ambassador, both of whom subscribed to neoconservative ideas. In contrast to the Carter administration, which tended to criticize "friendly" US partners violating human rights, the Reagan administration focused on unfriendly communist regimes. Reagan's appointee to the UN Commission on Human Rights, Michael Novak, hence distinguished

---

[31] Schmidli 2011, 348.   [32] Forsythe 1990.   [33] Bon Tempo 2012, 227.
[34] Feffer 2004, 32.   [35] Bon Tempo 2012, 228.   [36] Bon Tempo 2012, 233.
[37] Mertus 2004, 33.

between "totalitarian" and "authoritarian" nations.[38] This distinction partially explained the inconsistent human rights policy of the Reagan administration: continued economic and military support for authoritarian right-wing dictatorships such as South Korea and the Philippines, while criticizing totalitarian communist regimes such as Cuba and North Korea for human rights violations.

The Reagan administration helped institutionalize a human rights discourse which not only espoused the national interest, but shifted the liberal left's comprehensive understanding of human rights to one focused "narrowly on the civil and political rights familiar to the American system."[39] This sentiment was echoed by Freedom House's John Richardson and Raymond Gastil, who recommended that the United States base its policies on the promotion and protection of political and civil rights and avoid "stretching the term human rights to cover all sorts of human wants from sound nutrition to formal schooling."[40]

An Emerging North Korean Human Rights Discourse

While the direction of human rights in US foreign policy during the 1970s and 1980s involved input from nonstate actors, state actors were largely responsible for steering the discourse and framework for the human rights agenda in the United States. As the debate over human rights unfolded in the late 1970s, a nascent North Korean human rights discourse also quietly emerged. No lobby or advocacy group on behalf of North Korean human rights existed yet in the United States. In fact, human rights groups were more preoccupied with violations under the South Korean dictatorship rather than North Korea. Nevertheless, Congress, as a part of their broader investigation into human rights abuses globally, held a hearing on September 9, 1976, to discuss the human rights situation in North Korea.

Despite the absence of information, the image painted of North Korea is clear. As Rep. Fraser argued, "Among all [countries] . . . North Korea seems to be in a class by itself – a totalitarian regime of the extreme left of the spectrum, a closed society in the truest sense of the term."[41] Oscar Armstrong, the Deputy Assistant Secretary for East Asian and Pacific Affairs, described North Korea as "the most closed society in the world."[42] Reiterating on four different occasions the "controlled" nature of North Korean society, Armstrong declared that "[v]irtually nothing is heard from this tightly closed society except what

---

[38] Carleton and Stohl 1985, 72.   [39] Mertus 2004, 33.   [40] Bon Tempo 2012, 231.
[41] United States Congress 1976, 2.   [42] United States Congress 1976, 3.

the totalitarian regime permits."[43] The hearings often digressed to issues only tangentially related to North Korean human rights, including United States–North Korea relations and the North Korean economy, but the bulk of discourse centered on the lack of freedom in the areas of speech, religion, assembly, and movement.

In 1979, the US Department of State included North Korea in its annual human rights report to Congress. Similar to the 1976 hearings, the report focused almost entirely on political and civil rights. Topic headings included torture; cruel, inhuman, or degrading punishment; arbitrary arrest or imprisonment; denial of fair public trial; invasion of the home; freedom of movement; freedom of religion, free speech, press, and assembly; and freedom to participate in the political process.[44] By the end of the 1970s, the nascent discourse on North Korean human rights described North Korea as an isolated, totalitarian state denying its people the most basic of freedoms.

The first major NGO report devoted to North Korean human rights in the United States did not appear until 1988.[45] Motivated by the dearth of information in North Korea, researchers from the Minnesota Lawyers International Human Rights Committee, and assisted by members at Asia Watch (a predecessor to HRW), attempted to systematically explore North Korean human rights abuses. The research team gathered information from interviews with former North Korean residents and defectors, tourists, and open-source publications on North Korea.[46] The following year, Amnesty International published its own background report on North Korean human rights.[47] NGO reports, along with periodic mention of North Korean human rights in the media, were part of the broader *communicative discourse* in presenting and legitimizing ideas about North Korea as a totalitarian, isolated, and evil regime.

The language used to frame North Korean human rights during this period resonated closely with the foreign policy ideas of Jacksonite neoconservatives in the 1970s and right-wing Republicans in the early 1980s. In effect, policy elites were taking part in *coordinative discourse* – creating, elaborating, and justifying emerging ideas about North Korean human rights within a geopolitical context. Although North Korean human rights advocacy would remain largely dormant in the United States until the early 2000s, a ready-made discursive structure existed which an emerging North Korean human rights campaign could build on.

---

[43]   United States Congress 1976, 2.   [44]   United States Department of State 1980, 471.

[45]   However, in 1979, the first English-language NGO publication on North Korean human rights appeared from Amnesty International based on the first-hand account of Venezuelan poet Alí Lameda, who was imprisoned in North Korea from 1967 to 1974. See Lameda 1979.

[46]   Kagan et al. 1988.   [47]   Amnesty International 1989.

The North Korean famine and nuclear crisis in the 1990s provided potential opportunities to raise human rights issues in North Korea. However,
human rights were relegated to the background. For instance, even as the
Clinton administration linked food aid to security talks, there was no similar
offer of US aid in response to improved human rights.[48] As Hawk argues,
US officials were set on delinking human rights from the peace and security
process out of fear that North Korea might end the ongoing discussion with
the United States.[49] The absence of North Korean human rights discourse at
the policy level was also indicative of its relative absence among civil society.
For sure, human rights groups such as Amnesty International and HRW
reported on abuses. Smaller organizations such as DFF launched programs
in 1996 to bring North Korean defectors to the United States to speak and
testify about North Korean human rights.[50] However, a major advocacy
network on behalf of North Korean human rights in the United States had
yet to emerge.

An Emerging US Advocacy Network and the North Korean Human Rights Act of 2004

Although North Korean human rights discourse and advocacy made little
headway during the twin crises of the 1990s, by the late 1990s a loose coalition
of actors pushed the human rights agenda into the policy realm.[51] A key
player in this coalition was the National Endowment for Democracy (NED),
established during the Reagan years to promote democracy and democratic
institutions in mostly Soviet bloc countries. NED began building its North
Korea portfolio in 1998 by sponsoring a workshop in Seoul on liberalization
and market reform in North Korea.[52] According to estimates from Song and
Hong, between 1999 and 2010, NED allocated between $6.7 and
$11.9 million of Congressional funding to North Korean human rights
organizations.[53] Most of these organizations were based in South Korea,
most notably the Citizens' Alliance for North Korean Human Rights,
which provided an important transnational link between organizations in
the United States and South Korea. More specific to the United States,
according to John Feffer, NED "aligned itself with 'regime change'

---

[48] Feffer 2004, 33.   [49] Hawk 2010, 8, 11, 18–19.
[50] Defense Foundation Forum, n.d. Author obtained copy during NKFW 2015.
[51] Feffer 2004, 34.
[52] Interview with Lynn Lee, Senior Program Officer, National Endowment for Democracy,
     Washington DC, August 28, 2009.
[53] Song and Hong 2014, 46.

advocates against 'engagement' supporters" and retained close ties to US organizations which adopted hawkish positions on North Korea.[54]

Central among this group was the Defense Foundation Forum (DFF), and later the NKFC. Comprised of former Reagan officials and staffers, DFF began in 1987 as an organization committed to promoting national security and a strong national defense. Over the years, however, the organization turned its attention to "promoting freedom, democracy, and human rights abroad."[55] DFF involvement in North Korean human rights began in 1996 by inviting defectors and prison camp survivors to speak in the United States. By the early 2000s, DFF ramped up its policy advocacy work while supporting grassroots organizations aimed at helping North Korean refugees escape from China to South Korea or another third-party country. In addition to DFF, a bipartisan group of foreign policy and human rights experts launched the HRNK in October 2001, with the explicit purpose of making human rights "a major component" of the North Korea policy discussion.[56]

The early 2000s served as an important juncture in the evolution of North Korean human rights discourse and advocacy. As Feffer speculates, had the 2000 presidential election "brought a Democrat to the White House, the role of the NED and other groups opposed to engagement with North Korea might have remained marginal. When George W. Bush became president, a number of Scoop Jackson protagonists returned to power."[57] The revival of neoconservative foreign policy ideas thus presented an opportunity for activists to tap into a human rights discourse already familiar within elite policy circles. Meanwhile, as international aid workers and North Korean refugees revealed first-hand accounts of conditions inside North Korea, activists began drawing greater attention to the appalling human rights situation.

Congress, firmly under Republican control at the beginning of the George W. Bush administration, also paid more attention to the issue of human rights and North Korean refugees. As Lee and Miles argue, "Early in the Bush presidency, an idea began to circulate in Washington that North Korea could be forced to collapse by encouraging a mass exodus of refugees."[58] This approach gained attraction from conservative groups such as the Hudson Institute and DFF, and later even among some moderate Republicans who, perhaps less vocal on the prospect of regime change, nevertheless were willing to support a policy of resettlement for North Korean refugees.[59]

---

[54] Feffer 2004, 345.
[55] See DFF webpage: www.defenseforumfoundation.org/history-and-mission.html.
[56] Later, HRNK would drop the USA to reflect the transnational nature of North Korean human rights. HRNK intentionally selects board members from across partisan lines.
[57] Feffer 2004, 35.   [58] Lee and Miles 2004, 196.   [59] Lee and Miles 2004, 196.

With support from advocacy groups, Congress renewed its attack on the previous administration's engagement policy by concentrating on the issue of North Korean human rights and North Korean refugees.[60] HRNK executive director Debra Liang-Fenton called on Congress to implement legislation on North Korean human rights in June 2003.[61] DFF also organized the NKFC that same month in alliance with 21 organizations to support passage of a North Korean Freedom Act of 2003.[62] HRNK, NKFC, and other coalitional partners managed to elevate North Korean human rights onto the Congressional agenda by meeting with Congressional staffers, hosting forums and conferences, providing testimony at hearings, and raising public awareness about human rights violations.

Although the Freedom Act included provisions for humanitarian aid and placed human rights at the forefront of any negotiations with North Korea, the bill's scope was wide-ranging. Key Democrats in the Senate interpreted sections of the bill as designed to promote regime change rather than human rights. Unable to pass legislation in its current form, and with Congressional leaders ironing out a leaner, toned-down, renamed version of the bill, NKFC established NKFW to mobilize public support for the North Korean Human Rights Act of 2004. The presence of a clear, objective goal to channel mobilization – passage of the Human Rights Act – and support for North Korean human rights from high ranking government leaders helped solidify the North Korean human rights movement in the United States. Moreover, the passage of the North Korean Human Rights Act provided additional funding for human rights and defector organizations as well as institutional support through the appointment of a special envoy for North Korean human rights in the State Department.

In addition to the rapid rise of North Korean human rights advocacy groups in the United States and renewed activity in Congress in the early 2000s, President Bush himself would ultimately become a key supporter of North Korean human rights. Deeply moved by North Korean defector Kang Chol Hwan's autobiography *The Aquariums of Pyongyang*, a book Bush described as one of the most influential books he had read during his presidency, the president extended a personal invitation to Kang to visit the White House in 2005.[63] President Bush wrote in his memoir, "Kang's story stirred up my deep disgust for the tyrant who had destroyed so many lives, Kim Jong Il . . . In the long run, I am convinced the only path to meaningful change is for the North Korean people to be free."[64]

---

[60] Lee and Miles 2004.
[61] Author's interview with Debra Liang-Fenton, Washington DC, October 21, 2015.
[62] Lee and Miles 2004, 197.   [63] Cha 2012, 168–70.   [64] Bush 2011, 422.

The image of North Korea as a repressive, murderous regime certainly fit with the Bush administration's views on Kim Jong Il as part of the "axis-of-evil." Additionally, North Korea's appalling human rights record gave neoconservatives within the Administration all the more reason to promote policies directed at undermining the North Korean regime. This included support for North Korean defectors to seek asylum in the United States and greater funding to increase information flow into North Korea. In a throwback to the human rights discourse of the Regan years, right-wing influential policymakers close to the White House were eager to point to rights violations committed by the regime.

Transnational Discourses and the Road to the COI

Congressional legislation and interest from the White House helped raise public awareness of North Korean human rights abuses in the United States, which provided increased visibility to grassroots organizations. However, human rights issues were often overshadowed by the ongoing Six Party nuclear negotiations in the mid–2000s. The push for passage of the North Korean Human Rights Reauthorization Act of 2008 helped advocacy networks gain additional leverage with the elevation of the special envoy on North Korean human rights to an ambassadorial position and greater focus on North Korean refugee assistance.[65]

Insiders within the movement commented on a perceived shift in the tone and discourse of North Korean human rights advocacy by the late 2000s. For instance, longtime North Korean human rights advocates such as Hawk observed a shift from "regime change" rhetoric in the early 2000s to a focus on "accountability."[66] Ambassador Robert King, the US Special Envoy for North Korean Human Rights, also described the early 2000s as a period when NGOs and activists galvanized around "liberation and rescue" efforts for North Korean refugees, whereas advocacy groups in recent years focused on accountability and bringing fundamental change to North Korean human rights practices.[67] Some attribute this shift to the change in government from the Bush to the Obama administration. While this may explain part of the story, the greater transnationalization of the advocacy network by the late 2000s and the push to address North Korean human rights within the framework of the

---

[65] Wiscombe 2008.
[66] Author's interview with David Hawk, Washington DC, December 3, 2015.
[67] Author's interview with US Special Envoy for North Korean Human Rights, Amb. Robert King, Washington DC, December 17, 2015.

UN also influenced the direction of activists in the United States.[68] The conjoining of human rights organizations with different agendas required some level of frame alignment. The establishment of the International Coalition to Stop Crimes Against Humanity in North Korea (ICNK) in 2011, and the emphasis on crimes against humanity, created political space for bringing together groups in the naming-and-shaming camp, defector rescue and refugee organizations, and more moderate voices focused on international legal accountability. Major US organizations such as NKFC and HRNK were included as member organizations of ICNK.

The broader internationalization of North Korean human rights brought "mainstream" NGOs (i.e., HRW), think-tanks (i.e., CSIS), and research-based advocacy organizations such as HRNK into the limelight on North Korean human rights issues. Grassroots organizations which dominated the North Korean human rights scene in the United States in the early 2000s, such as NKFC, focused more on support for defectors and defector organizations and lobbying Congress than on legal accountability at the UN. Of course, grassroots organizations also raised issues of accountability. Additionally, they supported the COI process by providing expert testimony and connecting defectors to the Commission to share their oral testimony. Yet grassroots groups such as NKFC continue to hold NKFW annually and organize vigils and rallies which advocate policies intended to destabilize the regime and bring about immediate political change in North Korea. The politically charged naming-and-shaming rhetoric continues to be a significant part of discourse for early North Korean human rights pioneers such as NKFC, even if this discourse has not been at the core of North Korean human rights advocacy in the United States since the release of the COI.[69] What may have once been perceived in the United States as a movement dominated by vocal, right-wing conservatives focused on regime change is now seen as a more diverse transnational campaign supported by advocates across a wider range of the political spectrum and legitimated by the UN.

Different cleavages thus appear to exist within the North Korean human rights network, but no clear-cut divisions are apparent among US-based actors given their overlap within the network and solidarity in coalition movements such as ICNK. Multiple, but not necessarily competing discourses on North Korean human rights exist in the United States, even as the broader

---

[68]   I do not mean to suggest that US-based advocacy networks were simply co-opted by transnational coalitions. Indeed, groups such as HRNK were at the forefront in building a wider, global North Korean human rights network.

[69]   Feffer 2004, 69.

transnational North Korean human rights discourse shifts toward the language of accountability. By taking a more comprehensive approach to human rights (that is, greater inclusion of social and economic rights) one finds more moderation in the tone and rhetoric of some North Korean human rights groups in the United States than in the past. But at the same time, observers will still sense currents of belligerent rhetoric toward the regime reminiscent of the early days of human rights advocacy in US foreign policy which emphasized political and civil rights.[70]

The Human Rights–Security Nexus

Whichever direction transnational activists decide to take North Korean human rights advocacy and discourse in the future, in the United States national security concerns will continue to lurk in the foreground of North Korean human rights. The US government's fixation on the nuclear issue, more so than perhaps other countries, makes the advocacy network in the United States more prone to linking human rights with security concerns.

Such linkages were apparent in the 2000s, but in a mostly negative light. For instance, critics of the 2003 North Korean Freedom Act argued that by linking nuclear negotiations to improvement in human rights, hardliners were effectively blocking the path of nuclear engagement given Pyongyang's unwillingness to address human rights concerns.[71] The perceived regime-change agenda of the Bush administration also created the impression that the United States was using the human rights issue as a club to beat North Korea with and impede the resumption of nuclear negotiations.[72]

If human rights was previously associated with regime removal and not raised in conjunction with nuclear engagement, around 2010 the opposite argument began to gain greater airplay: human rights should be raised during security dialogue with North Korea. Most notably, a report authored by longtime human rights activist David Hawk specifically called on the US government to include human rights in any negotiations – nuclear or otherwise – with Pyongyang. For Hawk, the logic was simple: North Korea will not denuclearize without improvement in US–North Korea relations. Human rights violations in North Korea impede improved relations. Therefore, the human rights obstacle needs to be addressed

---

[70] This was observed at a conference event hosted on March 27, 2017, by the American Enterprise Institute, HRNK, and Yonsei Center for Human Liberty Under the theme "North Korea's Human Rights Abuses: The Crimes of a Belligerent State."

[71] Lee and Miles 2004, 198.   [72] Klingner 2007, 28.

proactively by the US government in any nuclear negotiation with North Korea.[73]

Such views have gained traction in the US policy and NGO community, as attested by a major conference in Washington DC in January 2016, *North Korea: The Human Rights and Security Nexus*.[74] A report on North Korea policy and strategy authored by former Clinton and Bush administration officials Robert Gallucci and Victor Cha, respectively, also laid out the case for addressing human rights and security issues in tandem.[75] This strategy eventually made its way into legislation under the North Korea Sanctions and Policy Enhancement Act of 2016 (H.R. 757). It is significant that a bill largely intended as a punitive response to North Korea's nuclear and missile tests included an entire section solely on the promotion of human rights (section III). This included: a) plans for making available unrestricted mass electronic communications to the North Korean people; b) reporting on North Korean political prison camps; c) submitting a report detailing US strategy to address human rights in North Korea; and d) compiling a sanctions list of individuals found responsible for committing serious human rights abuses.[76] Strong bipartisan support for the bill in Congress suggests that the human rights–security nexus framing has become embedded across partisan lines.

The fourth and fifth nuclear tests in 2016, as well as more than two dozen missile tests the same year, have helped sustain the more security-laced rhetoric once prevalent among conservative foreign policy proponents in Congress. Such findings suggest that advocacy networks in the United States will retain their American-flavored strong national security orientation to human rights advocacy, even as they accept the more measured, comprehensive legal approach articulated under the COI report. Amid heated discussion regarding US policy toward North Korea's nuclear progress throughout the first half of 2017, the returned comatose body, and subsequent death, of American student Otto Warmbier, who spent 18 months in captivity in North Korea, continued to demonstrate the meaningful intersection of security and human rights in US discourse on North Korea.

CONCLUSION

In the transnational advocacy literature, activists and NGOs set the agenda, raise awareness, and frame the human rights debate. Meanwhile, states exist as

---

[73] Hawk 2010, 51.
[74] The conference was sponsored by CSIS, HRNK, NED, and the George W. Bush Institute.
[75] Cha and Gallucci 2016.   [76] United States Congress 2016.

the recalcitrant target of movements or allies of activists, rarely taking on the role of the main protagonist. Of course, state and nonstate actors form a symbiotic relationship in human rights advocacy. However, given that the early stages of human rights campaigns – agenda-setting and movement framing – is often credited to NGOs, much less attention is drawn toward the role of state actors within transnational advocacy networks.

As demonstrated here, however, the state appeared to play an earlier role in shaping the trajectory of North Korean human rights discourse in the United States. Broader policy debates during the Cold War influenced the anticommunist tone and political content of North Korean human rights discourse and the strong orientation toward political–civil rights espoused first by the state, and then by NGOs. More concretely, the vision of human rights as conceived by conservatives in the 1970s and especially the 1980s had a strong bearing on North Korean human rights discourse and advocacy in the early 2000s. North Korean human rights had already been tied to an anticommunist discursive structure, allowing activists to tap into the same moral language and disdain for the regime used by their predecessors to describe other adversaries, such as the Soviet Union and China. Indeed, several key North Korean human rights advocates within HRNK, and especially DFF/NKFC, trace their ideological roots to the early Reagan years.

Even when opportunities arose in the 1990s to shift North Korean human rights discourse and advocacy toward a more comprehensive approach to human rights by addressing humanitarian needs, the dominant discourse overwhelmingly focused on political and civil issues such as political prison camps. Although some activists and policymakers were open to including humanitarian provisions as part of a broader human rights effort or at least prevent human rights legislation from jeopardizing humanitarian aid provisions to North Korea, many North Korean human rights advocates often distinguished humanitarian issues from human rights.[77]

The North Korean human rights agenda in the United States is steered by nonstate actors such as HRNK and NKFC, but this direction is often in alignment with or shaped by both opportunities and constraints created by state actors and institutions. Although this chapter focused on the United States, it is likely that North Korean human rights discourse in other domestic settings – South Korea and Japan, in particular – are also heavily influenced by state discursive structures. It is no coincidence that North Korean human rights activism in South Korea has grown and received greater attention from

---

[77] Author's interview with former Senate Foreign Relations senior staff, Missoula, Montana, October 3, 2015.

conservative governments and politicians. Japan's fixation on abductions of its citizens as the central narrative of North Korean human rights in Japan may also be driven as much by state as by nonstate actors. That organizations and individuals from different domestic political contexts are able to coalesce into a sustained transnational campaign (factions and cleavages notwithstanding) is, therefore, a major testament to the mobilizing power and commitment of the North Korean human rights transnational advocacy network.

REFERENCES

Amnesty International. 1989. *Democratic People's Republic of Korea (North Korea): Background to Human Rights Concerns*. London: Amnesty International.
Amnesty International. 2010. *The Crumbling State of Health Care in North Korea*. London: Amnesty International.
Bob, Clifford. 2005. *The Marketing of Rebellion: Insurgents, Media, and International Activism*. New York: Cambridge University Press.
Bon Tempo, Carl. 2012. From the Center–Right: Freedom House and Human Rights in the 1970s and 1980s. In *The Human Rights Revolution: An International History*, edited by Akira Iriye, Petra Goedde, and William I. Hitchcock, 223–44. New York: Oxford University Press.
Bush, George W. 2011. *Decision Points*. New York: Crown.
Carleton, David, and Michael Stohl. 1985. The Foreign Policy of Human Rights: Rhetoric and Reality from Jimmy Carter to Ronald Reagan. *Human Rights Quarterly* 7 (2): 205–29.
Carpenter, R. Charli. 2011. Vetting the Advocacy Agenda: Network Centrality and the Paradox of Weapons Norms. *International Organization* 65 (1): 69–102.
Cha, Victor D. 2012. *The Impossible State: North Korea, Past and Future*. New York: Ecco.
Cha, Victor, and Robert L. Gallucci. 2016. *Toward a New Policy and Strategy for North Korea*. Dallas: George W. Bush Institute, December 9.
Cohen, Roberta. 1979. Human Rights Decision-Making in the Executive Branch: Some Proposals for a Coordinated Strategy. In *Human Rights and American Foreign Policy*, edited by Donald P. Kommers and Gil Loescher, 216–46. Notre Dame: University of Notre Dame Press.
Defense Foundation Forum, n.d. *Programs Promoting Freedom and Human Rights in North Korea*. www.defenseforumfoundation.org/pdf/DFFNKFlyer07_12.pdf
Feffer, John. 2004. The Forgotten Lessons of Helsinki: Human Rights and US–North Korean Relations. *World Policy Journal* 21 (3): 31–9.
Ferree, Myra Marx. 2003. Resonance and Radicalism: Feminist Framing in the Abortion Debates of the United States and Germany. *American Journal of Sociology* 109 (2): 304–44.
Forsythe, David P. 1990. Human Rights in US Foreign Policy: Retrospect and Prospect. *Political Science Quarterly* 105 (3): 435–54.
Goedde, Patricia. 2010. Legal Mobilization for Human Rights Protection in North Korea: Furthering Discourse or Discord? *Human Rights Quarterly* 32 (3): 530–74.

Hawk, David. 2003. *Hidden Gulag: Exposing North Korea's Prison Camps.* Washington DC: US Committee for Human Rights in North Korea.

Hawk, David. 2010. *Pursuing Peace While Advancing Rights: The United States Approach to North Korea.* Washington DC: US–Korea Institute at SAIS.

Hong, Christine. 2013. Reframing North Korean Human Rights. *Critical Asian Studies* 45 (4): 511–32.

Human Rights Watch. 2006. *North Korea: Workers' Rights at the Kaesong Industrial Complex.* New York: Human Rights Watch.

Kagan, Richard, Matthew Oh, David S. Weissbrodt, Minnesota Lawyers International Human Rights Committee, and Asia Watch Committee. 1988. *Human Rights in the Democratic People's Republic of Korea (North Korea).* Minneapolis; Washington DC: Minnesota Lawyers International Human Rights Committee; Asia Watch.

Keck, Margaret E., and Kathryn Sikkink. 1998. *Activists Beyond Borders: Advocacy Networks in International Politics.* Ithaca: Cornell University Press.

Klingner, Bruce. 2006. North Korea: 2007 and Beyond. Paper presented at The Brookings Institution, September 14.

Lameda, Alí. 1979. *A Personal Account of the Experience of a Prisoner of Conscience in the Democratic People's Republic of Korea.* London: Amnesty International.

Lee, Karin, and Adam Miles. 2004. North Korea on Capitol Hill. *Asian Perspective* 28 (4): 185–207.

Mertus, Julie. 2004. *Bait and Switch: Human Rights and US Foreign Policy.* New York: Routledge.

Meyer, David, and Debra Minkoff. 2004. Conceptualizing Political Opportunity. *Social Forces* 82 (4): 1457–92.

Moon, Katherine. 2008. Beyond Demonization: A New Strategy for Human Rights in North Korea. *Current History* 107: 263–8.

Moon, Katherine. 2010. *Dialogue on North Korea Highlights Core Tasks Facing Donors.* March 15.

Schmidli, William M. 2011. Human Rights and the Cold War: The Campaign to Halt the Argentine Dirty War. *Cold War History* 12 (2): 345–65.

Schmidt, Vivien A. 2008. Discursive Institutionalism: The Explanatory Power of Ideas and Discourse. *Annual Review of Political Science* 11 (1): 303–26.

Shipper, Apichai W. 2013. Influence of the Weak: The Role of Foreigners, Activism, and NGO Networks in Democratizing Northeast Asia. *International Studies Quarterly* 56 (4): 689–703.

Song, Dae Han, and Christine Hong. 2014. Toward the Day After: National Endowment for Democracy and North Korean Regime Change. *Critical Asian Studies* 46 (1): 39–64.

Tarrow, Sidney G. 2005. *The New Transnational Activism.* New York: Cambridge University Press.

UN Human Rights Council. 2014. *Report of the Commission of Inquiry on Human Rights in the Democratic People's Republic of Korea.* A/HRC/25/63. February 7.

United States Congress. 1976. Subcommittee on International Organizations of the Committee on International Relations. *Human Rights in North Korea* 94th Cong., 2d sess., September 9.

United States Congress. 2002. *Congressional Record, 107th Cong., 2d sess.* 148 (95). Washington DC: GPO. www.congress.gov/congressional-record/volume-148/daily-digest/page/D95-97.

United States Congress. 2003. *Congressional Record, 108th Cong., 1st sess., June 5.* 149 (95). www.congress.gov/congressional-record/2003/6/25.

United States Congress. 2016. North Korea Sanctions and Policy Enhancement Act of 2016. *Public Law No: 114–122, February 18.* www.congress.gov/bill/114th-congress/house-bill/757.

United States Department of State. 1980. *Country Reports on Human Rights Practices for 1979. Report Submitted to the Committee on Foreign Affairs.* Washington DC: GPO.

Wiscombe, Steve. 2008. North Korean Human Rights Reauthorization Act of 2008 Passes in Congress. *NK News,* September 24. www.dailynk.com/english/read.php?cataId=nk00100&num=4104.

Yeo, Andrew. 2014. The Politicization of North Korean Human Rights in US Foreign Policy. *North Korean Review* 10 (2): 71–87.

4

Linking Abductions Activism to North Korean Human Rights Advocacy in Japan and Abroad

Celeste L. Arrington

In September 2002, North Korean leader Kim Jong Il surprised visiting Japanese prime minister Koizumi Junichiro by admitting that North Korean agents had kidnapped 13 Japanese nationals in the 1970s and 1980s. Since then, Japanese officials and advocacy groups have raised the abductions issue with North Korea and other countries, bilaterally and multilaterally. Officials still wear the blue ribbon pins created as a reminder that the Sea of Japan and the sky are the families' only connections to their abducted relatives. Abductees' families also receive regular briefings from the Cabinet Headquarters for the Abductions Issue, which was formed in 2006 so that, in the words of one official, the families and the government could be as aligned "as the wheels of a car."[1] Samuels uses the double entendre of "kidnapping politics" to describe how the parochial abductions issue "captured" Japanese foreign policy after 2002.[2] The abductions also captivated the public. More than ten million Japanese have signed a petition urging their government to rescue all abductees.[3] Opinion polls indicate that the abductions issue consistently outweighs all other concerns vis-à-vis North Korea, including the nuclear and missile programs (see Figure 4.1).

Yet the conventional wisdom about the abductions issue's dominance in Japan overlooks how the issue also became part of broader concerns about North Korean human rights, both in Japan and internationally. Japan's 2006 Act on Handling the Abductions and Other Human Rights Issues Related to the North Korean Authorities (hereafter the North Korean Abductions and Human Rights Act, NKAHRA) was an early codification of this connection. The NKAHRA aimed to increase awareness about North Korean human rights but prioritized the abductions. The link was even clearer in the 2014 report of the COI on Human Rights in the DPRK, which followed a decade of

---

[1] Interview J-103, Tokyo, July 19, 2007. [2] Samuels 2010. [3] See www.sukuukai.jp.

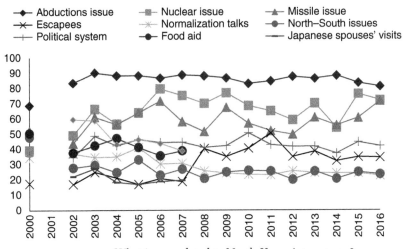

FIGURE 4.1 What issues related to North Korea interest you?

annual UN resolutions that condemned North Korea's human rights record and were cosponsored by Japan since 2004. Among the human rights violations that the report pins on the DPRK are "the systematic abduction, denial of repatriation and subsequent enforced disappearance of persons from other countries on a large scale and as a matter of State policy."[4] The COI report compiled an unprecedented body of evidence of human rights abuses in North Korea. However, the report is also a testament to the efficacy of Japanese state and nonstate actors' efforts to make the abductions issue a part of the story on North Korean human rights.

This chapter examines how Japanese state and nonstate actors strategically used international forums to raise the abductions issue, thereby interweaving the abductions and human rights issues. In so doing, I argue that Japanese actors successfully integrated the abductions issue as a core part of the broader North Korean human rights discourse, bolstering advocacy for both the particular issue of Japanese abductees and the more general issue of North Korean human rights. The legacies of Japan's complicated history with the Korean peninsula help explain the mobilization of four types of actors to advocacy in Japan: repentant leftists, foreign policy hawks, people already interested in the Korean peninsula, and newcomers to activism. Though these categories are not mutually exclusive, they illuminate the diverse interests and networks behind DPRK-related advocacy in Japan.

4   UN Human Rights Council 2014, 317 (see also: 270–318, 345–9).

Most of these actors prioritized the abductions, which clearly violated Japanese national sovereignty and victims' human rights. However, tapping into human rights language had strategic value because it could advance the abductions issue and give it a larger platform. It also helped counter efforts to portray the abductions as a strange but short-lived policy by over-zealous DPRK agents, as described by Kim Jong Il. Instead, the abductions were contextualized as yet another of North Korea's systematic human rights violations. A smaller but significant subset of Japanese NGOs active on North Korea issues emphasized North Korean human rights as more commonly understood in South Korea and the West. They included the plight of North Korean escapees (*dappokusha*), especially those individuals with prior ties to Japan.[5] Japanese activists' distinctive normative commitments, incentives, networks, and their interaction with the government and broader transnational advocacy groups have shaped the trajectory of North Korean human rights advocacy in Japan and the discursive frames they employ at the domestic and transnational levels.

To elucidate these overtones, this chapter maps the networks of nonstate actors involved in North Korean human rights advocacy and the abductions issue in Japan. As Morris-Suzuki correctly observes, the ascendancy of the abductions issue since 2002 engendered "a closing off of memory, consigning to oblivion many aspects of the past century of complex interaction between Japan and the northern half of the Korean peninsula."[6] This chapter reopens this history to trace the networks and cleavages among groups active on issues concerning abductions, North Korean escapees, and North Korean human rights prior to 2002. It then demonstrates how this complex history gave rise to a handful of NGOs that imbued Japan's North Korean human rights discourse with several layers of meaning in the wake of Kim Jong Il's admission about Japanese abductions. Relying on activist groups' publications, government reports, and interviews with key players, I analyze the effects of interactions among diverse state and nonstate actors in Japan on activists, networks, and public perceptions of the abductions and North Korean human rights, both in Japan and abroad.[7] In particular, I explore these interactions at two critical junctures for North Korean human rights in Japan: the 2006 NKAHRA and the COI process in 2013–14.

---

[5] I use the term "escapee" to emphasize that Japan does not recognize them as refugees and to avoid the political overtones of the term "defector."

[6] Morris-Suzuki 2009a, 2.

[7] Interviews targeted the main stakeholders and were open-ended. Notes are on file with the author.

ABDUCTIONS MANIA IN CONTEXT

In Japan, the abductions issue has understandably taken precedence over broader North Korean human rights concerns since 2002. Indeed, during two days of hearings in Tokyo by the COI, variations of the word "abduction" were heard 351 times, compared to just 47 mentions of the phrase "human rights."[8] During the Six Party Talks on North Korean denuclearization a decade earlier, observers noted how the abductions preoccupation constrained Japan's role in negotiations and curtailed policy debates. These insights are further supported by Lynn's study demonstrating how "television (and other forms of mass media) herded the public into a relatively constricted range of views [about North Korea] through narrow, biased saturation coverage."[9] Yet focusing on Japan's abductions mania fails to explain the intertwining of the abductions issue with broader North Korean human rights concerns, both in Japan and internationally. Even though the Japanese do not lead international North Korean human rights activism, Japan's distinctive conception of North Korean human rights – a blend of abductions and broader human rights concerns – has affected the global discourse, most visibly in the COI. The multivalence of North Korean human rights in Japan bears the imprint of Japan's complex history with the Korean peninsula and deserves analysis.

It is hard to overstate the rise in the influence and visibility of the abductions issue, abductees' families, and their supporters in Japan after 2002. Prime Minister Koizumi and Japanese officials involved in planning the summit meeting with Kim Jong Il in 2002 were ill-prepared for Kim's admission and the Japanese public's backlash. Criticism of the Japanese government began immediately, as officials were perceived to be unquestioningly relaying Pyongyang's account of how 8 of the 13 acknowledged abductees had died. Arguably, the abductees' families and their supporters enjoyed greater credibility and moral authority than did government officials. Politicians rushed to the families' side to avoid being lumped in with the Ministry of Foreign Affairs and other government officials, whose past attitude on the abductions was perceived as negligent.[10] Membership in the multi-partisan Diet Members' League to Help Japanese Abducted by North Korea (abbreviated to *Rachi Giren*) swelled by 100 lawmakers, and prefectural legislators' leagues for the abductions issue became more active.[11] Donations to abductions-related

---

[8]   From unofficial transcripts: www.ohchr.org/EN/HRBodies/HRC/CoIDPRK/Pages/PublicHe arings.aspx.

[9]   Lynn 2006, 484.   [10]   Lee 2016, 64–79.   [11]   Lynn 2006, 501.

organizations more than doubled between 2002 and 2003, to about $725,000 (USD).[12]

Saturation media coverage, lobbying, and grassroots mobilizing helped sustain public interest in the abductions.[13] Nearly 15 years after Kim Jong Il's admission, and after 6 nuclear tests (in 2006, 2009, 2013, twice in 2016, and 2017) and scores of missile tests, the abductions remain Japanese citizens' primary concern vis-à-vis North Korea (see Figure 4.1). Furthermore, whereas Kim Jong Il apologized for kidnapping 13 Japanese nationals, in contrast the DPRK has never admitted involvement in the abduction or detention of other foreigners, including 4,000 South Korean nationals since 1953 (though it agreed to release all but 516 after negotiations with South Korea) and more than 80,000 Koreans during the Korean War.[14] The Japanese government now puts the number of abducted Japanese citizens at 17, but is investigating nearly 900 other cases.[15] As a violation of Japan's sovereignty, the abductions also played into a national narrative of Japanese victimhood articulated by those who were weary of Japan being constantly labeled as the aggressor since World War II.[16] Additionally, the abductions captured the public imagination and made powerful news content. The poster child of the movement, Yokota Megumi, was just 13 years old when she was kidnapped, and the movement has leveraged her family's ordinariness and innocence. Nonetheless, informed observers sense public fatigue with the abductions issue. A one-time survey conducted by the Cabinet Office in June 2012 found that even though 96 percent of respondents knew about the abductions, nearly 60 percent were personally unwilling to participate in activities to raise awareness and address the abductee issue.[17]

Abducted Japanese nationals are not the only people with ties to Japan who were stranded in North Korea. Supporters of the other categories of people constitute a significant but often unacknowledged thread in Japanese activism related to North Korea. The largest group are the 93,340 ethnic Koreans who moved to North Korea with their families between 1959 and 1984. They represent about one-sixth of the Korean population remaining in Japan after immediate postwar return flows ebbed. This mass migration was called the "repatriation movement" (*kikan jigyō*), even though 95 percent of the resettlers were originally from the southern part of the Korean peninsula. Many were escaping discrimination and poverty in Japan. However, the DPRK, its

---

[12] Arrington 2016, 163.   [13] Arrington 2013.   [14] See Yamamoto 2011.
[15] For a recent list of the potential abductions cases, see The National Police Agency website: www.npa.go.jp/bureau/security/abduct/list.html.
[16] Williams and Mobrand 2010; Boynton 2016, 233.   [17] Cabinet Office 2012.

representatives in Japan, and arguably even the Japanese government also encouraged their repatriation.[18] For some "repatriates," wealth and political connections to *Chongryeon* (the pro-DPRK General Association of Korean Residents in Japan) in Japan gave them influence and status in North Korea but also left them vulnerable to political suspicion. Reports reaching repatriates' relatives in Japan beginning in the 1990s indicated that the DPRK sent a disproportionate number to political prison camps. Although the migration largely faded from public memory, nearly 7,000 of the "repatriates" were Japanese nationals, including some 1,800 Japanese wives (*nihonjinzuma*).[19] Families and friends of the ethnic Korean repatriates and especially the *nihonjinzuma* back in Japan formed organizations in the 1990s to lobby for home visits and their "human rights in both countries."[20]

In addition, several hundred other Japanese were trapped in North Korea. Scores remained in the northern part of the Korean peninsula after Japan's defeat in 1945, though most had passed away by the 1990s. The most notorious group of people in the DPRK with ties to Japan was the far-left Japanese Red Army Faction (*Sekigunha*), whose hijacked Yodogō airplane ended up in North Korea in 1970, and who gradually lured Japanese women to North Korea to become their wives.[21] Some of the wives who returned to Japan, their friends, and the *Kyūen Renraku Center*, which had provided legal aid to arrested leftist students since the late 1960s, advocated on their behalf in Japan.[22] A few Japanese citizens in North Korea classified under such categories have been able to return to or visit Japan, as groups of *nihonjinzuma* did in the 1990s. However, most remain in North Korea, while a few others have fled the country much like other North Korean defectors, via China or in rare cases by boat to Japan.

Coincidentally, the issue of North Korean defectors rose to prominence in Japan just a few months before Kim Jong Il's bombshell announcement elevated the status of abductees as the primary victims of North Korean human rights abuses in Japan. In May 2002, a group of five North Koreans, including a four-year-old girl named Hanmi, rushed into the Japanese Consulate General in Shenyang, only to be violently dragged out by Chinese police. The episode was filmed by a Japanese NGO and shocked Japanese audiences after it was aired on Japanese television.[23] Public criticism grew over Japan's reluctance to recognize asylum seekers. The word *dappokusha* (escapee) was introduced into Japanese from the Korean word *talbukja*. Outcry over the "*Hanmi-chan*

---

[18]   See Morris-Suzuki 2007; Kikuchi 2009.   [19]   Morris-Suzuki 2009b, 5.
[20]   Testimony, Yamada Fumiaki, COI hearing, Tokyo, August 30, 2013.   [21]   Steinhoff 2004.
[22]   Boynton 2016, chapter 14.   [23]   Funabashi 2007, 17; Wan 2003.

(little Hanmi) Incident" catalyzed a quiet but significant shift in Japanese policy to protect North Korean escapees in its embassies and consulates and help them get to Japan. The target population was broadened beyond Japanese citizens to include former participants of the repatriation movement and their descendants up to the third generation. For a few years, the Chinese government also permitted North Korean defectors with prior ties to Japan to be transferred into Japanese custody, rather than returning them to North Korea.[24] Thus, in the early 2000s, the number of defectors arriving in Japan grew. Given their connections to Japan, they were granted special permanent residency status rather than recognition as refugees. Although Tokyo has not released the official number of North Korean escapees in Japan, to date more than 200 are estimated to have resettled in Japan.[25] Proponents supporting a broader conception of North Korean human rights in Japan tend to support such escapees.

It is worth noting that respondents to the Cabinet Office's annual foreign policy survey could select multiple options when asked for their top concerns about North Korea (see Figure 4.1). Close to half of respondents selected the *dappokusha* (escapee) or food aid options (the latter option appears subsumed under the former after it was removed from the survey in 2007), indicating a smaller but still significant concern among Japanese for North Koreans' well-being. The option of Japanese spouses in North Korea (*nihonjinzuma*) was removed after 2007, but it also sustained interest from about 20 percent of respondents.[26]

Yet, among the groups of people connected to Japan residing in North Korea, those most narrowly identifiable as Japanese and presumed innocent (perceived as not having gone of their own accord) are the abductees. The bulk of Japanese advocacy and attention has thus been bestowed on this group since 2002. Morris-Suzuki calls this privileging of Japanese citizens' rights in North Korea policy "human rights nationalism."[27] Narrow conceptions of *whose* human rights deserve most attention and/or for *whose* protection the Japanese government bears responsibility can also be attributed to the fact that resource-poor citizen groups, rather than the Japanese government, were the primary advocates of people stranded in North Korea and of human rights more broadly. Before Kim Jong Il's admission in 2002, even abductee families

---

[24] Author's interview with Ishimaru Jirō, journalist, by telephone, January 25, 2017.
[25] Email correspondence, Katō Hiroshi, LFNKR, January 26, 2017.
[26] This survey has yet to include "North Korean human rights" as an option, despite efforts to frame the abductions as human rights violations and use the UN to criticize the DPRK's human rights record.
[27] Morris-Suzuki 2009a.

recall being "laughed out the door" (*monzenbarai*) by Japanese officials.[28] Their organization, which was formed in early 1997, had no staff and relied on volunteers from the small supporter groups that formed in each victim's hometown.[29] As elaborated in the next section, advocates for the various categories of people stranded in North Korea started by campaigning on behalf of their specific plight, and not as part of a broader North Korean human rights campaign. But human rights rhetoric later facilitated cooperation among Japanese NGOs at times.

JAPAN'S COMPLEX RELATIONSHIP WITH NORTH KOREA

Tokyo had little incentive to help advocacy groups for the abductees and others stranded in North Korea expand their focus beyond each group's narrow issues. A more cohesive movement might have undermined quiet efforts to pursue diplomatic relations with North Korea. Until the early 1990s, Japan practiced a "two Koreas" policy of normalized relations (after 1965) with South Korea but continued unofficial political, economic, and cultural interactions with North Korea. Hence, prior to 2002, the framing of North Korean issues in Japan was contested Leading the dialogue faction was the Diet Members' League for the Promotion of Japan–North Korean Friendship (*Nitchō Giren*), which had formed in 1971 and whose members' constituents had interests in exports, cement, fishing, and *Chongryeon*. League members served as unofficial diplomatic conduits to Pyongyang. Additionally, relatives of repatriates fought to retain the right to visit their families, which was first granted when Japan created the category of "special permanent resident" (*tokurei eijūken*) after signing the Refugee Convention in 1981.[30] The Japanese government was wary of North Korean agents infiltrating Japan through such visits. They were also suspicious of the pro-DPRK *Chongryeon* (or *Chōsen Sōren* in Japanese) in Japan which today represents about a quarter of *zainichi*[31] Koreans. Yet for many North Korean relatives, the visits were an important source of staples and money; an estimated $100 million USD per year flowed from *zainichi* Koreans to the DPRK.[32] Overall, the idea of eventually normalizing relations with the DPRK remained relatively common in Japan until 2002.

Proponents of pressuring the DPRK seized the upper hand in Japanese politics after Kim Jong Il's admission in 2002. Rumors about North Korea's

---

[28] Interview J-103, Tokyo, July 19, 2007.   [29] Arrington 2016, 158–9.   [30] Ryang 2016.
[31] *Zainichi* here refers to ethnic Koreans living in Japan.
[32] Eberstadt 1996, 523, 528; Noland 2000, 104.

involvement in mysterious disappearances had sporadically surfaced since 1980.[33] In 1996 and 1997, however, new evidence emerged about Yokota Megumi's abduction from Niigata. Hardliners against the DPRK then gained strength in the late 1990s as domestic economic and strategic factors, including North Korean provocations, heightened public unease and added fuel to discussions about bolstering Japan's foreign and defense policymaking.[34] Institutional and administrative reforms also facilitated more frank discussions of Japan's security policy.[35] An emerging "pressure faction" within the Liberal Democratic Party (LDP) cited the 1998 North Korean Taepodong missile launch over the Japanese archipelago and two suspicious ship (*fushinsen*) incursions into Japanese waters in 1999 and 2001 as further proof of the North Korean threat.[36] After Kim Jong Il admitted North Korean culpability in 2002, many of the more hawkish "revisionists" active in these debates saw an opportunity and began to "integrate into the political mainstream ideas that were once quite marginal."[37] Some emboldened political allies of the abductee families called for textbook revisions that allegedly whitewashed history, a crackdown on pro-DPRK Korean residents of Japan, a bolder defense posture, and a constitutional change to Article 9. Samuels reports that two-thirds of the newly elected Diet in 2003 favored harsher policies toward the DPRK.[38] But the post-2002 period also witnessed unprecedented collaboration among Japanese NGOs working on behalf of abductees, "repatriates," *nihonjinzuma*, and the growing number of escapees. The remainder of this chapter analyzes these activists and their networks.

NORTH KOREA-RELATED ACTIVIST NETWORKS IN JAPAN

Due to Japan's complex history with the DPRK, the networks of people active on the abductions, human rights, and North Korean escapee issues sometimes include an unlikely combination of four types of activists and organizations. They include activists with a prior interest in the Korean peninsula, repentant former leftists, foreign policy hawks, and people with no prior experience in activism. These categories are not mutually exclusive, as this section demonstrates. But they shed light on the diverse moral commitments and priorities that different actors bring to advocacy. Although each group has tended to focus on its narrow cause, such as the abductees or the *nihonjinzuma*, their interactions help explain the multiple interpretations of North Korean human rights in Japan. Table 4.1 provides a list of the main organizations active on North Korea-related issues in Japan.

---

[33] Johnston 2004.   [34] Green 2001, 17.   [35] Shinoda 2005.   [36] Leheny 2006, 158.
[37] Samuels 2010, 366.   [38] Samuels 2007, 150.

TABLE 4.1. *Main Japanese NGOs and state actors active on North Korean human rights*

Abductions-Focused Groups	Founded	Membership, Aims
Kazokukai or Association of Families Kidnapped by North Korea (AFVKN)	1997	Recognized abductees and their families
Sukūkai or National Association for the Rescue of Japanese Kidnapped by North Korea (NARKN)	1998	Federation of local groups supporting Kazokukai
Chōsakai or Investigation Commission on Missing Japanese Probably Related to North Korea (COMJAN)	2003	Unrecognized abductees' families
Lawyers' Association for the North Korean Abductions and Human Rights Issues	2003	Lawyers who work with COMJAN and escapees
Rachi Giren or Diet Members' League to Help Japanese Abducted by North Korea	1997, 2002	Diet members from all parties
Cabinet Headquarters for the Abductions Issue	2006	Centralized policy coordinating body

Escapee/Returnee-Focused Groups		
Mamorukai (Society to Help Returnees to North Korea)	1994	For repatriates and *nihonjinzuma*
Life Funds for North Korean Refugees (LFNKR, or *Kitachōsen Nanmin Kyūen Kikin*)	1998	Helps North Koreans escape and resettle (in Japan or elsewhere)
Mindan's Escapee Assistance Center (*Dappokusha Shien Senta*)	2003	Office in the pro-ROK Korean residents association
Modu Moija (Korea of All, KOA)	2014	Association of escapees in Japan
International Parliamentarians' Coalition for North Korean Refugees and Human Rights (IPCNKR)	2002	Cofounded by Japanese lawmakers with other countries' lawmakers

Others		
No Fence	2008	To publicize and abolish prison camps in the DPRK
Human Rights Watch-Japan	2006	Japan office of HRW was key to COI
International Coalition to Stop Crimes Against Humanity in North Korea (ICNK)	2011	A coalition of NGOs from around the world campaigning for a COI and accountability of the DPRK

The most influential organizations active on North Korean issues in Japan are the core of the abductions movement: the Association of Families Kidnapped by North Korea (AFVKN, or *Kazokukai*) and the National Association for the Rescue of Japanese Kidnapped by North Korea (NARKN, *Kitachōsen ni Rachi sareta Nihonjin wo Kyūshutsu suru tameno Zenkoku Kyōgikai* or *Sukūkai*). The *Kazokukai* was formed in March 1997 with help from Satō Katsumi, who led the Modern Korea Research Institute. Until the mid-1960s, Satō had supported the repatriation movement, closer Japan–DPRK ties, and the Japan Communist Party (JCP). But he became disillusioned with the DPRK and leftist thought, and he describes his activism for abductees as atoning for past wrongs.[39] In April 1997, a group of lawmakers from multiple parties founded the *Rachi Giren* to support the *Kazokukai*. Prefectural legislators formed similar leagues over the next few years.

In addition, in April 1998, Satō helped form the *Sukūkai* as a national federation of 39 local "[abductee] rescue associations," which are small citizen groups concerned about the abductions. Kojima Harunori, a friend of Satō's, had founded the first "rescue association" with 20 friends and neighbors in Niigata in early 1997. Kojima had worked with Satō to facilitate the repatriation movement in the early 1960s from Niigata, and subsequently became an advocate for the rights and return visits of *nihonjinzuma*.[40] Kojima's association, the Group of Promoters of an Inquiry into Yokota Megumi's Abduction (*Yokota Megumi-san Rachi Kyūmei Hakkinin Kai*), helped Megumi's parents "produce and distribute flyers in Niigata and collect signatures to petition the Japanese government."[41] Many members of rescue associations lacked prior activism experience and merely wanted to help a neighbor, as was the case with *Asagao-no-Kai*, which neighbors formed to manage the Yokotas' voluminous mail. Such localized "supporter groups" (*shien dantai*) are a common organizational form in Japan and constituted the backbone of earlier leftist activism.[42] Although the national *Sukūkai* is more politically active and considered rightist, its grassroots network of rescue associations has been critical in keeping the issue alive. They epitomize what Avenell calls Japan's "victim-centered model of activism," which is less focused on abstract principles (such as human rights) than on affected and identifiable individuals.[43]

Several NGOs have worked alongside the abductee families and their supporters. For example, in 2003, *Sukūkai* member Araki Kazuhiro founded the Investigation Commission on Missing Japanese Probably Related to North

---

[39] Morris-Suzuki 2009a, 7–8.   [40] Boynton 2016, 97–103.
[41] Author's interview with Yamazaki Haruya, former group member, Tokyo, March 26, 2009.
[42] Steinhoff 1999.   [43] Avenell 2012.

Korea (COMJAN, or *Chōsakai*) to press the Japanese government to recognize additional suspected abductions. Araki is relatively hawkish and has a
longstanding interest in the Korean peninsula. *Kazokukai/Sukūkai* and
COMJAN sometimes collaborate on public events with nonabductions
groups because, as Araki put it, "Japanese citizens and the government should
care about all different North Korean human rights issues; it would be strange
to single out the abductions."[44] COMJAN, which is quite active, receives legal
support from the Lawyers' Association for the North Korean Abductions and
Human Rights Issues (*Kitachōsen ni yoru Rachi Jinken Mondai ni torikumu
Hōritsuka no Kai*). This group of about two dozen lawyers was formed in 2003
by Kawahito Hiroshi, who first learned about the abductions issue while
representing Japanese citizens accused of aiding DPRK agents in the early
1980s. Most of Kawahito's other pro bono activities focus on the issue of *karōshi*
(death by overwork), and he noted that the abductions issue's "conservative
overtones turned off many of [his] lawyer friends."[45] The lawyers' group and
COMJAN persuaded the Japanese government to recognize a seventeenth
abduction case in 2006 and reopen investigations into hundreds of other
potential cases in 2012. After 2004, the lawyers' group also lobbied the Japan
Federation of Bar Associations – one of Japan's staunchest defenders of human
rights – to pay more attention to North Korean human rights.

Other Japanese organizations focus on North Korean human rights issues
beyond the abductions and were founded years before the abductions movement took off.[46] Among their members, some were repentant former leftists
who had become disillusioned with North Korea; many had a longstanding
interest in the Korean peninsula. Two organizations stand out. The first,
founded in 1994, is *Mamorukai* (Society to Help Returnees to North Korea,
or *Kitachōsen Kikokusha no Seimei to Jinken wo Mamorukai*).[47] As its name
indicates, *Mamorukai* advocates for the welfare and human rights of repatriates and *nihonjinzuma*, as well as other North Korean human rights issues.
Mamorukai's current director, Yamada Fumiaki, is a Professor in Osaka who
used to have leftist sympathies but more recently has been arrested in China
for aiding North Korean defectors.[48] On the other hand, its vice director,
Miura Kotarō, is an "anti-communist" who learned of the repatriation movement through his work with Araki and Satō at the Modern Korea Institute and

---

[44] Author's interview, Araki Kazuhiro, COMJAN, Tokyo, March 24, 2009.
[45] Author's interview, Kawahito Hiroshi, lawyer, Tokyo, June 8, 2009.
[46] Over time, some Japanese NGOs related to North Korea have fallen into abeyance. One
      example is Rescue of the North Korean People (RENK), which a Korean resident of Japan
      founded in 1993.
[47] See hrnk.trycomp.net/index.php.   [48] *The Japan Times* 2003.

advocates limits on escapee acceptance in Japan.[49] *Mamorukai* actively supports repatriate escapees, but only once they arrive in Japan, and has branches in Tokyo and Osaka. It has also long focused on raising awareness of the plight of repatriates from Japan in North Korea.[50] Disagreements about how to best address the North Korean human rights situation as it worsened with the famine in the late 1990s led some *Mamorukai* members to reorient or form new organizations. Most notable is Life Funds for North Korean Refugees (discussed in the next paragraph), which directly helps people flee from North Korea.[51] Another *Mamorukai* leader, Hagiwara Ryō, has recently become active in a marginal movement to ban *Chongryeon* from Japan. His involvement in *Mamorukai* can be traced back to his time as the Pyongyang correspondent for the Japan Communist Party newspaper, *Akahata*, in the 1970s, when he witnessed human rights abuses. Ogawa Haruhisa, another founding leader of *Mamorukai*, helped organize the inaugural International Conference on North Korean Human Rights and Refugees in Seoul in 1999. Ogawa and several associates also formed the Japanese organization No Fence in 2008 to publicize prison camps in the DPRK and fight to abolish them. No Fence members frame North Korean human rights as activists in South Korea and the West do, work closely with Korean NGOs, seek to tap into transnational advocacy networks related to North Korean human rights, and express shame that Japanese activists are so late in promoting human rights in North Korea.[52]

Since splitting from *Mamorukai* in 1998, Life Funds for North Korean Refugees (*Kitachōsen Nanmin Kyūen Kikikn*, LFNKR) has taken its place alongside *Mamorukai* as one of the most active groups on North Korean human rights in Japan, although it adopts a different approach. This self-described "human rights and humanitarian NGO" started with 20 members and facilitates North Koreans' escape and their resettlement in Japan or elsewhere. LFNKR runs largely off volunteers and small donations. Several of its members have been arrested in China while helping more than 200 escapees (to date), including about half of those now residing in Japan. Katō Hiroshi, one of its founders, had ties to Japan's Korean community since childhood and explained that his activity with LFNKR was motivated by "shame for having indirectly encouraged the repatriation movement."[53] His

---

[49] Author's interview, Miura Kotarō, Mamorukai, Tokyo, June 11, 2009.
[50] It does not work closely with the organization of families of *nihonjinzuma* (*Nihonjinzuma Jiyū Ōrai Jitsugen suru Undō no Kai*), which reportedly has leadership overlap with the Japan branch of the Unification Church.
[51] Email correspondence, Katō Hiroshi, LFNKR, January 31, 2017.   [52] See www.nofence.jp.
[53] Author's interview, Katō Hiroshi, Tokyo, March 27, 2009.

first experience of helping North Koreans seek asylum occurred in the early 1990s in the Russian Far East, while he was posted to Moscow as a journalist for the right-leaning magazine *Bungei Shunju*. He emphasizes that "the distress, grief, hatred, and despair" and the human rights violations that abductees' families experience during their separation mirrors that of the 93,000 repatriates.[54] LFNKR won the Tokyo Bar Association's Human Rights Prize in 2008. It has also translated South Korean government reports on North Korean human rights into Japanese. In 2008, it began offering training seminars to Japanese bar associations that take up the North Korean human rights issue, and works with *Mindan* (the pro-South Korean association of Korean residents of Japan) and *Mamorukai* to help escapees settle in Japan. LFNKR is a member organization of the US-based North Korea Freedom Coalition and the International Coalition to Stop Crimes Against Humanity in North Korea (ICNK), and often partners with South Korean groups (see Chubb, Chapter 8 this volume).

There are also Japanese-based NGOs that focus on human rights writ large; they are relative late-comers to Japan's North Korea-related activism. The Tokyo office of Human Rights Watch (HRW), for instance, was only established in 2006, but subsequently played an important role in facilitating the COI process. The involvement of influential INGOs such as HRW and Amnesty International supplied skills and elite contacts to the relatively resource-poor Japanese NGOs active on North Korean human rights. Another example is *Rimjin-Gang*, a news outlet founded by Ishimaru Jirō and based on reporting from the undercover North Korean reporters he trains.[55] Ishimaru traces his activism to having supported the South Korean democratization process in the 1980s and feeling compelled to expose the reality in North Korea after several trips there in the 1990s.[56] *Rimjin-Gang* reporting is often used in international discussions about North Korean human rights.

Within Japan's Korean community and among North Korean escapees who have resettled in Japan, there are also several key organizations. First, the pro-ROK *Mindan* founded an Escapee Assistance Center (*Dappokusha Shien Senta*) in 2003 after the Hanmi-chan Incident.[57] The Japanese government aims to facilitate escapees' "return to an independent life" and does not supply shelter, food, clothing, or other things they might need.[58] Some local governments provide assistance, but *Mindan* picks up the slack as the main association of Korean residents of Japan. Unlike LFNKR, *Mindan* only helps escapees once they arrive in Japan, but also works closely with LFNKR and *Mamorukai*.

---

[54] Katō 2009.   [55] See www.asiapress.org/index.html.   [56] Choi 2015.
[57] See www.mindan.org/dappokusien/index_eng.htm.   [58] MOFA 2015, 5.

Initially, *Mindan* members were divided about helping escapees, but since the Center was established they have provided 100,000 yen (about $900 USD) per person, advice on navigating Japanese bureaucracy, help with medical and housing services, free Japanese language training, employment in *zainichi* businesses, and social gatherings for escapees.[59] In addition, escapees in Japan founded Korea of All (*Modu Moija*) in 2014 after the release of the COI report to raise awareness about the repatriation movement. It has since become part of the ICNK. Modu Moija receives legal advice from lawyers in Kawahito's firm and frames its activism in human rights terms. It remains small because escapees in Japan are generally reluctant to organize due to fears of retaliation against their families left in North Korea. But escapees often join social or mutual support meetings organized by *Mindan*, *Mamorukai*, or LFNKR.

This section mapped the diversity of organizations, individuals, and normative commitments at play behind North Korean human rights and abduction-related activism in Japan. Taken as a whole, they include interlocking networks with repentant leftists, foreign policy hawks, people with a longtime interest in the Korean peninsula, and newcomers to activism, including escapees themselves. As I argue in the next section, interactions among NGOs and with state actors helped shape policy outcomes and understandings of North Korean human rights in Japan and internationally.

NETWORKS IN ACTION

The 2006 passage of Japan's NKAHRA and the 2013–14 COI were critical developments that intertwined the abductions and North Korean human rights issues and provided opportunities to bolster domestic and transnational advocacy infrastructures for both issues. As this section details, both developments illuminate how different organizations and networks in Japan and beyond interacted and deployed distinctive conceptions of North Korean human rights in pursuit of these outcomes. Neither outcome would have been possible without collaboration from state actors, who brought their own normative commitments and priorities to the process.

The North Korean Abductions and Human Rights Act

When NGOs began lobbying for North Korean human rights legislation in Japan, groups supporting escapees, *nihonjinzuma*, and abductees (especially

---

[59] Author's interview, *Mindan*, Tokyo, March 30, 2009.

unrecognized ones) found an eager ally in the opposition Democratic Party of
Japan's (DPJ) Nakagawa Masaharu. Nakagawa was a leader of the party's
Abductions Issue Project Team for most of the 2000s and a member of the
Lower House's Special Committee on the Abductions Issue, but he was also
active on North Korean human rights issues. He and six other Diet members
had helped found the International Parliamentarians' Coalition for North
Korean Refugees and Human Rights in 2002 and hosted the group's second
meeting in Tokyo in August 2005. In the DPJ bill he submitted to the Diet in
early 2005, Nakagawa emphasized that Japan and South Korea needed legislation like the United States' 2004 North Korean Human Rights Act to facilitate
trilateral cooperation on DPRK policy, but defined North Korean human
rights as "the abductions issue and North Korean escapees."[60] In drafting the
bill, he drew on written recommendations and advice from LFNKR,
Mamorukai, and *Mindan*.[61] These organizations also lobbied parliamentarians from all parties, finding few who opposed the idea of such legislation.[62]

Indeed, the DPJ's bill prompted the ruling LDP to outline a similar plan.
Although the DPJ's bill was shelved at the end of the Diet session in 2005, the
DPJ and LDP submitted versions of a similar bill in February and April 2006,
respectively. The DPJ bill was titled the Act to Relieve North Korean Human
Rights Violations, without the word "abductions." The LDP's bill bore the title
that eventually became law: Act on Handling the Abductions and Other
Human Rights Issues Related to the North Korean Authorities. The LDP
bill was only one-third the length of the DPJ bill. While the DPJ's bill focused
on establishing institutions to aid abductees and escapees, the LDP bill
reflected a desire to create pressure on North Korea and stipulate triggers for
sanctions. Indeed, it was a joint effort by the LDP's Abductions Issue Team
and the LDP's North Korea Sanctions Simulation Team, with considerable
input from *Sukūkai*.[63]

North Korean human rights were more prominent in the DPJ bill.[64] The
DPJ bill would have made Japan more open to accepting North Korean
escapees and working with UN bodies to protect and assist them. However,
the bill lacked specific guidelines for implementation, especially regarding
assistance for escapees resettling in Japan. Instead, and reflecting *Kazokukai/
Sukūkai* lobbying of the DPJ, it was more explicit than the LDP bill about the
Japanese government's obligations regarding the abductions issue. Although

---

[60] Nakagawa 2005.   [61] Author's interview, *Mindan*, Tokyo, March 30, 2009.
[62] Author's interview, Katō Hiroshi, LFNKR, Tokyo, March 27, 2009.
[63] Author's interview, Shimada Yōichi, *Sukūkai*, Tokyo, November 20, 2008.
[64] For an English translation of the draft, see www.northkoreanrefugees.com/lawmaker-proposes
-human-rights-law-in-japan-diet.

the LDP draft differentiated itself from the DPJ one in stipulating sanctions as punishment for nonimprovement in North Korean human rights, it echoed the DPJ draft's call for an annual week to raise awareness about North Korean human rights (including the abductions), an Abductions Issue Headquarters in the Cabinet Office, and regular reporting to the Diet.

The NKAHRA that passed easily in 2006 is a relatively short statute and, as is usually the case with bills drafted by Diet members, does not allocate any budget.[65] Although it has been called "symbolic," it illustrates the centrality of the abductions to conceptions of North Korean human rights in Japan.[66] It urges the Japanese government to make "maximal effort" to resolve the abductions issue (Article 2) while also establishing a North Korean human rights Awareness Week every December (Article 4). In addition, the government must report to the Diet annually about how it has been working to address "abductions and other human rights violations committed by the North Korean authorities" (Article 5).[67] The national and local governments must work to spread information about these issues (Article 3). And the Japanese government should strengthen cooperation with foreign governments, international organizations, and domestic and foreign NGOs to craft effective policies to address the abductions and other human rights violations (Article 6). It also calls for unspecified measures to protect and support North Korean escapees, in cooperation with NGOs. To date, nothing has been done. Should North Korea's human rights situation fail to improve, Article 7 lists Japanese statutes which would call for sanctions. The NKAHRA thus reflects the competing interests of the politicians and NGOs that pushed for it. While the *Kazokukai*, the *Sukūkai*, and COMJAN focused on abduction-related provisions, LFNKR, *Mamorukai*, *Mindan*, and the lawyers' group focused on broader human rights concerns, especially related to North Korean escapees.

Despite lacking specifics, the NKAHRA was significant for several reasons. First, it created the Cabinet Headquarters for the Abductions Issue. The Headquarters institutionalized the predominance of the abductions issue in Japanese discussions of North Korea and North Korean human rights. With a $115 (USD) million budget (excluding compensation for its 40 staff members), the Headquarters devotes about three-fourths of its resources to "information gathering." It also pays for abductee families' transportation and conducts

---

[65]   In Japanese, *Rachi Mondai sonota Kitachōsen Tōkyoku ni yoru Jinken Shingai Mondai e no Taisho ni Kansuru Hōritsu* (law no. 96, June 23, 2006). For an English translation, see www.hrnk.org/uploads/pdfs/Japan_NKHRA_2005.pdf.

[66]   Author's interview with Ishimaru Jirō, by telephone, January 25, 2017 .

[67]   See MOFA 2015.

diverse public education efforts through brochures, an animated feature, advertisements, symposia in Japan, a radio broadcast into the DPRK, tours for foreign journalists in Japan, and events abroad to educate opinion leaders.[68] During North Korean Human Rights Awareness Week, the Headquarters frequently invites speakers from abroad or from Japanese NGOs such as LFNKR or *Mamorukai*, which do not focus on the abductions. One Headquarters official explained that such symposia helped "increase citizens' interest in North Korean human rights, starting with the abductions."[69]

Second, although the Headquarters' core policy objectives do not explicitly include North Korean human rights, the Headquarters and the Cabinet have prioritized international cooperation to address the abductions, as stipulated by the NKAHRA. As a result, Japan became a key player in UN initiatives addressing North Korean human rights. From 2004 onward, Japan wrote the first drafts of annual resolutions in the UN Human Rights Council (HRC, called the Commission on Human Rights until 2006) and later the UN General Assembly condemning North Korea's human rights violations. For North Korean human rights activists, persuading Japan to cosponsor and draft UN resolutions alongside European countries was a strategic decision to prevent the campaign from being seen as a biased, Western effort. At the time, the progressive South Korean government was wary of jeopardizing rapprochement with North Korea, and it was not a member of the HRC. Therefore, Japan was one of the few potential cosponsors from the Asian regional bloc.

For Japan, these resolutions presented an opportunity to dispel the notion that the abductions were isolated, bizarre episodes only relevant to Japan. Instead, Japan emphasized that the abductions were DPRK state policy and targeted people of various nationalities. As early as 1999, *Kazokukai/Sukūkai* had reached out to as-yet-unorganized South Korean abductees' families to define the Japanese abductees as victims of a broader pattern of North Korean state behavior. Japanese advocates also tried to tap into international treaty mechanisms by framing the abductions as "enforced disappearances" and violations of the rights of a child.[70] As most North Korea-related Japanese NGOs lack the means to engage in sustained UN advocacy, active backing from the Headquarters (and thus the Cabinet) has been helpful. Joint efforts by *Kazokukai/Sukūkai* and the Japanese government to raise international

---

[68] For the 2016 budget, see www.rachi.go.jp/jp/archives/2016/1222yosan.pdf.

[69] Email correspondence with an Abductions Headquarters official, January 31, 2017.

[70] Testimony, Yokota Shigeru, COI hearings, Tokyo, August 29, 2013.

awareness of the abductions exemplify what Tarrow calls "scale shift" or a change in coordinated activism "to a different focal point, involving a new range of actors, different objectives, and broadened claims."[71] Framing the abductions as violations of international norms, and later as crimes against humanity, had strategic value for Japanese state and nonstate actors seeking to hold the North Korean regime accountable. At the same time, the shift in the scale and scope of activism also added momentum to transnational efforts to expose and address North Korea's human rights abuses. Although most Japanese actors prioritize the abductions, they also helped broaden the conventional understanding of North Korean human rights violation to include the abductions.

Japan and the UN Commission of Inquiry

In fact, the most important international initiative regarding North Korean human rights to date – the COI – enshrined the abductions as one of the human rights violations for which North Korea is receiving increased international condemnation. Although Japan initially resisted the idea of a COI out of fear that it would jeopardize quiet diplomatic efforts with Pyongyang to elicit information about the missing abductees in 2012, Japan ultimately contributed to the COI process in significant ways. First, Japan cosponsored annual UN resolutions on North Korean human rights, as described earlier. The votes on the resolutions signaled rising international concern over North Korea's human rights record and culminated in the 2012 resolution, which passed by consensus. Second, Japan wrote the first drafts of these resolutions, including the resolution which ultimately commissioned the inquiry in 2013. Following a persuasive call from the UN High Commissioner for Human Rights for an inquiry (see Hosaniak, Chapter 6 in this volume) and a series of North Korean provocations, Japan's eventual decision to back a COI bolstered activists' efforts to convince other UN member states to do likewise. The COI process highlights the multiple meanings of North Korean human rights in Japan because it shows how Japanese state and nonstate actors prioritized the abductions issue, but, in so doing, also advanced the wider North Korean human rights cause.

The international campaign for the establishment of a COI began in 2011. Forty organizations worldwide launched the ICNK at an international conference in Tokyo in September 2011. They aimed to persuade the Japanese government to back a COI since Japan had already cosponsored the annual

---

[71] Tarrow 2005, 121.

resolutions on North Korean human rights and represented an influential non-Western member of the UN. Japanese public interest in the abductions issue was also considered complementary to the coalition's aims. Japanese member organizations included COMJAN, LFNKR, *Mamorukai*, the Lawyers' Association, and No Fence.[72] Despite being a relatively new organization, HRW's Tokyo office was well-positioned to host the conference given its global network, knowledge, and government contacts. However, HRW also depended on the issue expertise of local groups such as LFNKR and No Fence. After the conference, participants held demonstrations at *Chongryeon* headquarters. HRW's Tokyo office also organized meetings at the Ministry of Foreign Affairs for Japanese and international activists and defectors to urge Tokyo to support a COI.

Initially, Japan and abductions-related groups were reticent about a COI and potential referrals to the International Criminal Court (ICC). Backing the COI might jeopardize Japan–DPRK talks on the abductions and World War II–era Japanese remains in North Korea. After returning to the premiership in late 2012, Abe Shinzō, whose political ascent had been aided by his support for the abductees' families, prioritized resolving the abductions issue and thus maintained a back-channel to North Korea. Abductees' families also hoped that the intergovernmental talks, held in November 2012 for the first time in four years, might yield a breakthrough. However, North Korea's December 2012 missile test derailed follow-up talks.

Meanwhile, North Korea's noncooperation at the UN also bred frustration among other member states. For example, North Korea refused to implement any of the recommendations provided by other countries after it participated in the time-consuming Universal Periodic Review at the HRC in 2010. One expert called this "non-cooperation on steroids."[73] Coupled with the rising numbers of defectors in South Korea and elsewhere, including in Japan, the problem of North Korean human rights was also becoming harder to ignore.[74] The January 2013 call for a COI from the UN High Commissioner for Human Rights helped activists, especially from HRW's Tokyo office, to convince the Abductions Headquarters and Japanese NGOs that a COI could bolster pressure on North Korea. In fact, *Sukūkai* later applauded the COI report for labeling all abductions "crimes against humanity" and giving the Japanese government and international community leverage to secure the return of all remaining abductees, Japanese and otherwise.[75]

---

[72] See http://stopnkcrimes.org/.
[73] Author's interview with David Hawk, by telephone, January 30, 2017.
[74] Author's interview with Ishimaru Jirō, by telephone, January 25, 2017.
[75] *Sukūkai News* 2014.

North Korea's third nuclear test in February 2013 further strengthened the case for pressure and accountability. Once Japan agreed in late January to draft that year's resolution and include a COI, persuading European countries and others to get on board became easier. The HRC ultimately established the COI in March 2013.

NGOs and Japanese officials working on the abductions issue actively facilitated COI hearings in Tokyo in August 2013. Although *Mamorukai*, LFNKR, No Fence, escapees, and relatives of repatriates testified alongside COMJAN and abductees' relatives, the Commissioners asked why the witnesses thought the abductions had received more attention in Japan than other North Korean human rights and escapee issues. Witnesses pointed to a low level of public awareness about the repatriation movement and escapees' lives in Japan, as well as escapees' reluctance to speak out. Since many escapees had family remaining in the DPRK, they were loath to speak publicly, including at the COI hearings.[76] Partly to raise awareness about the plight of escapees in Japan, *Mamorukai* had backed a lawsuit by escapees against *Chongryeon* for allegedly tricking them into going to North Korea.[77] One of the plaintiffs explained that she had been "kidnapped from Japan" to link her plight to the abductions.[78] Ultimately, the COI's 2014 principal findings equated the abductions with other enforced disappearances, including those that happened during the Korean War and the "organized movement of ethnic Koreans from Japan to the DPRK."[79] And in December 2016, ICNK hosted a forum in Bangkok highlighting North Korean abductions from many countries. Thus, as argued earlier, transnational activism surrounding the COI signaled an upward scale shift in that it incorporated the abductions issue into the global North Korean human rights discourse.

From the vantage point of transnational human rights activists, however, mobilization for a COI also integrated universal human rights frames downward into Japan's domestic abductions discourse. Since the COI report, Japanese state and nonstate actors increasingly frame the abductions as one human rights violation among many that the DPRK commits. The abductions remain the priority, but the Abductions Headquarters has invited COI Commissioners to speak at annual international symposia at the UN in New York under such titles as "Human Rights Violations including Abductions by North Korea" and "Human Rights Situation in DPRK: Strategies Toward Restoration of Humanity." Its December 2016 international symposium in

---

[76]　Author's interview, Miura Kotarō, Mamorukai, Tokyo, June 11, 2009.
[77]　Testimony, Yamada Fumiaki, COI Hearings, Tokyo, August 30, 2013.
[78]　Mamorukai-No Fence event, Tokyo, July 7, 2009.
[79]　UN Human Rights Council 2014, 318.

Tokyo was similarly titled "International Cooperation to Seek Accountability for Human Rights Violations in North Korea, Including the Abductions Issue."[80] In the process of pursuing a COI, some abduction-related activists also increasingly embraced a wider conception of North Korean human rights. *Sukūkai*, for instance, now supports efforts to refer Kim Jong Un to the ICC and US sanctions for human rights violations, including the abductions.[81] And Japanese NGOs have strengthened their transnational network ties to North Korean human rights activists elsewhere. Whether the rhetorical shift is instrumental or reflects a growing acceptance of broader human rights norms, the intertwining of the abductions and North Korean human rights issues is unmistakable.

CONCLUSION

This chapter examined how Japanese organizations active on the North Korean human rights and abductions issues brought diverse interests and moral commitments to their activism because of Japan's complex history with the Korean peninsula and the DPRK. Interactions among Japanese NGOs and between nonstate and state actors help explain the distinctively multivalent quality of discussions about North Korean human rights in Japan. Morris-Suzuki accurately notes that Japan's North Korean human rights discourse is "riven with self-contradictions" due to its multivalence.[82] The discourse and related activism privilege the rights of Japanese nationals (for example, abductees or *nihonjinzuma*), and then those with past ties to Japan (for example, "repatriated" ethnic Korean former residents of Japan and their offspring). From this angle, human rights rhetoric carries instrumental value in that it advances the abductions cause. The NKAHRA illustrates the focus on the abductions issue in Japan and the influence of abductee families and their allies, often rightists, over the policymaking process. Escapee and repatriates' advocates were less visible, but still represented significant voices in the process of crafting human rights legislation. These Japanese NGOs also forged links with North Korean human rights activists in South Korea and the West in the lead up to the COI, broadening the Japanese groups' agendas. Both abductions groups and other North Korea-related NGOs in Japan contributed to issue framings and networks which enabled the abductions issue to gain traction internationally, thereby (albeit perhaps inadvertently) adding steam to transnational advocacy for North Korean human rights more generally, as

---

[80]   For a summary, see www.rachi.go.jp/en/archives/2016/1228gyoji.html.
[81]   *Sukūkai News 2016.*   [82]   Morris-Suzuki 2009a, 2, 6.

witnessed in the development of the COI. This interaction between the universal and the particular in Japan has helped reshape the claims of transnational and local activists, as well as the network structure and dynamics of North Korean human rights in Japan.

REFERENCES

Arrington, Celeste L. 2013. The Abductions Issue in Japan and South Korea: Ten Years after Pyongyang's Admission. *International Journal of Korean Studies* 17 (2): 108–39.

Arrington, Celeste L. 2016. *Accidental Activists: Victim Movements and Government Accountability in Japan and South Korea*. Ithaca: Cornell University Press.

Avenell, Simon. 2012. From Fearsome Pollution to Fukushima: Environmental Activism and the Nuclear Blind Spot in Contemporary Japan. *Environmental History* 17 (2): 244–76.

Boynton, Robert S. 2016. *The Invitation-Only Zone: The True Story of North Korea's Abduction Project*. New York: Farrar, Straus and Giroux.

Cabinet Office. 2012. Kitachōsen ni yoru Nihonjin Rachi Mondai ni Kansuru Tokubetsu Yoron Chōsa [Special Survey on the North Korean Abductions Issue]. https://survey.gov-online.go.jp/tokubetu/h24/h24-rachi.pdf.

Choi, Ha-young. 2015. On N. Korea by N. Koreans: The Rimjin-Gang Model. *NK News*, October 22. www.nknews.org/2015/10/on-n-korea-by-n-koreans-the-rimjin-gang-model/.

Eberstadt, Nicholas. 1996. Financial Transfers from Japan to North Korea: Estimating the Unreported Flows. *Asian Survey* 36 (5): 523–42.

Funabashi, Yoichi. 2007. *The Peninsula Question: A Chronicle of the Second Korean Nuclear Crisis*. Washington DC: Brookings Institution Press.

Green, Michael J. 2001. *Japan's Reluctant Realism: Foreign Policy Challenges in an Era of Uncertain Power*. New York: Palgrave.

Johnston, Eric. 2004. The North Korea Abduction Issue and Its Effect on Japanese Domestic Politics. *JPRI Working Paper* 101. www.jpri.org/publications/workingpapers/wp101.html.

Katō, Hiroshi. 2009. Japanese Government Urged to Accept All North Korean Defectors to Solve Abduction Issue. *LFNKR*. www.northkoreanrefugees.com/2009–04-accep tall.htm.

Kikuchi, Yoshiaki. 2009. *Kitachōsen Kikoku Jigyō: "Sodai Na Rachi" Ka "Tsuihō" Ka [North Korean Repatriation Enterprise: "Mass Abduction" or "Exile"]*. Tokyo: Chūkō Shinsho.

Lee, Seung Hyok. 2016. *Japanese Society and the Politics of the North Korean Threat*. Toronto: University of Toronto Press.

Leheny, David R. 2006. *Think Global, Fear Local*. Ithaca: Cornell University Press.

Lynn, Hyung-Gu. 2006. Vicarious Traumas: Television and Public Opinion in Japan's North Korea Policy. *Pacific Affairs* 79 (3): 483–508.

MOFA. 2015. *Rachi Mondai No Kaiketsu Sonota Kitachōsen Tōkyoku Ni Yoru Jinken Shingai Mondai E No Taisho Ni Kansuru Seifu No Torikumi Ni Tsuite No Hōkoku [Report on Government Initiatives Regarding the Resolution of the Abductions Issue and Other Human Rights Violations Committed by North Korean Authorities]*.

Northeast Asia Division, Ministry of Foreign Affairs. www.mofa.go.jp/mofaj/files/000099426.pdf.

Morris-Suzuki, Tessa. 2007. *Exodus to North Korea: Shadows from Japan's Cold War.* Lanham: Rowman & Littlefield Publishers, Inc.

Morris-Suzuki, Tessa. 2009a. Refugees, Abductees, Returnees: Human Rights in Japan–North Korea Relations. *The Asia-Pacific Journal* 7 (13, 3): 1–23.

Morris-Suzuki, Tessa. 2009b. The Forgotten Japanese in North Korea: Beyond the Politics of Abduction. *Japan Focus/ Asia-Pacific Journal* 7 (43, 2). www.japanfocus.org/-Tessa-Morris_Suzuki/3241.

Nakagawa, Masaharu. 2005. *Nagatachō Kawaraban No. 238.* www.masaharu.gr.jp/data/pdf/kawaraban/1705323928.pdf.

Noland, Marcus. 2000. *Avoiding the Apocalypse: The Future of the Two Koreas.* Washington DC: Peterson Institute for International Economics.

Ryang, Sonia. 2016. The Rise and Fall of Chongryun – From Chōsenjin to Zainichi and Beyond. *The Asia-Pacific Journal* 14 (15, 11). apjjf.org/2016/15/Ryang.html.

Samuels, Richard J. 2007. *Securing Japan: Tokyo's Grand Strategy and the Future of East Asia.* Ithaca: Cornell University Press.

Samuels, Richard J. 2010. Kidnapping Politics in East Asia. *Journal of East Asian Studies* 10 (3): 363–95.

Shinoda, Tomohito. 2005. Japan's Cabinet Secretariat and Its Emergence as Core Executive. *Asian Survey* 45 (5): 800–21.

Steinhoff, Patricia G. 1999. Doing the Defendant's Laundry: Support Groups as Social Movement Organizations in Contemporary Japan. *Japanstudien: Jahrbuch Des Deutschen Instituts Für Japanstudien* 11: 55–78.

Steinhoff, Patricia G. 2004. Kidnapped Japanese in North Korea: The New Left Connection. *The Journal of Japanese Studies* 30 (1): 123–42.

Sukūkai News. 2014. "Kokuren Jinkeni ga, 'Kitachōsen ha sukunakutomo 100nin anmari no Nihonjin wo Rachi' to Hōkoku [UN Human Rights Commission Reports North Korea Kidnapped at least 100 Japanese]. February 18. www.sukuukai.jp/mailnews/item_3903.html.

Sukūkai News. 2016. Kitachōsen saishin Jōsei to Kyūshutsu Senryaku [The Latest Situation in North Korea and Rescue Strategy]. August 3. www.sukuukai.jp/mailnews/item_5495.html.

Tarrow, Sidney. 2005. *The New Transnational Activism.* Cambridge: Cambridge University Press.

The Japan Times. 2003. Don't Send North Koreans Back, August 13. www.japantimes.co.jp/news/2003/08/13/national/dont-send-north-koreans-back/.

UN Human Rights Council. 2014. Report of the Commission of Inquiry on Human Rights in the Democratic People's Republic of Korea. A/HRC/25/63. February 7.

Wan, Ming. 2003. Tensions in Recent Sino-Japanese Relations: The May 2002 Shenyang Incident. *Asian Survey* 43 (5): 826–44.

Williams, Brad, and Erik Mobrand. 2010. Explaining Divergent Responses to the North Korean Abductions Issue in Japan and South Korea. *The Journal of Asian Studies* 69 (2): 507–36.

Yamamoto, Yoshi. 2011. *Taken!: North Korea's Criminal Abduction of Citizens of Other Countries.* Washington DC: Committee for Human Rights in North Korea. www.hrnk.org/uploads/pdfs/Taken_LQ.pdf.

5

North Korean Human Rights Discourse and Advocacy: The European Dimension

Rajiv Narayan

This chapter considers the European dimension of human rights advocacy and discourse on the DPRK. Europe's human rights landscape is home to some of the oldest human rights civil society organizations (CSOs). These organizations have, over time, developed close relations with their governments at the local and national levels; they brief legislative institutions, courts, and bureaucracies including the diplomatic corps. CSOs in Europe have also developed strong relationships with interregional institutions which uniquely define the European human rights landscape, including the EU and its relevant institutional bodies, such as the European Commission, the European Parliament, and the European Council.

Following the two World Wars, which generated enormous human tragedies including genocide, mass casualties, and large-scale displacement of millions of people, the EU has embedded the values of human rights[1] – human dignity, democracy, freedom, equality, and the rule of law – as a central part of its international relations. For example, a human rights clause is included in all EU trade and cooperation agreements with non-EU countries, numbering more than 120 agreements. The EU also pursues human rights dialogues with more than 40 countries and organizations, including Russia, China, the DPRK, and the African Union. Meanwhile, CSOs work hard to ensure that human rights remain at the core of EU policies. These

---

[1] Fundamental rights are guaranteed nationally by the constitutions of individual countries and at the EU level by the EU Charter of Fundamental Rights (adopted in 2000 and binding on EU countries since 2009). The EU's official website on human rights policy includes the following: working to promote the rights of women, children, minorities, and displaced persons; opposing the death penalty, torture, human trafficking, and discrimination; defending civil, political, economic, social, and cultural rights; defending the universal and indivisible nature of human rights through full and active partnership with partner countries, international and regional organizations, and groups and associations at all levels of society. See European Union, n.d.

nonstate actors play a proactive role, influencing decision-makers, and monitoring the implementation of human rights measures taken up by the EU.

In addition to formal institutions, Europe's human rights landscape includes CSOs. CSOs in Europe tend to have a strong research and advocacy orientation, in part due to their close links with national governments and the EU institutions. The handful of European CSOs focusing on North Korean human rights include more established CSOs such as Amnesty International (AI), Christian Solidarity Worldwide (CSW), and the Brussels-based Human Rights Without Frontiers (HRWF). The London-based AI has worked on North Korean issues as early as the 1970s, reporting on political prisoners and harsh prison conditions in the DPRK. In the aftermath of the devastating famine (referred to by the North Koreans as the "Arduous March") in the mid-1990s, AI has been joined by individual activists such as the French author Pierre Rigoulot, parliamentary groups including the UK's All-Party Parliamentary Group on North Korea (APPG), and new organizations devoted specifically to North Korean human rights such as the European Alliance for Human Rights in North Korea (EAHRNK). These nonstate actors have formed transnational solidarity with other CSOs based in South Korea, Japan, and the United States. They also work with North Korean survivors, including the estimated 1,400 North Korean refugees residing in Europe as of 2014.[2]

This chapter aims to highlight the European flavor of mobilization and human rights discourse regarding the DPRK. The first section presents an overview of the institutional landscape in which North Korean human rights issues unfold in Europe, describing the relationship between European political institutions and the DPRK. The second section profiles several important European CSOs which address North Korean human rights. Relying on interviews with key players in these organizations, the third section describes the nature of relationships within the North Korean human rights network, and in particular between CSOs and state actors. The fourth section uses a case study to illustrate these relationships, highlighting recent work in addressing labor conditions of overseas workers from the DPRK in Europe. Of particular interest is how CSOs use formal political channels – national legislatures, the European Parliament, the UN including the Office of the High Commissioner for Human Rights and its bodies and the UN General Assembly (UNGA), and the International Labor Organization (ILO) – to pursue North Korean human rights advocacy.

[2] Burt 2015.

THE EU AND DPRK RELATIONS

The EU's Common Foreign and Security Policy prioritizes democracy, human rights, and the rule of law on a global scale.[3] However, the EU has difficulty speaking as a single voice on foreign policy matters, given the inherent complexities of representing 28 member states whose sovereign rights, powers, and individual foreign policy prerogatives must also be recognized.[4] Furthermore, Europe's complex network of institutions, with their differing mandates, roles, and competing agendas, has resulted in different approaches to handling human rights. Nevertheless, these institutions provide multiple platforms for CSOs to influence European policies, including the policy toward North Korea. This relationship appears to be "[b]acked by a policy of 'critical engagement' which relies on regular political dialogue and development assistance programs on the one hand, and diplomatic pressure and sanctions on the other"[5] The core of the European Commission's engagement strategy with the DPRK includes aid through technical assistance, humanitarian assistance, and food aid. Such engagement has been coupled with political dialogue encouraging the North Korean government to respect and eventually adopt human rights measures.

Since 1998, political contact between the EU and the DPRK has taken the form of regular dialogue. The most recent round, the fourteenth session of political dialogue,[6] was held in June 2015 in Pyongyang. During this and

---

[3] The key document guiding the EU's actions in human rights – the 2012 Strategic Framework on Human Rights and Democracy – highlights certain priorities in line with Europe's commitment to these rights as enshrined in the Lisbon Treaty. The Framework explicitly focuses on freedom of expression, opinion, assembly, and association; freedom of religion; the death penalty; fair and impartial administration of justice; human rights defenders; and civil society. To implement the Framework, the EU has elaborated different tools and mechanisms. For instance, the EU's *Annual Report on Democracy and Human Rights*, elaborated under the guidance of the High Representative, and adopted by the Council, represents an important pillar of the EU's human rights policy.

[4] Kratz 2016.

[5] The EU's involvement with the DPRK, including a core human rights component, took root in October–November 2000 when the European Council committed its approach to the Korean peninsula and North Korea by supporting the inter-Korean reconciliation process and providing assistance to the DPRK. Interestingly, the EU has no delegation in the DPRK. Its local representation is ensured by one of the seven member states (Bulgaria, Czech Republic, Germany, Poland, Romania, Sweden, and the United Kingdom) that have resident embassies in the country. In total, 26 member states have diplomatic relations with the DPRK. The DPRK embassy to the UK follows EU affairs, although this may change if the country leaves the EU.

[6] The EU "delegation led by Mr. Gerhard Sabathil, Director for North East Asia and the Pacific in the European External Action Service, visited Pyongyang between 19 and 24 June 2015 and held meetings as part of the political dialogue with the authorities of the DPRK . . . The scope

previous dialogues, the EU reportedly raised human rights concerns, including the existence of prison camps, the use of torture, and the lack of freedom of expression and other political freedoms.

The first EU–DPRK human rights dialogue took place in Brussels in June 2001. Following this meeting, officials from the DPRK's Ministry of Foreign Affairs acknowledged the importance of human rights. However, they argued that they had "their own standards and that their priority concerns were the right to subsistence, right to development, and equality."[7] During the second round of EU–DPRK talks in June 2002, the EU expressed concern that the DPRK government lacked official information on human rights. Another concern was the DPRK's denial of access to vulnerable populations for NGOs and UN human rights rapporteurs. The following year, the EU cosponsored a resolution on North Korea at the UN Commission on Human Rights in Geneva. The North Korean authorities announced that this would have a negative impact on their human rights dialogue.

There are questions surrounding the effectiveness of these dialogues in alleviating the human rights situation of ordinary North Koreans given the DPRK's reluctance to seriously commit itself to democracy and human rights. As one analyst argued, "[p]rogress on the talks on human rights and democratization remains very unlikely in the near future, given North Korea's reluctance to discuss the issue at all. Indeed, such talks are considered to be 'regime threatening' in Pyongyang, and are therefore off the agenda."[8] Moreover, the EU's goals of improving human rights in the DPRK is predicated (or subsumed) under the broader policy of supporting a lasting de-escalation of tensions on the Korean peninsula and in the Northeast Asian region. At the most recent EU–DPRK political dialogue, there was again no progress toward improvements in human rights in line with international standards.[9] Recent nuclear and missile tests under the Kim Jong Un administration have further limited Europe's engagement policy.

Despite a temporary freeze in EU–DPRK bilateral relations, at the multilateral stage, in particular at the UN Human Rights Council (HRC) and the UNGA, the EU and its relevant institutions have been leading global efforts to

of discussions covered all the issues of concern to the EU and the international community: non-proliferation (nuclear/WMD and ballistic missile programs), regional stability and security, and the respect of human rights ... The exchange of views was frank and comprehensive." See EEAS Press Release 2015.

7   Ford 2008, 141.   8   Berkofsky 2003.
9   EEAS Press Release 2015. The discussions in the political dialogue in June 2015 covered all the issues of concern to the EU: nonproliferation, regional stability and security, the humanitarian situation in the country and the respect of human rights.

keep the issue of human rights in North Korea high on the international agenda. The EU codrafted and became a key sponsor of all resolutions of the HRC and the UNGA relating to the situation of human rights in the DPRK since the first resolution at the Commission on Human Rights in 2003. As longtime North Korean human rights activist Willy Fautré argues, due to political reasons, such resolutions could not officially come from South Korea or the United States, despite their active work on North Korean human rights. Instead, such resolutions were usually initiated by Japan with the EU. Fautré states, "[t]he EU is considered a soft power and less entangled in the geopolitics of the region."[10] These resolutions resulted in the establishment of a UN Special Rapporteur for the situation of human rights in the DPRK in 2004, and the COI in 2013. As Justice Michael Kirby, the Chair of the COI remarked, the EU has been "extremely supportive and active"[11] in the promotion of North Korean human rights.

For example, in March 2014, the EU followed up on the COI report by codrafting a resolution referring North Korea to the ICC. The EU and Japan also drafted a UNGA resolution in November 2014, which supported the findings of the COI report and called on the UN Security Council to refer North Korea to the ICC. These resolutions moved forward despite a North Korean diplomatic initiative to block any such referral to the ICC.[12] The North Koreans even traveled to Europe during this period to persuade the EU to drop references to the ICC. In October 2014, Kang Sok Ju, a member of the DPRK's Politburo and director of the Korean Workers' Party's International Affairs Department, met with the EU Special Representative for Human Rights, Stavros Lambrinidis, and offered to hold a dialogue on human rights at the end of the year.[13] Following this series of resolutions at the HRC and the UNGA, in December 2014, the UN Security Council discussed for the very first time the human rights situation in North Korea, and followed this up with another meeting in 2015.

---

[10] Author's correspondence with Willy Fautré, by email, June 7 2017.
[11] Author's correspondence with Justice Michael Kirby, by email, June 19, 2017.
[12] In response, in October 2014, North Korea offered greater human rights engagement with the UN and international actors. For the first time, North Korean diplomats met with Marzuki Darusman, then in his capacity as UN Special Rapporteur, on the situation of human rights in the DPRK. The meeting was historic as it gave de facto recognition by North Korean authorities to the post of the Special Rapporteur on the situation of human rights in the DPRK; the North Koreans had not recognized this post before. The North Koreans offered an incentive to Special Rapporteur Darusman; they even "envisaged" inviting him to visit the country if he could help in influencing the member states from referring North Korea to the ICC. However, this invitation was withdrawn after the UNGA vote had passed.
[13] The North Korean effort did not succeed.

Although questions continue to exist regarding the efficacy of North Korean human rights advocacy, the EU cannot be faulted for lack of trying. Over the past decade, the EU has engaged the DPRK in political dialogue, raising human rights issues directly. The EU and its members have also worked through multilateral channels at the UN to maintain international pressure. It is under this formal institutional template that European CSOs and activists operate.

CIVIL SOCIETY ORGANIZATIONS IN EUROPE ADVANCING NORTH KOREAN HUMAN RIGHTS

Although intergovernmental and state actors such as the EU, the European Parliament, the European External Action Service, national parliamentary members, and the diplomatic corps in European countries play a significant role in North Korean human rights issues, their thinking and actions are also influenced by CSOs invested in human rights. CSOs provide regular briefings and regularly interact with government officials; launch awareness campaigns throughout European capitals including Brussels, London, and Paris; and organize testimonies of North Korean survivors at the various EU institutions. They also sway parliamentary deliberations in EU member states through their research, expert testimony, and organizing visits with key figures in the North Korean human rights network, including members of the COI and the UN Special Rapporteur on human rights to the DRPK. In addition to working through formal channels and with government actors, CSOs have also organized protests outside of North Korean embassies in EU member state capitals. The work of CSOs has helped build a strong consensus within the EU and European institutions regarding the gravity of the human rights situation in the DPRK. This consensus is conveyed through the many resolutions on North Korean human rights drafted by and sponsored by the EU and their member states. The remainder of this section profiles several key CSOs which have been active on North Korean human rights issues in Europe.

Amnesty International

Amnesty International has addressed North Korean human rights since the 1970s, when the organization published a report based on testimony by the Venezuelan poet Alí Lameda, an inmate of Sariwon prison camp between

1968 and 1974.[14] Alí Lameda's experiences echo the human rights violations faced by prisoners in the prison camps even today. In the 1990s, AI raised concerns on public executions, abductions, forced disappearances of individuals, and torture.[15] In the mid-1990s, prior to the awakening of North Korean human rights transnational advocacy, AI conducted research and organized a campaign raising concerns about the plight of overseas workers from the DPRK in Russian logging camps. In particular, AI documented human rights violations inflicted upon those individuals who had fled the logging camps and who had been caught and forcibly returned to DPRK.[16]

Between 2000 and 2010, AI issued research reports and raised concerns on the vulnerability of North Korean "refugees" who had crossed the border to China in search of food,[17] the human rights impact of the food crisis in the DPRK,[18] the crumbling health sector in the DPRK, and the drastic lack of access to basic health facilities by the millions of ordinary North Koreans whose health was already severely affected by the persistent food crisis.[19] AI has also repeatedly raised serious concerns about the lack of freedom of expression, the lack of freedom of movement, and the death penalty.

In recent years, the rise of testimonies by North Koreans who have settled outside the DPRK detailing life inside prison camps, as well as improved satellite technology, have enabled AI to refocus its research and advocacy on political prison camps, with particular attention to Political Prison Camp 15 at Yodok.[20] AI's campaign led to more than 150,000 letters of protest signed by its members. These letters were delivered to the DPRK embassy in London and placed in front of the Permanent Mission of the DPRK to the UN in Geneva. AI's research also highlighted the practice of guilt-by-association, the *yeon-jwa-je* system,[21] as highlighted by AI's campaign launched in 1993 on behalf of Shin Sook Ja and her two daughters. These women were imprisoned in Political Prison Camp 15 at Yodok following the "defection" of Shin's husband

---

[14] Amnesty International 1979. Alí Lameda's case highlighted the multitude of civil and political human rights violations in the form of poor prison conditions, the lack of an independent judicial process, and the severe punishment meted out to even foreign nationals who expressed criticism of the leadership that would have been accepted as ordinary criticism in most other countries.

[15] See Amnesty International 1993; Amnesty International 1994; Amnesty International 1995; Amnesty International 1997.

[16] See Amnesty International 1996.   [17] See Amnesty International 2000.

[18] See Amnesty International 2004.   [19] See Amnesty International 2010.

[20] See Amnesty International 2011.

[21] A system whereby relatives of those suspected of committing a political crime are also imprisoned in political prison camps.

in the 1980s. Their cases were brought to the attention of the UN Working Group on Arbitrary Detention, who then sent a query to the DPRK authorities.[22]

Amnesty International is represented by a large, well-established membership in European countries represented by its local branches (known as "sections") who have developed channels of influence in government bodies and the media. AI's sections in Europe and its office in Brussels have used its reports and case studies to brief and lobby the foreign ministries of their home countries and EU institutions to promote human rights as a core aspect of critical engagement with the DPRK. AI met and briefed the UN Special Rapporteurs and OHCHR staff on the situation of human rights in the DPRK on several occasions. These meetings aided the drafting of the reports by the Special Rapporteurs. AI also joined the International Coalition to Stop Crimes Against Humanity in North Korea (ICNK), calling for the establishment of the COI.

Christian Solidarity Worldwide

According to its East Asia Team Leader Ben Rogers, CSW's work on the human rights situation in North Korea DPRK emerged around 2000. CSW published a widely circulated report, *North Korea: A Call to Answer, A Call to Act*, in 2007. The report chronicled crimes against humanity, including murder, extermination, enslavement or forced labor, imprisonment or other severe deprivation of physical liberty, torture, and the enforced disappearance of persons. Most importantly, it called on "[t]he establishment of a strong commission of inquiry mandated to clarify facts, to establish responsibility and to propose suitable responses by appropriate UN bodies and others which would be a first crucial step."[23] CSW was one of the first organizations to call for a commission of inquiry, and it helped mobilize the ICNK to this end.

Human Rights Without Frontiers

The Brussels-based HRWF also began work on North Korean human rights around the year 2000. According to its director Willy Fautré, the French

---

[22] In response to this query, in April 2012 the DPRK government stated that Shin Sook Ja had died of complications linked to hepatitis. They also claimed that her daughters did not want any contact with their father Oh Kil Nam, who is now based in the Republic of Korea. However, it was not clear when Shin died or where. The fate and whereabouts of her two daughters remain unknown.

[23] See Christian Solidarity Worldwide 2007, 91.

human rights activist Pierre Rigoulot, who helped pen North Korean defector Kang Chol Hwan's autobiography, *Aquariums of Pyongyang*, motivated Fautré and his organization to get involved.[24] As Fautré argued regarding HRWF:

In Brussels, the capital of the EU, and in Europe, Human Rights Without Frontiers has been the only NGO to monitor on a regular basis the situation of human rights in the DPRK in the last 15 years. We have successfully developed advocacy at the European Parliament (by organizing conferences) and in other EU institutions. Our work has certainly contributed to the regular involvement of the EU in resolutions concerning the DPRK at the UN in Geneva and in New York.[25]

Free North Korean Association in EU

As a more recent CSO addressing North Korean human rights, Free North Korean Association in EU (EUFreeNK) was founded in January 2015 to represent North Korean refugees in Europe. EUFreeNK aims to help North Korean refugees settle successfully in European countries and to build an international environment conducive to the defense of human rights reforms, liberation, and the democratization of North Korea. EUFreeNK hosted the "World Congress for North Korean Defectors" on April 25, 2017, in Brussels, where the Brussels Declaration was launched. The Declaration highlighted eight priorities focusing on human rights and basic freedoms denied to North Korean citizens.[26] EUFreeNK enables North Korean refugees to contribute to the overall discourse of North Korean human rights in Europe. As one North Korean refugee in the UK articulated, "[a]s a witness to the violation of human rights abuses in North Korea, we were able to see the devastation of human rights abuses in North Korea. Through the European Parliament, UN organizations in Geneva, and European NGOs, refugees [have strengthened] the activities of the EU and international organizations to improve human rights in North Korea."[27] Europe provided a unique space for North Korean refugees since it did not have the burden of belonging to hostile countries as perceived by the DPRK leadership, such as South Korea, the United States, and Japan.

---

[24] Author's correspondence with Willy Fautré, by email, June 11, 2017.
[25] Author's correspondence with Willy Fautré, by email, March 5, 2017.   [26] Kostaki 2017.
[27] Author's correspondence with Kim Joo Il, dated June 21, 2017 (translation from Korean to English by author).

European Alliance for Human Rights in North Korea

Another relatively new CSO, the EAHRNK, was established in January 2013 by a group of young activists, North Korean refugees and asylum seekers, journalists, and academics in the United Kingdom and across Europe. EAHRNK "seeks to inform policies that lead to the improvement of human rights in North Korea . . . through advocacy, providing practical policy advice, conducting informed research, and raising awareness on the key issues affecting North Koreans."[28] In 2017, the two areas of EAHRNK's focus were transnational justice (and the prospects of developing a truth commission) and forced North Korean labor within the EU.

NETWORK DYNAMICS OF NORTH KOREAN HUMAN RIGHTS ADVOCACY IN EUROPE

Relations Between CSOs

CSOs working on North Korean human rights issues and their respective contributions have evolved over time. To understand the nature of their relationships and characteristics, key actors with first-hand experience of these organizations were interviewed.[29] Only a handful of CSOs follow the situation of North Korean human rights on a regular basis. However, the intensity of interaction increases when working on certain specific individual cases and issues, including lobbying for the establishment of the COI, supporting the work of the COI, and, more recently, investigating labor violations among overseas North Korean workers, especially those working in Europe.

In contrast to network dynamics among North Korean human rights groups in other domestic settings such as South Korea and the United States, or even within the broader transnational advocacy network, relationships within the European network have been relatively less contentious. As European activist Fautré argues, "[e]ach organization has its own agenda or specificity and although they work separately, they are all complementary."[30] Stronger

---

[28]   See EAHRNK's website: www.eahrnk.org/.

[29]   The following email correspondence and personal interviews were conducted by the author. Email correspondences: Lord Alton of Liverpool, February 25, 2017; Ben Rogers (CSW), March 9, 2017, and June 11, 2017; Willy Fautré (HRWF), March 5, 2017, and June 11, 2017; Pierre Rigoulot, June 15, 2017; Justice Michael Kirby, June 19, 2017; Kim Joo Il, June 21, 2017. Personal interviews: Dr. Joanna Hosaniak, April 4, 2017; Park Ji Hyun, April 2, 2017; Former UN Special Rapporteur Marzuki Darusman, June 3, 2017; Professor Remco Breuker, June 10, 2017.

[30]   Author's correspondence with Willy Fautré, by email, March 5, 2017.

cohesion might partly be explained by the relatively small number of CSOs in Europe dedicated to North Korean human rights, and also because the EU provides an institutional context for advocacy which helps minimize politicization. However, even though some CSOs are closely linked to their national parliaments or the European Parliament, activists perceive a need to develop closer ties among CSOs given the dearth of organizations solely working on North Korean human rights (EUFreeNK and EAHRNK being two such organizations).

Relations Between CSOs, EU, and National Parliaments

The European CSOs, noting that their work focus and strengths are complementary, have developed a relationship which is, in general, marked by cooperation and coherence. Interestingly, there are no struggles for funding among European CSOs, a reason that could be attributed to the fact that there is very little EU funding for working on human rights issues on the DPRK. Within the European context, organizations such as HRWF have focused their advocacy on the DPRK at the European Parliament, in Brussels-based think-tanks, and in the European and US media. The European Parliament has been a target for activists because of its tradition of adopting a human rights approach and its influence in addressing issues relating to accountability and in securing formal investigations such as the COI. At the national level, CSOs have worked closely with organizations such as the UK's APPG in recognition of the influence of parliamentarians in guiding governments. The APPG has also visited the DPRK on a few occasions and raised concerns regarding its human rights record and, in turn, has invited its counterparts from the DPRK to the UK.[31] However, CSOs have expressed dissatisfaction at the lack of stronger action from the EU and other state actors. In the case of overseas workers from the DPRK, which I highlight in the next section, the inadequacies of the European and national parliaments prompted activists to take the issues to the ILO.[32]

In a sense, the collaboration between European CSOs and interregional organizations such as the EU, and with national governments, is an acknowledgment of the lack of physical access to the DPRK and the difficulty of conducting investigations of human rights violations freely and unconditionally

---

[31] In March/April 2011, the Speaker of the DPRK Assembly, Choe Tae Bok, and four others, visited London and, accompanied by then Ambassador Ja Song Nam, met with senior government officials including the Speakers of the House of Commons and House of Lords – at which human rights were the main focus for discussion. Alton 2011.

[32] Author's interview with Professor Remco Breuker, by telephone, June 10, 2017.

in North Korea. At times, UN agencies have adopted approaches to engage with North Korea and to gain access and work inside the DPRK, especially on issues relating to humanitarian and development assistance, thus creating limitations for CSOs to wage war on the human rights front. In some instances, CSOs realize that on particular issues, working with their individual national governments and through EU institutions provides greater possibilities for human rights action than going through the UN.

However, the high point of North Korean human rights activism in recent years has still revolved around the UN, where European CSOs converged with their counterparts in South Korea, Japan, and the United States in establishing the COI. A division of labor appears to exist, built by past experience with governments which have depended on CSOs for information and updates. Testimonies from CSOs in meetings and side-events during UN sessions at the HRC in Geneva and at the UNGA resolutions in New York help governments and the UN shape resolutions. For instance, several European activists played a central role in helping the COI secretariat during their investigation, arranging for testimonies by North Korean refugees during hearings conducted by the COI in London. They also supplied evidence of rights violations in the DPRK which later appeared in the periodic reports published by the Special Rapporteur and the UN Secretary General. Former UN Special Rapporteur on Human Rights in North Korea and COI member Marzuki Darusman sums up the agenda-setting role European CSOs played in raising the spotlight on North Korean human rights within the EU, the UN, and throughout European member states:

> The European NGOs have been very instrumental in drawing international attention to the situation there. If it wasn't the persistent efforts of these NGOs, then what is happening there would have not been spotlighted in a way that now arouses outrage. I think for NGOs, especially the major ones, North Korea has become a major matter and become a benchmark of the extent of the seriousness of its human rights violations throughout the world.[33]

EUROPEAN CSOS IN ACTION: NORTH KOREAN OVERSEAS WORKERS IN EUROPE

A concrete example of North Korean human rights advocacy in Europe, illustrating the contributions, character, and degree of network coherence experienced

---

[33] Author's interview with Marzuki Darusman, former UN Special Rapporteur, by email, June 3, 2017.

by European actors, is the recent research and advocacy highlighting the vulnerable situation of North Korean overseas laborers employed in EU member states. According to a 2014 study by Go Myung Hyun and Shin Chang-Hoon, titled *Beyond the UN COI Report on Human Rights in DPRK*, the DPRK has sent an estimated 50,000–60,000 laborers overseas to approximately 40–45 countries,[34] earning an estimated $1.2–2.3 billion USD on behalf of the state.[35] The current UN Special Rapporteur, Tomás Ojea Quintana, found in his report of February 22, 2017, that the earnings of overseas workers reportedly constitute a significant source of foreign currency for the DPRK government. Moreover, a substantial portion (60–90 percent) of their salaries is reportedly deducted by the state in the form of "loyalty funds" and used to support the operating costs of North Korean companies deploying the workers.[36]

In the EU, the number of work permits issued to North Korean workers reportedly increased to around 500 permits per year, accumulating to a total of 2,783 work permits granted between 2008 and 2015. In the EU, North Korean workers were found to be mostly working in Poland and Malta. According to a 2016 report led by Professor Remco Breuker of Leiden University, titled *Slaves to the System: Researching North Korean Forced Labour in the EU*, three North Korean firms – Korea Cholsan General Corp, Korea Rungrado General Trading Corp, and Korea South–South Cooperation Corp – were identified as deploying workers who were then assigned to two Polish companies, Alson sp. z o.o. and Armex sp. z o.o., as cheap labor.[37] Both Polish companies included North Korean nationals on their boards.

On September 22, 2016, in a presentation to the Organization for Security and Cooperation in Europe, HRWF found that notable shipbuilding companies including Crist SA and Nauta SA, based in Gdynia, relied on North Korean labor. Crist used North Korean workers on vessels for European companies located in Denmark, France, Germany, the Netherlands, Spain, and the UK, among others, and additionally for other non-EU countries including Norway. Nauta, which conducted work on NATO military vessels and is NATO certified, also employed North Koreans.[38]

On August 29, 2014, a North Korean national, Chun Kyungsu, suffered fatal injuries while welding pipelines inside a tank in a dry dock at the Crist Shipyards.

---

[34] Shin and Go 2014.
[35] This figure is disputed by North Korea observers such as the economist Marcus Noland, who estimates that the earnings estimate could be much lower, amounting to a few hundreds of millions of US dollars. See Noland 2015.
[36] Do et al. 2016, 477–80.   [37] Breuker et al. 2016.
[38] Author's correspondence with Willy Fautré, by email, June 7, 2017.

Polish labor-standards officers investigated his death and concluded that the victim had worn flammable clothing provided by Armex. However, labor officials were unable to prosecute the company. The North Korean workers were documented as self-employed workers and thus remained outside of Polish legal jurisdiction.

The UNGA and the HRC have expressed serious concerns regarding the conditions and exploitation of workers sent abroad by the DPRK, which it states amount to forced labor. This was recognized by the UNGA in its resolution 71/202, which passed without a vote on December 19, 2016.[39] The UNGA resolution was echoed by the following HRC resolution on the situation of human rights in the DPRK, passed on March 20, 2017. The resolution raised serious concerns at "the exploitation of workers sent abroad from the Democratic People's Republic of Korea to work under conditions that reportedly amount to forced labor."[40]

In the European Parliament, the Dutch Labor Party (PvdA) asked questions regarding poor working conditions meted out to overseas workers from North Korea in Poland, which PvdA characterized as "exploitation." The authors of the Leiden University report on overseas workers from North Korea directly approached European Parliament members Agnes Jongerius and Kati Piri, who raised questions on May 25, 2016, as to whether the European Commission was planning to take action at the EU level to identify member states and companies hiring North Korean workers. They also inquired if the Commission was planning to set up a systematic control mechanism concerning work contracts offered to North Korean workers and their implementation. In her response on behalf of the European Commission, Marianne Thyssen, the Commissioner for Employment, Social Affairs, Skills, and Labor Mobility, stated:

> The Commission condemns forced labor and recalls the EU Charter of Fundamental Rights, which prohibits slavery, forced labour and trafficking in human beings for all forms of exploitation. The Charter also sets out the

---

[39] The UNGA, in its Resolution 71/202 on the Situation of Human Rights in the Democratic People's Republic of Korea (UN General Assembly 2016), based on the report of the Third Committee (A/71/484/Add.3), Paragraph 2 x, expressed its serious concern at "Violations of workers' rights, including the right to freedom of association and effective recognition of the right to collective bargaining, the right to strike as defined by the obligations of the Democratic People's Republic of Korea under the International Covenant on Economic, Social and Cultural Rights ... as well as the exploitation of workers sent abroad from the Democratic People's Republic of Korea to work under conditions that reportedly amount to forced labor."

[40] HRC Resolution on the Situation of Human Rights in the Democratic People's Republic of Korea (UN Human Rights Council 2017, paragraph 3).

right of workers to working conditions which respect their health, safety and dignity ... In the EU and irrespective of the status of EU or third-country nationals, the rules on working conditions, health and safety at work as well as legislation against trafficking in human beings apply. It is the responsibility of the national authorities to ensure that the rules are enforced. The Commission may launch infringement procedures in case of breach of Union law. The use of ERDF [European Regional Development Fund] and ESF [European Social Fund] funds must be consistent with the activities, policies and priorities of the Union, including the Charter. The Commission is in contact with the Member States to check possible irregularities. In the event of infringement of EC law by an economic operator, the Commission can make financial corrections by cancelling all or parts of the financial contribution to the programme.[41]

In response to civil society pressure and possible action by the EU, the Polish government decided to investigate a local shipbuilding company employing North Korean workers at its sites.[42] According to the Polish Foreign Ministry, "not one work visa was issued to a North Korean national after the tests (including the nuclear test in January and the long-range missile launch in February 2016). In 2015, 156 work visas and 482 work permits were issued."[43] Fautré explains the nonissuance of visas to North Korean nationals as a result of pressure exerted on Poland in the preceding few years. As Fautré describes,

> The Polish government recognized last year that there were North Korean workers in a number of private companies in their country and decided to freeze the issuance of visas to North Korean workers. It was a good example of the impact on agenda setting [by European CSOs]. Other countries stopped giving work visas to North Korean workers because of international pressure: Malta in 2015 and the Czech Republic around 2005.[44]

The Dutch Parliament also stated they had not issued work visas to North Koreans since February 2016.

However, CSOs continued to push national governments toward greater accountability. Researchers at Leiden University questioned the Dutch Parliament's response and the Polish government's statement that North Korean workers remained outside their jurisdiction of remedial action. In a letter to the Dutch Parliament, the researchers stated:

[41] Do et al. 2016, 477–80.   [42] Shim 2016.
[43] Shim 2016; UN Human Rights Council Resolution on the Situation of Human Rights in the Democratic People's Republic of Korea (UN Human Rights Council 2017, paragraph 3).
[44] Author's correspondence with Willy Fautré, by email, March 5, 2017.

The Polish Labor Inspection has knowledge of at least 77 cases of illegal employment. Although the Polish Labor Inspection states that it does not have the jurisdiction to check for forced labor, it has observed features of forced labor at the work sites … Finally, the Polish government has not stopped issuing work permits to North Koreans. In the second half of 2016, 182 work permits have been granted to North Koreans.[45]

In May 2017, following in-depth reportage by the Norwegian magazine *Josimar* which highlighted the dreadful working conditions at the St. Petersburg World Cup site, the presidents of the Swedish, Danish, Norwegian, and Icelandic Football Associations (FA) wrote to Fédération Internationale de Football Association (FIFA) President Gianni Infantino raising their concerns. The article reported that the workers, including those from North Korea, were accommodated in crowded storage containers outside the stadium. The journal also cited local reports that a North Korean worker was found dead in one of the storage containers, having suffered a heart attack. In his letter responding to the four FA presidents, dated May 22, 2017, President Infantino stated that FIFA was aware of and "firmly condemns the appalling labor conditions under which North Korean workers are employed in various countries around the world."[46] He acknowledged that under FIFA's labor monitoring system, which had been established to address concerns about human rights abuses, a team had conducted an investigation following this report. The investigation revealed "strong evidence for the presence of North Korean workers on the construction site in St. Petersburg."[47] The issues discovered were subsequently raised with the respective company and the general contractor, and a follow-up inspection in March 2017 found no more North Korean workers employed at the site.[48]

CSOs have recognized that the presence of overseas workers from the DPRK presents visible opportunities to campaign and raise concerns about human rights, especially when these workers are employed in European countries which are also ILO member states. The actions by these organizations have received media interest and reactions from the EU, the European Parliament, the UN, and several national governments. Actions taken against the exploitation of DPRK overseas workers were made possible due to the close networking between CSOs and EU actors in Europe, including the countries hosting North Korean workers.

---

[45] Letter from the Leiden Asia Centre on the issue of "Slaves to the System" Research Group's response to the answers regarding Parliamentary Questions about North Korean forced labor in the EU, as provided by the Dutch Ministries of Foreign Affairs and Social Affairs and Employment, author's correspondence.

[46] Conn 2017. [47] Conn 2017. [48] Conn 2017.

CONCLUSION

The voice of European organizations on North Korean human rights was first heard from AI in the 1970s. As concerns about the situation of human rights in the DPRK has increased, the role of European CSOs has since grown in importance because of their strong research orientation, long-established contacts with member state governments in the EU, and connections within European political institutions and the UN. Their influence can be seen in the work conducted by national parliaments, and in resolutions passed by the European Parliament and the HRC. Beyond the region, European CSOs have built transnational linkages with other groups in South Korea, the United States, Japan, and beyond. European CSOs have been successful in the sense that a consensus has emerged among EU policymakers and institutions and in national parliaments in Europe that the situation of human rights in the DPRK is very grave, very widespread, and systemic – hence, the need for international accountability on North Korean human rights is greater than ever. Although, given the current 28-member composition of this political body, EU institutions do not always speak in the same voice, member states have come together on the North Korean human rights issue more easily than on other matters pertaining to foreign policy. Some countries, such as the UK, have the added advantage of having active parliamentary groups such as the APPG, making the UK more active on the North Korean human rights front than other European countries.

In navigating strategy between an action-oriented versus a more gradual, institutional approach, more established CSOs, through their experience working in previous campaigns, understand how to work through formal institutional channels such as the UN and the EU to bring about change. This often involves a gradual process of dialogue, resolutions, and démarches. This is in contrast to smaller, defector-oriented North Korean human rights victims' groups who wish for more "action." European CSOs have established coherent, better-coordinated networks on specific areas such as the establishment of the COI and the plight of overseas workers from the DPRK, especially in European countries. However, given their limitations in number, networking capabilities, and financial resources, and that they are working in a closed country such as the DPRK, European CSOs of all stripes recognize the need for collaboration as they draw on their comparative advantages. For these reasons, European CSOs have also developed strong transnational linkages with states and groups outside of the region. This, in essence, is the European flavor of human rights advocacy and action by CSOs and by European institutions in relation to North Korean human rights.

REFERENCES

Alton, David. 2011. 2011 North Korean Delegation in London. *Davidalton.net*, April, 9. davidalton.net/ 192011/04/09/2011-north-korean-delegation-in-london/.

Amnesty International. 1979. *A Personal Account of the Experience of a Prisoner of Conscience in the Democratic People's Republic of Korea.* ASA 24/002/1979, January. London: Amnesty International.

Amnesty International. 1993. *North Korea: Summary of Amnesty International's Concerns.* ASA 24/003/1993, October. London: Amnesty International.

Amnesty International. 1994. *North Korea: The Death Penalty.* ASA 24/001/1994, April. London: Amnesty International.

Amnesty International. 1995. ASA 24/012/1995, December. *Democratic People's Republic of Korea, Human Rights Violations Behind Closed Doors.* London: Amnesty International.

Amnesty International. 1996. *Democratic People's Republic of Korea/Russian Federation: Pursuit, Intimidation and Abuse of North Korean Refugees and Workers.* ASA 24/006/1996, September. London: Amnesty International.

Amnesty International. 1997. *Democratic People's Republic of Korea: Public Executions Converging Testimonies.* ASA 24/001/1997, January. London: Amnesty International.

Amnesty International. 2000. *Democratic People's Republic of Korea: Persecuting the Starving: The Plight of North Koreans fleeing to China.* ASA 24/003/2000, December. London: Amnesty International.

Amnesty International. 2004. *North Korea: Starved of Rights: Human Rights and the Food Crisis in the Democratic People's Republic of Korea.* ASA 24/003/2004, January. London: Amnesty International.

Amnesty International. 2010. *North Korea: The Crumbling State of Health Care in North Korea.* ASA 24/001/2010, July. London: Amnesty International.

Amnesty International. 2011. *North Korea: Political Prison Camps.* 24/001/2011, May. London: Amnesty International.

Berkofsky, Alex. 2003. *EU's Policy Towards the DPRK – Engagement or Standstill?* BP 03/01, August. Brussels: European Institute for Asian Studies. http://nautilus .wpengine.netdna-cdn.com/wp-content/uploads/2011/12/eudprkstandstill.pdf.

Breuker, Remco, Marte Boonen, Klara Boonstra, Christine Chung, Imke van Gardingen, Kim Kwang-cheol, Oh Kyuwook, and Anoma van der Veere. 2016. North Korean Forced Labour in the EU, the Polish Case: How the Supply of a Captive DPRK Workforce fits our Demand for Cheap Labour. *Findings from the Slaves to the System Project*, 6 July. Leiden: Leiden Asia Center.

Burt, James. 2015. *A Case for Clarification: European Asylum Policy and North Korean Refugees.* London: European Alliance for Human Rights in North Korea.

Conn, David. 2017. World Cup 2018: FIFA Admits Workers Have Suffered Human Rights Abuses. *The Guardian*, May 25. www.theguardian.com/football/2017/may/25/ fifa-world-cup-2018-workers-human-rights-abuses.

Christian Solidarity Worldwide. 2007. *North Korea: North Korea: A Case to Answer – A Call to Act.* London: Christian Solidarity Worldwide.

Do, Kyung-ok, Soo-am Kim, Kyu-chang Lee, Dong-ho Han, Min Hong, and Ye-jun Lim. 2016. *White Paper 2016.* Seoul: Korea Institute of National Unification.

European External Action Service (EEAS) Press Release. 2015. EU-DPRK Political Dialogue – 14th Session. Brussels, Belgium. June 25, 2015. https://eeas.europa.eu/h eadquarters/headquarters-homepage/6336/node/6336_pl.

European Union. n.d. *EU by Topic: Human Rights*. europa.eu/european-union/topics/ human-rights_en.

European Union. 2016. Exploitation of North Korean Overseas Workers. Paper presented at the OSCE Human Dimension Implementation Meeting, September 22, Warsaw.

Ford, Glyn. 2008. *North Korea on the Brink*. London: Pluto Press.

Kostaki, Irene. 2017. North Korean Refugees Announce 'Brussels Declaration.' *New Europe*, April 27. Brussels.

Kratz, Agatha 2016. North Korea: A Role for the EU on Human Rights, *European Council on Foreign Relations*, January 6.

Noland, Marcus. 2015. The Exportation and Exploitation of North Korean Labor. *Peterson Institute for International Economics*, July 30.

Shim, Elizabeth. 2016. Poland Banned North Korea Workers after Provocations, Warsaw Says. *UPI*, June 7.

Shin, Chang- Hoon and Myong- Hyun Go. 2014. Beyond the UN COI Report on Human Rights in DPRK. The Asian Institute for Policy Studies, November 3.

UN General Assembly. 2016. *Resolution 71/202 on the Situation of Human Rights in the Democratic People's Republic of Korea*. A/RES/71/202, December 19. New York: UN General Assembly.

UN Human Rights Council. 2014. *Report of the Commission of Inquiry on Human Rights in the Democratic People's Republic of Korea*. A/HRC/25/63. February 7.

UN Human Rights Council. 2017. *Resolution on the Situation of Human Rights in the Democratic People's Republic of Korea*. A/HRC/34/L.23, March 20. Geneva: UN Human Rights Council.

PART II

TRANSNATIONAL NETWORKS

6

NGOs As Discursive Catalysts at the United Nations and Beyond
An Activist's Perspective

Joanna Hosaniak

A Korean saying reminds us that the hardest part of lighting up a vast plain is to ignite the first spark. This metaphor is frequently invoked by Benjamin Hyun Yoon, the founder of Citizens' Alliance for North Korean Human Rights (Citizens' Alliance, or NKHR) and the "father" of the North Korean human rights movement. The first spark of activism on the North Korean human rights issue took place in a cold, unwelcoming environment where attempts to talk about North Korean human rights were met with reluctance. This was particularly the case in South Korea, where after decades of democracy activism, civil society was refocusing its energies on developing a strong democratic state. In 2017 – just two decades since Yoon founded his fledgling NGO, and only 15 years since strategic advocacy aimed at the United Nations (UN) began – the issue of North Korean human rights violations is now an official agenda item at the UN Security Council. From an activist perspective, this represents an outstanding success story.

The transnational North Korean human rights movement has achieved this great success despite significant hurdles. In South Korea, where the movement began, the advocacy network remains small and without any stable donor base. Additionally, it is not a very united movement; commonly (mis)labeled as a "conservative" movement, members in fact come from a range of ideologically diverse backgrounds, and their missions and motives often compete. These diverse backgrounds range from organizations whose founding members have roots in pro-democracy activism in South Korea, some of which were connected with the radical left wing of South Korea's anti-authoritarian dissident movement during the 1970s and 1980s,[1] to far-right groups

[1] In reaction to South Korea's authoritarian dictatorship, pro-democracy, human rights activists in South Korea sometimes aligned themselves with a pro-North Korean agenda, sympathetic to

associated with a strong anticommunist, democracy promotion agenda. In this chapter, I explore strategies taken by Citizens' Alliance and the decision to move advocacy outside the South Korean context in light of the constrained advocacy space. The internationalization of the North Korean human rights agenda that ensued resulted in the issue gaining credibility at the UN level. In doing so, I draw on my 15 years' experience as a human rights activist, the majority of which time I have worked with the advocacy team at Citizens' Alliance in Seoul.

THE ORIGINS AND RATIONALE OF THE NORTH KOREAN HUMAN RIGHTS MOVEMENT IN SOUTH KOREA

A number of factors contributed to the early transnationalization of the movement, which ultimately resulted in the placement of North Korean human rights high on the agenda of the UN. First, the early organizations were established by experienced advocates, who understood well the benefits of transnational organizing as an established advocacy method.[2] Second, the North Korean human rights movement experienced initial difficulties in finding support for its cause among either the public or the progressive governments in South Korea, and thus it looked to find such support abroad from early on. As the progressive and radical-left circles in South Korea were reluctant, or even outwardly hostile, to raising the issue of North Korean human rights, the split with those circles initiated the establishment of organizations devoted solely to the North Korean human rights issue. These groups then decided to shift their focus and turn attention to gaining support for their cause outside of South Korea. Finally, there is no grassroots civil society in North Korea and international human rights organizations are not permitted to work on the ground there. The only way to hold North Korea accountable has been through the UN system, of which North Korea is a member and has in fact voluntarily ratified various human rights treaties. This has enabled a small coalition of NGOs to expose the North Korean human rights problem to a large forum of states and other actors through the UN in a systematic manner and within a relatively short time.

The first organization established in South Korea was the Citizens' Alliance, founded in 1996, which initiated the transnationalization of the North Korean human rights issue. Its founder, Yoon, had a long history of

---

anti-US, *Juche* ideology. For more on the effect this radical human rights activist history has had on North Korean human rights activism today, see Chubb 2014, 137–48, 165–75.

[2]   These activists had previously participated in South Korean pro-democracy activism.

human rights activism in South Korea: from 1969, he was vice chairman of Korea's Civil Rights Struggle Committee, after which he joined the National Council of Advocacy for Democracy. In 1972 he founded the South Korean Amnesty International section, which he led, supporting the prisoners of conscience who later stood at the forefront of South Korean democratization and became political leaders. It was during his time with Amnesty International that Yoon first encountered the North Korean human rights issue. In July 1979, Amnesty International published a book entitled *A Personal Account of the Experience of a Prisoner of Conscience in the Democratic People's Republic of Korea*.[3] The writer, Alí Lameda, a poet and a member of the Venezuelan Communist Party, had worked for the North Korean government's publication agency in Pyongyang since 1966. There, with Jacque Sedillot, a former French soldier, they criticized the idolization of Kim Il Sung, for which they were later arrested and imprisoned.

Yoon often credited that first account as a turning point that prompted him to ultimately establish an organization that would advocate on behalf of North Korean political prisoners. He explained that in the 1970s and 1980s, as activists were preoccupied with fighting South Korea's military regime, they were initially unable to turn their eyes toward North Korea, but that the situation changed after South Korea democratized and significantly advanced its human rights situation in the 1990s. However, given its role in fighting for democracy in South Korea, Amnesty Korea and other organizations were for the most part populated by activists with a "progressive" agenda, and had a membership base with similar political leanings. According to Yoon, these groups were often unwilling to raise the issue of North Korean human rights due to their relationship with *Juche* ideologists and were considered favorable to the North Korean dictatorship. As a result, they viewed North Korean human rights advocacy by the South as confrontational and antithetical to the progress of peaceful reunification on the Korean peninsula. When establishing Citizens' Alliance in 1996, Yoon made a public statement that challenged this view and represented a radical departure from how his fellow South Korean human rights activists framed the North Korean human rights issue:

> How meaningful would reunification of Korea be without ensuring respect for basic civil and political rights? How will I answer the cries of the victims of North Korea's political prison camps and their families, the number of whom might be more than 200,000 when they ask me, "What did you do when you knew we were dying?"[4]

---

[3] Amnesty International 1979.   [4] Yoon 1996.

TRANSNATIONALIZATION OF THE NORTH KOREAN HUMAN RIGHTS ISSUE

South Korean NGOs initially focused on building an international network which would amplify victims' voices beyond the South Korean context.[5] Collecting victim testimony, documenting violations in North Korea, and disseminating this information to NGOs, targeted governments and the UN was a strategy adopted by Citizens' Alliance to raise international concern about the situation in North Korea.[6] As I discuss in this chapter, this strategy proved successful. It provided stimulus for independent investigation by international organizations and NGOs. It also created opportunities to press for change in North Korea's human rights record through bilateral channels of "engagement" from foreign countries, and using naming-and-shaming tactics at the UN.

Bringing victims' voices to the attention of the international community was a necessary strategy to counter North Korea's suppression of information, which enabled the regime to sustain abuses of power. NGOs also targeted the international community with the hope that raising the profile of the issue would prompt international experts and institutions to initiate independent investigations into the abuses and provide greater credibility to the claims of South Korean NGOs working on North Korean human rights. The early reports of these NGOs were subjected to accusations of bias and equated with the hostile anti-North Korea agenda propagated by South Korea's previous authoritarian regimes. For example, Minnesota Lawyers International and Asia Watch, which later became part of Human Rights Watch (HRW), stated in a 1988 report: "The Republic of Korea has ... engaged in a systematic pattern of issuing misinformation and inaccurate information about the DPRK ... As a result, any material which derives directly or indirectly from

---

[5] In that early period from 1996 to 2003 (when the first UN Resolution on North Korean human rights was adopted), there were only few South Korean organizations focusing on North Korean human rights. Initial international advocacy began with the activities of the Citizens' Alliance for North Korean Human Rights, which was later occasionally joined by NKnet: Network for North Korean Democracy and Human Rights, or Free NK Gulag (now NK Watch), established by survivors of the North Korean political prison camps. Another organization, North Korea Database Center, focused primarily on documentation of abuses and dissemination of information. Some international advocacy work was later conducted by media groups which broadcast radio into North Korea, or by organizations focusing on specific issues, such as unions of families of South Korean citizens abducted by North Korea.

[6] The term "defector," which is commonly used to refer to North Koreans escaping their country, carries a highly political connotation and does not belong to the official UN terminology. In addition, NGOs focused on presenting testimonies and conducting advocacy with people who experienced some forms of human rights abuses. Hence, the word "victim" has been used here.

South Korean sources must be checked and rechecked against independent data."[7] Similar arguments were often used by the progressive media and civil society in South Korea, and by some international scholars and government officials. Such skepticism only began to dissipate after the report of the COI for DPRK in 2014.

Faithful to his previous work on political prisoners in South Korea, Yoon and his team, including former Amnesty colleague (and current Director-General) Young Ja Kim, decided to first expose the violations in North Korean political prison camps. Thus, the initial name of the organization was Citizens' Alliance to Help Political Prisoners in North Korea.[8] In the autumn of 1996, *Life & Human Rights*, a quarterly publication aimed at revealing the brutality of North Korea's political prison camps to the world, was first distributed to the international community. The journal was the first in the world to carry North Korean victims' voices, informing international governments, NGOs, and the UN about the situation inside the country. Published in Korean, English, and Japanese, and totaling 57 editions, the journal greatly contributed to the dissemination of the then unfamiliar voices of North Korean victims and vivid descriptions of the grave human rights situation in North Korea.

However, dissemination of information alone was not enough to tackle the international community's silence on the situation in North Korea, and Yoon teamed up with Professor Haruhisa Ogawa of the Japanese NGO Society to Help Returnees to North Korea, and French scholar Pierre Rigoulot, to hold an international forum on North Korean human rights. Hence, Citizens' Alliance's annual international conferences focusing exclusively on North Korean human rights were born, conceived as a platform to link NGOs, experts, government officials, and media to spread awareness about the situation. On December 1, 1999, the First International Conference on North Korean Human Rights and Refugees opened in Seoul, involving eight organizations from five countries, and with a large audience of 1,000 people. For this inaugural public event, Citizens' Alliance put the spotlight on the plight of North Korean refugees in third countries where they could not receive asylum. The topic was chosen to highlight the international nature of the issue and mobilize an international network of actors. The most notable outcome of this first conference was the formation of an international network for the improvement of human rights in North Korea, called NKHR (Citizens' Alliance) Friends Network. More than 140 experts from 10 countries joined

---

[7]   Kagan, Oh, and Weissbrodt 1988, 3.
[8]   The current name has been used since 2001: Citizens' Alliance for North Korean Human Rights.

this early initiative, and later 31 intellectuals from European countries including France, Romania, Czech Republic, Spain, and Belgium adopted an international appeal. This expanding international network of experts and NGOs participating in the first three conferences allowed the organizers to move the forum beyond Asia, as more and more organizations were interested in including North Korean human rights in their research and campaigning, and therefore became natural partners to host the conferences.

Thus, the fourth conference was held in Prague, Czech Republic, in March 2003. Citizens' Alliance deliberately targeted postcommunist countries in Europe, believing that recent memories of communism and their lived experiences of transition to democracy would evoke solidarity and heightened interest from the governments, media, and public of these countries. With the help of the Czech People in Need Foundation, Citizens' Alliance coordinated a meeting of North Korean victims with President Vaclav Havel – himself a former human rights activist – and members of parliament. During the meeting, President Havel remarked:

> I often meet with human rights activists from different countries. The reason I do so is because, although the issue of human rights carries political overtone, the dignity of human beings and freedom is something more meritorious than political understanding. The power elite of North Korea would be displeased with me to meet with North Korean human rights activists like you. But I do not care what they think of me since the respect for human dignity and freedom is the noblest duty that mankind should never neglect.[9]

From that moment on, President Havel, a symbolic figure in the fight for human dignity under communist dictatorship, became a high-profile supporter of the North Korean human rights movement and continued to raise the issue of North Korean human rights at every opportunity until his death in 2011.

After this initial success with moving the conferences abroad, Citizens' Alliance cohosted similar conferences in Poland with the Helsinki Foundation for Human Rights; in Norway with the Rafto Foundation (where the conference accommodated new approaches engaging with actors that worked in North Korea on various projects – from business through artistic cooperation to humanitarian aid); in the UK with Chatham House; in Australia with the support of members of the Federal Parliament; in Canada with HanVoice, in Switzerland with HRW and Conectas Human Rights; and in Indonesia with HRW, Conectas Human Rights, and KontraS. The final meeting was held in Germany with the Union der Opferverbände kommunistischer Gewaltherrschaft (Union of the

---

[9]   Citizens' Alliance for North Korean Human Rights 2009, 39.

Victims of Communism) in 2013. In many cases, conference locations were chosen simply because the foreign partners were interested in cohosting the forum. There were also strategic choices: Geneva was chosen to test the ground for the future call for a COI, while Indonesia was chosen because it is a seat of ASEAN that holds a regular forum of Southeast Asian countries also involving North Korea.

The strategy of holding meetings on North Korean human rights in foreign countries provided the impetus for international independent research, media coverage, books, and documentaries in various languages, all of which raised the profile of the North Korean human rights issue across the world.[10] More concretely, this activity contributed to the creation of an advocacy network that would raise the issue of North Korean human rights violations with governments in Europe, the United States, and Japan, as well as at the UN level. The most effective result of creating the transnational network of NGOs and individuals working on North Korean human rights through these conferences was the individual and collective advocacy work with foreign governments and UN agencies. The conference created opportunities for advocacy, as officials from the government where the conference was hosted, as well as officials from embassies present in the country, often participated. Aside from the conference, Citizens' Alliance and North Korean victims would often meet individually with government officials, members of parliaments, foreign embassies, and media. To this end, activists acted as facilitators, allowing victims' voices to bear witness to the atrocities taking place inside North Korea.

As the years progressed, this work to raise the profile of the North Korean human rights issue started to yield results. Activists felt confident that the time had come to move advocacy to the level of the UN. In 2003, Citizens' Alliance board member Professor Man Ho Heo and staff member Hae Young Lee, along with former Amnesty researcher David Hawk,[11] went to Geneva and engaged in a series of concerted lobbying efforts, clearing the way for future UN advocacy. That year, the first "Resolution on the Situation of Human

---

[10]   To name just few examples of such activities, the first accounts of North Koreans who participated in NKHR's conferences appeared in books by Pierre Rigoulot (Kang and Rigoulot 2001), or by Barbara Demick (2010). Initial documentaries about the North Korean situation were the result of the connection in the NKHR's conference network, such as "Seoul Train" by Lisa Sleeth and Jim Butterworth and "Yodok Stories" by Andrzej Fidyk. Anti Slavery UK published a report ("An Absence of Choice") on the trafficking of North Korean women and pursued an international campaign to put pressure on the UNHCR to protect North Korean refugees. Muico 2005.

[11]   Hawk authored the highly cited report *Hidden Gulag*, the first systematic account of the North Korean political prison camp system. Hawk 2003.

Rights in the DPRK" was passed at the UN Human Rights Commission. In 2004, after the Citizens' Alliance's Conference in Warsaw, an even larger advocacy team was assembled to lobby for the establishment of the mandate of the UN Special Rapporteur for the Situation of Human Rights in the DPRK. The team involved not only members of Citizens' Alliance and Hawk, but also members of several European organizations: the author of this chapter, who joined at this time as a member of the Helsinki Foundation for Human Rights in Poland, which co-organized the conference; Jubilee Campaign representative, Ann Buwalda; and Elizabeth Batha from UK Christian Solidarity Worldwide. This group organized the first parallel meeting on North Korean political prison camps during the 60th Session of the UN Human Rights Commission in Geneva. As the international advocacy grew, the conferences that were held in Geneva in 2011 and in Jakarta in 2012 served as an opportunity to build strategy with HRW and Conectas Human Rights, and to test the ground for a future call for the COI for DPRK.

By the time of the conference in Germany, Citizens' Alliance had successfully lobbied with partner NGOs for the COI, established in March 2013 by a UN Human Rights Council Resolution. Citizens' Alliance decided that this conference would be the last. The International Conferences had achieved great success over the years and had fulfilled their original purpose, allowing the organization to focus its energies on the next step: strengthening its UN advocacy efforts. The success of the International Conferences was well illustrated in a message sent by the 14th Dalai Lama to the participants of the First International Conference in 1999 at a time when the world was completely silent on human rights abuses happening in North Korea:

> Speak up for the Voiceless! In order to achieve genuine happiness, every society needs to guarantee the right to freedom of thought, conscience, and expression. Human rights can flourish only where the soil is built on confidence, trust and freedom from fear. Yet, around the world, we still see many people who are deprived of their own basic rights and freedoms. They cannot but remain voiceless.[12]

NGO ADVOCACY AT THE UN: ESTABLISHING A NORTH KOREAN HUMAN RIGHTS DISCOURSE

The DPRK became a member state of the UN simultaneously with the Republic of Korea in 1991. It was a political decision and the result of years-long negotiations to accept both Koreas at the same time.[13] The DPRK had

---

[12]   The XIV Dalai Lama 1999.   [13]   Pak 2000, 64–75.

acceded to some of the human rights treaties much earlier, namely the International Covenant on Civil and Political Rights and the International Covenant on Economic, Social and Cultural Rights in 1981, followed by the Convention on the Rights of the Child in 1990, and the Convention on the Elimination of All Forms of Discrimination Against Women (CEDAW) in 2001.[14] In contrast, with the exception of CEDAW, the Republic of Korea declined to ratify these instruments until the early 1990s, when the country was undergoing democratic transition. During the 1970s and 1980s, the South Korean government, which at the time was faced with an active civil society community protesting the lack of human rights and democracy inside the country, was unwilling to submit itself to the scrutiny that accession to the human rights treaties would have invited. In 1981, North Korea, on the other hand, did not harbor an active dissident community and was keen to gain access to the UN. Ratifying these treaties allowed it to do so without any immediate consequences. North Korea was so poorly integrated into the international community that it is likely that Pyongyang considered such a move to be risk-free, not expecting that decades later they might be called to account for the human rights obligations that came with membership of the international human rights legal framework. And indeed, such scrutiny did not come for many decades, and only after the first South Korean NGOs were established in the late 1990s to monitor the situation in the country, high-lighting the testimonies of North Korean human rights victims for the attention of the international community.[15] Even then, UN officials and member states would not officially recognize the seriousness of the situation in North Korea for another decade.

South Korean NGOs quickly discovered that they could not bring about meaningful change at the UN while working alone. While the first resolutions on North Korean human rights were adopted by the UN Sub-Commission on the Promotion and the Protection of Human Rights in 1997 and 1998,

[14] With the exception of CEDAW, which South Korea ratified in 1984, Seoul did not ratify these human rights treaties until after democratic transition had begun: the Civil and Political and Economic, Social and Cultural Rights Covenants in 1990, and the Rights of the Child Convention in 1991.

[15] Competition between the two Koreas to be recognized as the legitimate Korean state and responsible member of the international community could have also played a significant role. North Korea was initially objecting both Koreas being simultaneously accepted to the UN. North Korea also wanted to prevent the situation whereby South Korea is recognized as the only legitimate Korean state by the UN (see discussion on membership attempts in Pak 2000). The fact that North Korea tried to withdraw from the UN Core Covenants in 1997 upon first scrutiny by NGOs and the UN speaks volumes about North Korea's logic in using earlier ratifications only as a strategic move.

following the commencement of first advocacy efforts in Geneva by Citizens' Alliance, the political effect of these resolutions was ultimately minimal. The Sub-Commission was a recommending body made up of experts and did not have the authority to bring states to account. To elevate the issue, Citizens' Alliance turned its attention to the development of a transnational network of NGOs and individuals. This network was built year by year, international conference by international conference.[16] Thus, collective strategic advocacy work with foreign governments and the UN agencies started in 2003, leading to the first full-fledged UN Resolution on the Situation of Human Rights in the DPRK[17] being adopted by the member states of the UN Commission on Human Rights. The Resolution was an important watershed, as the network of NGOs realized that greater collective mobilization could lead to an international change of stance toward the North Korean human rights issue. Thus, in 2004, after Citizens' Alliance's international conference, a large international advocacy group was formed to try to increase the number of states supporting the Resolution and to create a UN independent expert panel mandated to investigate and report on the human rights situation. Human Rights Commission Resolution 2004/13 established the mandate of the UN Special Rapporteur on the Situation of Human Rights in the DPRK.[18]

NGO advocacy work involved consultations on the text of the Resolution with the drafting states (namely EU countries and Japan) and individual meetings with diplomats covering the Asian, African, and South American regions to request their support for the North Korean resolution. This is where the involvement of larger numbers of individual activists from an enlarged advocacy group started to play a role, as no single NGO could cover the 30–40 member states of the Commission.

There were many obstacles to advocacy at this beginning stage. Some states were against country-specific resolutions and country-specific mandates, viewing it as an obstacle to cooperation with a state in the spirit of the UN. This is often the position of authoritarian countries, which do not wish to be singled out for exposure, and hence oppose country mandates. As a result, many

---

[16] Membership of the network was fluid, but during the first three years the core members were Citizens' Alliance, NKnet, Jubilee Campaign, Christian Solidarity Worldwide and David Hawk. After 2009, the core members were Citizens' Alliance and HRW, with other network members either acting alone or through the umbrella organization ICNK. The network largely developed organically, with efforts made to ensure that at least some members were groups with ECOSOC consultative status, in case attendance at official UN events was required.

[17] UN Commission on Human Rights 2003.   [18] UN Commission on Human Rights 2004.

diplomats from Asian or African countries which maintained friendly relations with the DPRK government declined to even speak to the activists.

Advocacy on the Resolution, however, was only a small portion of the early UN advocacy. The criticism of North Korea's human rights record had to be substantiated with hard evidence, little of which was available at the international level. It was at this point that Citizens' Alliance started to utilize UN mechanisms based on North Korea's earlier accession to several human rights treaties. While the DPRK continually rejected the mandate of the UN Special Rapporteur on the Situation of Human Rights in the DPRK established by the relevant country Resolution, claiming it was politically driven action against the DPRK, it was obliged to fulfill the regular reporting obligations to the Committees monitoring the implementation of the treaties. For NGOs, this created a new advocacy opportunity, and the North Korean human rights network gathered evidence to submit to the Committees, briefed the relevant experts and monitored the reviews of the country.

North Korea was reviewed in 2001 by the Human Rights Committee monitoring implementation of the International Covenant on Civil and Political Rights; in 2003, the Committee on Social, Economic and Cultural Rights reviewed the DPRK delegation based on the International Covenant on Economic, Social and Cultural Rights; in 2005, the CEDAW Committee reviewed the implementation of Convention on the Elimination of All Forms of Discrimination Against Women in North Korea; and in January 2009, the Committee on the Rights of the Child (CRC) questioned North Korea on the status of children's rights based upon the Convention on the Rights of the Child.

The UN Committees relied heavily on NGOs to help gain an understanding of the scope and nature of the human rights problems inside North Korea. North Korea's own reporting lacked credibility, failing to meet minimum requirements on technical issues (such as reliable statistics). Gaining an alternative view from inside the country is, of course, impossible, given the lack of an independent civil society, and NGOs were able to provide briefings and written submissions on a range of issues around gender discrimination, trafficking, and access to food and medical services. It was clear that DPRK officials were not prepared for the level of scrutiny that followed the submission of their Committee reports. After both the CEDAW and CRC Sessions in 2005 and 2009, respectively, the concluding observations of the Committees expressed concern about the poor level of human rights compliance inside the country. Such problems were further elaborated in the reports of the UN Special Rapporteur on the Situation of Human Rights in the DPRK. Seeing the increasing criticism, North Korea stopped submitting the reports to the Committees and switched to use the Universal Periodic Review (UPR) instead, which is a much simpler, diplomatic peer review created by the UN Human Rights Council. The UPR process allows NGOs to submit stakeholders' submissions, which is compiled by the Office of the High Commissioner for Human Rights. Before the 2010 and 2014 reviews of North Korea, NGOs extensively used this channel to voice their concerns and to make recommendations, often meeting in official briefings with the states preparing their statements for the Review. It is now chiefly through the UPR mechanism that the UN is able to conduct a dialogue with North Korea regarding its human rights obligations.[19]

At the turn of the century, the international community knew little about the human rights situation in North Korea. By 2012, after more than a decade of concerted research, reporting, and advocacy, the international community had substantial information about the situation in North Korea coming from NGOs and the UN experts. North Korea's noncooperative attitude with the Office of the UN High Commissioner for Human Rights, overdue reports to the Committees monitoring their obligations with conventions, copy-pasted answers on individual complaint cases, and their rejection of all recommendations from the states during the UPR in 2010, coupled with ongoing military provocations, gave North Korea little room to maneuver. Even Pyongyang's usual supporters, who in the past had argued that North Korea should be "given a chance" to work within the UN system, fell silent.

The international alienation of North Korea was most visible during the annual votes on the UN Human Rights Resolution on the Situation of Human Rights in the DPRK. While the number of supporters was slowly rising over the years (as Tables 6.1–6.3 in this chapter illustrate), the real breakthrough came in 2012 when the annual resolutions calling for improvements in the human rights situation passed by consensus, meaning that even the traditional supporters of North Korea, such as China, Russia, and their satellite countries, did not encourage discussion or call for a vote. This was a surprising development even to the NGOs, but understandable given North Korea's continued uncooperative attitude. The clear trend of support for the Resolution (with 88 states voting yes in 2005 and 122 states voting yes in 2011) is illustrated in Table 6.1, which represents votes at the UN General Assembly where all member states have a seat. As membership in the UN Human Rights Council (and earlier Commission) membership rotate, the

---

[19] After a long hiatus and international pressure related to COI's report, North Korea submitted overdue reports to CEDAW and CRC in 2016. In addition to these Committee submissions, NGOs also submitted information to other thematic mandates: in particular, the UN Working Group on Enforced or Involuntary Disappearances. North Korea did not cooperate on these matters.

TABLE 6.1. *UN General Assembly voting records on the resolution of the situation of human rights in the DPRK, 2005–11*

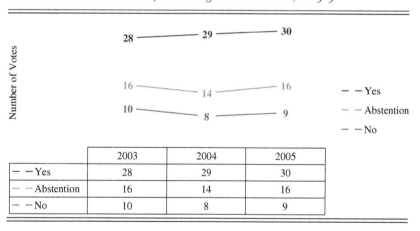

	2005	2006	2007	2008	2009	2010	2011
– –Abstention	60	56	59	63	63	57	50
– –Yes	88	99	101	94	99	106	122
– –No	21	21	22	22	20	20	16

TABLE 6.2. *UN Commission on Human Rights voting record on the resolution on the situation of human rights in the DPRK, 2003–5*

	2003	2004	2005
– –Yes	28	29	30
– –Abstention	16	14	16
– –No	10	8	9

numbers in Tables 6.2 and 6.3 represent different states voting at different times. Table 6.1 does not include states that were absent during the votes.

When these resolutions passed by consensus at the UN Human Rights Council and the UN General Assembly, it sent a signal to the network of NGOs working on North Korean human rights that the timing might be right to demand more from the international community and establish the COI.

TABLE 6.3. *UN Human Rights Council voting records on the resolution on the situation of human rights in the DPRK, 2008–11*

	2008	2009	2010	2011
– –Yes	22	26	28	30
– –Abstention	18	15	13	11
– –No	7	6	5	3

Year

TOWARD ACCOUNTABILITY: BEYOND THE COI

In international diplomacy, timing is a crucial element of success. In order for the UN to establish a COI on North Korean human rights, it was essential that NGOs pick their moment strategically. As the UN resolutions addressing human rights violations in North Korea passed by consensus, coincidentally China and Russia's terms at the UN Human Rights Council were coming to an end. Citizens' Alliance, HRW, and Conectas Human Rights thus seized this opportunity to launch a concerted advocacy effort for the establishment of the COI for DPRK.

On December 3, 2012, the author of this chapter, as the head of International Campaign and Advocacy at Citizens' Alliance, led the delegation that included two victims of North Korean political prison camps to meet with Navi Pillay, the then UN High Commissioner for Human Rights. The meeting was coordinated with the Geneva office of HRW, and supported by HRW director, Juliette de Rivero. Never before had a South Korean NGO working on North Korean human rights issues or prison camp victims from North Korea had the opportunity to meet privately with the UN High Commissioner for Human Rights. During the meeting, the victims told their stories, illustrated with maps and drawings, and requested that the international community act now, reminding the High Commissioner of the situation toward the end of WWII when advancement of the Allied Forces revealed the full extent of the Holocaust after entering abandoned concentration camps and recording the horrific sites on tape.

During the meeting, the activists explained that the UN Resolution on North Korean Human Rights was by itself insufficient given both the extent of North Korean human rights abuses as well as the lack of cooperation on the part of the North Korean government. The author explained that the full scale of the problems ongoing for more than half of the century in the country could not be revealed with just the yearly update of the Special Rapporteur in his reports. The organizations encouraged the Commissioner to support the launch of a full investigation into North Korean violations and to prioritize North Korean human rights, especially the situation in political prison camps and unresolved abductions.

Following the meeting, the Office of the High Commissioner issued a statement calling for an investigation into possible crimes against humanity in North Korea. From the statement it was clear that the High Commissioner's interest in the subject was greatly influenced by the December meeting:

> In December, the High Commissioner met with two survivors of DPRK's elaborate network of political prison camps which are believed to contain 200,000 or more people. Their personal stories were extremely harrowing ... They described a system that represents the very antithesis of international human rights norms. We know so little about these camps, and what we do know comes largely from the relatively few refugees who have managed to escape from the country. The highly developed system of international human rights protection that has had at least some positive impact in almost every country in the world, seems to have completely bypassed DPRK, where self-imposed isolation has allowed the government to mistreat its citizens to a degree that should be unthinkable in the 21st century ... For years now, the Government of DPRK has persistently refused to cooperate with successive Special Rapporteurs on the situation of human rights in the DPRK appointed by the Human Rights Council, or with my Office ... For this reason, and because of the enduring gravity of the situation, I believe an in-depth inquiry into one of the worst – but least understood and reported – human rights situations in the world is not only fully justified, but long overdue.[20]

The next step for activists was ensuring that the call for the COI was supported by member states. It was clear that some states held doubts that a COI was the best way to approach this issue. At the time, Japan, which was one of the main drafting states, was engaged in ongoing bilateral discussions with the DPRK on the issue of abductions. It was thus not clear whether the Japanese Cabinet – under pressure from home to resolve the abductions issue quickly – would support the call for investigation. The EU, which codrafts the Resolution, is

[20]   UN Office of the High Commissioner for Human Rights 2013.

a large entity, in which states supportive of the investigation were opposed by other states. Some EU states with embassies and projects in North Korea were worried about the fallout of the COI. The toughest advocacy work in terms of individual EU states had to be resolved on the "consultation line": Brussels – Geneva – Seoul – Pyongyang. That is, lobbying work at an individual state level did not take place solely in Brussels or Geneva. Activists had to ensure that they were relaying a consistent message to all members of each country's missions, including those based at the EU, the UN, and the Seoul and Pyongyang embassies. Finally, activists had to engage in lobbying at the EU level. HRW led this advocacy effort, in cooperation with Citizens' Alliance.

The political departments of some EU countries were concerned about the diplomatic ramifications of such an inquiry. EU dialogue with the DPRK, which took place in 2001 and 2002, was stalled in 2003 after the first UN Resolution on North Korean human rights. In early 2013, just two years after the transition of power in North Korea, many were hopeful that the new leader, educated in Europe, would be open to dialogue. Additionally, many EU countries indicated to NGOs that they did not believe a full-fledged inquiry would add value to the current mechanisms available, namely the UN Special Rapporteur on North Korean human rights. They cited concerns that the COI would only undermine the Special Rapporteur's mandate. They were concerned that the call for a COI would turn some countries away from supporting the annual Resolution, and thus it was better to continue the steady road than to take a risky approach.

The author of this chapter, who conducted many such individual and EU-level meetings, responded that actions should not be based on wishful thinking and hopes for unknown future developments, but on the current situation. The reality was that North Korea had defied the UN system for years, showing disregard for human rights norms it should have adhered to. It had also failed to cooperate in various UN multilateral efforts, especially with regard to reporting to UN treaty bodies and the UPR process, stalling the treaty bodies' reviews with several overdue reports.

NGOs argued that there should be a meaningful measure of engagement; simply showing up or submitting a report should not be considered as such. Rather, North Korea should be held accountable to its obligations and follow through with the recommendations. Activists further argued that leniency under such circumstances had fostered a sense of impunity on the part of DPRK officials. This set a dangerous precedent. At the time, for example, North Korea was the only country among all UN member states that rejected visits of thematic rapporteurs, such as the Special Rapporteur on the Right to Food. We argued that improving human rights conditions, the existence of which Pyongyang continued to deny, was not a dialogue, but a one-way communication.

Finally, activists argued that a COI would strengthen the mandate of the Special Rapporteur, which at the time had few resources, only one part-time assistant, and no means to conduct in-depth research. The COI, on the other hand, would have the resources required to conduct a meaningful inquiry. Even if some countries switched their votes to "abstentions" or "no," the annual Resolution would still pass with an overwhelming number of votes in favor.

The final result surpassed everyone's expectations and was affirmed by the Human Rights Council by consensus, without any requests for the matter to go to a vote. Michael Kirby, the Chair of the COI, describes the Council's response to the president's call for a COI as follows:

> So it was in 2013 the HRC, for the first time without a call for a vote, established a COI to carry out an extensive mandate concerned with issues of human rights in DPRK. Before the matter was declared resolved, the President of the HRC ... repeatedly paused to allow for a vote to be called for. But no such call arose. This fact, and the subsequent response of the HRC to the report of the COI, indicates the level of exasperation that the recalcitrant conduct of the DPRK had occasioned. The COI was established. The mandate given to it by the HRC was of the widest possible dimension.[21]

The establishment of the COI meant that South Korean organizations would have to come together to help the COI's secretariat and the Commissioners to fulfill their mandate, whether through access to victims or specific documentation, or cross-checking of facts that could come up during the unofficial interviews and public hearings. South Korean NGOs thus played a vital facilitative role in support of the COI by providing office space, or even interpretation when official interpreters lacked knowledge of specific North Korean vocabulary. When public hearings began, the foreign press was still unaware of the venue and how to apply for access passes, and so South Korean NGOs mobilized to share the information with the public. Even the venue for the hearings was too difficult for many victims to find, such that NGOs had to assist them to find it.

The Commission's 2014 report on human rights abuses in North Korea caused a discursive shift on the international level toward accountability. This new paradigm shifted attention to responsibility for the crimes and the necessity of processes which would provide justice to the victims. In this sense, the report's findings of "systematic, widespread and grave human rights violations

---

[21] Kirby 2014a, 5.

occurring in the Democratic People's Republic of Korea and a disturbing array of crimes against humanity," which the Commission stressed "had no parallel" in the modern world, were extremely significant.[22] NGOs again mobilized extensive advocacy, with the individual states drafting the text to ensure that the annual Resolution on the Situation of Human Rights in North Korea would fully reflect the conclusions and recommendations of the COI and that there would be widespread support for the Resolution and condemnation of the crimes committed by the North Korean regime.

Even though the Resolution of the UN Human Rights Council, reflecting COI recommendations and adopted in March 2014, did not pass by a consensus, there were 30 votes in favor, 11 abstentions, and only 6 negative votes. This reflected the usual level of support before the COI was established. Given the strong language contained in the Resolution, this was an enormous success. There was also a change in the voting position of some of the targeted African and Asian countries. Algeria, which previously voted no, switched its vote to abstention, and Cote d'Ivoire, Philippines, and the United Arab Emirates changed their votes in favor of the resolution instead of abstention. Botswana has cut diplomatic ties with North Korea altogether. The final count on the UN General Assembly Resolution A/RES/69/188 was also excellent and comparable to the vote in previous years, which is remarkable considering that this Resolution called on the UN Security Council to place the North Korean human rights issue on its official agenda. Armenia, Burkina Faso, Chad, and Somalia changed their votes in favor of the resolution. Other countries which had recently changed their vote in favor of the resolution maintained their "yes" vote despite strong pressure to change. These were Thailand, Tajikistan, Cote d'Ivoire, Rwanda, Seychelles, and Barbados. Countries which switched from long-term "yes" votes to abstention were El Salvador, Eritrea, Gabon, Libya, St. Lucia, Solomon Islands, Togo, and Tanzania. As a result, the UN Security Council officially discussed the North Korean human rights violations for the first time in December 2014 and has continued in the ensuing years.

UN ADVOCACY ON NORTH KOREAN HUMAN RIGHTS AND THE IMPACT ON NORTH KOREA

Despite North Korea's ongoing recalcitrance toward UN criticisms of its human rights record, it is clear that ongoing advocacy at the UN level has raised the level of awareness of member states toward North Korea's human

---

[22] Kirby 2014b.

rights record. This is significant in light of North Korea's ongoing development of its nuclear weapons program, which tends to overshadow human
rights issues. It has also had some impact on North Korea's relationship with
the concept of human rights and the way it talks about human rights at the
UN, particularly with regards to the rights of specific groups in the country.

In 1997, the year Citizens' Alliance began advocacy in Geneva, North Korea
was reproached by the UN Human Rights Committee. Responding angrily,
North Korea tried to withdraw from the UN Covenant on Civil and Political
Rights but was told this was not possible.[23] The country tried similar angry
approaches with the UN Human Rights Commission and UN Human Rights
Council, denouncing resolutions addressing its human rights record as usually
a product of political trickery fabricated by the forces hostile to the North
Korean government. It rejected the mandate of the country's Special
Rapporteur and did not accept technical cooperation from the Office of
High Commissioner for Human Rights.

Yet, the NGOs documenting abuses in North Korea observed certain
changes after 2004, which some victims credited to international pressure.
The North Korean Criminal Code was amended to lighten the punishment
for border-crossers, female victims reported fewer beatings, and there were
fewer forced abortions and infanticides in detention centers. Some victims
also reported signing documents stating that their "human rights were not
violated" upon release from detention. Although this evidence is anecdotal
and some of these policies have been reversed in recent years, with human
rights further deteriorating following the 2011 political transition of power in
the country, international pressure seems to have had some impact on North
Korea.[24]

The international community's scrutiny on the treatment of women and
children in particular has had a demonstrable effect on North Korea, with the
country hurriedly adopting two laws on women's rights and children's rights in
2010 before its UPR, and including the words "human rights" in its
Constitution. North Korean diplomats, however, learned quickly that these
nonsubstantive changes would not satisfy UN processes. For example, North
Korea caused a real uproar at the UN Human Rights Council when it did not
clarify which of the 117 recommendations it would accept: this move was
understood as a rejection of all of them. Countries demanded a break of

---

[23] In the same year, the UN Economic and Social Council's Sub-Commission on Prevention of
Discrimination and Protection of Minorities also attempted to address the situation in North
Korea; see UN Economic and Social Council 1997.

[24] See Goedde (Chapter 7 of this volume) for more on North Korea's legal changes pertaining to
human rights issues.

Council and gathered in front of the red-faced DPRK Ambassador. Even states such as Brazil that had famously defended North Korea's efforts to go through the UPR process as a sign of engagement, and which had switched their vote from "yes" to "abstention" as a sign that a North Korean human rights resolution is counterproductive, were deeply embarrassed by this attitude.

After the COI was established, North Korea at first responded angrily. When this did not prove a productive strategy, North Korean diplomats then engaged in a charm offensive. During the Interactive Dialogue with the COI at the Human Rights Council in March 2014, the DPRK Ambassador stormed out of the room in protest after attempts to disturb the session. A few months later, the DPRK changed tack and proposed that it would grant access to the Special Rapporteur for North Korean human rights and re-establish human rights dialogue if the EU countries removed the language on accountability from the Resolution that was to be tabled at the UN General Assembly in 2014. Cuba attempted to table a separate resolution, proposing cooperation with DPRK instead of calling for accountability, but countries which opposed country-specific resolutions said they would not vote for such a resolution, and other countries argued that it was too early to undertake such an exercise of trust given that North Korea had not shown any goodwill to participate faithfully in UN processes before the establishment of the COI. Finally, in October 2014, Citizens' Alliance initiated and co-organized a parallel meeting with HRW, the Jacob Blaustein Institute for the Advancement of Human Rights, and the Committee for Human Rights in North Korea, and cosponsored by Australia, Panama, and Botswana. A large North Korean delegation appeared at the meeting and engaged for the first time in heated discussion with the Chair of the COI, Michael Kirby. The exchange was broadcast by UN TV.

Despite North Korea's angry efforts and charm offensive tactics, the pressure did not subside after the COI. In 2016, the yearly UN Human Rights Council's Resolution established the Panel of Experts on Accountability in the DPRK. In the past, North Korea had ceased submitting reports to the UN Committees monitoring implementation of human rights treaties in defiance of the review processes. After the 2016 Resolution, North Korea suddenly submitted overdue reports to UN CEDAW and CRC Committees and was expected to undergo a review on women's and child's rights in late 2017. The country also ratified the UN Convention on the Treatment of Persons with Disabilities. It is likely that these reports were submitted as part of an effort to regain some credibility at the UN. Yet, North Korea's tactics of anger mixed with a charm offensive, cooperation, and withdrawal has not seen pressure on the country's human rights situation subside. In the absence of real change, it will probably be very difficult for North Korea to regain the trust of the international community.

CONCLUSION

North Korea is probably the most difficult country for NGOs to work with. Usually, NGOs provide support to the UN system "on the ground" inside target countries, observing and monitoring implementation of international and domestic law and gathering testimony. Even though the majority of this typical NGO work cannot be done inside North Korea, these obstacles have not prevented NGOs such as Citizens' Alliance from engaging in activism at the UN level since 1997. NGO-driven actions and North Korean human rights NGOs' milestone achievements include advocacy work at the UN Human Rights Commission, the UN Human Rights Council, and the UN General Assembly, lobbying for support on the Resolution condemning human rights violations in North Korea, and advocacy to establish the respective mandates of the UN Special Rapporteur on Human Rights Situation in the DPRK, the COI for DPRK, and finally the UN Panel of Experts on Accountability.

South Korean NGOs often did not have the human or financial resources to establish local branches in various countries, and South Korea itself has historically been a hostile environment for North Korean human rights NGOs. For many years, Citizens' Alliance was operating from a dilapidated building with no heating during winter, no hot water, and with just a few passionate members who worked on a voluntary basis. It was necessary to build an international network to carry out advocacy work in countries where South Korean organizations could not be present.

At the beginning of its work, Citizens' Alliance included everyone who was interested, building a diverse network of North Korean human rights NGOs. But over time many groups naturally parted as the movement became mature and specialized. Thus, Citizens' Alliance started to form close partnerships with organizations that shared its strong human rights focus and regional networks that shared its thematic focus, such as the Asian Federation Against Enforced Disappearances and the Asia Pacific Refugee Network. It was always careful not to be affiliated politically and to be viewed as concerned exclusively with the upholding of international human rights norms. Because of this deliberate decision to not align itself, the NGO was often attacked by both sides in South Korea and abroad. When, in its international platform, it included different approaches and organizations that worked inside North Korea and were thus engagement-oriented, Citizens' Alliance was accused by some of not being critical enough of the North Korean regime. At the same time, the group was confronted with conspiracy theories and accused of being used by foreign intelligence agencies to bring about "regime change" in North Korea. Those leveling these criticisms never made any efforts to liaise with the organization itself, and knew little of the history of the founders of the North Korean human rights movement, for whom fighting for respect for the human rights of their fellow North Koreans was a natural extension of their previous work to promote human rights and democracy in South Korea. For the founding activists of Citizens' Alliance, human rights had universal value and not selective value dependent on the South Korean government's policies toward North Korea.

The success, thus far, of the North Korean human rights movement at the UN proves that the nexus between NGOs, the UN, and member states allows even a small NGO to place issues high on the agenda of the UN and other governments. International advocacy on North Korean human rights has been influenced by testimonies and pleas of victims and witnesses. Yet, despite the weight of evidence available with regard to human rights abuses in North Korea, the political environment necessitated the wielding of much tact and diplomacy in order to convince states to use the information and recommendations presented by NGOs.

The result of this advocacy is that comments, reports, and recommendations made by NGOs are delivered directly to the government of North Korea in accordance with the UN Resolution, or through foreign governments and experts speaking at the UN. Given the lack of a domestic civil society inside North Korea, this is the only form of communication possible between human rights NGOs and the North Korean government at the moment. Even though this communication is indirect, its impact cannot be underestimated. Of course, the true testimony of advocacy efforts will come when human rights organizations and victims' associations in South Korea are able to bring about real justice for the crimes committed in North Korea, including through access to truth, naming of the nameless victims, and compensation to those who lost everything.

REFERENCES

Amnesty International. 1979. *Alí Lameda: A Personal Account of the Experience of a Prisoner of Conscience in the Democratic People's Republic of Korea.* ASA 24/02/79. London: Amnesty International.
Chubb, Danielle. 2014. *Contentious Activism and Inter-Korean Relations.* New York: Columbia University Press.
Citizens' Alliance for North Korean Human Rights 2009. *A 10 Year's History: 1996–2006.* Seoul: Life and Human Rights Books.
Demick, Barbara. 2010. *Nothing to Envy.* New York: Spiegel & Grau
Hawk, David. 2003. *The Hidden Gulag: Exposing North Korea's Prison Camps.* Washington DC: US Committee for Human Rights in North Korea.

Kagan, Richard, Matthew Oh, and David Weissbrodt. 1988. *Human Rights in the Democratic People's Republic of Korea.* Washington DC: Minnesota Lawyers International and Asia Watch.

Kang, Chol-Hwan, and Pierre Rigoulot. 2001. *The Aquariums of Pyongyang: Ten Years in a North Korean Gulag.* Translated by Yair Reiner. New York: Basic Books.

Kirby, Michael. 2014a. United Nations Commission of Inquiry on North Korea – Creation, Methodology, Conclusions and Prognosis. No. 2733. www.michaelkirby .com.au/content/2014.

Kirby, Michael. 2014b. *Statement by Mr. Michael Kirby, Chair of the COI on Human Rights in the DPRK to the 25th Session of the Human Rights Council.* March 17. Geneva: UN Office of High Commissioner for Human Rights.

Muico, Norma Kang. 2005. *An Absence of Choice: The Sexual Exploitation of North Korean Women in China.* London: Anti-Slavery International.

Pak, Chi- Young. 2000. *Korea and the United Nations.* The Hague: Kluwer Law International.

The XIV Dalai Lama. 1999. *Message to Participants of The 1st International Conference on North Korean Human Rights & Refugees.* Seoul: Citizens' Alliance for North Korean Human Rights Archives.

UN Economic and Social Council. 1997. *Situation of Human Rights in the Democratic People's Republic of Korea.* E/CN.4/1998/2. August 21.

UN Commission on Human Rights. 2003. *Situation of Human Rights in the Democratic People's Republic of Korea.* E/CN.4/RES/2003/10. April 16.

UN Commission on Human Rights 2004. *Situation of Human Rights in the Democratic People's Republic of Korea.* E/CN.4/RES/2004/13. April 15.

UN Office of the High Commissioner for Human Rights. 2013. Pillay Urges More Attention to Human Rights Abuses in North Korea, Calls for International Inquiry. *Press Statement,* January 14.

Yoon, Benjamin Hyun. 1996. *Founding speech, Citizens' Alliance to Help Political Prisoners in North Korea.* May 4. Seoul: Citizens' Alliance for North Korean Human Rights Archives.

7

Human Rights Diffusion in North Korea
The Impact of Transnational Legal Mobilization

Patricia Goedde

The COI report in 2014 has elevated the North Korean human rights issue into the global political arena with unprecedented gravity.[1] It is a turning point for the transnational advocacy network for human rights protection in North Korea, which has mobilized the legal framework of the UN's complex and international human rights law treaties to pressure the North Korean government into abiding by human rights principles. Advocating for international criminal liability, the COI report has propelled further legal activities, such as evidence collection toward accountability, the passage of domestic legislation in South Korea and the United States, and other efforts to address human rights violations by the North Korean government in its territory and abroad.[2] But the paradox lies in whether this approach has been effective for the actual diffusion or institutionalization of human rights in North Korea, especially without a domestic advocacy structure in place. This chapter addresses the North Korean human rights narrative from a transnational legal perspective, asking (1) how the UN and the NGO community have mobilized the legal institutional framework to address and protect human rights within North Korea, and (2) how North Korea contends with transnational legal norms of human rights in relation to its national security. Reaching beyond the accountability paradigm, the

[1] This chapter is a revised version of an article published in *Asian Journal of Law and Society* and is reproduced here with permission. See Goedde 2017.
    The author would like to thank Edward Baker, Roland Bleiker, Sandra Fahy, Andrew Yeo, Danielle Chubb, and Markus Bell for reading the earlier versions of this paper and providing extremely helpful comments. She would also like to thank Jinyoung Lee for her research assistance, and those who were interviewed for this study.
[2] For example, European initiatives have also become more visible since publication of the COI report, such as EU dialogue with North Korea, the All-Party Parliamentary Group on North Korea, and the Leiden Asia Centre project on North Korean forced labor in EU countries (Breuker et al. 2016).

chapter concludes with a discussion of alternative discourses and channels for human rights engagement with and within North Korea.

THEORETICAL FRAMEWORKS ON HUMAN RIGHTS AND LAW

The spiral model of human rights has been a popular theoretical framework to study transnational human rights advocacy in relation to North Korea.[3] As Chubb and Yeo discuss in this volume's opening chapter, North Korea challenges the model in a number of ways. First, the spiral model assumes a local advocacy counterpart to work from the "bottom up" with an international advocacy network.[4] While many countries have rights advocacy actors who can mobilize and work with a transnational network, this is not evident in North Korea.[5] While the transnational human rights advocacy network for North Korea is a strong and expansive one, its members and activists exist outside of North Korea with their strongest nodes in the capitals of South Korea and the United States. With the exceptions of subversive information infiltration and underground religious activism, North Korean human rights advocacy is active extraterritorially rather than domestically in North Korea. When successful, the spiral model assumes a transition from a reluctant state's concessional phase toward institutionalization of human rights protection.[6] However, the absence of a domestic civil society and accompanying structures for legal mobilization means that there is blockage from the concessional phase to the institutionalization phase in North Korea. This absence of a rights structure, as well as rights consciousness within North Korea, makes human rights diffusion in North Korea deeply challenging.

Law is a critical component to the observance of human rights in terms of representation, legislation, and enforcement of rights. Research in law and society studies also emphasizes the importance of having supportive domestic advocacy structures in place if meaningful change is to occur. The fight for human rights advancement usually goes hand-in-hand with political liberalism and often involves a vanguard of activists and lawyers to contest state practices by framing grievances as rights violations.[7] This type of advocacy is usually empowered by allying with international organizations such as human rights NGOs, UN human rights mechanisms, and international or regional courts when available. Legal mobilization comprises a dynamic structure of

---

[3] Chubb 2014; Song 2010, 190.   [4] Risse et al. 1999; Keck and Sikkink 1998.
[5] In contrast, South Korean civil society engaged closely with international human rights groups to facilitate democratization in the 1980s.
[6] Risse et al. 2013.   [7] Halliday et al. 2007, 34–37.

a coalition of actors who frame grievances, usually within a rights discourse, and mobilize other legal actors, networks, institutions, and legal or political processes to implement change.[8] Cause-lawyering literature also explains the transformative role of the legal profession as critical actors in rights advancement,[9] with scholars noting the particular challenges of legal mobilization under authoritarian governments.[10] Tam argues that "legal mobilization under authoritarianism requires both the legal complex and the rights support structure,"[11] referring to rights advocacy groups, government-funded legal programs, a bar association, and an independent judiciary within these categories. A general rights consciousness among the population would also be needed to implement the rule of law via the legal complex and rights support structure. While a legal infrastructure in terms of courts, prosecutors, and lawyers exists in North Korea, these are state mechanisms that do not support politically contentious petitions against the government.

Despite participation in the UN and having signed six major international human rights treaties, North Korea appears to have resisted the "norms cascade" of international human rights.[12] This is not entirely surprising from a global perspective given that signature or ratification may often be a low-cost symbolic gesture as opposed to actual implementation via domestic legislation.[13] Naming-and-shaming has worked to bring attention to human rights violations in North Korea and yielded some tactical concessions, but the question remains as to how to constructively persuade the North Korean government to improve human rights protection.

LEGAL MOBILIZATION VIA UN MECHANISMS

Given the intransigence of North Korea's position on human rights, institutional participation on the part of the UN vis-à-vis North Korea has escalated over the past decade (see Hosaniak, Chapter 6 of this volume). Beyond the treaty body reporting system and the Universal Periodic Review, the DPRK

---

[8]   Halliday et al. 2007, 34–37; Epp 1998.   [9]   Sarat and Scheingold 1998; McCann 1994.
[10]   Tam 2013; Moustafa 2007, 193–217; Fu and Cullen 2008.   [11]   Tam 2013, 25–6.
[12]   Sunstein 1996. North Korea had acceded to three international human treaties: the International Covenant on Civil and Political Rights (ICCPR) and the International Covenant on Economic, Social, and Cultural Rights (ICESCR) in 1981, and the Convention on the Rights of the Child (CRC) in 1990. It later acceded to the Convention on the Elimination of Discrimination Against Women (CEDAW) in 2001, acceded to the Optional Protocol to the Convention on the Rights of the Child on the sale of children, child prostitution and child pornography in 2014, and ratified the Convention on the Rights of the Persons with Disabilities (CRPD) in 2016.
[13]   Simmons 2009; Hathaway 2007.

COI represents an emerging legal mechanism within the UN apparatus, moving beyond treaty monitoring toward fact-finding and prosecution. The UN Human Rights Council has made use of commissions of inquiry in a variety of cases over the past 20 years. This involves sending fact-finding missions to investigate violations of international humanitarian law and international human rights law in armed conflict areas.[14] Each commission of inquiry has had a slightly different character, scope, and methodology according to its respective mandate, but all are basically tasked to identify legal violations, ensure accountability, and propose remedies. In this sense, they have evolved from their original purpose of fact-finding for mediating and conciliatory purposes between two parties at conflict with each other to one of "*de facto* law-applying authorities."[15]

The case of North Korea represents the most recent culmination of this increasingly juridical trend where the COI has moved well beyond merely fact-finding to applying the law and proposing legal remedies of accountability.[16] This is evident in its mandate to "investigate the systematic, widespread and grave violations of human rights in the [DPRK] . . . with a view to ensuring full accountability, in particular where these violations may amount to crimes against humanity."[17] This mandate is instructive in that it presupposes human rights violations and tasks the Commission to find full, essentially criminal, liability for those violations deemed crimes against humanity.[18] In listing evidence of human rights violations as crimes against humanity, and in stating that the North Korean leadership must be held internationally accountable for its criminal culpability, the COI report represents what Sikkink identifies as the emerging global, juridical norm or "new

---

[14]   These include the former Yugoslavia (1992–4), East Timor (1999), Togo (2000), Darfur (2004), Timor-Leste (2006), Lebanon (2006), Guinea (2009), Cote d'Ivoire (2011), the Syrian Arab Republic (2011–14), the Occupied Palestinian Territory (2012), DPRK (2013) Central African Republic (2013), Sri Lanka (2014), among others.

[15]   Van den Herik 2014, 509.   [16]   Van den Herik 2014, 510.

[17]   UN Human Rights Council 2013.

[18]   Under Article 7 of the Rome Statute, crimes against humanity refer to the following: (a) Murder; (b) Extermination; (c) Enslavement; (d) Deportation or forcible transfer of population; (e) Imprisonment or other severe deprivation of physical liberty in violation of fundamental rules of international law; (f) Torture; (g) Rape, sexual slavery, enforced prostitution, forced pregnancy, enforced sterilization, or any other form of sexual violence of comparable gravity; (h) Persecution against any identifiable group or collectivity on political, racial, national, ethnic, cultural, religious, gender . . . or other grounds that are universally recognized as impermissible under international law . . .; (i) Enforced disappearance of persons; (j) The crime of apartheid; (k) Other inhumane acts of a similar character intentionally causing great suffering, or serious injury to body or to mental or physical health.

orthodoxy" that calls for accountability of those responsible for genocide, war, crimes, and crimes against humanity.[19]

The DPRK COI report has helped to further propel UN institutional mechanisms. The DPRK COI recommendation to create a UN field office to continue investigations and documentation of North Korean human rights abuses sustains the accountability mechanism. After some politicking about the location, the UN field office opened in Seoul in 2015 for the practical need to access and interview North Koreans, given its mandate to "[s]trengthen monitoring and documentation of the situation of human rights as steps towards establishing accountability in the DPRK."[20] With only half a dozen staff, the UN Seoul office is limited in its capacity. Therefore, other UN mechanisms were employed, such as sustaining the Special Rapporteur position with the 2016 appointment of Argentinian lawyer Tomás Ojea Quintana, as well as designating two independent experts to "explore appropriate approaches to seek accountability" and "recommend practical mechanisms of accountability ... including the International Criminal Court" over a period of six months.[21] Quintana has encouraged the North Korean government to continue engaging with the existing UN human rights mechanisms,[22] while independent experts Sonja Biserko and Sara Hossain advanced the discourse on accountability by mapping the complexities and options for prosecution and transitional justice, ultimately recommending more extensive probing of international and domestic tribunal options.[23] Unofficially, the COI members and former Special Rapporteurs, along with other senior advocates, have launched a "Sages Group on North Korean Human Rights" to continue their active role in recommending strategies for human rights improvement in North Korea, including international prosecution.[24]

Publication of the COI report has also made it easier to push through human rights legislation in both South Korea and the United States. In South Korea, the North Korean Human Rights Act was enacted on March 3, 2016, after more than ten years of various bills being introduced to the National Assembly.[25] The passage of the law represents a certain degree of bipartisan concession that the issue of North Korean human rights needs to

[19]   Sikkink 2011, 13–18.
[20]   UN Human Rights of the Office of the High Commissioner (Seoul), "About Us," seoul.ohchr .org/EN/Pages/ABOUT%20US.aspx.
[21]   UN Human Rights Council 2016, Articles 10, 11, and 12.
[22]   UN Human Rights Council 2017a.   [23]   UN Human Rights Council 2017b.
[24]   These include former ICC President Song Sang Hyun, US Special Envoy for North Korean Human Rights Ambassador Robert R. King, and ROK Ambassador for Human Rights, Lee Jung-Hoon.
[25]   Republic of Korea National Assembly 2016.

be addressed in a more formal and unified approach by the South Korean government. The North Korean Human Rights Act creates three new institutions: a North Korean human rights advisory committee under the Ministry of Unification; a North Korean Human Rights Foundation to help research, strategize, and fund for human rights improvement in North Korea; and the appointment of a North Korean human rights ambassador-at-large by the Ministry of Foreign Affairs.[26] The Act also calls for the development of a government database to keep track of North Korean human rights abuses. This is to be retained by the Ministry of Unification and the Ministry of Justice,[27] thereby also preserving documentation for accountability and transitional justice measures in the future.

In the United States, a number of pieces of legislation relate to North Korean human rights issues. The North Korean Human Rights Act of 2004 has been reauthorized through 2017 to fund humanitarian assistance to North Koreans, information dissemination into North Korea, and NGO programs supporting "human rights, democracy, rule of law, and development of the market economy in North Korea."[28] The North Korea Sanctions and Policy Enhancement Act, which passed into law in February 2016, focuses on trade sanctions but also embeds conditions that human rights improvements need to meet before suspension or termination of sanctions (for example, repatriation of abducted or unlawfully held citizens, improvement in prison conditions, release of political prisoners).[29] While the preexisting North Korean Human Rights Act stands as separate legislation to promote human rights improvement in North Korea, the new law has made the lifting of US sanctions conditional on human rights improvement. This permanently and effectively ties human rights to the security issue of North Korea, satisfying past calls for moving US and North Korean dialogue toward a Helsinki-type process.[30]

NORTH KOREA'S CONCEPTION OF HUMAN RIGHTS AS "LAWFARE"

The North Korean government is, of course, the biggest critic of the COI report, viewing it as explicitly and implicitly calling for the prosecution – and

---

[26] Republic of Korea National Assembly 2016, Articles 5, 9, 10.
[27] Republic of Korea National Assembly 2016, Articles 6, 13, 15.   [28] Lilley and Solarz 2012.
[29] North Korea Sanctions and Policy Enhancement Act of 2016, Title III, Secs. 302–03, 401, 402.
[30] Januzzi 2013. The 1975 Helsinki Accords initiated multilateral dialogues toward resolving the Cold War. Issues of security, economics, human rights, and implementation were addressed concurrently, allowing for more linkages and openness between organizations in Eastern and Western Europe, thus diminishing Soviet influence and eventually ending the Cold War.

thus removal – of the North Korean leadership. It considers the COI report a direct personal attack upon its leader Kim Jong Un, and by extension an attack on its national sovereignty and thereby a threat to its national security.[31] A discussion of how North Korea perceives the globalized discourse of human rights as a form of "lawfare," and how this collides with its localized conception of rights and duties, can help illuminate its vehement stance.

The concept of lawfare is edifying as a broader lens to study North Korea's reaction to UN reporting on the human rights situation inside the country. The term "lawfare" refers to the use of legal mechanisms to achieve strategic goals. It was first coined in the late 1990s in the United States, when the country failed to ratify the Rome Statute establishing the ICC, thus resisting universal jurisdiction by international, national, and regional courts in any attempt to try US and Israeli officials.[32] This conceptualization of lawfare by the United States is similar in logic to the North Korean view of avoiding or defending against extraterritorial jurisdiction regarding rights violations committed in the name of national security. Perugini and Gordon explain this growing phenomenon of categorizing human rights in and of itself as a national security threat:

> One of the most common ways of challenging the existing human rights discourse is by pitting it against national security concerns and against real and constructed existential threats. This strategy has become pervasive among conservatives who attempt to limit the impact of human rights campaigns by reframing events ... as a security threat to the government's authority or the country's territorial integrity.[33]

This excerpt can be easily referenced not only with respect to North Korea, but also to any other state that has breached human rights in the name of national security or evaded court jurisdiction in the name of national sovereignty.[34] Accordingly, "human rights" are fighting words to the North Korean government and are considered a threat to national security. This is stated explicitly in a number of official DPRK statements, such as the following:

> It is of the view that as human rights are guaranteed by sovereign States, any attempt to interfere in others' internal affairs, overthrow the governments and change the systems on the pretext of human rights issues constitutes violations of human rights. ... [T]he DPRK holds that human rights immediately mean national sovereignty.[35]

---

[31] KCNA 2014.   [32] Perugini and Gordon 2015, 55–56.   [33] Perugini and Gordon 2015, 54.
[34] For the history and an analysis of US policy toward the ICC, see Fairlie 2011.
[35] DPRK, National Report Submitted in Accordance with Paragraph 15(A) of the Annex to Human Rights Council Resolutions 5/1, A/HRC/WG.6/6/PRK/1 (August 27, 2009), II(2)(15).

Human rights are perceived to be a mere pretext or to have an instrumental purpose in the ultimate goal of deposing the current head of government and its administration:

> In the confrontation between the DPRK and US, the US learned that it was impossible to overthrow the people-centred system by mean of political and military threats and pressure as well as the economic blockade. What they found next was the human rights issue.[36]

The international discourse of human rights gains little traction in North Korea because they are not seen as legitimate to the survival of the North Korean state, which prioritizes security over rights. Perugini and Gordon point out that "the politics of human rights acquires an even more profound connection with sovereign politics since human rights is equated with the state's security."[37] Threats to national security often result in an "increase in discretionary authority," usually through "broad legislative authorizations or through the invocation of emergency powers."[38] In North Korea's case, the discretionary authority is based on the founding family's fiat and de facto emergency powers. As Jay Song explains, "externally, the [North Korean] regime is trying to abide by international human rights standards where they are acceptable and safe enough to defend the security of the regime."[39] This explains why the same rights it grants to its dutiful citizens are not applied equally to the hostile classes or those who flout government directives, which include those charged with crimes against the state. And yet it is precisely the manner in which the state deals with those charged with crimes against the state that equates to crimes against humanity.

Rather than summarily dismiss the idea that North Korea has no conception of human rights, however, some scholars have tried to understand the nation's socialist history of rights conception, differentiating the different evolution and conception of human rights in North Korea from that of the Western liberal democratic tradition.[40] Song argues that "the evolution of North Korean rights thinking is not at odds with the broad understanding of 'international' human rights,"[41] especially in noting how North Korea prioritizes cultural relativism over universalism, collective interests over individual rights, socio-economic rights over civil and political rights, and duties before rights:

---

[36] Report of the DPRK Association for Human Rights Studies, 2014, at 129.
[37] Perugini and Gordon 2015, 14. [38] Roth 2008, 289. [39] Song 2010, 184.
[40] Song 2010; Kim 2008; Hwang 2014. [41] Song 2010, 178.

[T]he contemporary form of rights thinking in the DPRK, "our style" of human rights, takes priority in cultural relativism, post-colonial sovereignty, collective interests, materialistic pragmatism and a duty-based language of human rights.[42]

This manner of thinking draws from a longer socialist tradition, whereby international human rights law is considered an instrumental tool of the Western imperialist bourgeois class, rather than a locally sensitive mechanism to protect workers' rights.[43] Instead of the rule of law which defines most liberal democracies, North Korea follows the Stalinist version of socialist legality, whereby the ruler's decrees are considered law and rights are earned or granted in exchange for the citizens' loyalty to the Korean Workers Party line. This socialist conception is combined with a revolutionary zeal and monarchical tradition particular to the sociopolitical history of the Korean peninsula. This is evident in the *Ten Great Principles of the Establishment of the Unitary Ideology System* (Ten Principles), which has more legal authority and popular observance than the nation's constitution. Promulgated in 1974 by Kim Jong Il, the Ten Principles constitute a doctrine that all North Korean citizens must memorize and follow in revering Kim Il Sung and his revolutionary thoughts above all else. As stated in one of the subprinciples:

> Great Leader Comrade Kim Il Sung's instructions must be viewed as a legal and supreme order and unconditionally realized without excuses or trivial reasons, but with endless loyalty and sacrifice.[44]

The Ten Principles continue with other terms, such as unconditional acceptance, holy duty, and collective spirit, with the words "revolutionary" and "fight" liberally interspersed. As some of the clauses state, the Great Leader must be protected from attacks and criticism; others are to be judged according to their degree of loyalty to the Great Leader; and there should be no departure from or struggle against the Great Leader's sole leadership. Violating the Ten Principles is equivalent to *lèse-majesté*,[45] subjecting transgressors to consequences ranging from subjection to self-criticism sessions (at which one can publicly confess their minor transgressions in order to preempt being informed against) to punishment under the North Korean Criminal Code for crimes against the state or treason. Though Kim Il

---

[42] Song 2010, 190.   [43] Tunkin 1974.

[44] Article 5(1), *Ten Great Principles of the Establishment of the Unitary Ideology System*. (English translation by Citizens' Alliance for North Korean Human Rights.)

[45] *Lèse-majesté* is a crime against the sovereign power of a state, usually treason, but minor offenses against the dignity of the state, such as insulting or defaming images of the sovereignty, may also be punishable.

Sung is now deceased, the creed lives on as part of the dynastic legacy and continues to apply to his successors Kim Jong Il and Kim Jong Un.[46] The Ten Principles override the North Korean Constitution, which has a different function. While constitutions in liberal democracies are the predominant foundations of rights formation and implementation, this is not the case in North Korea. North Korea's Constitution is similar to many Asian constitutions, which are amended numerous times and usually in accordance with the policy objectives of a newer administration.[47] Its constitution illustrates the sacrosanctity of Kim Il Sung, outlines the structure of the government and policy objectives, and delineates citizens' rights in relation to their duties and loyalty to the state.[48] It is certainly not akin to a bill of rights, as is commonly the case in liberal democracies. In contrast, the North Korean Constitution explains that:

> The laws of the DPRK are a reflection of the intents and interests of the working people and serve as a basic weapon in state administration. Respect for the law and its strict observation and execution is the duty of all organs, enterprises, organizations, and citizens. The state shall perfect the socialist legal system and strengthen the socialist law-abiding life.[49]

Thus, rights consciousness is not an intuitive or learned concept in North Korea, given that rights are not promoted in North Korea in the same way they are in liberal democracies that emphasize constitutional rights or civil liberties via history and classroom education. Instead, North Korea's legal creed is the Ten Principles, which requires allegiance to the Great Leader above all else.

At the UN, North Korea's treaty reports refer to its constitution, not the Ten Principles, in claiming that the government has a legal framework of human rights.[50] This is not a new development. In his speech at the Supreme People's Assembly on the adoption of a new socialist constitution in 1972, Kim Il Sung stated:

> The new Socialist Constitution correctly reflects the achievements made in the socialist revolution and in building socialism in our country, defines the

---

[46] Han 2015, 50.   [47] Goedde 2004.   [48] Yoon 2004.
[49] The official English translation of the 2009 Constitution as provided by a North Korean government source is available at www.servat.unibe.ch/icl/kn00000_.html. However, this text is taken from the more accurate translation available at asiamatters.blogspot.kr/2009/10/north-korean-constitution-april-2009.html. Original Korean texts of the DPRK Constitutions are available on the ROK Ministry of Legislation's North Korea Laws Information Center, at world.moleg.go.kr/KP/law/23273?astSeq=582.
[50] For example, Democratic People's Republic of Korea, National Report Submitted in Accordance with Paragraph 15(A) of the Annex to Human Rights Council Resolution 5/1, A /HRC/WG.6/6/PRK/1 (August 27, 2009), Sec. III(1)(A).

principles to govern activities in the political, economic and cultural fields in socialist society and the basic rights and duties of citizens, and stipulates the composition and functions of the state organs and the principles of their activities. Its purpose is to protect by law the socialist system and the dictatorship of the proletariat established in the northern half of the Republic and to serve the revolutionary cause of the working class.[51]

Rights are mentioned from the beginning, but only in relation to duties and in preserving the socialist state and "the dictatorship of the proletariat." The Constitution was revised in 2009 to read that "the state . . . shall safeguard the interests of, and respect and protect the human rights of the working people,"[52] introducing the words "human rights" into the constitution for the first time. However, the conception of human rights here is being used within the North Korean socialist context. North Korean human rights discourse is based upon Marxist, Confucian, and *Juche* foundations, which prioritize collective, familial, and sovereign state interests over those of the individual.[53] North Korea's history presents an argument for cultural relativism in the same vein as that of the Chinese government's longstanding critiques of Western human rights norms and the infamous Lee Kuan Yew "Asian values" debate, placing North Korea firmly within a family of nations that continue to contend with theories of universal human rights on the principle of subjugating individual rights for the greater collective good.[54] This suggests further academic space to discuss the domestic conceptualization of North Korean human rights from a comparative, socialist constitutional perspective, especially in relation to China, Russia, Vietnam, and other socialist states.

The North Korean government perceives international human rights discourse to be an aggressive, instrumentalist tool used to justify interference with its state sovereignty. Rights discourse as used by the international community in censuring North Korea is at fundamental odds with the North Korean perception of rights, which prioritizes state sovereignty as the basic foundation and the subjugation of individual rights to the collective. The international community has struggled to engage North Korea on human rights due to what is interpreted as simple intransigence on the part of the North Korean government, but the latter's response derives essentially from their deeply embedded perception of rights discourse as a threatening political tactic to undermine their statehood. The next section suggests how human rights discourse might be reframed to converge with localized conceptions of rights protection in North Korea.

---

[51] Kim 1972, 29.   [52] DPRK Constitution, Art. 8.   [53] Weatherley and Song 2008.
[54] Weatherley and Song 2008; Zakaria and Lee 1994.

REFRAMING THE HUMAN RIGHTS NARRATIVE

As Justice Kirby has stated, at "the heart of the COI" is the "dilemma or paradox of reconciling two streams of accountability and promoting engagement."[55] Chubb also asks the important question of how to balance its two seemingly conflicting goals, these being "efforts to bring about accountability and efforts to bring about verifiable progress" versus "careful engagement designed to bring about changes in policy and the eventual institutionalization of human rights norms in North Korea."[56] Specifically, Chubb asks "can both these sets of goals be carried out simultaneously, or does progress in one area (for example, referral to the ICC) inevitably lead to a stalemate in another (for example, greater disengagement due to DPRK hostility over the ICC referral)?" Sharp contemplates this on a global scale: "To what extent should human rights reporting in the twenty–first century be (1) largely limited to shaming and denunciation, and (2) constructively propose and engage with the hard and pragmatic policy choices necessary to build a world where fuller enjoyment of human rights is genuinely possible?"[57] He argues that the two choices should be treated as "poles on a continuum rather than a simple binary," and that moving the discourse toward constructive engagement constitutes "an increasingly critical component of global governance."[58] The resulting question is not *whether* to engage constructively with North Korea, but *how* this can best be carried out.

While the accountability track is gathering momentum, engagement with North Korea is at a standstill. This refers us back to the spiral model, wherein North Korea has been sufficiently shamed globally to cause it to respond with some tactical concessions but not with significant transformations to protect its citizens' fundamental human rights as required under ratified international human rights treaties. According to the latest Database Center for North Korean Human Rights investigations, the human rights situation within North Korea does not appear to have improved since the publication of the COI report.[59] As COI member Marzuki Darusman has iterated, "The bottom line is we must make a difference for the people on the ground in North Korea. If we do not do that, then we have not succeeded."[60] Human rights lawyer Jared Genser puts it more bluntly: "Justice in accountability is not going to change the lives of the North

---

[55] Panel comments at "The Launching of 'The Sages Group on North Korean Human Rights'," UN Seoul Office One-Year Anniversary Commemorative Symposium: "North Korean Human Rights: Shifting Gear on Accountability," Seoul, Korea (June 27, 2016).
[56] Chubb 2014, 69. [57] Sharp 2015, 74. [58] Sharp 2015, 74.
[59] Database Center for North Korean Human Rights 2016. [60] Cha and DuMond 2015, 13.

Korean people."[61] Thus, the next priority is addressing how to engage with North Korea for the practical effect of improving human rights, given that the language of international human rights discourse is perceived inside the country as a repertoire of war.

Some advocates claim that accountability creates pressure on the North Korean state to respond to accusations of human rights violations and to be vigilant about its current and future behavior on this front, due to what they call "accountability anxiety."[62] This has arguably led to the North Korean government's increasing attention to human rights issues, such as responding to the latest Universal Periodic Review and submitting treaty reports for CEDAW and CRC.[63] While the accountability mechanism forces the DPRK government to respond on some level, the accountability angle alone is not sufficient in changing the human rights landscape in North Korea. These are essentially tactical concessions, and the deeper challenge is in creating rights consciousness within North Korean society.

Given the provocative nature of human rights discourse with the North Korean government and the lack of rights consciousness within the general population, the next stage of discourse could contemplate reframing human rights discourse in more relatable contexts without sacrificing or negotiating away fundamental human rights principles. As stated by one participant during a European Parliament workshop, it is "important to connect to North Korea with its own narrative."[64] Scholars across disciplines – political science, sociology, and anthropology – recognize the importance of localizing international human rights legal norms within domestic cultural contexts for more successful norm diffusion. For example, Hafner-Burton argues that foreign proponents of human rights can risk failure or backlash if they "use their power to coerce or persuade – without attention to the local context, perspectives of local partners, or preexisting normative frameworks."[65] Acharya calls localization a "congruence-building process" which focuses on the agency of "norm-takers," and includes the processes of framing language and grafting norms consistent with a "preexisting local normative order."[66] He explains that norm diffusion is quicker when the norm "resonates with historically constructed domestic norms."[67]

---

[61] Panel presentation on "Accountability: Feasible Options and Instruments," UN Seoul Office One-Year Anniversary Commemorative Symposium: "North Korean Human Rights: Shifting Gear on Accountability," Seoul, Korea (June 27, 2016).
[62] Walsh and Cha 2015. [63] Hosaniak 2016. [64] Pardo 2016.
[65] Hafner-Burton 2013, 153–4. [66] Acharya 2004, 242–3.
[67] Acharya 2004, 12 (citing Checkel 1998, 6).

Legal anthropologist Sally Engle Merry has also argued that it is crucial to translate global human rights discourse into the local vernacular for local adaptation to occur. She pushes beyond the spiral model's focus on the relationship between transnational activists and governments by examining "the interface between global ideas and those of local groups."[68] Merry makes the same argument that "[t]his is the paradox of making human rights in the vernacular: in order to be accepted, they have to be tailored to the local context and resonate with the local cultural framework."[69] In her comparative study of gender violence, Merry is concerned with how transnational knowledge of rights becomes localized: "Human rights must become part of local legal consciousness in order to fulfill their emancipatory potential, yet activists in several countries told me that the knowledge of human rights within village communities was quite limited."[70] In the case of North Korea, the challenge for activists involved with the legal mobilization of human rights change is how to bring about meaningful outcomes in the absence of local domestic institutions that can support such change.

The words "human rights" are not in the daily lexicon of the North Korean population. When questioned upon arrival in South Korea, North Koreans do not say they left North Korea because of human rights violations.[71] They left, according to their own accounts, for reasons of hunger, poverty, to support family members or in search of family, to escape imprisonment, or to have better life opportunities for themselves or their children. The language of international human rights law, institutional mechanisms, and procedures is far removed from the informational realm and daily lives of most of the North Korean populace. This gap in discourse that exists between elite transnational North Korean human rights activists and local North Korean communities is not unique to the North Korean case; other human rights movements have experienced this sort of disconnect.[72] In the case of North Korea, the transnational movement is managed mostly by educated elites, often consisting of politicians, UN officials, lawyers, NGO leaders, religious leaders, academics, and North Korean defectors. The actual interaction between this group and citizens inside North Korea is minimal at best, and any such interactions occur at great risk for the latter. As a result, the discourse at the center of the North Korean human rights movement has developed largely without the North Korean people, domi-nated by advocacy nodes in Seoul, Washington DC, New York, Geneva, and London, reaching a global audience far more effectively than it does the

---

[68] Merry 2006, 221–2. [69] Merry 2006, 221. [70] Merry 2006, 178. [71] Han 2016.
[72] Hafner-Burton 2013, 152–4.

North Korean people themselves.[73] Thus, the critical issue is how to introduce or transform the language of international human rights into a more culturally relatable discourse for the North Korean population, while at the same time searching for depoliticized entry points for human rights engagement with the North Korean government.

RECOMMENDATIONS

To address Sharp's continuum of accountability and engagement, the challenge lies in contextualizing human rights in more relatable terms to different sectors of North Korea: its government, its elites, and its mass population. For resonance with preexisting cultural norms, this would require framing human rights in terms more consistent with socialist ideology (for example, referencing social and economic rights) and even with a sociohistorically Asia-centered approach to collective rights. Another way to engage in rights protection and improvement may be to employ alternative frameworks that incorporate human rights principles without necessarily using the words "human rights." This is not to say that the language of "human rights" cannot or should not ever be used in interacting with North Korea, but that rights diffusion may be more successfully localized if it resonates within an easily understood cultural context. Human rights objectives can be and often are addressed in many alternative discourses and frameworks, such as social welfare, development, health and safety, crime prevention, public interest, modernization, education, quality of life, governance, equality, social justice, access to justice, professional standards, international best practices (in socialist countries if necessary), and the UN Sustainable Development Goals.[74] The next section offers some initial recommendations in framing, grafting, and localizing human rights norms.

Information Campaigns

One effort toward increasing the international awareness of the North Korean population has been through information dissemination, such as radio

[73] An important partial exception to this is the role played by North Korean defectors, an issue considered by Song in Chapter 9 of this volume.

[74] In the United States, for example, local narratives of gender violence are usually contextualized and addressed in terms of crime prevention, personal safety, gender equality, or feminist jurisprudence, rather than in terms of international human rights (though advocates try to leverage this); see Merry 2006. Abolishing the practice of female genital circumcision translated better with some local African communities in terms of personal health and safety rather than what was perceived as a Western cultural condemnation when wielding the language of human rights violations (Steiner and Alston 2000, 409–24).

transmissions, leaflets, DVDs, and USB drives containing content such as US and Korean films, South Korean Wikipedia, pro-democracy materials, and news about leader Kim Jong Un.[75] Calls have been made to add human rights literature such as the Universal Declaration of Human Rights, international human rights treaties, accounts of postwar history, and easy-to-read summaries of the COI report to these information packages.[76] The question is whether the literal transplanting of these texts or smuggling-in of information via USB sticks would be adequate in translating the international human rights discourse into the cultural vernacular of the larger population, much less that of the rural poor who are likely most at risk in terms of a lack of human rights protections. One recommendation may be to circulate North Korea's own laws and regulations more frequently, highlighting the portions claiming to provide for the economic and social welfare of the people, or even more specific provisions on the protection of workers, women, children, and the disabled.

Sustaining UN Mechanisms

North Korea's relationship with the United Nations regarding human rights is more multifaceted than it first appears, mainly because the North Korean government is involved with different UN agencies, channels, and programs, some with relatively more success than others. On the one hand, the relationship seems contentious given North Korea's resistance to human rights monitoring and compliance, as seen with UN General Assembly resolutions and the COI report. On the other hand, North Korea has been a constant recipient of humanitarian assistance since the 1970s, and especially during the famine periods of the 1980s and 1990s (though on a restricted basis), which means long-term engagement and projects with UN aid agencies that address issues of economic and social welfare, such as famine, child and maternal health, sanitation, environmental protection, and other sustainable development projects.

The Strategic Framework for Cooperation Between the UN and the DPRK (2017–2021) explains the range of programs with approximately a dozen UN agencies to achieve the UN Sustainable Development Goals.[77] The North Korean government has participated in numerous projects with these agencies

---

[75]   See, for example, the work of the Unification Media Group (www.unificationmediagroup
.org) regarding radio broadcasts.
[76]   Lee 2016, 145; Cha and DuMond 2015, 25.
[77]   The UN Sustainable Development Goals for 2030 can be found at sustainabledevelopment
.un.org/?menu=1300.

on issues related to health, education, environmental protection, sustainable development, trade, and other training programs related to best practices. Programs consist of on-the-ground involvement in North Korea, as well as bringing North Korean officials to third-party countries for education and training workshops. The North Korean government views humanitarian agencies as politically less threatening, referring to technical cooperation as "an important tool of international cooperation for human rights."[78] Thus, smaller-scale aid projects have allowed more on-the-ground interaction with North Korea because they are couched in terms of humanitarian priorities and technical assistance under the umbrella of economic and social rights for the goals of alleviating poverty, famine, and medical issues.

Humanitarian projects are fundamentally about human rights protection and improvement, but frequently operate without the words "human rights."[79] Many rights protection issues in North Korea could be framed within the above contexts in relation to vulnerable groups such as women, children, the disabled, the elderly, and the infirm, especially the detained and imprisoned among these. Roberta Cohen, whose expertise covers both human rights and humanitarian protections in North Korea, has suggested that UN agencies such as WHO, UNICEF, and WFP could initiate programs to help these particularly vulnerable groups.[80] Within these types of frameworks, UN agencies can continue to introduce global standards and comparisons, and provide technical assistance and follow-up where necessary. Meanwhile, thematic rapporteurs and treaty body experts will have to continue to push to assist in monitoring and evaluations of subject groups, such as women, children, the disabled, and especially those who are detained. This can be achievable on an incremental level, as illustrated by the visit of the Special Rapporteur on the Rights of Persons with Disabilities, Catalina Devandas Aguilar, in May 2017, at the invitation of the North Korean government.

Professional and Cultural Exchanges

Nonpolitical, people-to-people exchanges continue to be instrumental in building bridges and exposure in the fields of science, sports, arts, music, and environmental protection between North Korea and other

[78]   The Universal Periodic Review (UPR) of North Korea's National Human Rights Report and Related Documents of the South Korean Government, NGOs and INGOs: 334–5. See National Human Rights Commission of Korea 2010.

[79]   Benelli 2014, 13.   [80]   Cohen 2015.

nations.[81] Creative, critical, and nonpoliticized engagement should be explored and pursued with institutional bodies and individuals with a more neutral presence in North Korea, such as the Red Cross Red Crescent Movement, longstanding humanitarian groups, and educators. In terms of collaborative venues, it may help to continue to organize further dialogue and programs via UN agencies and other IGOs, academic institutions, and think-tanks in countries such as Vietnam, China, and Mongolia with their socialist traditions, or Singapore, Sweden, Norway, and the Netherlands with their experiences of hosting or interacting with North Korea.[82]

Precedents exist for UN assistance in the fields of judicial and legal reform, such as with UN Development Programme (UNDP) projects on "strengthening legal capacity" in Vietnam.[83] Yanbian University, Pyongyang University of Science and Technology, or other North Korean universities could be sites for educational or professional workshops. The Mongolian government offers some channels for influence and engagement. For example, Mongolian president Tsakhiagiin Elbegdorj gave a speech at Kim Il Sung University mentioning freedom, fundamental human rights, and judicial reform,[84] and the Ulaanbaatar Dialogue on Northeast Asian Security in 2017 was attended by both North and South Korean delegates. Legal exchanges should, in particular, be encouraged and funded for purposes of exposure and to share best practices in both the public and the private sectors of law, especially concerning judicial processes and remedies. In addition, it is important to integrate the voices and experiences of North Koreans and to train and empower future generations of North Koreans who can act as professional, legal, and cultural mediators between the two Koreas.

CONCLUSION

The transnational advocacy network on North Korean human rights has mobilized the legal framework of the UN, international human rights law treaties, and international criminal law to address human rights infringements in North Korea, but to minimal practical effect. Thus far, the North Korean

---

[81] Examples include sports exchanges between the two Koreas; concert performances between North Korea and the United States; North Korean art exhibitions in China, United States, and Europe; and UN regional environmental projects.

[82] For example, see Vietnam's potential role in King 2016. See also the role of NGOs such as Choson Exchange in holding professional training workshops in Singapore and Pyongyang for North Koreans, at www.chosonexchange.org/.

[83] Gillespie and Nicholson 2012, 211–13.   [84] Green 2013.

human rights discourse has fixated increasingly on accountability. The current trajectory of transnational legal mobilization assumes international prosecution of the North Korean leadership, and thus regime termination from the North Korean perspective, which causes further political retrenchment both with and within North Korea on the subject of international human rights. The North Korean government perceives human rights discourse to be part of a war repertoire, especially any dialogue emanating from Washington DC or Seoul. The paradox is the effectiveness of the accountability approach for actual diffusion or institutionalization of human rights in North Korea. The practical issue is how to overcome this security dilemma and engage North Korea on human rights protection if domestic legal advocacy and a rights structure are not in place.

The accountability paradigm is to some degree productive in extracting tactical, symbolic concessions from the North Korean government, but it is largely counterproductive in achieving on-the-ground results for rights protection of the general population. It is possible the North Korean government would like to reform its human rights record, as evidenced by its attempts to revise laws, regulations, and policies in response to treaty body reports and processes. Yet even if such a benign reading of North Korea's intentions is accurate, NGO and defector accounts suggest that, despite treaty participation, the state has done little to improve the daily lives of North Koreans throughout the nation. This consequently calls for a more comprehensive approach to effect change. Embedded in the larger context of a divided Korea, the issue of human rights is difficult to resolve without also addressing national sovereignty, ideological warfare, national security, and military priorities involving regional and allied states. Nonetheless, if engagement openings such as those recommended in the COI are to be pursued, human rights discourse must concurrently be reframed in more localized and relatable narratives for the North Korean people and government by neutral parties other than entities based in the United States and South Korea. This would mean working from the perspective of North Korean human rights as understood historically in terms of social, economic, and cultural rights; informing North Koreans of the rights they possess to hold their own government accountable on the entire spectrum of economic, social, civil, and political rights; simultaneously pursuing rights protection within existing UN mechanisms, including the discursive framework of the UN Sustainable Development Goals; and continuing cultural and professional exchanges for exposure to global best practices.

REFERENCES

Acharya, Amitav. 2004. How Ideas Spread: Whose Norms Matter? Norm Localization and Institutional Change in Asian Regionalism. *International Organization* 58 (2): 239–75.

Benelli, Prisca. 2014. Human Rights in Humanitarian Action and Development Cooperation and the Implications of Rights-Based Approaches in the Field. *ATHA Advanced Training Program on Humanitarian Action.* atha.se/content/human-rights-humanitarian-action-and-development-cooperation-and-implications-rights-based.

Breuker, Remco, Marte Boonen, Klara Boonstra, Christine Chung, Imke van Gardingen, Kim Kwang-cheol, Oh Kyuwook, and Anoma van der Veere. 2016. North Korean Forced Labour in the EU, the Polish Case: How the Supply of a Captive DPRK Workforce fits our Demand for Cheap Labour. *Findings from the Slaves to the System Project,* July 6. Leiden: Leiden Asia Center.

Cha, Victor, and Marie DuMond (eds). 2015. North Korean Human Rights: The Road Ahead. *A Conference Report of the CSIS Korea Chair.* Washington DC: Center for Strategic and International Studies.

Chubb, Danielle. 2014. North Korean Human Rights and the International Community: Responding to the UN Commission of Inquiry. *Asia-Pacific Journal of Human Rights and the Law* 15 (1–2): 51–72.

Cohen, Roberta. 2015. Must UN Agencies Also Fail in North Korea? *38North,* April 21. www.38north.org/2015/04/rcohen042115/.

Database Center for North Korean Human Rights. 2016. *An Evaluation Report of the North Korean Human Rights Situation after the 2014 UN Commission of Inquiry Report.* Seoul: Database Center for North Korean Human Rights.

Epp, Charles. 1998. *The Rights Revolution: Lawyers, Activists and Supreme Courts in Comparative Perspectives.* Chicago: University of Chicago Press.

Fairlie, Megan. 2011. The United States and the International Criminal Court Post-Bush. *Berkeley Journal of International Law* 29 (2): 528–76.

Fu, Hualing, and Richard Cullen. 2008. Weiquan (Rights Protection) Lawyering in an Authoritarian State: Building a Culture of Public-Interest Lawyering. *The China Journal* 59: 111–27.

Gillespie, John, and Pip Nicholson. 2012. *Law and Development and the Global Discourses of Legal Transfers.* Cambridge, UK: Cambridge University Press.

Goedde, Patricia. 2004. Law "of Our Own Style": The Evolution and Challenges of the North Korean Legal System. *Fordham International Law Journal* 27 (4): 1265–88.

Goedde, Patricia. 2017. Human Rights Diffusion in North Korea: The Impact of Transnational Legal Mobilization. *Asian Journal of Law and Society:* 1–29. DOI: 10.1017/als.2017.20.

Green, Chris. 2013. Mongolian President's Speech Raises Eyebrows. *DailyNK,* November 15. www.dailynk.com/english/read.php?cataId=nk00100&num=11185.

Hafner-Burton, Emilie. 2013. *Making Human Rights a Reality.* New Jersey: Princeton University Press.

Halliday, Terence C., Lucien Karpik, and Malcolm Feeley. 2007. *Fighting for Political Freedom: Comparative Studies of the Legal Complex and Political Liberalism.* Oxford: Hart Publishing.

Han, Dong-Ho. 2016. Accountability: Feasible Options and Instrument. Paper presented at the North Korean Human Rights: Shifting Gear on Accountability Conference, June 27, Seoul.

Han, Myung Sub. 2015. Main Contents and Problems of North Korean Human Rights Laws. In *Report on Human Rights in North Korea*, edited by Korean Bar Association, 48–65. Translated by International Bar Association. Seoul and London.

Hathaway, Oona A. 2007. Why Do Countries Commit to Human Rights Treaties? *The Journal of Conflict Resolution* 51 (4): 588–621.

Hosaniak, Joanna. 2016. UN Human Rights Mechanisms for the Protection of Women's Rights in the DPRK. Paper presented at the 2016 International Symposium on North Korean Human Rights, May 19, Seoul.

Hwang, Jae Ok. 2014. North Korea's Human Rights Policy. In *Report on Human Rights in North Korea*, edited by Korean Bar Association, 18–45. Translated by International Bar Association. Seoul and London.

Januzzi, Frank. 2013. The Road to Pyongyang Goes Through Helsinki. *Foreign Policy*, April 12. http://foreignpolicy.com/2013/04/12/the-road-to-pyongyang-goes-through-helsinki/.

Keck, Margaret E., and Kathryn Sikkink. 2014. *Activists Beyond Borders: Advocacy Networks in International Politics*. Ithaca: Cornell University Press.

KCNA. 2014. *Report of the DPRK Association for Human Rights Studies*. September 13. Report on file with author.

Kim, Il Sung. 1972. Let Us Further Strengthen the Socialist System of Our Country. *On the Socialist Constitution of the Democratic People's Republic of Korea*. Pyongyang: Foreign Languages Publishing House.

Kim, Soo-Am. 2008. *Conceptions of Democracy and Human Rights in the Democratic People's Republic of Korea*. Seoul: Korea Institute for National Unification.

King, Llewellyn. 2016. Vietnam Wants to Be America's Bridge to North Korea, *Inside Source*, August 4.

Lee, Dong Bok. 2016. *Human Rights and National Unification*. Paper presented at the Seoul Dialogue for Human Rights, Seoul.

Lilley, James R., Ambassador, and Stephen J. Solarz, Congressman. 2012. North Korea Human Rights Reauthorization Act of 2012. 22 USC. §7801.

McCann, Michael W. 1994. *Rights at Work: Pay Equity Reform and the Politics of Legal Mobilization*. Chicago: University of Chicago Press.

Merry, Sally Engle. 2006. *Human Rights and Gender Violence: Translating International Law into Local Justice*. Chicago and London: University of Chicago Press.

Moustafa, Tamir. 2007. Mobilising the Law in an Authoritarian State. In *The Legal Complex and Struggles for Political Liberalism*, edited by Terence C. Halliday, Lucien Karpik, and Malcolm Feeley, 193–217. Oxford: Hart Publishing.

National Human Rights Commission of Korea. 2010. The Universal Periodic Review (UPR) of North Korea's National Human Rights Report and Related Documents of the South Korean Government, NGOs and INGOs Seoul, Korea.

Pardo, Ramon Pacheco. 2016. Paper presented at Human Rights in North Korea: Accountability vs. *Engagement? Workshop of the European Parliament*, Directorate–General for External Policies, Policy Department.

Perugini, Nicola, and Neve Gordon. 2015. *The Human Right to Dominate*. New York: Oxford University Press.

Republic of Korea National Assembly 2016. *Bukhan-ingweon-beom* (North Korean Human Rights Act). Law No. 14070. Enacted March 3, 2016. Entry into force September 4, 2016.

Risse, Thomas, Stephen C. Ropp, and Kathryn Sikkink, eds. 1999. *The Power of Human Rights: International Norms and Domestic Change*. Cambridge, UK: Cambridge University Press.

Risse, Thomas, Stephen C. Ropp, and Kathryn Sikkink, eds. 2013. *The Persistent Power of Human Rights: From Commitment to Compliance*. Cambridge, UK: Cambridge University Press.

Roth, Brad R. 2008. Retrieving Marx for the Human Rights Project. In *Marx and Law*, edited by Susan Easton, 265–302. London: Ashgate.

Sarat, Austin, and Stuart Scheingold. 1998. *Cause Lawyering: Political Commitments and Professional Responsibilities*. New York: Oxford University Press.

Sharp, Dustin. 2015. Human Rights Fact-Finding and the Reproduction of Hierarchies. In *The Transformation of Human Rights Fact-Finding*, edited by Philip Alston and Sarah Knuckey, 69–87. New York: Oxford University Press.

Sikkink, Kathryn. 2011. *The Justice Cascade: How Human Rights Prosecutions Are Changing World Politics*. New York: W. W. Norton.

Simmons, Beth A. 2009. *Mobilizing for Human Rights: International Law in Domestic Politics*. Cambridge, UK: Cambridge University Press.

Song, Jay. 2010. *Human Rights Discourse in North Korea: Post-Colonial, Marxist and Confucian Perspectives*. New York: Routledge.

Steiner, Henry J., and Philip Alston. 2000. *International Human Rights in Context: Law, Politics, Morals: Text and Materials*. Oxford: Oxford University Press.

Sunstein, Cass R. 1996. Social Norms and Social Roles. *Columbia Law Review* 96 (4): 903–68.

Tam, Waikeung. 2013. *Legal Mobilization Under Authoritarianism: The Case of Post-Colonial Hong Kong*. Cambridge, UK: Cambridge University Press.

Tunkin, Grigory I. 1974. *Theory of International Law*. Cambridge, MA: Harvard University Press.

UN Human Rights Council. 2013. Situation of Human Rights in the Democratic People's Republic of Korea. A/HRC/RES/22/13. April 9.

UN Human Rights Council. 2016. Resolution Adopted by the Human Rights Council on 23 March 2016. A/HRC/RES/31/18. April 8.

UN Human Rights Council. 2017a. Report of the Special Rapporteur on the Situation of Human Rights in the Democratic People's Republic of Korea. A/HRC/34/66. February 22.

UN Human Rights Council. 2017b. Report of the Group of Independent Experts on Accountability. A/HRC/34/66/Add.1. February 24.

Van den Herik, Larissa. 2014. An Inquiry into the Role of Commissions of Inquiry in International Law: Navigating the Tensions between Fact-Finding and Application of International Law. *Chinese Journal of International Law* 13 (3): 507–37.

Walsh, Christopher and Victor Cha. 2015. Creating Accountability Anxiety in North Korea. *Foreign Policy*, April 28.

Weatherley, Robert, and Jay Song. 2008. The Evolution of Human Rights Thinking in North Korea. *Journal of Communist Studies and Transition Politics* 24 (2): 272–96.

Yoon, Dae-Kyu 2004. The Constitution of North Korea: Its Changes and Implications. *Fordham International Law Journal* 27 (4): 1289–305.

Zakaria, Fareed, and Lee Kuan Yew. 1994. Culture Is Destiny: A Conversation with Lee Kuan Yew. *Foreign Affairs* 73 (2): 109–26.

8

The Politics of Networking
Behind the Public Face of the Transnational North Korean Human Rights Movement

Danielle Chubb

During the summer of 2014, a group of North Korean human rights activists traveled to Geneva and New York.[1] These activists, from the Seoul-based Citizens' Alliance for North Korean Human Rights (Citizens' Alliance) and elsewhere, joined forces with Human Rights Watch (HRW), North Korean prison camp survivors, individual country missions, and other NGOs over the course of several months. Bit by bit, the activists expanded their support networks within the UN, meeting with government representatives and organizing events at the sidelines of UN meetings.

For some of these activists, this lobbying push represented the culmination of many years of quiet, behind-the-scenes work within the UN system. Following the publication of the COI report earlier that year, activists were now garnering support for a General Assembly resolution. This resolution would, for the first time, call on the UN Security Council (UNSC) to place the issue of North Korean human rights on its official agenda. The final goal was to see the UNSC refer North Korea to the ICC. Throughout the remainder of 2014, these groups worked quietly, but doggedly, through the diplomatic channels available to them.[2] On December 18, 2014, the General Assembly passed the resolution. Shortly thereafter, on December 22, the UNSC met in New York and voted to place the North Korean human rights issue on its agenda for ongoing attention.[3]

---

[1] The author would like to thank Leonid Petrov, Jennifer Hadden, Sandra Fahy, Joanna Hosaniak, Andrew Yeo, and Jay Song for providing helpful comments on earlier versions of this paper. She would also like to thank Michael Hatherell for his research assistance with the hyperlink analysis.
[2] For details of these activities, see: Citizens' Alliance for North Korean Human Rights 2015. See also the account by Hosaniak (Chapter 6, this volume).
[3] United Nations 2014.

A few months later, on Capitol Hill in Washington DC, a group of activists gathered for the 12th North Korea Freedom Week. As part of this annual awareness raising event organized by the North Korea Freedom Coalition (NKFC), the Defense Forum Foundation (DFF) hosted a Congressional defense and foreign policy forum, entitled "Ending the Kim Regime's Reign of Terror in North Korea." Similar to their counterparts working at the UN level, many of these activists were veterans of the North Korean human rights movement. But the focus here was noticeably different. Introducing the speakers, DFF president and NKFC chairwoman Suzanne Scholte acknowledged the UN COI process as a watershed moment in the movement's history. Thanks to the COI, she reminded the gathering, activists no longer have to make the case that crimes against humanity are being committed in North Korea: "There is no disputing that fact [of crimes against humanity] at this time in history, at this time in the struggle."[4] Yet, despite the centrality of the UN report to their work – and the involvement of many of the forums' participants in the COI process – the activists at this gathering were not interested in working through the UN's legal mechanisms. Instead, these activists were more interested in bringing about an improvement in the human rights situation through a more direct approach: regime change by peaceful means. "The challenge we face now," Scholte told the gathering, "is that we know these atrocities are happening but nothing is going to change in North Korea unless we act – we must [help] these North Korean defectors do the job of reunifying the Korean Peninsula peacefully."[5]

The UN COI has been embraced by activists across the North Korean human rights network as an important juncture in the movement's history. And given what we know about the contentious nature of social movements, it is perhaps unsurprising that the question of "where to go next?" is approached from a wide variety of perspectives by different actors within this network. We know that the call for a COI into North Korean human rights came about after decades of concerted efforts by a range of activists to raise the profile of the issue. The actors involved, as the various chapters in this volume document in detail, come from a wide range of backgrounds, operate within different domestic political contexts, and bring a diverse array of motivations and goals to their activism.

The transnational advocacy literature tells us that such actors succeed when they come together in solidarity to achieve a shared goal. The value of forming a social network is particularly pronounced when the issue at hand is characterized by "high value content and informational uncertainty," and

---

[4] Defense Forum Foundation 2015a.   [5] Defense Forum Foundation 2015a.

when advocacy networks tend to feature the sharing of information as a key activity.[6] Other scholars have refined this description of advocacy networks to identify transnational advocacy networks of activists "aiming to affect political behavior through moral argument."[7] These actors are thus norm entrepreneurs: strategic actors whose ability to effect change on the international stage challenges the state-centric nature of traditional International Relations theory.

A common conception in the literature is that human rights advocacy campaigns rely on a shared understanding, among network actors, of how rights are to be perceived, prioritized, and pursued regarding the particular issue at hand. Local actors play an important role in the development of these shared understandings, providing important contextual input to the broader transnational coalition, and in this way help shape key network decisions.[8] Yet when it comes to North Korean human rights advocacy, these decisions are made at a distance given the absence of domestically located North Korean voices directly shaping the campaign network. As a result, North Korean human rights advocacy is an interpretive and contentious area; lack of access to the target state or society brings with it a range of normative and analytical questions for activists.

As we discuss in Chapter 1 of this volume, the North Korean human rights movement is a divided one. In this chapter, I turn my attention to the nature of interactions between the actors in this divided movement, and the interplay between these interactions and advocacy outcomes. I start with the following question: Which actors were most influential in attaining the support for the North Korean human rights issue at the level of the UN Office of the High Commissioner for Human Rights, from where the call for the Commission of Inquiry eventually arose?[9] We would expect actors with the greatest social power within the North Korean human rights network to have played a central role in bringing about this outcome. Yet, the preliminary hyperlink analysis performed in this chapter shows that this isn't the case. Those activists who focused their advocacy efforts at the UN level turn out to be only loosely linked within the network based on an analysis of activist or organizational web pages.

How, then, does the network function? The absence of key actors from the core network suggests that factors beyond network structure are important for understanding how advocacy networks function and understanding the

---

[6] Keck and Sikkink 1998, 2. [7] Carpenter 2007, 101. [8] Risse and Sikkink 1999, 5, 20.
[9] The OHCHR is a gatekeeper insofar as it can help determine which issues "make it" to the human rights agenda of the United Nations, thereby providing issues with a level of international attention difficult to replicate elsewhere. For a discussion of the governing role of gatekeepers in the human rights advocacy space, see Carpenter 2010.

agendas adopted by members. Looking beyond network structure allows us to highlight the central role played by ideas, beliefs, and network dynamics. Before I turn my attention to this issue, I first provide an overview of what the extant literature tells us about transnational advocacy network dynamics. I then map out the North Korean human rights network through hyperlink analysis and discuss the findings of this mapping, as well as the benefits and limitations of such an exercise. This chapter thus represents a preliminary attempt to unpack some of the complex intranetwork dynamics that animate North Korean human rights activism. These dynamics are likely, as we discuss in Chapter 1, to influence movement outcomes in terms of North Korean human rights compliance, yet are incorporated so deeply into the way the network functions that they are often invisible to the external observer, and hold a taken-for-granted status among network members.

TRANSNATIONAL NETWORKING IN THE HUMAN RIGHTS REALM

Scholarship documenting the spread of human rights norms and the central role played by transnational activists has focused by and large on norm emergence on the world stage, as well as norm-adoption and adherence in target states.[10] Less attention has been paid to the ways in which the nature of the network itself might influence the employment of particular normative frameworks by activists, or lead to the adoption of certain policy advocacy choices over others. Carpenter and her colleagues argue that the focus of the transnational advocacy network literature on the *network as actor* has failed to incorporate the importance of the *network as social structure* "composed of nodes of various actors connected by ties of different types and strengths."[11]

In response to this conceptual and empirical gap in the research agenda, a newer body of work examines the intranetwork dynamics of transnational activism.[12] Largely motivated by what scholars perceive to be significant power imbalances inside the networks themselves, this work asks why some issues "make it" to the global agenda while others – arguably equally worthy and pressing – do not. Research into these questions reveals the sometimes contrary ways in which actors within networks can work at odds with each other, and the circuitous routes to norm-adoption that can ensue. This work examines the question of power from two different perspectives: at the

[10]   Gready 2003; Hafner-Burton 2013; Khagram, Riker, and Sikkink 2002; Risse, Ropp, and Sikkink 1999, 2013; Sikkink 2011; Simmons 2009.
[11]   Carpenter et al. 2014, 467.
[12]   See for example: Bob 2005; Carpenter et al. 2014; Hertel 2006.

international level, and at the intranetwork level. The first of these scrutinizes international agenda-setting practices through the lens of "gate-keeping" organizations and networks, and the role that these play in determining which causes, of all the worthy causes seeking an international response, "make it" to the global agenda.[13] Gatekeepers play a governing role at the international level, insofar as they have the power to both define normative frameworks in a particular issue space, and select which issues should be adopted and which shouldn't. This work looks at the different types of power wielded by gatekeepers, the role gatekeepers play in structuring and governing the global agenda, and what the normative and practical implications of this are for transnational civil society.[14]

From the intranetwork perspective, scholars seek to uncover the framing strategies used by grassroots organizations to gain the attention of NGOs and other gatekeepers, and thus effect change through influencing which issues become part of the global agenda. This work shifts the focus to the network level. It looks closely at how less powerful actors within a transnational network help shape the normative agendas of transnational campaigns. While these actors may lack the social or institutional power of other actors within their networks, they are highly adaptive. In this sense, localized actors have been able to make significant changes to the normative benchmarks that frame advocacy campaigns. Research undertaken by Hertel, for example, rejects the assumption that power dynamics prevent grassroots influence over a campaign's normative frame. She identifies two key mechanisms – blocking and backdoor maneuvers – applied by local actors when they wish to challenge and shape the way a network thinks and talks about an issue. Hertel documents the success of such mechanisms, finding that local actors are in fact able to play an important and often powerful role in shaping campaign agendas, even when there is resistance to such normative change from more powerful actors within their network.[15]

In addition to the work described above, other research continues to emphasize the importance of network structure (and actor position) in determining advocacy function and outcomes. Much of this work highlights the public good provided by transnational advocacy networks, such as resources, access, profile, or influence. Actors are thus seen to make networking decisions in order to benefit from this public good.[16] Murdie and Davis's analysis of human rights networks draws from both social network studies and the literature on transnational advocacy, and illustrates some of the ways network

---

[13] Carpenter 2010.   [14] See, for example, Carpenter 2007, 2010; Wong 2012.
[15] Hertel 2006. See also Bob 2005.   [16] Murdie 2013, 2.

characteristics can both enable and constrain actors and network outcomes. The position of an actor (such as a human rights NGO) within that network is found to have a significant influence on how successful that actor is in achieving its goals. Conversely, actors that do not have the capability to immerse themselves fully into the network are unable to benefit from the public good. As a result, their lack of connectivity within the broader network impedes their ability to achieve their advocacy goals.[17] This also seems to corroborate Hafner-Burton, Kahler, and Montgomery's claim that network centrality can act as a form of social power; it allows actors situated within central nodes to access benefits from other network members, and grants disproportionate influence to these actors in terms of shaping collective understandings of interests and norms.[18]

Applying these insights to the North Korean human rights network, we need to interrogate the constitution of the network, determine the position of various actors within the network, analyze the strategies and normative frameworks adopted by network actors, and examine efficacy and advocacy outcomes. In this respect, the analysis starts with the network's most high-profile outcome: the decision by the UN High Commissioner for Human Rights to launch an inquiry into human rights violations in North Korea. In terms of the literature on transnational advocacy, this achievement can be interpreted as the securing of gatekeeper support, and thus international legitimacy, for the North Korean human rights movement.

NETWORK MAPPING (AND ITS LIMITATIONS)

To gain insight into network structure, I have chosen to undertake a preliminary hyperlink analysis, focusing on the way the North Korean human rights network appears on the web. For these groups, Internet presence is important as North Korean human rights is an issue that seeks to transcend borders and bring together a variety of actors. Thus, for groups interested in enacting change beyond borders and engaging in transnational activism, a well-maintained English-language version of their website is a reasonably high priority. One of the pitfalls of hyperlink analysis is that it fails to encompass groups that do not place priority on maintaining a public profile. However, given that this analysis seeks to ascertain the connectivity within the network of actors we already know to have a good international profile, I do

---

[17]   Murdie and Davis 2012, 3, 198–9. Murdie and Davis's research also found that this was true of
       networks operating across a variety of issue areas (human rights, environment, and health).
[18]   Hafner-Burton, Kahler, and Montgomery 2009, 570.

not expect this to be a confounding factor; these groups do not suffer from a lack of technical expertise. Rather, the absence of these actors should be seen as deliberate. One final caveat is necessary at this stage: this mapping exercise is necessarily preliminary. An in-depth analysis of the social structure of a network requires the application of a variety of methods: hyperlink social-network analysis, content and discourse analysis, focus groups, and interviews.[19] Such a comprehensive mapping of the North Korean human rights network is beyond the scope of this chapter. Instead, I take as my starting point hyperlink analysis, collected with the help of a web crawler.[20] A preliminary mapping exercise such as this is valuable for what it tells us about the network, based on its externally focused presentation and the way its connections manifest on the web.

The Internet is fundamentally a networking tool, in both a technical and a social sense. Just as physical protests bring together like-minded individuals, so too does Internet activism draw together individual citizens who share interests, concerns, or values.[21] For human rights organizations, the act of linking is part of a broader politics of association.[22] As such, a hyperlink analysis which looks at linking practices within a network can potentially tell us a lot about network dynamics, issue-framing, and points of fragmentation. It gives us a snapshot of how organizations within a network are connected on the web, and tells us something about the way an organization presents itself to the world. For a human rights organization wishing to bring about change, networking and profile-raising are high priorities. In this sense, a strong web presence not only acts as an outreach and publicity tool, it also allows organizations to shape their identities through deliberate linking practices, indicating an association and shared purpose with other like-minded groups. It provides groups with some of the public goods discussed earlier, such as profile and legitimacy. When one organization links to another, this is more than an act of convenience. Rarely are these links required for an under-standing of the content of a stand-alone website. For human rights organiza-tions, the act of linking is more often a form of political statement.

In order to interrogate the politics of association around North Korean human rights activism, I undertook a hyperlink analysis of the activist network as it appears on the Internet. A snapshot of linking practices was produced using Issue Crawler software which identifies network connectivity through the creation of

---

[19] For a rigorous demonstration of such an approach, see Carpenter et al. 2014.
[20] See Scenarios of use for NGOs and other researchers, n.d. http://www.govcom.org/scenarios_use .html.
[21] Gurak and Logie 2013, 40.   [22] Rogers and Ben-David 2008.

maps that visualize organizations' linking practices.[23] To perform the analysis and commence the "crawl," 17 NGO websites were selected as "starting points." Table 8.1 provides a list of the organizations and websites selected. These starting points were selected following Rogers and Ben-David's "public trust" heuristic: web sites that an interested, non-issue expert would trust for the purposes of educating themselves about an issue, for learning more about other organizations involved with the issue, and possibly for obtaining information about how to get involved.[24] All groups in the starting-points list are single-issue organizations that focus exclusively on North Korean human rights issues. Finally, only the English-language versions of websites were used as starting points, given this study's interest in the transnational organizing of these groups.[25]

The North Korean human rights network is a broad and diverse one. The groups selected as the starting points represent this diversity, encompassing organizations from the USA, South Korea, Japan, Canada, and Europe, as well as defector-run groups based in Seoul. We know that the groups most directly involved in advocacy around the establishment of the COI were Citizens' Alliance and the International Coalition to Stop Crimes Against Humanity in North Korea (ICNK).[26] Further, given the centrality of NKFC[27] and the Committee for Human Rights in North Korea (HRNK) to a number of other network outcomes over the past two decades, and given the involvement of these latter groups in promoting the COI report's outcomes, we expect to find a North Korean human rights network with reasonably strong linkages between these actors. We also expect to see actors not included in the original starting-points list appear in the network. Table 8.2 provides a list of these actors, to help the reader identify them on the hyperlink network map.

---

[23]   In this particular analysis, only organizations that are linked to by at least two other websites (colinked) in the network appear on the map. It is thus possible to identify which actors can reasonably be said to exist within a network, and then to identify their level of connectivity therein. Additionally, the crawl will uncover other common linking practices of network actors, revealing any preferences or linking strategies shared by network members. The analysis was performed at a depth of two: it crawled two levels deep into every site.

[24]   Rogers and Ben-David 2008, 509.

[25]   The common language used by groups when networking tends to be English.

[26]   Roberta Cohen, in her account of the factors leading to the UN High Commissioner decision to adopt the North Korean human rights issue, lists a number of indirect (background advocacy conditions) and direct factors, but does not name Citizens' Alliance as a central player in the UN setting, instead pointing toward HRW and ICNK, for whose creation she credits HRW (Cohen 2013). HRW certainly played an important role in these intensive advocacy activities, as did a few key activists, such as Hosaniak (see her account in Chapter 6) from Citizens' Alliance. Other groups involved include Christian Solidarity Worldwide and Conectas Human Rights. These groups are multi-issue, international human rights organizations and thus excluded from the original starting points list.

[27]   See North Korea Freedom Coalition, n.d., nkfreedom.org.

TABLE 8.1. *Hyperlink analysis starting points*

Organization	Starting Point URL
All-Party Parliamentary Group on North Korea (APPG-NK)	https://appgnk.org/
Citizens' Alliance for North Korean Human Rights	http://eng.nkhumanrights.or.kr/
Database Center for North Korean Human Rights (NKDB)	http://nkdb.org/en/main.php
European Alliance for Human Rights in North Korea (EAHRNK)	www.eahrnk.org/about
Free North Korea Radio	www.fnkradio.com/
Helping Hands Korea	www.helpinghandskorea.org/
International Coalition to Stop Crimes against Humanity in North Korea	www.stopnkcrimes.org
Justice for North Korea	www.justice4nk.org/en/
Liberty in North Korea (LiNK)	www.libertyinnorthkorea.org/ and linkglobal.org
Life Funds for North Korean Refugees (LFNKR)	www.northkoreanrefugees.com/
Network for North Korean Democracy and Human Rights (NKnet)	http://en.nknet.org/
North Korea Freedom Coalition (NKFC)	www.nkfreedom.org/
North Korea Intellectuals Solidarity (NKIS)	http://nkis.kr/
North Korea Strategy Center (NKSC)	http://en.nksc.co.kr/
People for Successful Corean Reunification (PSCORE)	www.pscore.org/xe/en_home
The Committee for Human Rights in North Korea (HRNK)	www.hrnk.org/
The Council for Human Rights in North Korea (Canada)	http://www.hrnkcanada.org/

The first thing we learn from the snapshot provided by the hyperlink analysis (Figure 8.1)[28] is that the Office of the UN High Commissioner for Human Rights (OHCHR) COI web page features at the center of the network, receiving 67 total links from the crawled population.[29] While the OHCHR does not link back into the network at all, it remains at the center. The centrality of the OHCHR to the network suggests that activists across

---

[28] To identify organizations on the map, see the list of starting points. Organizations which appear on the map but not in the starting points list can be found in Table 8.2.

[29] Link count data on file with author.

TABLE 8.2. *Key to identifying nonstarting point organizations*

Site	Name	Type
amnesty.org	Amnesty International	International Organization
dailynk.com	Daily North Korea	Information (News)
freekorea.us	One Free Korea	Blog
hrw.org	Human Rights Watch	International NGO
hrwf.net	Human Rights Without Frontiers International	International Organization
Jubileecampaign.org	Jubilee Campaign	International Organization
kimjongiliathemovie.com	Kim Jong Ilia – the movie	Information (events/movies)
nkeconwatch.com	North Korea Economy Watch	Information (Blog)
nkgenocide.net	North Korea genocide exhibit	Information (events/movies)
nkgulag.org	Democracy Network Against the North Korean Gulag	North Korean human rights NGO
ohchr.org	Office of the High Commissioner for Human Rights	International Organization
psaltnk.org	Prayer Service Action Truth Love for North Korea	North Korean human rights NGO
rfa.org	Radio Free Asia	Information (News)
Seoultrain.com	Seoul Train Documentary	Information (events/movies)

the spectrum tend to link to the 2014 COI Report. This is unsurprising. As discussed earlier, the establishment of the UN COI is now the centerpiece of the North Korean human rights campaign, representing the single biggest success the network has achieved in terms of securing international legitimacy and visibility for the North Korean human rights campaign.

More surprising is the discovery that some of the groups that worked specifically on the establishment of the Commission drop out of the hyperlinked network, in particular, the ICNK and Citizens' Alliance. ICNK is a coalition developed with the specific goal of holding North Korea accountable for crimes against humanity through UN processes, and has worked closely with key members of Citizens' Alliance to this end. Its members include many of the groups that feature heavily in the hyperlinked network, such as the NKFC, Network for North Korean Human Rights, HRW, Liberty in North Korea (LiNK), North Korea Intellectuals Solidarity (NKIS), and

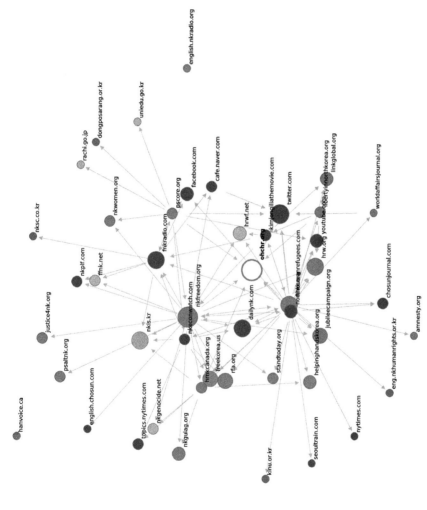

FIGURE 8.1 Hyperlink analysis of the North Korean human rights network

187

HRNK.[30] Yet ICNK, despite its coalition status and own linking practices, is not linked back to the core network by other groups. Citizens' Alliance, which lobbied the High Commissioner for Human Rights directly and played a central role in setting up the COI, features only at the periphery of the network.

Two other South Korea-based starting-point organizations drop out of the hyperlinked network, as well as two European groups. The Seoul-based NGO Network for North Korean Democracy and Human Rights (NKnet) is likely absent due to a lack of activity on the English-language version of its website.[31] Alternatively, DailyNK (an online English- and Korean-language news source focusing on North Korea issues), which was originally formed under the umbrella of NKnet, features as a strongly linked website. This organization, as a news media organization rather than a human rights group, did not appear on the original starting points list. The Database Center for North Korean Human Rights (NKDB) also fails to appear in the hyperlinked network. This correlates with the longstanding goal of the organization to remain politically neutral and focus on data collection,[32] thus accounting for its lack of connectivity to the network.[33] Finally, it appears that the two European-based advocacy groups – the European Alliance for Human Rights in North Korea, and the All-Party Parliamentary Group on North Korean Human Rights – are also not closely linked into the main US–South Korean network of human rights advocates. While they are part of the broader network, they do not appear to publicly broadcast these connections and do not appear on this map.

The single-issue organizations that remain (from our original set of starting points) in the hyperlinked networks exhibit a high public level of connectivity. These include FreeNK Radio (FNKR), NKIS, Helping Hands Korea, and LiNK. They refer to each other's work, campaign together on issues of shared

---

[30]   *ICNK*, n.d., stopnkcrimes.org.
[31]   While the Korean-language version is still active, comments on the English version indicate that NKnet's transnational advocacy efforts (and presumably resources) have been redirected toward ICNK. NKnet was a founding member of ICNK, according to its website, whose establishment roughly coincides with the downturn in activity on en.nknet.org. See *Overview*, en.nknet.org/about/overview/.
[32]   Author's interview, number one, Seoul, 2008.
[33]   NKDB has previously received funding from the National Endowment for Democracy. Organizations receiving funding from NED have been criticized by scholars who claim that they are part of a wider, politically motivated imperialist effort, orchestrated by the US Congress, to bring about regime change in North Korea (Song and Hong 2014). However, NKDB's actual activities, which focus on data collection and expert analysis, do not support the contentions made by Song and Hong. This is further supported by the lack of NKDB connectivity to the network, which (as I discuss in this chapter) allows the group to maintain some distance from the overtly political agendas of other network members.

importance, and seek to draw strength and legitimacy from the existence of such a network. They draw heavily on the mobilization capital provided by network membership. These groups work closely with the NKFC and its organizer and veteran conservative North Korean human rights campaigner, Suzanne Scholte, and the bipartisan HRNK. Scholte, who has been working on raising the profile of the North Korean human rights issue within the US Congress since the late 1990s, focuses largely on elevating the voices of defector-activists and mobilizing defector organizations. Some of these groups have radical, transformative agendas whereby they believe the realization of human rights in North Korea to be impossible within the current structure of the North Korean state.[34] HRNK, by contrast, is often considered one of the most balanced and trusted sources of research, information, and advocacy on North Korean human rights. Self-consciously bipartisan, its board of directors includes leaders on the North Korean human rights issue from across the political spectrum.[35] HRNK thus plays a central role in the public face of North Korean human rights activism.

The most surprising outcome of the hyperlink analysis is that the key single-issue groups involved in efforts to secure the support of the High Commissioner for Human Rights and raise the profile of the North Korean human rights cause through the UN – that is, Citizens' Alliance and ICNK – do not display high levels of connectivity within the broader North Korean human rights network. This throws into doubt assumptions that strong network ties and organizational centrality within the network are harbingers of greater international advocacy outputs. We expect groups working on the same advocacy issue to seek closer ties to the network in order to gain the mobilization capital (and social power) that the network provides. Murdie goes so far as to suggest that because the network is assumed to provide a "public good that matters for global advocacy,"[36] the absence of organizations from the network might limit their advocacy potential. Yet this tentative map of the North Korean human rights movement on the web shows us that those groups we know to have achieved significant outcomes and to have been central to securing the UN High Commissioner's support are not closely connected to the network at the time of mapping. In order to understand why this is so, we need to move beyond structural analysis. What is the nature of these network ties, in a qualitative sense? What does the public good that the

---

[34] See, for example, the letter written by the NKIS to participants in the 2012 Seoul Nuclear Security Summit, which emphasizes the *inherent* brutality and inhumanity of the North Korean regime (North Korea Intellectuals Solidarity 2012)

[35] See *The Board of Directors*, n.d., hrnk.org/about/board-of-directors.php.

[36] Murdie 2013, 4.

network provides its member organizations actually look like? The next section takes these two questions on board, in order to ascertain what it is about the network that results in a structural analysis with such seemingly counterintuitive results.

IDEAS, BELIEFS, AND NETWORK DYNAMICS

While the North Korean human rights network provides its members a clear public good, particularly in terms of profile raising and information gathering, it is at the same time a highly politicized space. Of course, human rights campaigns are by their very nature political. Yet, the deep roots of North Korea–US and North Korea–South Korea relations in both the Cold War context and in the struggle of South Korean human rights activists against their authoritarian government mean that this is an issue that is particularly ideologically polarized.[37] The North Korean human rights movement is strongly identified with conservative, anticommunist politics, and this is a profile embraced by some of the most vocal organizations that we find at the center of the hyperlinked network. Networks can constrain as well as enable actors. To understand the ways in which the North Korean human rights network constrains an organization's action or behavior, and why groups sometimes choose to drop out of the network when communicating with certain audiences rather than remain and gain the full benefit of the network's mobilization potential, we need to interrogate a central claim made within the transnational advocacy literature – namely, that actors within advocacy networks share a common framework of beliefs and values, and that this enables them to act effectively as a collective.

The body of work examining transnational advocacy networks is, as described earlier, based on a formulation that sees actors coming together, motivated by "shared principled ideas or values."[38] This draws on an earlier distinction between causal and principled beliefs, which Sikkink refers to in her argument that human rights networks are distinguishable from other nonstate interest groups insofar as they are driven by "ideas about what is right and wrong – rather than shared causal ideas or instrumental goals."[39] Less discussed has been the distinction between ideas and values, with the two often conflated. Yet the North Korean human rights case reveals that this is, in fact, an important distinction, and that groups whose work is motivated by values may behave very differently, and appeal to very different audiences when compared with groups motivated by a normative commitment to principled ideas. Human rights NGOs motivated

---

[37] Chubb 2014.   [38] Keck and Sikkink 1998, 1–2, 30.
[39] Sikkink 1993, 411–12. See also Goldstein and Keohane 1993, 8–11.

FIGURE 8.2 Organizations and normative frameworks

primarily by moral principles or values draw their legitimacy from the inherent "morality" of the issue they are involved with, and their constituencies likewise tend to be committed to strongly held ideas about right and wrong. This is particularly true in the case of faith-based human rights activists and constituencies. On the other hand, a human rights NGO motivated by a less value-laden agenda and driven by principled ideas regarding right and wrong, and the pursuit of justice in a legal or normative sense, relies on a different set of criteria to retain its legitimacy in the eyes of its constituency. This, I argue, is evident in the North Korean human rights campaign, and can account for the lack of cohesiveness apparent in the hyperlinked network.

The actors involved in the international North Korean human rights campaign are diverse, but not necessarily independent of one another. It is thus helpful to distinguish actors along a spectrum, placed across a range of ideas or values, rather than attempt to place organizations in distinct categories. This is illustrated in Figure 8.2. The distinction here is not based on strategies, normative positioning, or political affiliation, but on motivation, as described earlier. At one end of the spectrum are organizations that are motived by what can be described as a moral mandate – values. In many cases, this moral mandate is drawn from a faith-based (namely, Christian) interpretation of the human rights situation in North Korea, but has appeal beyond the Christian community and has its roots in the United States. These groups include the NKFC, whose members include many Christian organizations and which draws capital and membership from the American evangelical and Korean–American Christian communities. These groups lobby Congress, and hold public meetings, prayer groups, rallies, and seminars. FNKR, a defector-led radio station founded by defector Kim Seung Min, also sits on this side of the spectrum. The station seeks to break down the information blockade in North Korea through its shortwave radio broadcasts. Alongside the transmission of news, defector stories, and human rights issues, FNKR supports Gospel broadcasts funded by grassroots Christian churches in the United States.[40] The moral

---

[40] By way of example, see the 2015 DFF leaflet advertising the opportunity for American Christians to sponsor Gospel programming to North Korea (Defense Forum Foundation 2015b).

motivation is not restricted to faith-based organizations. The DFF is a non-profit foundation whose commitment to democracy promotion forms part of its core mission and derives from its neoconservative, Cold War–era roots. In this sense, the commitment to human rights and democracy is a deeply embedded value in the organization.[41] The DFF has been the key sponsor of North Korean defector activism, led by the efforts of Suzanne Scholte, since the late 1990s.[42]

Groups that sit somewhere in the middle of this spectrum tend to be US-based, nonpartisan, nonreligiously affiliated groups that draw capital both from values-driven and principles-driven individuals and organizations. HRNK self-consciously styles itself in this way, as does the student-focused LiNK, both of which feature strongly in the hyperlinked network. And while the North Korean human rights issue is certainly politicized in the US context, this sort of "middle road" approach has proved highly successful for groups such as HRNK and LiNK.

At the other end of this spectrum are those groups motivated by a strong commitment to international legal norms – principled ideas – and which are thus devoted to resolving the North Korean human rights crisis through the UN and the international legal tools available to the international community. These include Citizens' Alliance, ICNK, and the European organizations, which, as we saw in the hyperlink analysis above, are not closely linked within the online network. In Chapter 6 of this volume, Hosaniak outlines in detail the strategies undertaken by Citizens' Alliance, which positions itself as a "non-profit, non-governmental, non-religious human rights organization." The group's founder, Benjamin Yoon (Yoon Hyun), himself the former director of the national Korean Section of Amnesty International (1972–85), believed that his new North Korean human rights NGO should adopt a similar style of advocacy to that of Amnesty International. Citizens' Alliance's board members, many of whom are tenured professors at South Korean universities, were attracted to the NGO by its tendency toward research-based advocacy based on the principles of international law. Citizens' Alliance board member Hong Seong Phil describes how, at its foundation, the group's board committed itself to a movement based on the principle of the rights of the individual. This offered the organization a sense of political neutrality, making it less susceptible to accusations of

---

[41] Neoconservative ideology, as it was enshrined in the Reagan-era *Committee on the Present Danger*, saw hostile states such as North Korea as a moral and strategic threat to American values and power and held regime change as a core goal, on the basis that negotiating with such states was futile: Kagan and Kristol 2000, 66. For more on this, see Reus-Smit 2004, 27–31.

[42] See Yeo's account of DFF in the US foreign policy process, including its involvement in the North Korean human rights issue (Chapter 3 of this volume).

harboring regime-change motives.[43] While the organization initially worked with US-based groups such as the DFF, in the early 2000s the group turned its attention to Europe.[44] The behind-the-scenes work of Citizens' Alliance, alongside like-minded groups, led ultimately to the 2012 meeting between UN High Commissioner Navi Pillay, two political prison camp survivors, and staff from Citizens' Alliance and HRW. It was this crucial meeting that served as a tipping point.[45]

Actors such as Citizens' Alliance, which are driven primarily by "principled ideas," tend to target advocacy at multilateral organizations, such as the EU or the UN, rather than national governments, and rely on nonpartisan, evidence-based advocacy that accords with the international legal norms that guide decision-making and agenda-setting in these scenarios.[46] Rather than drawing on a faith-based or value-driven political framework, these actors seek to apply the existing normative frameworks that govern world politics and are enshrined in international human rights law. The dissemination of carefully considered, credible information is at the heart of these organizations' legitimacy, whereas groups with a constituency committed to a cause due to their dedication to a particular ideological or faith-based "value" are likely to remain loyal to an organization, even if information is at times discredited. As one HRW researcher explains, "all we have is our credibility,"[47] and that leads to a careful selection of strategies, public statements, and association choices.

CONCLUSION

The diversity of the transnational North Korean human rights movement extends beyond what its public profile – encapsulated in the hyperlink analysis portrayed in Figure 8.1 – might suggest. A closer inspection of the groups that drop out of the network reveals that ideological differences seem to shape network ties. Actors whose agendas are shaped by the pursuit of principled ideas make a strategic decision to disengage from the broader network, thus

---

43 Author's interview, number 2, Seoul, 2006.
44 For a discussion of the politics around the decision to direct large amounts of money into Freedom House conferences following the passing of the US–North Korean Human Rights Act, and the focus of the new European focused campaign, see Chubb 2014, 178–81.
45 See Cohen for an account of how this decision broke with the UN's position on the North Korean human rights issue under previous High Commissioners for North Korean Human Rights (Cohen 2013, 37–8).
46 European Alliance for Human Rights in North Korea and APPG–North Korea can be considered to sit under this umbrella.
47 Author's interview, number 3, Seoul, 2006.

foregoing the mobilization capital that association with the network affords.[48] What does this mean for advocacy? Is there a competing or complementary effort, or a strong broker that can help overcome any constraints that these networking choices may place on the overall movement? For now, it appears that variation in the advocacy movement has benefited the agendas of all actors. Those organizations at the "principled" ideas end of the spectrum have benefited indirectly from the mobilization capital generated by the network. The aggressive lobbying style of campaigning undertaken by values-driven actors has raised the profile of the issue; it allowed for the passing of North Korean human rights-focused legislation through a variety of national legislatures, and provided resources for defectors to broadcast their messages to wide audiences. Without these efforts, it seems unlikely that the quieter lobbying activities undertaken at the UN level would have been quite so effective. On the other hand, actors who have long expressed skepticism at the utility of UN-level advocacy and prefer more direct forms of action to bring about change in North Korea have embraced the COI outcome. While some of these groups joined ICNK, indicating a degree of solidarity with the UN track, these groups have traditionally focused their energies elsewhere, leaving the resource-heavy work of lobbying at the UN to others. Once the COI was announced, however, these actors embraced the additional profile the COI provided their campaign, participated in the reporting process, and highlighted the report as a tool of legitimacy in their own campaigns. This is evident in the anecdote that this chapter opens with, wherein actors in Washington DC who otherwise eschew the UN as a useful actor in the North Korean human rights space nonetheless celebrate the COI report as a watershed. The effort of actors across the spectrum appears to be complementary, albeit in an ad hoc manner. This is at least partly due to the involvement of groups at the center of the spectrum – HRNK, as well as INGOs such as HRW – who continue to build network relations with actors on all sides.

Critics of the North Korean human rights movement have failed to account for the wide range of sometimes contending perspectives, motivations, and strategies that have characterized the North Korean human rights campaign. In her introduction to a two-part special issue on North Korean human rights, Hong accuses North Korean human rights activists of promoting "imperial violence." Hong argues that "[t]he North Korean human rights project . . . has allowed a spectrum of political actors – US soft-power institutions, thinly renovated Cold War defense organizations, hawks of both neoconservative and liberal varieties, conservative evangelicals, anticommunist Koreans in

---

[48] I draw this insight from Lang's work on women's advocacy groups in the EU. Lang 2014, 48.

South Korea and the diaspora, and North Korean defectors – to join together in common cause," and that "the past decade has been witness to the consolidation of a US funded transnational advocacy, propaganda, and intelligence network under the elastic banner of North Korean human rights."[49] It is clear that this assessment of the transnational movement derives from a thin understanding of the overall campaign. While its public face, as witnessed through the hyper-linked map, favors values-driven organizations, these groups constitute just one component of what is, in fact, a complex transnational movement. Far from representing a hegemonic discourse on rights in the DPRK, activists display a remarkable ability to negotiate a contested normative frame. The COI report, arguably the movement's most prominent milestone to date, was largely driven by groups that seek the amelioration of North Korean human rights through diplomacy and legal tools – a far cry from the imperialist neoconservatism denounced by Hong and colleagues.[50]

This chapter's analysis has revealed that, at present, network members worried about the possibility of competing advocacy strategies have overcome this concern through deliberate networking practices, through which non-linking practices have provided their work a certain degree of autonomy. The question for activists now is whether network division will continue to allow for success. Moving beyond the COI, the attention of activists turns to the question of compliance and how the networks can bring about real human rights change in North Korea. A critical question for scholars of North Korean human rights activism which needs to be further explored is whether there is a point at which efforts at the UN to engage North Korea more closely with the fabric of international society will be undermined by the naming-and-shaming strategies adopted by network counterparts adhering to a value-driven inter-pretation of human rights advocacy. Or, alternatively, is it possible that the pursuit of multiple mechanisms of change (see Figure 1.1 in Chapter 1 of this volume) will result in positive human rights outcomes in North Korea? Whether intended or not, for now, it appears that the existence of two different networks within the North Korean human rights advocacy space has worked to the advantage of the activists' cause.

REFERENCES

Bob, Clifford. 2005. *The Marketing of Rebellion Insurgents, Media, and International Activism.* Cambridge: Cambridge University Press.

[49] Hong 2013, 511, 518. [50] See Song and Hong 2014.

Carpenter, Charli, Sirin Duygulu, Alexander H. Montgomery, and Anna Rapp. 2014. Explaining the Advocacy Agenda: Insights from the Human Security Network. *International Organization* 68 (2): 449–70.

Carpenter, R. Charli. 2010. Governing the Global Agenda: Gatekeepers' and "Issue Adoption" in Transnational Advocacy Networks. In *Who Governs the Globe?*, edited by Deborah D. Avant, Martha Finnemore, and Susan K Sell, 202–37. Cambridge: Cambridge University Press.

Carpenter, R. Charli. 2007. Setting the Advocacy Agenda: Theorizing Issue Emergence and Nonemergence in Transnational Advocacy Networks. *International Studies Quarterly* 51 (1): 99–120.

Chubb, Danielle. 2014. *Contentious Activism and Inter-Korean Relations*. New York: Columbia University Press.

Citizens' Alliance for North Korean Human Rights. 2015. NKHR Advocates at the UN General Assembly as the General Assembly Considers Resolution Seeking Referral of North Korea to the ICC. *News Board*, May 18. eng.nkhumanrights.or.kr/eng/news/press_list.

Cohen, Roberta. 2013. Human Rights in North Korea: Addressing the Challenges. *International Journal of Korean Unification Studies* 22(2): 29–62.

Defense Forum Foundation. 2015a. Ending the Kim Regime's Reign of Terror in North Korea: What Must Be Done? *Defense Forum Foundation Congressional Defense and Foreign Policy Forum.* May 1. defenseforumfoundation.net/images/stories2017/2015 May1NKFWForum.pdf

Defense Forum Foundation. 2015b. Special North Korea Missions Opportunity: Sponsor a Gospel Message and Broadcast to North Korea. defenseforumfoundation .org/images/stories/FreeNorthKoreaRadioChristianSponsors2015.pdf

Goldstein, Judith, and Robert Keohane, eds. 1993. *Ideas and Foreign Policy: Beliefs, Institutions, and Political Change.* Ithaca: Cornell University Press.

Gready, Paul. 2003. The Politics of Human Rights. *Third World Quarterly* 24 (4): 745–57.

Gurak, Laura J., and John Logie. 2013. Internet Protests, from Text to Web. In *Cyberactivism: Online Activism in Theory and Practice*, edited by Martha McCaughey and Michael D. Ayers, 25–46. New York: Routledge.

Hafner-Burton, Emilie. 2013. *Making Human Rights a Reality*. Princeton: Princeton University Press,.

Hafner-Burton, Emilie M., Miles Kahler, and Alexander H. Montgomery. 2009. Network Analysis for International Relations. *International Organization* 63 (3): 559–92.

Hertel, Shareen. 2006. *Unexpected Power: Conflict and Change Among Transnational Activists.* Ithaca: Cornell University Press.

Hong, Christine. 2013. Reframing North Korean Human Rights: Introduction. *Critical Asian Studies* 45 (4): 511–32.

Kagan, Robert, and William Kristol. 2000. The Present Danger. *The National Interest* 59: 57–69.

Keck, Margaret, and Kathryn Sikkink. 1998. *Activists Beyond Borders: Advocacy Networks in International Politics.* Ithaca: Cornell University Press.

Khagram, Sanjeev, James Riker, and Kathryn Sikkink, eds. 2002. *Restructuring World Politics: Transnational Social Movements, Networks and Norms*. Minnesota: University of Minnesota Press.

Lang, Sabine. 2014. Women's Transnational Advocacy in the European Union: Empowering Leaders, Organizations, or Publics. In *Women in Leadership: Can Women Have it All?*, edited by Christiane Lemke. New York: Max Weber Conference.

Murdie, Amanda. 2013. The Ties That Bind: A Network Analysis of Human Rights International Nongovernmental Organizations. *British Journal of Political Science* 44 (1): 1–27.

Murdie, Amanda, and David R. Davis. 2012. Looking in the Mirror: Comparing INGO Networks across Issue Areas. *The Review of International Organizations* 7 (2): 177–202.

North Korea Intellectuals Solidarity. 2012. Open Letter to the Leaders of States Participating in the Seoul Nuclear Summit. March 3. http://nkis.kr/board.php?board=ennkisb401&command=body&no=18.

Reus-Smit, Christian. 2004. *American Power and World Order*. Cambridge: Polity Press.

Risse, Thomas, Stephen Ropp, and Kathryn Sikkink, eds. 1999. *The Power of Human Rights: International Norms and Domestic Change*. Cambridge: Cambridge University Press.

Risse, Thomas, Stephen Ropp, and Kathryn Sikkink. 2013. *The Persistent Power of Human Rights from Commitment to Compliance*. Cambridge: Cambridge University Press.

Risse, Thomas, and Kathryn Sikkink. 1999. The Socialization of Human Rights Norms into Domestic Practices. In *The Power of Human Rights: International Norms and Domestic Change*, edited by Thomas Risse, Stephen Ropp, and Kathryn Sikkink, 1–38. Cambridge: Cambridge University Press.

Rogers, Richard, and Anat Ben-David. 2008. The Palestinian–Israeli Peace Process and Transnational Issue Networks: The Complicated Place of the Israeli NGO. *New Media & Society* 10 (3): 497–528.

Sikkink, Kathryn. 1993. Human Rights, Principled Issue–Networks, and Sovereignty in Latin America. *International Organization* 47 (3): 411–41.

Sikkink, Kathryn. 2011. *The Justice Cascade: How Human Rights Prosecutions Are Changing World Politics*. New York: W. W. Norton.

Simmons, Beth. 2009. *Mobilizing for Human Rights: International Law in Domestic Politics*. New York: Cambridge University Press.

Song, Dae Hun, and Christine Hong. 2014. Toward "the Day After": National Endowment for Democracy and North Korean Regime Change. *Critical Asian Studies* 46 (1): 39–64.

United Nations. 2014. Security Council, in Divided Vote, Puts Democratic People's Republic of Korea's Situation on Agenda Following Findings of Unspeakable Human Rights Abuses. SC/11720, December 22.

Wong, Wendy H. 2012. *Internal Affairs: How the Structure of NGOs Transforms Human Rights*. Ithaca: Cornell University Press.

PART III

NORTH KOREAN VOICES

9

The Emergence of Five North Korean Defector-Activists in Transnational Activism

Jay Song

Three of the objectives of this volume are to identify the main actors working on the issue of North Korean human rights violations, identify their networks, and track discursive changes within these networks. This chapter focuses on North Korean defectors or refugees as one of the main drivers to shape and transform international discourses on North Korean human rights, using their social and professional networks across national borders.[1] The ultimate goal of this transnational activism would be the North Korean regime changing its state behavior and fully complying with international human rights law. While activists all share this goal, they differ on the means of its achievement: some argue for regime collapse; others for the referral of Kim Jong Un to the ICC; still others have focused their energies on the creation of three international institutional establishments. The first of these was the 2004 North Korean Human Rights Act, signed in the United States; the second was the 2004 appointment of Vitit Muntarbhorn as first UN Special Rapporteur on the Situation of Human Rights in the DPRK/North Korea; and the third was the 2013 establishment of the COI by the UN Human Rights Council to investigate human rights in North Korea. The COI published their report in 2014, accusing the North Korean leader, Kim Jong Un, of committing serious human rights violations and crimes against humanity, and calling for referral of the case to the ICC.[2]

[1] This chapter is a revised version of an article published in *Australian Journal of International Affairs* and is reproduced here with permission. See Song 2017.

The author would like to thank Edward Baker, Roland Bleiker, Sandra Fahy, Andrew Yeo, Danielle Chubb, and Markus Bell for reading the earlier versions of this paper and providing extremely helpful comments. She would also like to thank Jinyoung Lee for her research assistance and those who were interviewed for this study.

[2] South Korea and Japan have also passed domestic legislation pertaining to North Korean Human Rights. However, for the purposes of analysis in this chapter, these are not considered. The US legislation had significant influence on the trajectory of North Korean human rights

There is limited academic work on transnational activism against North Korean human rights violations. Some scholars have worked on public discourses,[3] victim narratives,[4] and transnational activism.[5] Additionally, Hong and Smith provide a critique of the North Korean human rights project from a critical perspective as part of a double special edition of *Critical Asian Studies*, dedicated to the issue of North Korean human rights.[6] Missing from the literature is an in-depth study of how defector-activists have influenced the trajectory of North Korean human rights activism, and the approach adopted by the international community. This is important because, in the absence of an active civil society inside North Korea, external actors have necessarily been the dominant actors in this particular activism.

The testimonies of defectors have been used in the place of first-hand witness accounts and evidence by independent human rights observers. A series of questions arise. To what degree are the voices of North Korean defectors voices a legitimate reflection of North Korean society as a whole? How have other actors sought to use defector testimony to their advantage, and to forward their own agendas? How are defectors treated within the international activist community? Are their testimonies honored, or are there instances when defector-activists have been undermined, selectively chosen to further particular causes, or, alternatively, abandoned when the claims do not fit a particular narrative? In other words, whose voices do we hear, what broader political, ideological or personal agenda do these voices reflect, and which narratives are missing? These are important questions because the testimonies of defectors have been central to lending legitimacy to three important institutions developed in response to the work of transnational activists: the American North Korean Human Rights Act (2004); the position of the UN Special Rapporteur on the Situation of Human Rights in the DPRK; and the 2013 establishment of the COI inquiry and its subsequent 2014 report.

In this chapter, I focus on the role North Korean defector-activists have played (and continue to play) in this particular transnational activism and the transformation of international discourses on North Korean human rights over time, from a bottom-up, agent-centric perspective. While individual behavior is shaped by environment and opportunities, actors' identities and inherent capabilities also transform public discourses and activism. As I explain

activism, while the South Korean and Japanese cases were more significant for domestic outcomes.

[3] Weatherley and Song 2008; Song 2010; Yeo 2014.   [4] Choi 2014; Fahy 2012; Fahy 2015.
[5] Chubb 2014; Kim 2006; Kim 2010.   [6] Hong 2013; Smith 2014.

throughout this chapter, this is best characterized as a spiral process, evolving through iterated interactions and feedback loops. It is spiral, not linear, as the process evolves to the next level under certain conditions. When the conditions are not met or maintained, the process can either become stuck at one point or even regress to the previous stage. The conditions are continuously shifting due to who individuals meet and interact with, and what kind of information feedback they receive and process internally. I argue here that the role played by defector-activists has not been confined to the type of legal incorporation of testimony, such as was the case during the COI process. Rather, who speaks matters, and public international discourses have been shaped by more than the words of defectors: individual traits, experiences, relationships, and motivations have all played a discernable role in shaping the North Korean human rights narrative. In the sections that follow, I first outline the data and methodology used in this chapter. I then explain the individual traits of the five selected defector-activists, before I demonstrate how each agent has formed his/her own professional networks and what these connections have meant for the broader transnational activism and international discourses. Finally, I draw some implications for future studies on network-discourse analyses.

DATA AND METHODOLOGY

The five individuals that form the focus of analysis in this chapter are Kang Chol Hwan (Kang), Shin Dong Hyuk (Shin), Kim Joo Il (Kim), Park Yeon Mi (Park YM), and Park Ji Hyun (Park JH). These individuals have been selected on the basis of two criteria. First, each publicly identifies as a human rights activist. Second, each is deemed to have a high level of influence, being the most highly mentioned North Korean activists in the media between 1998 and 2015, based on both English and Korean newspapers searched during this period. All five have actively engaged in public discourses on North Korean human rights by self-consciously transforming their identities from "victims" or "survivors" of human rights abuse to activists for change, operating in South Korea and the West. They have built their professional networks and appeared in the media, foreign parliaments, and international organizations as witnesses of the abusive and isolated North Korean regime.

I used a computer-based qualitative data analysis tool, Atlas.ti, to detect patterns in the five defector-activists' discourses and activism between 1998 and 2015, and drew partial networks based on the results. Over 2,000 Korean and English materials were gathered featuring these five defector-activists in this period, and I analyzed the qualitative data of the texts, and the video and

audio materials. Bennett emphasizes the relevance of computer-assisted content analyses in today's discourse analyses and the importance of mixed
sources from text, audio, and video materials:

> Computer-assisted searches can quickly identify patterns in vast amounts of
> text and provide clues on which particular texts (and silences) merit a close
> reading and interpretation in context, and scholars versed in discourse ana-
> lysis are adept at making such interpretations. Researchers from these two
> communities, who at present rarely cite one another's work, have much to
> learn from each other, and much to gain by working together.[7]

Finally, publicly available mixed sources were gathered and overlapping
contents deleted. Sources were reduced to 118 total sources on Kang, 122 on
Shin, 54 on Kim, 17 on Park JH, and 16 on Park YM. The data was supple-
mented by my own personal face-to-face and email interviews with four of the
five human subjects for this study (Kang, Shin, Kim, and Park JH) which took
place between January 2011 and January 2016.

INDIVIDUAL TRAITS AND NETWORKS OF DEFECTOR-ACTIVISTS

Based on the collected data, I draw simple transnational networks for each
defector-activist (featured as the middle node of each figure), formed over the
past two decades. Each node is connected to another, based on simple rela-
tional principles such as *meets with* (low interaction), *invites* (medium), or
supports (high), and institutional links such as *heads* or *part of*. The networks
show how each defector-activist is connected to other state and nonstate actors
in the system of international human rights activism.

   One of the first North Korean defector-activists in South Korea who started
his career as a human rights activist is Kang Chol Hwan (Figure 9.1). Kang was
born in Pyongyang in 1968. His grandparents were well-known communist
leaders of the North Korean community in Japan. He was detained along with
his grandparents and parents in the *Yoduk* camp from 1977 to 1987, escaped
from North Korea, and arrived in South Korea in 1992. He graduated from
Hanyang University with a trade's degree and worked for the Korea Electric
Power Corporation for some time. In 1998, he started speaking at the
US Congress, giving testimonies concerning North Korean political prisons.
After a series of international testimonies and the 2005 publication of
Aquariums of Pyongyang, Kang became a public international figure as
a direct witness and victim of the political prison in North Korea.

---

[7]   Bennett 2015.

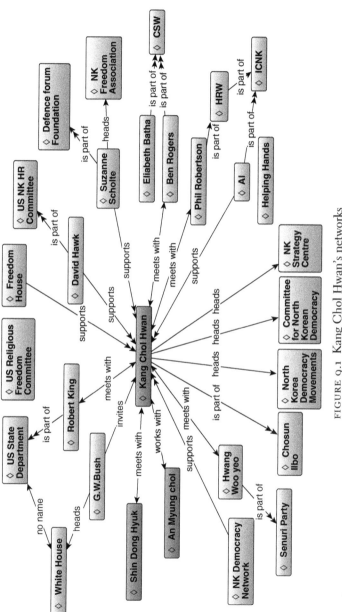

FIGURE 9.1 Kang Chol Hwan's networks

As shown in Figure 9.1, Kang's networks are largely based around South Korean and US conservative politicians, and their respective political parties (Senuri Party in South Korea)[8] and administrations (George W. Bush in the United States). Kang became a journalist with a conservative South Korean newspaper, *Chosun Ilbo*, and established several advocacy groups, which provided him with a solid domestic foundation for his activism in South Korea. For many years, Kang's work on human rights was supported exclusively by North Korean human rights groups (such as the North Korea Freedom Coalition[9] and the US Committee for North Korean Human Rights); international human rights NGOs such as Amnesty International (AI) and Human Rights Watch (HRW) did not work directly with Kang (or Shin, as detailed below), as they were concerned about the reliability and verifiability of his human rights claims. This changed in 2011, when HRW and AI became involved with the broader North Korean human rights coalition movement.

Like Kang, Shin Dong Hyuk (Figure 9.2) was also incarcerated inside a North Korean political prison. Shin was born in 1981 in North Korea. He claimed that the North Korean government detained him in Camp 14, reputedly the most heavily securitized prison in North Korea. However, Shin later revealed that he spent more time in Camp 18 than in Camp 14. Camp 18 is described as a "somewhat less strict and less severe prison–labor colony [than camp 18]."[10] No North Koreans in South Korea had been imprisoned in Camp 14 before, and therefore no one could testify against his prison experience. His book was published in 2012, and quickly became a bestseller. Shin's rise as an international best-selling author and human rights activist was much faster than Kang's. Shin left North Korea in January 2005 and arrived in Seoul in August 2006. Less than a year later, in June 2007, Shin started talking to the UK government and parliamentarians. He published a memoir in Korean in 2007. While it took Kang 13 years to publish his English memoir, Shin needed only six years. Shin's rapid rise as an activist – gaining international legitimacy and fame after just one year outside North Korea – can be attributed to his ability to learn from the experience of his predecessor, Kang. Repeated interactions, feedback loops, and accumulated learning are important mechanisms for the evolutionary process of defector-activists which becomes faster with each iteration.

---

[8] In Figure 9.1, "Senuri Party" refers to the South Korean conservative party (*Saenuri-dang*), which was the ruling party at the time this analysis was undertaken. The conservative party went by this name from 2012 to 2017. The party has since split into two and the main body changed its name to Liberty Korea Party (*Jayu-hanguk-dang*).

[9] This is referred to as "North Korea Freedom Association" in Figure 9.1.   [10] Hawk 2012, 70.

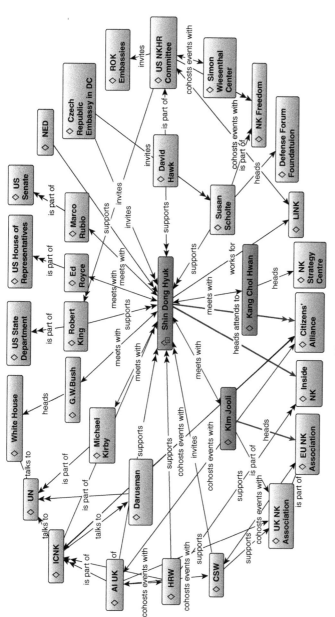

FIGURE 9.2 Shin Dong Hyuk's networks

As is evident in Figure 9.2, Shin's networks are more dense and international than Kang's. Shin has broadened the number of support groups for North Korean human rights issues from Kang's rather limited key organizations. Shin's networks include, for example, not just the US State Department but also legislative bodies and both the Senate and House of Representatives. Key individuals such as Ed Royce and Marco Rubio (both from the Republican Party), supported Shin's campaigns against North Korean political prisons. Shin has internationalized human rights activism against the North Korean regime. Shin is linked to various foreign governments and parliaments, such as the United States, the UK, and the Czech Republic, as well as international human rights NGOs and the UN. His memoir in English, which became a bestseller, has played a significant role in broadening his networks and transnational activism. Shin's networks are built upon Kang's and linked to both Kang (earlier activist) and Kim (later activist). The US State Department and the White House continues to support former political prisoners such as Kang and Shin.

Figure 9.3 combines two North Korean defector-activists in the UK as they have many points in common. Both work as human rights activists, representing different groups: the former is the founder of the UK North Korean Association, and the latter works as a coordinator for the European Alliance for Human Rights in North Korea. Kim and Park JH's identities and networks demonstrate a few key differences when compared with those of Kang and Shin. Firstly, neither Kim nor Park JH were political prisoners. Kim was a soldier, and Park JH was a trafficking victim in China. Secondly, they have internationalized the networks of North Korean human rights beyond South Korea, the United States, and Japan by building European networks. Kim and Park JH have almost no interactions with South Korean groups and exclusively run their campaigns in Europe. Thirdly, the networks became more sophisticated and professional, especially once Park JH became involved.

Like many North Korean refugees living in the UK, Kim came from South Korea to seek "second asylum" in the UK with his family.[11] He was already active in South Korea as an anti-North Korea campaigner, and had appeared in the local South Korean media in 2003.[12] Less than a year after his arrival in the UK in October 2007, Kim founded the UK North Korean Association and the European North Korean Association in May 2008.[13] Kim also publishes

---

[11]   For a discussion of the secondary migration patterns of North Koreans, who choose to leave South Korea and seek asylum in a third country, see Song 2015, 410–11.

[12]   *Son Sok Hee's sison chipjung* (Focus), 2003. Radio Program, August 15.

[13]   UK North Korean Residents Society at nkrs.org/purpose.

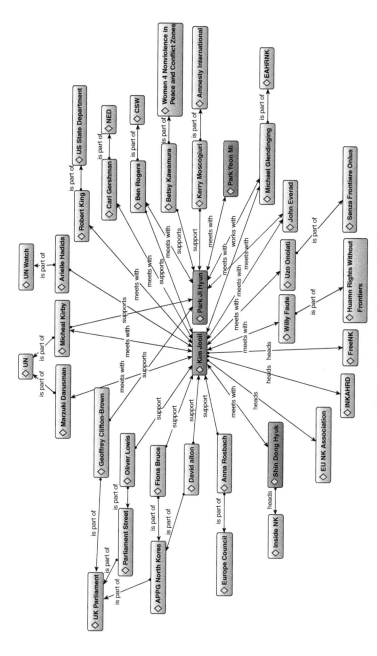

FIGURE 9.3 Networks of Kim Joo Il and Park Ji Hyun

Korean-language newspapers. In a series of interviews, he stated that the motivation to come to the UK was to set up human rights organizations against the North Korean regime as there were too many in South Korea and the United States to avoid competition.[14] Kim learned from his predecessors, Kang and Shin, that political prisons were both the topic that the international community were interested in, and a saleable story for the media, and hence he advocated against them at the beginning of his campaigns.

Kim was one of the first defector-activists to advocate publicly on a wider range of human rights issues, such as children's rights and disability rights. In this respect, being based in the UK enabled Kim to develop a narrative and campaign around what would create more locally acceptable and favorable conditions for him as an activist, using his own personal circumstances. He interacted with UK parliamentarians and human rights activists who provided him with international human rights education. Choosing child and disability rights was only natural as he had a daughter with developmental disabilities.[15] As was the case with Kang and Shin, Kim's endogenous identity and agency, alongside external factors such as interaction and learning from defector-activist predecessors and other actors, shaped his campaign agendas.

A more recent addition to North Korean human rights activism is Park JH, also based in the UK. Her emergence opened a new thread of networks in the international North Korean human rights movement as she brought women's rights actively into the movement's discursive frame. Unlike Kim, Park JH's motivation to become a human rights activist was not predetermined. Individual involvement in human rights activism is often unpredictable and non-deterministic. She became involved with human rights activism after her arrival in the UK and was granted refugee status, along with the rest of her family. In an interview, she said it was her teenage son who motivated her to become a human rights activist.[16] The initial motivation to join a human rights campaign (in Park JH's case) or shifting toward certain human rights agendas (in Kim's case) is often influenced by an individual's personal traits or circumstances. In both Kim's and Park JH's cases, it was their immediate family members who were the triggering factors.

What made Park JH different from the other three North Korean defector-activists was that she used English as the direct medium of communication with other non-Korean actors in the system of international human rights activism, and she worked directly with European activists in a UK-based

---

[14] Author's interview, Kim Joo Il, London, June 2014.
[15] Author's interview, Kim Joo Il, London, June 2014.
[16] Author's interview, Park Ji Hyun, London, January 14, 2016.

organization. She had strong personal motivations to integrate into British society. Park JH's networks are smaller than Kim's as she joined the movements much later, but they are likely to grow faster and become bigger than Kim's in the future due to her communication skills and active learning of international human rights laws.

The final subject for this study is Park Yeon Mi (Figure 9.4). She represents the new generation of North Koreans who can speak to an audience with more visual and emotional narratives. Park YM, then a college student in Seoul, initially appeared on a South Korean entertainment program that invited young North Korean women to tell their stories about their lives in North Korea. The image presented by Park YM was that of a privileged North Korean, part of the "Top 1%" elite who had been sheltered from the suffering of ordinary North Koreans. Her stage name was Park Ye Ju. Later, Park YM's narrative dramatically transformed from North Korea's "Top 1%" to that of a child victim of human trafficking. Park claimed that she was motivated to leave North Korea after watching the film *Titanic*, and that her mother was raped by Chinese traffickers in front of her eyes. She further claimed that her elder sister disappeared in China, and that she had buried her own father in China. Her sister was later rescued and brought to South Korea by the South Korean National Intelligence Service, whom Park YM thanked publicly.[17] The inconsistencies in her stories have been explored in detail in an article published by *The Diplomat*.[18]

Park YM is well connected to other defector-activists, old and young, and is linked to new organizations that are mainly focused on public events about North Korean human rights. In these forums, she relies heavily on her own highly emotional personal stories, such as witnessing her mother being raped by Chinese traffickers (individual criminal acts rather than human rights violations committed by a state), and life as a broker's mistress, while still a child. This approach creates sensational and entertaining effects for campaigns against North Korea and, to some extent, against China, rather than serving as evidence of state-sanctioned human rights violations. Rape is a criminal offense in both North Korea and China. Trafficking of persons is a transnational organized crime for which all relevant states are considered responsible and held accountable for their best efforts to prevent the crime, prosecute the traffickers, and protect victims. Rape and human trafficking are crimes committed by individuals, not by states. States are, however, responsible if they are not making sufficient efforts to improve such situations. Park YM's

[17] Seo 2014.   [18] Jolley 2014.

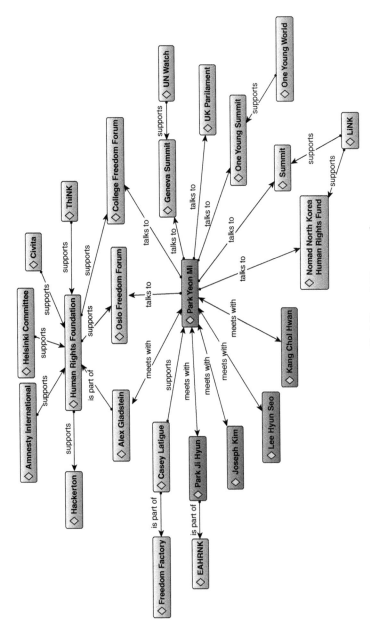

FIGURE 9.4 Park Yeon Mi's networks

story of her mother's rape was frequently repeated in public events, and she has quickly become a symbol: a girl-child trafficking victim. Having survived the harrowing experience of being a victim of child-trafficking in China, Park YM has shown a high level of agency and adaptability, and has thrived as an entertainer-turned-activist in South Korea. For individual North Korean defector-activists, human rights activism against North Korea is an opportunity for an alternative career, and represents a better means to survive in the long run than a short-lived entertainment career.

It is too early to offer a full analysis of Park YM's networks as it is unclear whether she will remain a human rights activist. Of the five individuals analyzed in this study, Park YM is the most active outside of South Korea. She is also the youngest. Like Kim and Park JH, Park YM has almost no connections with human rights groups in South Korea.

COEVOLUTION OF NETWORKS AND DISCOURSES

This section demonstrates the discursive changes over time from Kang to Park YM in relation to their networks. The sociopolitical environments in which defector-activists are embedded, and the professional and social networks in which they operate, influence their adaptation processes. I argue that during this process, each defector-activist self-selects their campaign agendas. The selection is path-dependent. It is based on their personal traits and individual experiences back in North Korea, as well as during their migratory journeys, settlement, and social/professional networking. Table 9.1 presents the results from defector-activists' public discourses in text format and the words most frequently used by each defector-activist, in both the Korean and English languages. The results are cross-checked with other audio and video materials for any outliers. Each defector-activist uses slightly different keywords, based partly on their endogenous traits, but also on the nature of their networks, shown in the previous section.[19]

Kang's discourse highlights: North Korea, defector, human rights, US, Kim Jong Il, prison, prisoner, South Korea, UN, government, Bush, regime, China, and international society. Kang's keywords show a clear inclination toward political terms. The same is true for his networks, which had connections with conservative politicians in South Korea and the United States. Kang criticized the Kim Dae Jung administration's engagement policy toward North Korea, and the Six Party Talks. Kang named specific political leaders, such as Kim Jong Il, George W. Bush, Kim Dae Jung, and Lee Myung Bak, and politicized

---

[19] They exclude all pronouns, prepositions, and auxiliary verbs.

TABLE 9.1. *Thematic keywords of the North Korean defector-activists*

	Kang	Shin	Kim	Park JH	Park YM
1	North Korea	North Korea	North Korea	North Korea	North Korea
2	defector	political prisoner	UK	human rights	human rights
3	human rights	human rights	human rights	UK	market
4	US	prison	defector	defector	defector
5	Kim Jong Il	defector	secretary-general	women	US
6	prison/ prisoner	US	political prisoner/ prison	programme coordinator	South Korea
7	South Korea	UN	UN	China	generation
8	UN	Camp 14	Europe	UN	English
9	government	Cooper	international	reality	RFA (Radio Free Asia)
10	Bush	South Korea	Chosun	trafficking in persons	UK
11	regime	mother	settlement	movies	freedom
12	China	2013	disability	settlement	movies
13	international society	escape	world	political prison	Internet

human rights in inter-Korean relations. His motivations were geared toward political activities in the South. To his disappointment, however, in the last general election the ruling conservative party appointed Cho Myong Chol, a North Korean elite and former professor at Kim Il Sung University, instead of him as the Party's representative member of parliament.[20] Cho is now a member of South Korea's parliament.

Kang's discourses and his focus on political prisons as the focal point of the North Korean human rights issue were soon reflected in broader international discourses on North Korean human rights. This can largely be attributed to the political capital he derived from his fame, which emerged in no small part from his authorship of a best-selling book and subsequent meeting with the then United States president, G.W. Bush. Shin followed Kang's trajectory closely, albeit with higher emotional intensity. He presented himself as a child

---

[20]   Kim 2012.

prisoner in the most notorious political prison in North Korea. Accordingly, Shin's discourse features: North Korea, political prisoner, human rights, prison, defector, US, UN, camp, South Korea, and mother. Camp 14, being the most heavily securitized, was his biggest "selling" point, distinguishing his stories from those of other political prisoners. Stories about child labor, torture against children, public executions in the prison, and family betrayal were highly personalized and dramatized. With Camp 14, Shin internationalized the campaigns against North Korean human rights. There is one more critical actor in Shin's transnational networks and activism that is revealed in his discourses: "Cooper" appeared as one of the most frequent keywords in Shin's discourses. Anderson Cooper, a CNN anchor, interviewed Shin in 2012 for a TV program called *60 Minutes*, bringing Shin fame in the United States. "Cooper," as one of the keywords in Shin's discourse, demonstrates the importance of the US media in spreading Shin's narratives to the world and marking him as a direct child victim of the North Korean state violations of human rights.

Not being a former political prisoner, Kim was more adaptable and flexible in shifting the topics of his campaigns. What is peculiar about Kim is evident in his discourse: UK, Europe, international, chosun, settlement, disability, and the world, demonstrating the expansion and internationalization of North Korean human rights campaigns from South Korea and the United States to Europe, and especially in the UK, where he resides as a refugee. Kim has brought a European dimension to the international campaigns for North Korean human rights. As previously explained, he had been involved in right-wing activism in South Korea under a different name, as Chang Kuk Chol. His motivation to become a human rights activist was to delegitimize the Kim Jong Un regime and bring about subsequent regime collapse. In social media, he openly talks about setting up a government in exile to replace the current North Korean regime.

Kim not only brought a European dimension to transnational North Korean human rights activism, he also diversified the topics by incorporating the disability rights issue. Disability was one notable theme developed later in Kim's discourse. The trigger was a random event in the UK in 2014. The North Korean government sent arts representatives with disabilities to the UK and France, including the Paralympian swimmer Rim Ju Song.[21] Kim criticized not only the UK government, but also the UK-based Korean community for supporting the events as they were deemed to indirectly help the North Korean regime by recognizing the state representatives who were part of the elite.[22]

---

[21] Freeman 2014.   [22] Kim KH 2014.

To Kim and his followers, Rim Ju Song represented the North Korean state. He then started advocating on behalf of ordinary North Koreans with disabilities who were severely discriminated against because of their conditions.[23]

The direction of Kim's campaign shifted suddenly and dramatically, triggered by North Korea's decision (which seems to have been made for reasons internal to the regime), and it has been influenced by Kim's interactions and connnections with UK-based governmental and nongovernmental organizations. Kim's activism on disability rights was not only unpredictable, but also rather random and constitutive of his interactions with other agents in the sociopolitical system within the UK.

In contrast, Park JH's initial involvement in North Korean human rights activism has been personal rather than political, as it was her son who motivated her to be an activist.[24] As seen in her networks, she chose to join an existing human rights organization in the UK to start her career as an activist. For her campaigns, she uses her identity as a woman and as a victim of human trafficking, as is evident in her narratives, represented as: human trafficking, forced abortion, forced repatriation, and women. Park JH has contributed to the feminization of international campaigns against North Korean human rights, as well as having broadened the thematic topics. Movies, films, and stories also appeared in her speech acts. Unlike many male defector-activists of her generation, Park JH speaks English and works directly with European activists, which is a powerful skill in her activism and beneficial to her social integration in the UK. Women represent up to 80 percent of the North Koreans who have arrived in South Korea since the mid-2000s. With more women participating in and engaging with international human rights activism networks, the discourses on North Korean human rights have increasingly focused on women's issues. Park JH has broadened the spectrum of activism, using her networks in the UK. The topics have diversified from Kang and Shin's political prisons to Kim and Park JH's children's rights, women's rights, and disability rights.

Given the shorter timeframe of Park YM's activism, her discourses are rather limited in terms of their substance. For Park YM, it is not so much that the contents of the discourses have become diverse and sophisticated, but that the tactics have become slicker, more popular, and more commercially successful. Over the years, Park YM has appeared on South Korean entertainment programs as someone who belonged to the "Top 1%" North Korean elite, with the stage name "Park Ye Ju."[25] Later, she changed her narrative to that of

---

[23] Kim BK 2014.   [24] Author's interview, Park Ji Hyun, London, January 14, 2016.
[25] A South Korean entertainment program, yije mannaro kapsida ("Let's go and meet them"), shows Park YM as Park Ye Ju. In this program, her mother says Park YM does not know much

a child victim of and witness to North Korean atrocities, as "Park Yeoh Mi,"[26] the name we are now more familiar with. There is a critical actor in Park YM's networks: Casey Lartigue, who coached her in English.[27] Her interactions with people such as Lartigue, alongside her experience in the South Korean television entertainment industry, have been formative have been formative. She has changed her narratives over the years in the formation of her public identity as a defector-activist.[28] Although it is still too early to draw definitive conclusions, there are clear differences in Park YM's discourses compared to those of the others. Out of the top 15: market, generation, English, UK, freedom, world, movie, and the Internet have emerged as new terms, representing Generation Y. She represents a new generation and appeals to a younger audience of college students. This is also evident in her networks: instead of joining or forming a human rights organization, Park YM works as a freelancer, focusing mainly on public events and performances, during which her book is often featured.

It is not yet clear what Park YM's changes in narrative and identity signify for broader transnational activism or international discourses on North Korean human rights. Her transformation from a television personality to a human rights activist adds a considerable theatrical element to campaigns against North Korean human rights violations. Her freelancing and active use of social media represents the new generation of North Korean activists, who are more likely to act individually than as part of a collective. Appealing to people directly rather than advocating through a more verified and organized mechanism of campaigns by human rights organizations reduces the validity of her claims. The emotional, sensational, and visual aspects of her campaign narratives create a constant feedback of reactive and short-term responses, which helps the public awareness of human rights issues in North Korea.

AGENCY AND IDENTITIES FOR DISCOURSES AND ACTIVISM

Defector testimonies were critical when it came to activists gaining support for both the 2004 US–North Korea Human Rights Act and the establishment of the COI in 2013. They also played a significant role in terms of evidentiary weight with regards to the 2014 COI report. Defector-activists, in the North Korean case, have proven themselves as individuals with highly adaptable

---

about North Korea and learns about it by talking with other North Koreans in South Korea (Channel A Home 2013).

[26] Pesta 2015.

[27] See the archived website of this partnership: *North Korea Today* at caseyandyeonmi.com/.

[28] Jolley 2014.

agency. Their purpose is to survive in the new liberal capitalist environments, which is impressive considering they spent their formative years deep inside the North Korean state. The five defector-activists analyzed here have demonstrated a high level of intelligence for survival and adaptation in the new liberal capitalist system in South Korea, where free flows of information and networks can intensify their personal capacity. They have maximized the use of the limited resources available and, over time, self-organized to survive in the political system through identity transformation, accumulated learning, network formation, and agenda-setting. The five defector-activists, as actors in the political system, used their networks as a means to achieve certain personal and political goals, often predetermined by the states at a system level. As a result of feedback loops, individuals adjust their discursive practices. It is an evolutionary process.

What we can learn from the case study is that the breadth and depth of agendas and shifts in thematic focus in the international discourses on North Korean human rights stem from the defector-activists' inherent identities. Other state and nonstate actors may discover their normative values for their own political and other interests; however, without the defector-activists' agency, neither the formation of transnational networks nor campaign narratives would have been possible. As more individuals have joined the campaigns and their narratives have diversified, international campaign agendas have shifted from focusing on gulags and political prisons to human trafficking and the rights of women, children, and persons with disabilities. North Korean defector-activists drew on aspects of their lives prior to defection as sociopolitical capital in the discourse of North Korean human rights. Personal traits and identities matter in the first place. Kang and Shin succeeded because of their identities as political prisoners. Kang's friend, Ahn Myung Chol, however, was not as successful as he was not a prisoner, but a prison guard. Another prison guard, Kwon Hyuk, who followed in Kang's footsteps and published a memoir, did not survive as a public figure, either.

The profile of victims have become younger and more female-oriented; the stories have become more dramatic and visual. Defector-activists watch and learn from their predecessors, working out what it takes to become a more successful activist at a faster pace. Shin was a child victim of a political prison. Shin's story perfectly fit the narrative of US–North Korean human rights activists, which portrayed North Korea as an evil, rogue, authoritarian regime that operated state-run gulags. His stories were thus able to fit easily into existing understandings and campaigns, opening an important opportunity structure for Shin, on which he capitalized with his book and subsequent activism. There were, however, some clear limitations to human rights campaigns against North Korea, particularly those which emphasized regime change: they were almost entirely based in the United States and South Korea. Kim helped open up new networks in Europe. Park JH, also based in Europe, built on this, and added professionalism to the movements as a female victim of human trafficking. Then there came Park YM, as a child victim of trafficking and witness to her mother's rape. Park YM often referred to the rape of her mother in terms of sacrifice: her mother sacrificed herself, for the sake of her child. Park YM's tactics were particularly successful in the sexualized consumer society of the United States. Today, she tours US universities to tell her story, and her videos still make the rounds on social media sites, years after their initial taping. She is truly a modern, sophisticated, twenty-first-century activist.

At the same time, over time the perpetrator profile has broadened from the state (the Kim regime) to include nonstate actors (criminal individuals). Accordingly, the types of violations have diversified, from arbitrary detention, torture, forced labor, and public executions to discrimination against disability, rape, forced abortion, and trafficking of persons.

The diversification of campaign agendas is done through adaptation and learning from accumulated interactions. The five chosen subjects are examples of "survival of the fittest," to borrow a term from evolutionary biology.[29] It is important to note this nonlinear evolutionary process of discourse formation among nonstate actors, and in particular defector-activists, as shown in this chapter. In the absence of an active civil society inside North Korea, defector-activists have granted the North Korean human rights campaign the legitimacy it needed to gain the attention of the international community (as discussed by Chubb and Yeo in Chapter 1 of this volume). Without an active civil society, the rise of defector-activists and writers has provided significant clues for understanding the main actors, institutions, and processes of transnational activism and international discourses in the past decade.

It is also important to consider the evolutionary process from a bottom-up micro-perspective in terms of how aggregated individual interactions, coupled with their own inherent traits, bring about the emergence of campaigns against North Korean human rights violations at an international level. NGOs and states are also important actors in international campaigns,

---

[29] This complexity thinking is deeply embedded in my analyses of most political affairs. A few complexity scholars have influenced me. See Gibson, Ostrom, and McKean 2000; Holland 2012; Kauffmann 1993.

but without these key individual witnesses and activists the campaigns would have no legitimacy. This chapter has shown how individuals' endogenous traits, intelligence, and learning capacity can liberate or restrict a person's contact with international campaigns. Not all victims survive; not all survivors choose to become activists. The second defector-activist, Shin, learned from the success of the first defector-activist, Kang, and, from very early on, he looked to publish a memoir as one of his survival tools.[30] In evolutionary biology, mimicking is a natural behavior for survival. The third defector-activist, Kim, also mimicked the first two by continuing the discourse on political prisons. However, he did not have the inherent trait of being a victim of political prison; he could not publish a memoir as his history as a former soldier did not carry enough power. Instead, Kim moved to the UK, where there was less competition, and positioned himself as the head of several human rights NGOs. He shifted campaign agendas from political prisons to disability rights, and co-opted a new agenda. The fourth defector-activist, Park JH, came to identify herself as a female victim of human trafficking, as awareness around this population grew. Instead of setting up her own organization as Kim did, she joined a European human rights group. The fifth defector-activist, Park YM, also emerged as a young female victim of trafficking and rape, with an emotional, vivid, and shocking story that was sought by the Western media. These individual adaptation processes are key to understanding what worked and what did not in transnational activism on North Korean human rights.

There is no central control tower in these campaigns. Defector-activists, along with other like-minded NGO activists and some state actors, operate under their own principles and calculations without necessarily knowing what others are doing in the system. There is one key condition to allow transnational activism and individual agency: the system's openness and permeability, which enables individuals to freely communicate across national boundaries. This is not possible in North Korea, and therefore no functioning civil society to lead domestic campaigns exists there. All five defector-activists analyzed here had access from South Korea to foreign activists, governments, parliaments, the media, and the UN. All have traveled widely, often funded by others. Communication in English also enables Park JH and Park YM to

---

[30]   A number of North Korea experts, including Yoon Yeo-Sang, founder of NKDB, an organization that works closely with defectors to collate information about human rights abuses in North Korea, recount that Shin was very insistent on publishing a memoir as soon as he was out of the resettlement center in Seoul in 2005. This was quite unusual for a 25-year-old North Korean man who came alone to South Korea without any family or friends.

communicate more freely with foreign actors outside the bounds of their own language.

CONCLUSION

This chapter examined the extent of individual agency in forming transnational networks and international discourses, and analyzed symbiotic coevolutionary relations between discourses and networks as a bottom-up process. What it did not do was look at more complex dynamics among NGOs, between NGOs and governments, and between governments and the UN. Going beyond the agent–structure debate in International Relations, I find that normative discursive changes were constituted by the nature of the networks – which were constantly updated – of individual actors within the system. At first, the actors' endogenous identities were influential in determining how individuals initiated their own campaign agendas and made discursive choices. Later, it became the environment and opportunities available to the individuals, their distinctive experiences, their interactions with other actors in the system, and, most importantly, their transnational networks that shifted the normative discourses over time and evolved toward a mission to survive and prosper in the system. In other words, individuals' endogenous identities have been critical for shaping international discourses on North Korean human rights in the first place. Then, it is the individual agencies and networks that have exponential power to strengthen the system of international human rights activism against North Korea.

The aim of transnational activism is ultimately to promote human rights in North Korea. There are several ways to achieve this aim. Kim Jong Un is certainly not the only North Korean problem. There are North Korean elites who have vested interests and have therefore buttressed the Kim regime. The prolonged armed conflict on the Korean peninsula without a peace treaty is also a fundamental structural problem. The ICC referral to charge Kim Jong Un with crimes against humanity is unlikely to proceed as China and/or Russia would veto this decision at the UN Security Council. In the field of International Relations, the purpose of liberal institutions and human rights activism is to empower individuals and allow them full agency. In order to achieve this in North Korea, where no civil society can grow, international society and those who advocate for the promotion of human rights in North Korea should do their best to help open its borders and grow networks, instead of imposing sanctions. The answer lies with individuals, their agency to talk to others in the system and to grow their networks, and what will emerge out of those networks.

REFERENCES

Bennett, Andrew. 2015. Found in Translation: Combining Discourse Analysis with Computer Assisted Content Analysis. *Millennium* 43 (3): 984–97.

Channel A Home. 2013. *Bukhanui sangryucheung yejuui nammoreul gomin!* [The Secret Anxieties of Yeju, a North Korean Upper Class Girl]. www.youtube.com/watch?v=qH6nUzWfTXU&feature=youtu.be.

Choi, Eunyoung. 2014. North Korean Women's Narratives of Migration: Challenging Hegemonic Discourses of Trafficking and Geopolitics. *Annals of the Association of American Geographers* 104 (2): 271–9.

Chubb, Danielle. 2014. North Korean Human Rights and the International Community: Responding to the UN Commission of Inquiry. *Asia-Pacific Journal on Human Rights and the Law* 15 (1/2): 51–72.

Fahy, Sandra. 2012. Communication Styles and Socio-Political Awareness in 1990s North Korea. *Food, Culture & Society* 15 (4): 535–55.

Fahy, Sandra. 2015. *Marching through Suffering: Loss and Survival in North Korea.* New York: Columbia University Press.

Freeman, Colin. 2014. British Government "Duped into Funding North Korean Athletes at London 2012 Paralympics." *The Telegraph*, December 11.

Gibson, Clark C., Elinor Ostrom, and Margaret A McKean. 2000. *People and Forests: Communities, Institutions and Governance.* Cambridge, MA: MIT Press.

Hawk, David. 2012. *The Hidden Gulag, Second Edition: The Lives and Voices of "Those Who Are Sent to the Mountains."* Washington DC: Committee for Human Rights in North Korea.

Holland, John. 2012. *Signals and Boundaries: Building Blocks for Complex Adaptive Systems.* Cambridge, MA: MIT Press.

Hong, Christine. 2013. The Mirror of North Korean Human Rights. *Critical Asian Studies* 45 (4): 561–92.

Jolley, Mary Ann. 2014. The Strange Tale of Yeonmi Park. *The Diplomat*, December 10.

Kauffmann, Stuart. 1993. *The Origins of Order: Self-Organization and Selection in Evolution.* Oxford: Oxford University Press.

Kim, Bong Ki. 2014. Ibabe Kokikuk Muknun Sesangeun Bukhandokjewa Ssaunundeso Onda [Fight Against the Kim Regime]. *The Tongil Shinmun*, September 1.

Kim, Hyuk-Rae. 2006. Transnational Network Dynamics of NGOs for North Korean Refugees and Human Rights. *Korea Observer* 37 (1): 57.

Kim, Jungin. 2010. A Study of the Roles of NGOs for North Korean Refugees' Human Rights. *Journal of Immigrant & Refugee Studies* 8 (1): 76–90.

Kim, Kuk Hwa. 2014. Bukhan Changein Kongyon, Talbukmin Dance Balkkun [North Koreans Angry with Disabled North Korean Art Performance]. *Radio Free Asia*, September 5.

Kim, Seong-weon. 2012. Bire Daepyo Talak Kang Chol Hwan [Kang Chol Hwan Fell Out with MP Candidate]. *Tongil Korea*, March 22.

Pesta, Abigail. 2015. I Escaped North Korea Only to Be Sold into Sex Trafficking: One Woman's Harrowing Journey to Freedom. *Marie Claire*, October 26.

Seo, Seong-weon. 2014. Talbukja Park Yeon Mi, "Imingapseo" 7–Nyeonmane Oenni Chateun Sayeon Gongae [Defector Park Yeon Mi Found Her Sister After 7 Years]. *Korea Daily*, October 22.

Smith, Hazel. 2014. Crimes Against Humanity? *Critical Asian Studies* 46 (1): 127–43.

Song, Jay. 2010. *Human Rights Discourse in North Korea: Post-Colonial, Marxist and Confucian Perspectives*. London: Routledge.

Song, Jay. 2015. Twenty Years' Evolution of North Korean Migration, 1994–2014: A Human Security Perspective. *Asia & the Pacific Policy Studies* 2 (2): 399–415.

Song, Jay. 2017. Co-Evolution of Networks and Discourses: A Case from North Korean Defector-Activists. *Australian Journal of International Affairs* 71 (3): 284–99.

Weatherley, Robert, and Jay Song. 2008. The Evolution of Human Rights Thinking in North Korea. *The Journal of Communist Studies and Transitional Politics* 24 (2): 272–96.

Yeo, Andrew I. 2014. Alleviating Misery: The Politics of North Korean Human Rights in US Foreign Policy. *North Korean Review* 10 (2): 71–87.

10

North Korea Responds to Transnational Human Rights Advocacy
State Discourse and Ersatz Civil Society

Sandra Fahy

This chapter examines how the North Korean state has responded to transnational advocacy. Drawing on state media and representatives' behavior at the UN, North Korea's response to advocacy claims of human rights violations is consistent and clear: the North Korean state is impervious to international efforts to force change through criticism of its human rights record. That is the message, but – as this chapter shows – how that message is conveyed demonstrates changes in North Korea's engagement with the international community.

The international community may assume that North Korea dismisses the COI categorically – indeed, North Korea has *said* as much; however, it has said and done much more than this, too. Precisely *how* North Korea has responded to the COI and to human rights accusations more generally is the focus of this chapter. Domestically and internationally, just prior to and in the wake of the COI, North Korea has been uncharacteristically outspoken on the topic of human rights, and it has made dramatic gestures in an effort to contest the COI findings. This chapter takes the reader on a journey into North Korean state discourse and actions. The mission of our sojourn is to ask simply: When North Korea talks about the COI, *what* does it say and *how* does it say it?

The major outcome of transnational advocacy for human rights in North Korea has been the COI and the tabling of the DPRK's human rights abuses permanently on the UN Security Council agenda. The regime's response indicates denial and minor tactical concessions, characteristics that place North Korea between stages two and three of the "spiral model" for human rights change outlined by Risse, Ropp, and Sikkink.[1] Examining the regime

[1]   Risse et al. 1999; Risse and Sikkink 1999.

side of the equation, this chapter shows that hyperconcern with image control, coupled with dramatic gestures aimed at refuting the COI allegations, could have the counter-effect of raising awareness of human rights domestically. To this end, this chapter makes three findings regarding North Korea's responses to its regime being a target of transnational advocacy.

Firstly, North Korea responds with discourse structured around state sovereignty as the bulwark of human rights. This is not unusual, and is arguably typical for a nation that identifies as postcolonial, in the nonaligned movement, and of the Global South. Appeals to national sovereignty and outright denial of rights violations are typical initial reactions of norm-violating states.[2] North Korea, by denying accusations, is at least in a process of international socialization. Secondly, North Korean discourse combines an emphasis on state sovereignty with a tireless reliance on *tu quoque* argument style – this Latin term identifies when the accused turns an accusation back on the accuser, also known as an appeal to hypocrisy. Words such as "hypocrisy" and "double-standard" appear many times in DPRK discourse and representatives' speeches to the UN; one speaker went so far as to say "mind your own business."[3] For North Korea, human rights are unthinkable without state sovereignty, and *tu quoque* irresistibly offers historic wrongs and contemporary missteps that name-and-shame North Korea's accusers – who are they to be giving tips on human rights? These first two findings are North Korea *par excellence*. Thirdly, North Korea relies on dramatic gestures to counteract the claims of the COI. Most intriguingly, it is the spoken and performed gestures of the state, embodied in sanctioned representatives, that hold the potential to precipitate North Korea into "self-entrapment" on the subject of human rights.[4]

The third finding of this chapter is the most concerning, yet it also holds potential for positive change. Since the publication of the COI, North Korea has produced a substitute imitation civil society, what I call an "ersatz civil society," which speaks the human rights discourse of the state. Circa November 2014, a North Korean ersatz civil society appeared and communicated via North Korean state media, echoing the state discourse. The ersatz civil society held a massive demonstration against the COI in Pyongyang's Kim Il Sung Square in late 2014. The Korean Central News Agency (KCNA) interviewed three key population groups about the COI and related topics.

2   Risse and Sikkink 1999, 23.
3   Human Rights Council 2015. DPRK Representative Mr. Kim Yong Ho addressed the panel, stating the UN should follow a proverb common in North Korea, "mind your own business."
4   Risse and Sikkink 1999, 27–8.

The three groups voicing their opinions included the man-on-the-street, family members of defectors, and return-defectors.[5] Analysis of discourse from the ersatz civil society shows a precise mirroring of state discourse in its entire subtle nuance. North Korea has adopted one of the most vital techniques in the rights advocacy playbook: the existential contingency of civil society for human rights advocacy. The ersatz civil society appears in North Korean news, as both mass and individuated, impersonating a domestic advocacy network. Like a ventriloquist, the state has thrown its voice into the masses and the individual, who flawlessly speak the regime's message. Prior to the COI, neither North Korean state representatives nor an ersatz civil society spoke about human rights to the international community.

A key argument in this chapter is that North Korea's primary comfort zone vis-à-vis human rights is in the control of its discourse: what is said, and how. And yet the COI and the international human rights norms process ushered North Korea into a discursive trap. The argument North Korea wielded at the UN was turned back on the regime like a boomerang. The trap for North Korea is that both its greatest strength and its greatest weakness rest on one argument leveled repeatedly at the UN: you have not seen violations directly, so you cannot say they exist. UN Special Rapporteurs on North Korean human rights have requested access and been denied. North Korea has engaged twice with the Universal Periodic Review (UPR). However, the state still controls the narrative.[6] By denying on-the-ground investigations, North Korea maintains control of its citizens' knowledge of human rights and how they react to their violation. Allegations of human rights abuse are suspended in the realm of debate by injecting the question of verifiability. However, by suspending human rights in this realm of debate, North Korea loops itself into a tricky and obvious contradiction. North Korea sets up a catch-22 for itself through over-reliance on discourse that excoriates other states for denying social and economic rights while touting its own respect for human rights. Their discourse is bound to clash with the day-to-day reality on the ground. Furthermore, as North Korea produces its ersatz civil society, it engages a portion of its population directly in voicing the state's version of human rights, however normatively flawed.

North Korea views the COI as a fabricated nuisance, yet it produced written, video, and oral responses to the claims as never before. North Korea *is* concerned about accusations of rights violations because they see these

---

[5] It is beyond the scope of this chapter, and perhaps the skill of any mortal, to truly know how people in North Korea interpret their state media.

[6] Chow 2016, 12.

claims as a threat to sovereignty. Thus, the regime is adapting how they respond to the international community's allegations of human rights abuses, evidenced in their media savviness and copious pages of state rhetoric.

NORTH KOREA'S TAKE ON RIGHTS ABUSE ALLEGATIONS

To capture North Korea's interpretation of the COI, this chapter draws on materials produced by the North Korean state in the public domain. The first source is the KCNA's *Rodong Shinmun* articles published online from January 1, 2014–May 27, 2015. This large corpus is taken as a representative sample of DPRK news. *Rodong Shinmun* published a total of 17,603 articles during the time under investigation, of which 1,038 mentioned human rights and 116 mentioned the COI (in Korean, *inkwon kyului*). I performed a corpus analysis on *Rodong Shinmun* articles, looking for the keywords "human rights" and "Commission of Inquiry report," but also collocated words (appearing before or after the words *"inkwon"* and *"inkwon kyului"*). Of the 17,603 articles between January 1, 2014, and May 27, 2015, only 1,038 (6 percent) cover the topic of human rights. Only 116 articles discuss the COI report directly (0.6 percent). The small fraction of articles covering human rights generally (1,038) do so in a manner that clarifies the definition, application, and constitutional features of North Korea's approach to human rights.

The second source of information I examined are the DPRK representatives' press conferences, Interactive Dialogue meetings, and written submissions to the UN. Portions of these events are transcribed here in the course of analysis. The third source is video materials in the public domain, both those produced by the DPRK as documentaries or news features and those North Korea has permitted foreign news sources to record inside its borders.

Drawing on the above data, my analysis shows that the North Korean state directs the following critique against the COI: a) citizens of the DPRK were not interviewed; b) UN officials doing the investigation did not visit the DPRK; c) interviews were conducted by enemy states, states that don't respect rights; d) interviewees from North Korea were "human scum," criminals paid by the US; e) the US/UN is using the COI as a plot to destroy the DPRK.

The timing of the COI is also interpreted as part of a conspiracy. Critique of North Korean human rights comes, they claim, at a time when the United States has tried all other methods to bring down the regime. The argument lobbied against the United States and the international community is as follows: a) sanctions did not work; b) isolation did not work; c) therefore, the

United States will try the "human rights racket" to destroy the social system of the DPRK.

The United States and South Korea, both nations and leaders alike, are variously described in hyperbolically negative ways which highlight the senseless cruelty and selfish ignorance toward their own people and the international community. The "human rights racket" is a ploy to destroy North Korea. Past cases where the United States evoked human rights as justification for international invasion (read Iraq) are put forward.

Not surprisingly, North Korea does not directly address the allegations of abuse raised in the COI report. North Korea does acknowledge the activities of the international community regarding an "anti-DPRK human rights racket" built on the "lies of human garbage" that are the "puppets of the US" and its followers, but none of the articles go into detail about the accusations of forced imprisonment, torture, famine, discrimination, and so on. At no point does *Rodong Shinmun* parse the accusations individually to discredit them. Rather, the COI report as a totality is discounted with the repeated phrase "a report based on lies." In international media, the length and exhaustive nature of the report are often mentioned. By contrast, if one only read *Rodong Shinmun*, one would think the COI report only comprised a couple of pages, with its contents based on the ramblings of criminal minds.

When words such as rape, torture, and prison camps do appear in the North Korean media, they are entirely collocated with the United States and South Korea.[7] Using the rhetorical argument style referred to as *tu quoque* (a technique that turns the accusation back on the accuser), the newspaper deflects and obfuscates through detailing atrocities committed by the United States and South Korea. The articles provide lurid details itemizing how the United States and South Korea fail to uphold even the most basic of rights. As such, the news articles reframe the COI as a hypocritical, anti-DPRK "plot."

Violence and discrimination in the United States, and committed by Americans abroad, is described in vivid detail. US military violence in South Korea toward South Koreans is a popular topic.[8] To encourage readers to imagine that descriptions are accurate, North Korean media hides the singularity of its narrative voice by injecting the perspective of other outsiders, such as *Juche* organizations abroad or other socialist (and former socialist) states. These other voices frame North Korean human rights

---

[7] I looked for the words hunger, famine, imprisonment, sexual violence, rape, torture, and prison camps because these so commonly appeared in the COI report.

[8] KCNA 2014d.

favorably and help to bolster the perspective offered by the North Korean media.[9] To diversify this narrative, sometimes the paper offers the view of an American, but here a special nuance is added. The Korean Central News Agency (KCNA) reported the reflections of a few unnamed US army officers who shared their preconceived notions about North Korea prior to visiting: "he [the US army officer] had been told when leaving Hawaii for the DPRK that it is a veritable hell on earth *but while staying there, he could realize that it is good to live in and what he heard from Western media and his seniors were all sheer lies.*"[10] These are written examples of how the North Korean state throws its voice into another subject to further strengthen its claims.

Rodong Shinmun draws attention to the United States' historic abuses in Iraq, Afghanistan, the former Yugoslavia, and in Korea during the Korean War. Other examples of abuse by Americans include the ongoing US military occupation in South Korea, US surveillance and wiretapping of allies in Europe, and US torture of illegally detained foreigners in off-shore prisons such as Guantanamo Bay. In addition to US abuses abroad, domestic problems are also raised to drive home the hubris of the United States accusing North Korea of human rights abuses. The killing of unarmed black men by white police officers throughout the United States is mentioned frequently.

These messages are conveyed in highly emotive language, which elicits fear and anger as it shapes knowledge of the topic. Not unlike other nations, North Korea's state rhetoric is highly emotional.[11] Through this technique, different worlds of experience are mediated for readers as the text elicits different emotional responses to events narrated.[12] Present in the newspaper, however, are also expressions of love, pride, and relief: life inside North Korea is safe from these outside forces. *Rodong Shinmun* distorts the foreign world by decontextualizing facts and events. Even when the newspaper is accurate in relaying facts, the context will be sacrificed. The discourse chosen for impact is often highly emotive as it "secures truths" through an emotional form of knowing.[13]

In *Rodong Shinmun*, the strongest word linkages with the COI are the names of nation states (see Figure 10.1). The term *most associated* with the report is United States, followed by the UN, and South Korea. Considering that the DPRK considers South Korea a colony of the United States, and the

[9]   KCNA 2014e.   [10]   KCNA 2015 (emphasis added).   [11]   Anker 2014.
[12]   See Ahmed 2004.   [13]   See Ahmed 2003.

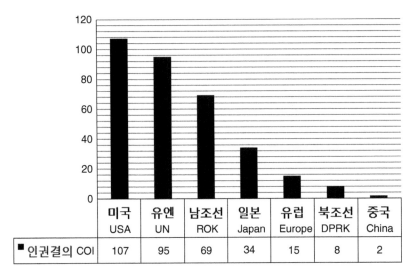

FIGURE 10.1 COI and associated nations

UN as equivalent to the United States, the following graph is stark in revealing which nation North Korea links most with the COI.[14]

The terms most frequently collocated with the COI were invasion and threat to peace. Other key terms of association are highly emotional, connected with suspicion and fear. Recalling that human rights are framed in North Korea as respect for the rights of the sovereign state to ensure the rights of individuals, it is clear that the COI is associated with the following: invasion, a threat to peace (*pyeong-hwa-leul wi-hyeob-ha-da*), a document based on lies, and a pretext for war (see Figure 10.2). This helps circulate an emotional understanding of the COI as a threat to the nation, the North Korean collective, and thus the North Korean individual. North Korea's KCNA explicitly calls the COI report a "new slogan for war."[15]

Emotions and their expression and cultural manifestations are all learned, and therefore pliable. They also include behavioral aspects. As Crawford argues, "aggressive nationalist and ethnocentric beliefs and their associated emotions are used to mobilize states' populations for war."[16] As Figure 10.3 indicates, emotive words most collocated with the United States and South Korea describe both behavior and character in

[14] The UN General Assembly states, "[the DPRK] establishes the equation that the UN equals the United States as the US troops are just the 'UN forces' on the Korean peninsula." United Nations General Assembly 2015, 5.

[15] KCNA 2014a. [16] Crawford 2000, 132.

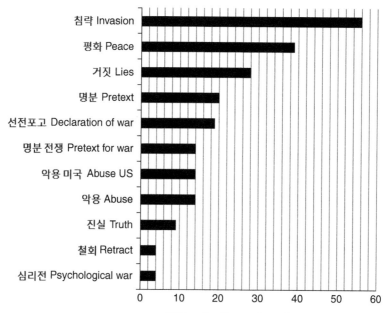

FIGURE 10.2 COI and collocated words

highly vituperative language.[17] The United States is associated with danger and scheming behavior. South Korea, officially known as the Republic of Korea (ROK), has these features too, but with fewer occurrences. Both are described as a dangerous threat to North Korea. The United States and ROK are characterized as diabolical, stupid, and nonsensical which raises the risk of unpredictable behavior.

Metaphor shapes how we conceive of concepts.[18] Metaphor delimits our conceptual foci. It establishes limits against considering aspects inconsistent with the metaphor. North Korea identifies the ROK and the United States as sovereign nations that are dangerous to the DPRK and their people. But two other elements are also included which fall within the realm of sovereignty and are necessary for human rights to be realized: the duty of the collective and the duty of the individual. North Korea identifies the role of the collective and the individual in terms of their duty toward

---

[17] The words "United States" and "dangerous" were collocated nearly 800 times in the newspaper, followed closely by "South Korea" and "dangerous" at over 700 collocations. Related words such as scheming, diabolical, unfortunate, fascism, and destructive appeared more than 200 times each; all were collocated with the United States and the ROK.

[18] Lakoff and Johnson 2003, 3, 5.

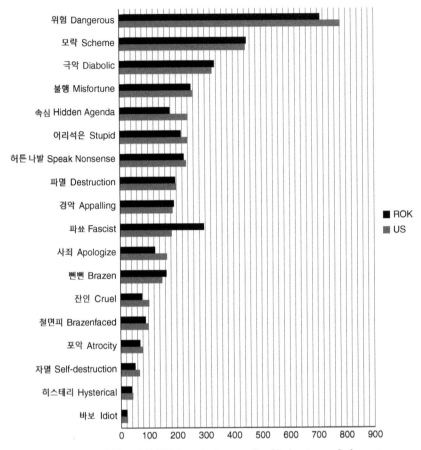

FIGURE 10.3 US and ROK descriptive words of behavior and character

human rights in the United States and the ROK. Figure 10.4 shows that both the collective and the individual in the ROK and the United States become victimized and victimizer, living in what North Korea calls a "tundra" of human rights violations. Through words depicting the quality of life, North Korea can highlight the unequal social and economic rights in the United States and South Korea. The corpus analysis demonstrates overwhelming reference to crime in the United States (more than 800 articles), and in the ROK (about 600 articles). Quality of life within these countries cannot be guaranteed, and the impact of these countries on other countries ensures the proliferation of rights abuses elsewhere.

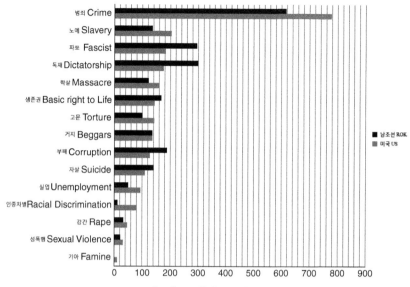

FIGURE 10.4 Quality of life words: ROK and USA

NORTH KOREA ADVOCATES FOR ITSELF AT THE UN

Prior to the publication of the COI report, an Interactive Dialogue was held with the COI on September 17, 2013. At this meeting, Justice Michael Kirby stated that North Korea was invited but declined to participate with the Commission.[19] In the audience, Mr. Kim Yong Ho, a representative of the DPRK, spoke from a prepared script. He stated that North Korea "totally rejects" the oral update from the COI because it is fabricated from "defectors and rivals" as part of a political plan to "sabotage our socialist system by defaming the dignified image of the DPRK ... under the pretext of human rights violations."[20] This was the first time North Korea's representatives spoke openly to discount human rights abuse allegations at the UN. Mr. Kim stated that the violations mentioned in the update "do not exist" in North Korea. He clarified that the Special Rapporteur and the COI are motivated by hostility. He concluded by stating that the COI would not result in any changes in the DPRK, but that his country honors dialogue and cooperation on human rights.

After the COI report was published, North Korean state representatives spoke up again. Their message was the same, but this time it had a little more

[19]   UN Web TV 2016b, at 1:26:15 minutes. Mr. Kim Yong Ho, as representative of the DPRK (concerned country) speaks at 00:17:39 minutes.
[20]   UN Web TV 2016b, at 17:49 minutes.

emotion. At the Interactive Dialogue with the COI on March 17, 2014, DPRK representative Mr. So Se Pyong stated that his delegation "categorically rejects" the COI because it is fabricated by the United States for "ill-minded political objectives."[21] The same items of criticism (mentioned earlier in this chapter) appeared again: fabricated stories from defectors and "criminals." As such, the report is "defective and unable to condemn" the DPRK. Mirroring the technique used in newsprint, the US-led wars in the Middle East and the Balkans were mentioned, in addition to the false documents used to support those wars. The decision to recommend the leader of the DPRK to the ICC was identified as the "desperate attempt to eliminate a social system by all means and ridiculous provocation." He stated that North Korea's social system "protects human rights and fundamental freedoms both legally and in practice" and that the DPRK will "faithfully fulfil its obligation in the international area of human rights." Mr. So's response traces similarities between the lies used to justify the US war in Iraq and the "fabricated" testimony of defectors.[22] These responses follow precisely the same structure as those found in *Rodong Shinmun*.

In October of 2014, a side event was held at the UN Headquarters in New York, organized by the UN Missions of Australia, Botswana, and Panama. The event included participation from North Korean defectors. Unusually, Mr. Kim Song, the DPRK Deputy Head of Mission, attended the event and challenged the COI report. He spoke openly and calmly without notes. He denied the allegations and denounced the "antagonistic style" of the panel-led approach. When he was given the opportunity to put questions to the panel, he took issue with the style of questioning used during the COI's information-gathering period. The testimony was gathered through a "leading fashion," according to Kim. Kim asked, "What does the panel think of this . . . what policy, at high level, is the source of crimes against humanity? Have you read the DPRK constitution? Have you read North Korea's human rights report?"[23] Unusually, these latter questions did deviate from the newsprint form, attacking the COI directly (though, notably, still not mentioning North Korea's alleged crimes).

Here we can observe the value of engagement and dialogue, even with "rogue states" such as North Korea. Mr. Kim's next critique is also one

[21] UN Web TV 2016b, at 00:16:46 minutes.
[22] UN Web TV 2016a. In 2003 a Western journalistic investigation produced a documentary called "Breaking the Silence: Truth and Lies in the War on Terror." The contents of this documentary were referenced by DPRK representatives and the title of the documentary resembles one made by the DPRK about the defector Shin Dong Hyuk, "Lie and Truth."
[23] See Kirby 2014.

proffered in DPRK newsprint, but it puts the regime in a catch-22. Mr. Kim accuses the COI of being an unfair process because the investigation was conducted without seeing things directly inside North Korea. From the two public events with North Korean representatives, then, we find that the DPRK is keeping pace with and responding to the accusations leveled against it by the UN.

North Korea held its own press conference at the UN on January 13, 2015, to inform journalists accredited to the UN, and to share a report sent to the United Nations. At the event, Mr. An Myong Hun, Deputy Permanent Representative of DPRK, asked that the United States temporarily halt the annual joint military exercises, and identified such exercises as a threat to human rights. If granted, North Korea would not hold a nuclear test.[24] In March 2015, for the first time, the DPRK foreign minister attended the Human Rights Council in Geneva to defend the DPRK's record. The DPRK also engaged in two rounds of the UPR process in 2008–11 and 2012–15. These can be identified as small changes in North Korea's response to international rights norms, but they should not be readily interpreted as positive. As former North Korea United Front Department propaganda writer Jang Jin Sung explained:

> Despite Pyongyang's deceptive ways, many people in the outside world continue to believe in the theoretical North Korea in which dialogue with the regime is seen as the way to [a]ffect change. But I know from my years inside the government that talking will not get Pyongyang to turn any corners, not even with the North's current leader, Kim Jong Un.[25]

Jang warns that the North Korean state cannot be trusted in diplomatic negotiations. If North Korea is negotiating with you, "it's a counter-intelligence operation … North Korea uses dialogue as a tool of deception rather than of negotiation."[26] The state uses international "negotiation" to buy time, gain access to things it wants, and to trap the enemy.[27]

In April 2015, the most heated exchange occurred between DPRK state representatives and defectors at a side event at the UN in New York. At the event, "Victims' Voices: A Conversation on North Korean Human Rights," North Korean representatives interrupted the event part way through.[28] Three

---

[24]   DPRK Press Conference 2015.   [25]   Jang 2014.
[26]   Jang identifies in his book three diplomatic tools of engagement, formally set by Kim Jong Il: "The US will buy any lie, as long as it is logically presented. Japan is susceptible to emotional manipulation"; and "South Korea can be ignored or blackmailed." Jang 2014, 253.
[27]   Choe 2017.
[28]   The event was held in conference room three as a member-state-run event, but not a UN-organized event, in New York on April 30, 2015. *North Korea Tech* 2015.

North Korean defectors were providing details about their lives. Joseph Kim, speaking in English, shared his story and thanked the audience for attending. Jo Jin Hye was about to speak when a man in the audience interrupted the proceedings. He was a DPRK representative, and was sitting with two other representatives. Initially speaking without a microphone, it was hard to hear him. The audience at the New York UN headquarters looked bemused. One of the North Korean panelists shouted at him, but the diplomat continued to read from his script without flinching. His microphone was turned on during his speech, when he was explaining that the United States had committed some of the world's worst human rights violations.

The DPRK representative continued apace without breaking from his speech, regardless of who was listening. US Ambassador Samantha Power asked for the control room to turn off his microphone, but then stated, "it's better to allow the DPRK to speak as it's a self-discrediting exercise."[29] Jo Jin Hye addressed the diplomat with poise and confidence, stating that he shouldn't bother speaking up just to tell lies. The panel speakers discussed whether UN security should be called, or whether they should let the DPRK representative speak. Despite all of this, he continued to read. Defectors in the audience shouted "out with you" collectively. Jo Jin Hye spoke up and began her story. She stated that she was now a US naturalized citizen, and held up her US passport. The audience clapped loudly. The North Korean representatives, cool, calm, and collected as diplomats par excellence, stood up together – the speech completed – and left the room.

In this case, it was the defectors, panelists, and audience who were provoked and came off looking rowdy and boisterous. Perhaps this was the intention. The speech echoed the state rhetoric precisely. A close listening of speeches at other events reveals precise echoing elsewhere. At a Regular Session of the Human Rights Council, the DPRK representative addressed the panel, stating that the UN should follow the proverb "mind your own business."[30] The representative spoke for five minutes (his allotted time) and managed to reiterate all of the same messages appearing in print media. He categorically rejected allegations of human rights abuses and claimed that the panel had nothing to do with human rights. Rather, the panel was part of a campaign with an agenda to eliminate the DPRK as "even Western media" outlets have identified that the human rights agenda is not genuine, but rather aimed at regime change. He further stated that the sponsors of the panel were "unqualified" to speak on issues related to the panel topic because panelists represented countries which had also

[29]   *North Korea Tech* 2015.   [30]   United Nations 2015.

committed human rights violations (here, he was referring to Japan on the Security Council). North Korean representatives held a second press conference on November 15, 2016, at the UN after the adjournment of the General Assembly's Third Committee meeting. The room was mostly empty, with representative Kim In Ryong (ambassador/deputy permanent representative to the UN), Kim Yong Ho (representative of DPRK, and self-identified human rights expert), and Ri Song Chul (counselor in the permanent mission) sitting at a table in the front. The representatives issued the same state response. However, they furnished more detail. The COI "reminds us of the time, thirteen years ago, when the United States was telling the lie that there were weapons of mass destruction in Iraq."[31] This press conference demonstrated that the DPRK was keeping up with the latest allegations of rights abuses. As stated in the press conference, "The resolution even touched on the nonexistent issue of exploitation of our workers sent abroad and nuclear weapon and ballistic missiles that have no relevance to human rights."[32] The representatives evoked contemporary issues for *tu quoque*, stating "The EU should rather pay attention to cleaning up their houses first by reflecting upon and bringing to justice those responsible for the crimes against humanity including xenophobia, Islamophobia, defamation of religion, and Neo-Nazism that are rampant in their own territories and the worst ever refugee crisis caused by the United States and Western countries themselves."[33] The press conference continued, itemizing Japan's past crimes against humanity as an area requiring compensation.

After the 12-minute speech, the group took questions from the press. Several questions sought perspectives on the US election results, abductions from Japan, missile tests, and nuclear facilities. Mr. Kim Yong Ho was tasked with answering the questions. He spoke without the assistance of notes and began by stating that he would answer questions related to human rights issues. This focus on rights was something new for North Korea's UN representatives. He began by stating that the abduction issue was resolved. On whether the current Special Rapporteur on human rights in North Korea, Tomás Ojea Quintana, would be permitted entry to the DPRK, Mr. Kim Yong Ho stated that he would always be welcome to the DPRK: *under the mandate of the UNSC as the Special Rapporteur he would never be permitted entry*, but as an individual he could visit Pyongyang.[34] This echoes the argument put forward by Chow in his analysis of North Korea's participation in the UPR: North Korea wants to be in

[31] United Nations 2015.   [32] United Nations 2015.   [33] KCNA 2016a.
[34] UN Web TV 2016a.

control of the narrative. That is why the UPR is acceptable, and a visit from the Special Rapporteur is not.[35] After the questioning period, Ambassador Kim In Ryong offered concluding remarks from a prepared document, the message of which did not deviate from print media on the topic of human rights.[36]

A third press conference was held by the DPRK on December 13, 2016, to give the standpoint of the DPRK on the human rights issue at the UNSC. Ambassador Kim In Ryong, Deputy Permanent Representative of the DPRK Mission to the UN, spoke from a prepared statement.[37] Again, the same messages were shared, with the added prescription that the UNSC be reformed.[38] Ambassador Kim's statement is nearly identical to an article published in the KCNA on December 11, 2016.[39] Several members of the press audience asked about North Korea's media rhetoric, identifying it as threatening. Mr. Kim's scripted answers did not address questions of rhetoric.

Keeping pace with developments, on November 23, 2016, North Korea's own state-run Association for Human Rights Studies forwarded an open questionnaire to the UN in response to the Third Committee of the seventy-first UN General Assembly resolution on human rights in North Korea.[40] The Korean-language version is worth mentioning here as it is significantly longer, and answers each of the questions itself, highlighting the failings of the United States and South Korea.[41] The Korean news article highlights the issue of North Korean overseas workers, an issue raised by the Asan Institute for Policy Studies in late 2014, and researched further by the Leiden Asia Center/ European Alliance for Human Rights in North Korea and the North Korea Database Center in years since.[42] The news article states that overseas workers are proud to be dispatched to help their motherland prosper. The article also praises North Korea's strong medical health system, contrasted with those in the United States and South Korea through granular detail on the price of medical exams, laboratory tests, and biopsies.

NORTH KOREA'S SELF-DISCREDITING DISCOURSE

North Korea's state discourse is self-discrediting and is evidentiary of rights-abuse sentiment. The state's tendency is to critique the interlocutor at a personal level and evoke sexist, racist, antidisabled, and homophobic justi-fication to defame/discredit the subject. Former president Park Geun Hye of

35 Chow 2016, 12.   36 UN Web TV 2016a.   37 UN Web TV 2016b.
38 United Nations Security Council 2016.   39 KCNA 2016e.   40 KCNA 2016b.
41 KCNA 2016c.   42 Shin and Go 2014; Park 2016; Yoon and Lee 2015.

South Korea is referred to as "[an] old prostitute coquetting with outside forces," and former president Barack Obama is her "American master reminiscent of a wicked black monkey."[43] Generally, the United States and the ROK are referred to as "mentally ill." Justice Kirby, the chief investigator for the COI, was also verbally abused:

Lurking behind [the COI] is a dishonest and political purpose of the US and its followers seeking to undermine the ideology and social system of the DPRK. Now, the forces hostile toward the DPRK regard the "human rights issue" as a main lever for stifling it since they had no way out over the "nuclear issue." After all, such political swindlers as Kirby were mobilized so as to internationalize the nonexistent "human rights issue" of the DPRK. As for Kirby who took the lead in cooking the "report," he is a disgusting old lecher with a 40-odd-year-long career of homosexuality. He is now over seventy, but he is still anxious to get married to his homosexual partner.[44]

The writing personalizes politics, removes it from the realm of the professional, and imbues it with nepotism by suggesting that personalities, basic urges, and instincts drive politics. Private aspects of Justice Kirby's life are phrased to create an image of him as a frustrated, sexually unusual suspect with an alternative agenda. This language is discrediting of North Korea because it supports inequality – straight from the mouth of the state. Hate speech, defamation, and violation of a person's honor and dignity occur not only with reference to Justice Kirby, but whenever former presidents Obama or Park are mentioned. The same is true when defectors are mentioned: they are often not even named, but instead referred to as "garbage" or "scum." Defectors who gave testimony about their experience of rights violations to the UN are subsumed under the term "human garbage" in state rhetoric. In Figure 10.5, the corpus analysis shows that of the 17,603 articles written between January 1, 2014, and May 27, 2015, *Rodong Shinmun* made few direct references to individual defectors, and rarely named them.

Defamation also occurs at the UN. In his statement read out at the press conference, Ambassador Kim refers to President Obama as a lackey who is defeated in office (as opposed to having fulfilled his maximum term of service). A state newspaper article and Mr. Kim's speech carry exactly the same words and errors:

A lackey of Obama [sic] who will soon be compelled to leave the Oval Office after sustaining his bitter defeat went so reckless [sic] as to dare hurt the dignity of the supreme leadership of the DPRK at the UNSC in a sinister bid

---

[43] KCNA 2014c.   [44] KCNA 2014b.

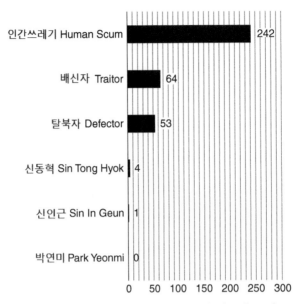

FIGURE 10.5 Defector references and related words

to tarnish its image and stir up the atmosphere of pressurizing it. But the lackey is sadly mistaken if he calculates that such ill-minded act can work on the DPRK and other countries.[45]

However, Ambassador Kim adds further insights which are not elaborated in the newsprint article:

> [In a] gangster like act of the US to insult the UN and its actor states, the US brought a small number of unknown NGOs and defectors, human scam [sic], at UN headquarters to fan [inaudible] the DPRK human rights racket even though most of the UN member states oppose such a politicized event. This shows clearly that the US is out all reasons [sic] and became the mental disabled who is not able to distinguish even the elementary things [sic].[46]

He further states that the UN cannot function due to US pressure to push its "ill-minded racket of slandering one of the sovereign member UN states."[47] Despite trying to obfuscate reality behind rhetoric, the discourse of the state, like the testimony of defectors, offers insights into violations that can be gleaned from forensic study of the discourse alone. On close examination, North Korea's state discourse is self-discrediting and is evidentiary of rights

---

[45] KCNA 2016e.   [46] UN Web TV 2016a.   [47] UN Web TV 2016a.

abuses. Likewise, defector testimony, in its variety and multiplicity, also bears traces of the truths inherent to lives lived in North Korea.[48]

AN ERSATZ CIVIL SOCIETY

North Korea has produced dramatic gestures in response to the COI to try to escape the "self-entrapment" or catch-22 created through its own discourse on human rights.[49] North Korea's critique that the Commissioners have not seen the violations directly catches the state in its own resistance to provide access. Thus, North Korea tries to provide access in its own way through the production of an ersatz civil society which speaks the human rights discourse of the state. The main weakness North Korea identifies in the COI, a weakness it readily evokes to cast the findings into doubt, is that it is based on the words of liars. Conversely, the same method is used to claim that their statements are true. A discursive loop – or noose, if you will – is created because it catches North Korea in a contradiction that it cannot escape without revealing more about its control of citizens and their rights. And the more the regime reveals through its response, the clearer it becomes that rights are being violated.

KCNA interviewed three key population groups about the UN human rights report: the man-on-the-street, family members of defectors, and return-defectors. All three groups voiced "their opinions" on the topic. Analysis of discourse from the ersatz civil society shows a precise mirroring of state discourse in its entire subtle nuance.

North Korea has adapted one of the most vital techniques in the rights advocacy playbook: the existential contingency of civil society for human rights advocacy. The ersatz civil society appears in the North Korean news both as a mass and individuated, impersonating a domestic advocacy network that explicitly promotes "state rights" over human rights. North Korea is compelled to try and escape the discourse trap. By creating an ersatz civil society, North Korea tries to address the contradiction inherent in suspending the human rights debate in discourse. It "gives access" to an ersatz society. North Korea is giving the international community what it has been demanding, but on its own terms: access to the people, with the voice of the state. The ersatz civil society created in this process introduces a tricky variable to the spiral model associated with human rights

---

[48]   Fahy 2015.   [49]   See Risse et al. 2007, 27–8.

advocacy because the domestic society advocating for rights are in fact advocating on behalf of the rights-violating state.[50]

On November 25, 2014, a massive rally took place in Pyongyang to denounce the UN resolution condemning North Korea's human rights record.[51] Thousands of protesters marched in Kim Il Sung Square, carrying preprinted banners in classic North Korean font, praising the leadership and ideology of North Korea. From photos and video footage, the audience appears to be almost entirely male and of a similar age group (30–40).[52] This domestic response is not unusual among autocratic polities. As Risse, Ropp, and Sikkink explain:

> The government may even succeed in mobilizing some nationalist sentiment against foreign intervention and criticism. Thus the initial "boomerang throw" often appears to be counterproductive because it allows the state to solidify domestic support. The presence of a significant armed insurgent movement in the target country can dramatically extend this stage, by heightening domestic perceptions of threat and fear.[53]

North Korea has begun to invite foreign media, who formerly would have been denied, to interview its people about human rights. In June of 2015, Will Ripley of CNN was invited to meet with eight individuals from North Korea in Pyongyang so they could speak about human rights in their country.[54] Ripley was told that each "asked to be there." The first man to speak challenges allegations about prison camps: "How could they have survived?" he asks.[55] However, this interview is insightful for addressing more recent accusations that North Korea exports forced labor overseas – an issue that was not covered in the otherwise extensive COI report. The men who are interviewed claim that they are happy to work overseas to earn money for their government. Will Ripley was invited to interview a family about their abducted daughter.[56] North Korea has also gathered family members to make video letters to defected family members in South Korea, demonstrating the agony of family left behind and the benevolence of the state should the wayward member return.

Recently, a returned defector tore up her published memoir as she was filmed by the KCNA.[57] North Korea is "showing" us what we otherwise could only hear about via word of mouth. Such stories are a boon for North Korea's position on the human rights accusations. Mrs. Son Ok Son tells state media that the memoir was written at the behest of enemies. It is

---

[50] Risse et al. 1999.   [51] Associated Press 2014.   [52] CGTN 2014.   [53] Risse et al. 1999, 23.
[54] CNN 2015.   [55] CNN 2015.   [56] CNN 2016.   [57] Rothwell 2016.

difficult to know how many North Koreans may have returned to North Korea after defecting to South Korea, but North Korea has filmed a few of them and broadcasted their stories domestically and in the public domain.[58] Stories of North Koreans defecting from North Korean restaurants in China are aired on state media, with the use of testimonies from family members, as abductions.[59]

KCNA television conducted man-on-the-street interviews with individuals (only one woman was interviewed), recording their views of the COI.[60] Each interview takes place in a different location. The message of each individual works collectively to echo the message carried in *Rodong Shinmun*, the UN letters submitted by the DPRK, and the DPRK Association for Human Rights Studies in the framework of their argument: a) the COI is a fabrication; b) it is an act of war that actually violates rights by threatening nations; c) the DPRK has great human rights, the United States has terrible rights; d) South Korea has terrible rights; e) human rights are a nation's rights; f) the United States and others should stop "or else."

The first citizen states that he is "furious from hearing what is reported in the news broadcasts. This fabricated report is a big political plot. It is political fraud and clownish play."[61] A second man states, "The UN COI report is an invasive attempt to eliminate everything we have, it is a declaration of war. Our sovereignty is severely violated. They have declared war on us and our military and citizens will never put up with this."[62] A third man states:

For me, living in a people's country, I enjoy genuine rights. I heard that the US fabricated a report about our human rights. Do they know anything about human rights to talk about it? Aren't we given free education, free medical treatment? Everything is guaranteed for the people. That is our system. The US tries to dominate the world with the logic that "I can live only by killing you."[63]

Finally, a woman is interviewed. She is very articulate as she responds:

[58] StimmeKoreas 2012.   [59] New China TV, May 4, 2016.
[60] In 2017, YouTube removed most of these videos from its site. The author had previously downloaded them for her records. For convenience they have been uploaded onto her YouTube account and are available at: for FN 61, Sandra Fahy, YouTube, April 4, 2018, DPRK Protest against United Nations Human Rights Report Pyongyang November 25 2014 https://www.youtube.com/watch?v=Or6XiIftMDo.
[61] Sandra Fahy, DPRK 8 O'Clock News November 25 2014, April 5 2018, https://www.youtube.com/watch?v=VAHZH5HX4jU&feature=youtu.be
[62] Sandra Fahy, DPRK 8 O'Clock News November 25 2014, April 5 2018, https://www.youtube.com/watch?v=VAHZH5HX4jU&feature=youtu.be
[63] Sandra Fahy, DPRK 8 O'Clock News November 25 2014, April 5 2018, https://www.youtube.com/watch?v=VAHZH5HX4jU&feature=youtu.be

They don't have any rights to speak of to criticize our rights. Truly, the South Korean puppet government should feel ashamed about human rights; they should hide their head in a mouse-hole. Everyone knows that they drowned the innocent young students in the sea. The Park government even cruelly suppresses the families of these victimized students, and then they talk about our human rights. This makes me angry.[64]

The fifth interviewee states:

Human rights are a nation's rights, and a nation's right is sovereignty. The human scum who betrayed our country and abandoned their family and ran away fabricated the human rights report. This is an intolerable challenge to our country. We are filled with a burning determination to protect our system and pursue the US and their followers to the end of the earth to punish them.[65]

The sixth interviewee argues:

We have been putting up with this for a long time. We should stop talking and start taking action. We have been building an extremely strong military and nuclear power for decades and these are not for decoration they are for today. The US is acting crazy, not knowing that it will die. We are going to let them taste the gun of the military-first North Korea. The US and its followers have responsibility of this result.[66]

Each speaker flawlessly echoes the official take on human rights.

CONCLUSION

North Korea sees state sovereignty as the bulwark of human rights, a typical reaction for norm-violating states.[67] DPRK discourse defends state sovereignty while tirelessly placing blame on other countries, calling them hypocrites. In its domestic newsprint media, North Korea obfuscates the message on human rights by itemizing the failings of other states. The findings of this chapter demonstrate that North Korea's comfort zone vis-à-vis the topic of human rights internationally and domestically rests in its control of discourse, specifically on *what* is said and *how* it is said. *Who* speaks about human rights is also something North Korea seeks to control. The prospect for human rights

---

64   Sandra Fahy, DPRK 8 O'Clock News November 25 2014, April 5 2018, https://www.youtube.com/watch?v=VAHZH5HX4jU&feature=youtu.be

65   Sandra Fahy, DPRK 8 O'Clock News November 25 2014, April 5 2018, https://www.youtube.com/watch?v=VAHZH5HX4jU&feature=youtu.be

66   Sandra Fahy, DPRK 8 O'Clock News November 25 2014, April 5 2018, https://www.youtube.com/watch?v=VAHZH5HX4jU&feature=youtu.be

67   Risse et al. 2007, 23.

reform in North Korea looks bleak. However, even though North Korea denies all accusations, it finds itself embedded, whether willingly or not, in a process of international socialization as it reveals and represents its views on human rights.

North Korea's savvy choice to put its voice into the "ordinary" citizen through an ersatz civil society may produce results contrary to its expectations. The manner in which the regime has responded to accusations – by utilizing defector's families in documentaries, permitting CNN to interview workers, and so on – may also inject an element of doubt, questioning, or curiosity about normative respect for human rights internationally, which the state may not completely contain.

Although North Korea seeks to remain in control of the narrative domestically and internationally, their dramatic efforts to maintain this messaging may be their undoing. The COI and the international human rights norms process ushered North Korea into a discursive trap that highlighted the argument North Korea wielded at the UN and turned it back on North Korea like a boomerang. The trap for North Korea is that both its greatest strength and its greatest weakness rest on one argument leveled repeatedly at the UN: international observers have not witnessed violations directly, so they cannot claim that such violations exist. UN Special Rapporteurs on North Korean human rights have requested access, and have been repeatedly denied. North Korea has engaged twice with the UPR. However, this enabled the state to control the narrative.[68] The regime has suspended human rights allegations in the realm of debate by continuously injecting the question of verifiability. Paradoxically, however, by suspending itself in the realm of debate, North Korea exposes itself to potential contradictions.

North Korea's over-reliance on discourse that excoriates other states for denying social and economic rights while touting its own respect for human rights precipitates the state into a catch-22. The discourse is bound to clash with the day-to-day reality on the ground. Furthermore, as North Korea *produces* its ersatz civil society, it literally engages the population directly in its own version of discourse about human rights, however normatively flawed. Although North Korea claims to view the COI as a fabricated nuisance, it continues to respond to transnational advocacy pressure regarding its human rights record in a dialectical fashion.

REFERENCES

Anker, Elisabeth R. 2014. *Orgies of Feeling: Melodrama and the Politics of Freedom.* Durham: Duke University Press.
Ahmed, Sara. 2003. The Politics of Fear in the Making of Worlds. *Qualitative Studies in Education* 16 (3): 377–98.

[68]   Chow 2016, 12.

Ahmed, Sara. 2004. *The Cultural Politics of Emotion*. Edinburgh: Edinburgh University Press.

Associated Press. 2014. North Koreans Protest Against UN Resolution on Human Rights. *The Guardian*, November 25. www.theguardian.com/world/2014/nov/25/-sp-north-korea-protest-un-resolution-human-rights.

Choe, Sang-Hun. 2017. North Korean Defector says Kim Jong-Un's Control is Crumbling. *New York Times*, January 25. www.nytimes.com/2017/01/25/world/asia/north-korea-defector.html.

Chow, Jonathan T. 2016. North Korea's Participation in the Universal Periodic Review of Human Rights. *Australian Journal of International Affairs* 71 (2):1–18.

CGTN. 2014. DPRK Protests Against UN Resolution on Human Rights, November 25. www.youtube.com/watch?v=bd-YHFCC5GQ.

CNN. 2015. North Korea Defends Human Rights Record, June 30. www.youtube.com/watch?v=eS3-8ErBYpQ.

CNN. 2016. North Korean Families Plead for Defectors to Return, May 11. https://youtu.be/Zqo2ulr_t2g.

Crawford, Neta C. 2000. The Passion of World Politics: Propositions on Emotion and Emotional Relationships. *International Security* 24 (4): 116–56.

DPRK Press Conference. 2015. *United Nations*, January 13. www.youtube.com/watch?v=evpTxoJvzYM.

Fahy, Sandra. 2015. *Marching through Suffering: Loss and Survival in North Korea*. New York: Columbia University Press.

Human Rights Council. 2015. 16th Meeting 30th Regular Session, North Korea on Human Rights. *UN 150921*, September 21. www.youtube.com/watch?v=WpbXvlkwcnk.

KCNA. 2014a. US "Human Rights" Racket Against DPRK's Sovereignty is Doomed to Failure: KCNA Report, March 26, Juche 103. www.kcna.co.jp/item/2014/201403/news26/20140326-17ee.html.

KCNA. 2014b. KCNA Commentary Slams Artifice by Political Swindlers, April 22, Juche 103. www.kcna.co.jp/item/2014/201404/news22/20140422-02ee.html.

KCNA. 2014c. Park Geun Hye Censured as Root Cause of Disasters of Nation, May 2, Juche 103. www.kcna.co.jp/item/2014/201405/news02/20140502-22ee.html.

KCNA. 2014d. Monstrous Crimes Committed by US Against Koreans Blasted, May 5, Juche 103. www.kcna.co.jp/item/2014/201405/news05/20140505-17ee.html.

KCNA. 2014e. West's Anti-DPRK Human Rights Abuses Rejected by Bulgarian Paper, July 20, Juche 103. www.kcna.co.jp/item/2014/201407/news20/20140720-05ee.html.

KCNA. 2015. KCNA Commentary Discloses Absurdity of US "Human Rights" Racket Against DPRK, March 11, Juche 104 www.kcna.co.jp/item/2015/201503/news11/20150311-17ee.html.

KCNA. 2016a. DPRK Delegate Rejects "Draft Resolution" A/C.3/71/L.23, November 17, Juche 105. www.kcna.co.jp/item/2016/201611/news17/20161117-11ee.html.

KCNA. 2016b. DPRK Association for Human Rights Studies Forwards Open Questionnaire to UN, November 23, Juche 105. www.kcna.co.jp/item/2016/201611/news23/20161123-29ee.html.

KCNA. 2016c DPRK's Human Rights Research Institute Responds to the United Nation's "North Korea Human Rights Report" as a Threat to the Nation, November 23, Juche 105. www.kcna.co.jp/calendar/2016/11/11–23/2016–1123-030.html.

KCNA. 2016d. North Korea's Human Rights Association on the United Nation's "North Korea Human Rights Report" a Threat to the Nation, November 23, Juche 105. www.kcna.co.jp/index-k.htm.

KCNA. 2016e. DPRK Foreign Ministry Spokesman Hits out at US-sponsored Anti-DPRK "Human Rights" farce at UNSC, December 11, Juche 105. www.kcna.co.jp /item/2016/201612/news11/20161211-14ee.html.

Jang, Jin Sung. 2013. The Market Shall Set North Korea Free. *New York Times*, April 27. www.nytimes.com/2013/04/27/opinion/global/The-Market-Shall-Set-North-Korea-Free.html.

Jang, Jin Sung. 2014. *Dear Leader*. Translated by Shirley Lee. London: Rider.

Lakoff, George and Mark Johnson. 2003. *Metaphors We Live By*. Chicago: University of Chicago Press.

Kirby, Michael. 2014. Epic Exchange Between Justice Kirby and DPRK Councillor Kim Song. *The Hon Michael Kirby AC CMG*. October 22. www.michaelkirby.com .au/content/epic-exchange-between-justice-kirby-and-dprk-councillor-kim-song-1.

North Korea Tech. 2015. More on UN Meeting, Silencing of DPRK Microphone, May 2. www.northkoreatech.org/2015/05/02/more-on-un-meeting-silencing-of-dprk-microphone/.

Park, Chan Hong. 2016. *Conditions of Labor and Human Rights: North Korean Overseas Laborers in Russia*. Seoul: Database Center for North Korean Human Rights.

Risse, Thomas, Stephen C. Ropp, and Katheryn Sikkink. 1999. *The Power of Human Rights: International Norms and Domestic Change*. Cambridge: Cambridge University Press.

Risse, Thomas, Stephen C. Ropp, and Katheryn Sikkink. 2013. *The Persistent Power of Human Rights: from Commitment to Compliance*. Cambridge: Cambridge University Press.

Risse, Thomas, and Kathryn Sikkink. 1999. The Socialization of Human Rights Norms into Domestic Practices. In *The Power of Human Rights: International Norms and Domestic Change*, edited by Thomas Risse, Stephen Ropp, and Kathryn Sikkink, 1–38. Cambridge: Cambridge University Press.

Rothwell, James. 2016. North Korean Defector Returns Home after 16 Years and Rips Up Her Memoirs on Camera. *The Telegraph*, January 21. www.telegraph.co.uk/ne ws/worldnews/asia/northkorea/12112246/North-Korean-defector-returns-home-after-1 6-years-and-rips-up-her-memoirs-on-camera.html.

Shin Chang-Hoon and Go Myong-Hyun. 2014. Beyond the UN COI Report on Human Rights in North Korea. *Asan Institute for Policy Studies*, November 3. en .asaninst.org/contents/asan-report-beyond-the-coi-dprk-human-rights-report/.

StimmeKoreas. 2012. North Korean defectors return after 4 Years in South Korea! *YouTube*, November 9. www.youtube.com/watch?v=x139pGGR_40.

Tonpomail. 2014. Juche Year 103, 2014, November 25, 8 O'clock News Report. *YouTube*, November 23. www.youtube.com/watch?v=Kw1S8KixbRg.

UN Web TV. 2016a. Kim In Ryong (DPRK) Press Conference, November 15. webtv.un .org/watch/kim-in-ryong-dprk-press-conference-15-november–2016/5211267770001.

UN Web TV. 2016b. Kim In Rong (DPRK) on Human Rights – Press Conference, December 13. webtv.un.org/watch/kim-in-ryong-dprk-on-human-rights-press-conference-13-december-2016/5246257589001#full-text.

UN Web TV. 2016c. Interactive Dialogue, Commission of Inquiry on DPRK 14th Meeting 24th Regular Session of Human Rights Council, December 13. webtv.un .org/watch/kim-in-ryong-dprk-on-human-rights-press-conference-13-december-2016/ 5246257589001#full-text.

United Nations. 2015. North Korea on Human Rights at the 16th Meeting 30, September 21. www.youtube.com/watch?v=WpbXvlkwcnk.

United Nations General Assembly. 2015. Statement by H. E. Mr. Ri su Young, Minister for Foreign Affairs of the Democratic People's Republic of Korea at the General Debate of the 70th Session of The United Nations General Assembly, October 1.

United Nations Security Council. 2016. The Situation in the Democratic People's Republic of Korea. S/PV.783, www.securitycouncilreport.org/atf/cf/%7B65BFCF9 B-6D27-4E9 C-8CD3-CF6E4FF96FF9%7D/s_pv_7830.pdf.

Yoon, Yeo-sang, and Lee Seung-Ju. 2015. *Human Rights and North Korea's Overseas Laborers: Dilemmas and Policy Challenges.* Seoul: Database Center for North Korean Human Rights.

11

Breaking Through
North Korea's Information Underground and Transnational Advocacy Networks

Jieun Baek

North Korea's restrictive information landscape is a key component of the regime's oppression.[1] All North Korean news and media, as mouthpieces of the government, go through several rounds of internal censorship before being published.[2] In order to uphold the state's fabricated history and exaggerated and fictitious biographies of the Kim family, and to justify its internal surveillance system and nuclear program to its people, the regime has gone to great lengths to prevent its citizens from accessing any unauthorized information. The possession, circulation, and viewing of unlawful information sourced from both inside and outside the country are heavily penalized.

Several external evaluations of the state's press and media underscore the repressiveness of the information landscape. Reporters Without Borders' 2017 rankings for press freedom placed North Korea last out of 180 countries.[3] In 2016, Freedom House's score of North Korea's press freedom was 97 out of 100 on a scale where 0 is best and 100 is worst. To capture a sense of North Korea's overall regime characteristics, the Polity IV Data Series' 2014 score for North Korea is –10, the lowest possible rating.[4]

These types of rankings appear to capture the domestic restrictions reflected in North Korea's bureaucratic, legal, and criminal code structures. Articles 193, 194, and 195 of the DPRK's Criminal Code explicitly prohibit the consumption, possession, and circulation of unauthorized media and

---

[1] This chapter is based on research published in the author's monograph with Yale University Press. See Baek 2016.

[2] Furthermore, the North Korean state media reports only on domestic issues that cast the party and state in a favorable light.

[3] Reporters Without Borders 2017.

[4] The range of the Polity IV Data Series is –10 to 10, where a score of –10 corresponds with the most autocratic and 10 corresponds with a consolidated democracy (Polity IV 2014).

information.[5] These articles appear to be actively enforced by bureaucratic units – such as Groups 109, 118, 1018, and 1019 – tasked explicitly with combating foreign media and information.[6]

Activists and policy practitioners now largely agree that information blockage contributes to maintaining the current dire situation of human rights violations in North Korea. For the most part, the North Korean people remain unaware of the rights afforded to them under international law. Additionally, as the number of defectors has swelled over the past two decades, more and more testimonies have surfaced which report the ways in which access to foreign information while living inside North Korea fundamentally impacted some defectors' ways of thinking and their *Juche*-centered belief system. Many defectors report that access to this information played a significant role in their decision to defect. Consequently, there is growing consensus within the international community that information flows into and out of North Korea ought to be championed to provide alternative information sources to North Koreans, and in an attempt to indirectly improve the human rights situation in North Korea.

This chapter will argue that North Koreans' repeat exposure to foreign information is creating consequential changes in the country. Such micro-changes may be economic and social in nature, rather than political, at the present time. However, these far-reaching and irreversible changes have been eroding citizens' trust and belief in the North Korean leadership, and may have a lasting impact by weakening this closed regime.

This chapter will proceed as follows: first, it will lay out the early, informal stages of the erosion of the North Korean regime's monopoly on information; next, it will briefly review and explain the proliferation of organizations focused on information access in North Korea since the early 2000s as a subset of the North Korean human rights transnational advocacy network;

---

[5]   According to the Seoul-based Citizens' Alliance for North Korean Human Rights, "this is a translation of the North Korean criminal law following its amendment which took place in 2009." Moreover, Article 222, which covers crimes pertaining to "fabrication and distribution of false rumor," is also a relevant article that can punish citizens for consuming and circulating foreign information, to the extent that the North Korean judicial system actually refers to the criminal code when trying alleged criminals. Article 222: Fabrication and distribution of false rumor: "A person who, without anti-state motives, concocts a false rumor that may lead to distrust of the state and cause social disruption shall be punished by short-term labor for less than two years. In cases where the person commits a grave offense, he or she shall be punished by reform through labor for less than three years." (Citizens' Alliance for North Korea Human Rights 2009.)

[6]   Do, Han, Hong, Kim, and Lee 2015, 248. Another group (or "*grouppas*") related to information and communication surveillance is the 127 *Grouppa*, which works to prevent the use of unauthorized cell phones.

then, it will lay out some theoretical and empirical implications of this phenomenon of foreign information continuing to erode the regime's information blockade, and capture some of the in-country micro-changes that can be causally linked to North Korean citizens' exposure to foreign information and media.[7] The chapter will conclude with a brief discussion of the limitations of the transnational advocacy network literature when applied to North Korea.

NORTH KOREAN INFORMATION ACCESS EFFORTS:
A SUBSET OF THE NORTH KOREAN HUMAN RIGHTS TRANSNATIONAL
ADVOCACY NETWORK

The Informal Beginnings of North Korea's Information Blockade Erosion

No one can know who first watched a foreign film or first listened to an unauthorized news source in North Korea, or when they first did so. There are anecdotes of diplomats sneaking VHS tapes into North Korea upon their return in the 1970s and 1980s. What we do know is that it was during the famine that hit North Korea in the mid-1990s that, for the first time, significant amounts of information about the outside world moved into and around North Korea. Throughout the famine, large numbers of North Koreans illegally fled to China in search of food and money, some of whom intended to return to North Korea with their procured resources to help their families.[8] During their time in China, these individuals witnessed China's comparative wealth. Chinese markets were abundantly stocked with food and clothing, and neon signs stayed brightly lit throughout the night. Conversations with Chinese citizens unearthed pity for starving North Koreans and criticism of Kim Jong Il.

---

[7] Much of the analysis in the chapter draws on the author's semistructured interviews with defectors, activists, and researchers and reports based on defector surveys. See Baek 2016 for more details of these interviews. As with most analyses of North Korea, defectors' experiences are not representative of all North Korean citizens, as they comprise an unrepresentative segment of people of the overall North Korean population. Over 80 percent of the 30,000 defectors in South Korea are from Yang-Gang province and North Ham-Kyoung province; the majority of defectors are female; and the very act of defection assumes a level of risk tolerance and life experiences among the people who successfully defected to a third country that may not be representative of all North Korean citizens. Nonetheless, however biased the information is that researchers are able to glean from a subset of defectors, it is essential that North Korean watchers continue to grapple with whatever data and sources are available for analysis to marginally enhance our understanding of this regime.

[8] Haggard and Noland 2007, 169.

Many of the thousands of North Koreans who fled to China eventually returned to North Korea, either of their own volition or through China's policy of forcible repatriation. These individuals took with them stories of what they had witnessed during their time in China: stories of plentiful food, even for domestic pets, bustling cities, and continuous electricity in private homes. Moreover, many people had watched television programs and movies, listened to international radio programs, and read materials that were forbidden in North Korea, but were safe to access in China. Such observations of wealth and exposure to newfound media and news led some North Koreans to ask themselves questions that were fundamentally disruptive to their belief in the state's propaganda. If North Korea was a socialist paradise, why was China so much richer? Why did ordinary North Koreans have to suffer through such poverty and famine while even China's poorest seemed to have plenty to eat? How come Chinese people felt free to criticize their Dear Leader?[9]

Those who did not return to North Korea either remained in hiding in China or escaped to South Korea and elsewhere, taking with them stories, memories, experiences, and testimonies of the realities of North Korea. The atrocious human rights situation that defectors' stories revealed in the late 1990s and early 2000s has captured the international community's attention ever since.[10] As the numbers of defectors who settled in South Korea increased throughout the 1990s and into the 2000s, small human rights groups, in addition to those in South Korea, emerged across the United States, Europe, and beyond. The shock value delivered by the stories of North Korea's prison camp survivors, family members affected by the guilt-by-association policy, and the victims of the regime's overall systematic human rights violations played an essential role in the nascent stages of small organizations that developed into what can now be labeled as a transnational advocacy network centered on raising awareness about, and trying to improve, the rights of North Korean citizens.

North Korean Human Rights 2.0: Information Efforts Building on North Korean Human Rights Advocacy

What is the significance of merely knowing about human rights violations in North Korea? Given high levels of awareness about the North Korean human

---

9 Baek 2016, 141.
10 Kang Chol Hwan's *Aquariums of Pyongyang*, published in French in 2000 and later translated into English (Kang 2001), was one of the first public accounts of North Korea's prison camps. *Seoul Train*, a 2004 documentary that traces the dangerous escapes of several defectors, was frequently screened across college campuses and churches around the world.

rights situation, and the high priority assigned to North Korean nuclear proliferation, how can actors within the North Korean human rights transnational advocacy network best advance their cause? Addressing this question, members of the existing North Korean human rights transnational advocacy network have laid a fertile ground for a subset of information-focused efforts to take further root.

If citizens *learning* about the human rights violations in North Korea comprise the phase "North Korean human rights 1.0," then perhaps citizens *taking action* to improve the human rights situation in the country are the next wave of activism among the North Korean human rights advocacy network. I label this new phase of action-based advocacy intended to directly impact North Korean citizens as "North Korean human rights 2.0."

Keck and Sikkink refer to transnational advocacy networks as networks of "activists, distinguishable largely by the centrality of principled ideas or values in motivating their formation."[11] Values are the essence of transnational advocacy networks, and this is certainly true of networks that have formed around the value of improving human rights for North Koreans through access to alternative sources of information, media, and news. To illustrate the significance of a shared value and vision in the North Korean human rights advocacy network, one could turn to various NGOs' driving vision statements. While they may differ in strategy and approach, the NGOs (many of which are in the next few paragraphs) are driven by the shared value and vision that North Korean people ought to live in a free democratic system that protects human rights.

In parallel to the increased attention on North Korea's human rights issues, more defector-led organizations surfaced largely due to South Korea's Sunshine Policy (1998–2008), which restricted human rights-focused activities to avoid antagonizing North Korea. Most South Korean government-led radio programs broadcasting into North Korea that had run for decades were ceased, and pressure was placed on high-profile defectors to stop airborne-leaflet campaigns into the North. Incredibly frustrated, North Korean defectors took it upon themselves to wage information campaigns as a substitute to the South Korean government's ceased information efforts. Many defectors believed that change in North Korea was urgent, and that it would only come about by providing more information to the North Korean people. As one such defector argued during a forum on Capitol Hill, "information is the best way to debilitate a communist regime ... it is the most effective way to inform the North Koreans of the

---

[11] Keck and Sikkink 1998, 1.

outer world and to bring them to rebel against the injustice in their own accord."[12]

In turn, coalitions of such groups with shared goals and values began to organize to reduce transaction costs and strengthen their collective organizing power. A well-known example of such a coalition is the North Korea Freedom Coalition (NKFC). Founded in 2003, NKFC has more than 70 member organizations, as well as private citizen members, that share the common belief that "promoting human rights for North Korea must be the central focus of any and all policy towards North Korea."[13]

NKFC's founding member and president, Suzanne Scholte, brought the first North Korean political prison camp survivors to Washington DC in the late 1990s to have them share their testimonies on Capitol Hill, and with the broader DC human rights and policy community. Since NKFC's inception, the organization has worked with individual defectors and defector-led organizations to raise awareness about human rights and to send information into North Korea, with the goal of changing the North Korean regime. A partner which NKFC works closely with and also supports is Free NK Radio (FNKR), the first defector-led radio station created in 2003 to broadcast into North Korea.[14] FNKR is an example of an organization that was founded partially out of frustration with South Korea's stance on stopping radio broadcasts into North Korea. Among other accomplishments, NKFC used its collective power to establish North Korea Freedom Week, an annual weeklong series of events in DC to raise awareness about the critical human rights conditions in North Korea. NKFC also played a major role in lobbying the US Congress to pass the North Korean Human Rights Act of 2004, which, among many other sections, includes clauses for the US government to provide "support for human rights and democracy programs," promote "radio broadcasting to North Korea," and take "actions to promote freedom of information."[15]

---

[12] The remarks were made by Choi Jeong-Hun, Broadcasting Director for Free NK Radio and Commander-in-Chief of North Korea People's Liberation Front (Defense Forum Foundation 2017).

[13] About the North Korea Freedom Coalition, n.d., nkfreedom.org/About-Us/About-Us.aspx.

[14] Led by defector Kim Seung Min, FNKR first started its programming on the Internet in 2003 and expanded to shortwave radio programming into North Korea in 2006.

[15] The North Korean Human Rights Act of 2004, sections 102, 103, and 104. The North Korean Human Rights Act which originally passed in 2004 was initially titled the North Korea Freedom Act. However, the original title implied regime change, and many in the US Congress still carried hopes for US–North Korean engagement. Therefore, the title, along with much of the legislative content, was changed to focus only on the human rights of North Koreans.

Difficulties of sending foreign information into the country include, but are not limited to, the challenges of disseminating media into and across North Korea, the interventions by the North Korean government to sabotage such efforts (for example, jamming radio and cellular waves, punishing smugglers who are caught), and deterrent measures imposed on citizens consuming information (unreasonable fines, sentences to detention centers or political prison camps, physical punishment, or even death). Despite such challenges, information initiatives have included both privately and publicly funded efforts. In addition to government-backed radio stations such as the Voice of America and Radio Free Asia, more informal organizations have also been sending information leaflets and USBs across the demilitarized zone and into North Korea for many years.[16]

Since the early 2000s, there has been an increase in the number of NGOs whose primary mission is to send information to this closed regime through digital, radio, and paper leaflet means. These groups are motivated by shared values of democracy, freedom, and the desire to bring a sense of truth and enlightenment to North Korean citizens. South Korean-based groups that send, or claim to send, information into North Korea include the Unification Media Group,[17] North Korea Intellectual Solidarity, North Korea Strategy Center, No Chain, FNKR, Fighters for Free North Korea, Now Action Unity Human Rights, small churches that support individual initiatives, and other small private groups. Moreover, there are approximately 50 "balloon warriors" in South Korea, many of them defectors, who send leaflets into North Korea without drawing public or media attention.[18]

Shiokaze is a Japanese shortwave radio station set up by the Investigating Committee on Missing Japanese Probably Related to North Korea (COMJAN) to broadcast into North Korea to target mainly Japanese abductees therein, as

---

[16] There have been several rounds of US State Department grants that support information access into North Korea emphasizing human rights, democracy, and other liberal values. Voice of America and Radio Free Asia have been broadcasting into North Korea for decades. KBS is a South Korean international broadcasting station that also broadcasts into North Korea. The British Broadcasting Corporation announced in 2016 that they will expand their broadcasting program to cover North Korea, and their program will commence soon. The UK parliament's All-Party Parliamentary Group on North Korea has recently raised the profile of information access projects by hosting public events to discuss this topic. *Furusato no Kaze* and *Nippon no Kaze* are Japanese government-funded shortwave radio broadcast programs that target Japanese abductees who are suspected to still be alive in North Korea.

[17] Unification Media Group has no relation to the ROK Ministry of Unification.

[18] While these activists tend to operate below the radar, a rare news report does highlight their work. See, for example, Choe 2016.

well as the general North Korean population.[19] European-based groups include the European Alliance for Human Rights in North Korea, and Human Rights without Frontiers. Both of these groups work to generate discussion and raise awareness about the human rights situation in the country. Across North America, the Bush Center for Freedom's North Korea program, Canadian Han Voice, Lumen, and Human Rights Foundation are some of the groups that aim to either raise awareness about or directly support projects that send information into North Korea. By no means is this a comprehensive list, but it is provided here to highlight the breadth of the groups that exist centered on the shared vision of ultimately bringing liberal values into this country.

From a practical perspective, the network enables groups to quickly share and distribute information. The North Korean information access groups embedded in the larger North Korean human rights transnational advocacy network are no different. A shared vision and mission to broaden the minds of the North Korean people, and to encourage critical thinking and questioning of their political status quo, drives activists and practitioners alike. A distinct feature of information access efforts is the extreme sensitivity of the work, as it places North Korean information consumers at high risks. As such, these networks do not always reveal or publicize best practices or other aspects of their work. And despite the interpersonal and interorganizational rivalries that afflict these networks, along with most advocacy movements and networks, actors do frequently exchange information to reduce general transaction costs.[20]

Contemporary realities of people-powered revolutions, pluralization of the creation of information, and the lowered cost of information dissemination with social media have engendered creative ideas about information access, free expression, and press freedom. In the world of North Korean human rights advocacy, information access initiatives have been brought to the foreground.

North Korea's Information Underground Today

Despite North Korea's severe deterrents against citizens' consumption of foreign information and media,[21] the domestic demand for banned information is growing, and the supply to meet the demand is diversifying and

---

[19]   COMJAN's mission is to investigate cases of Japanese citizens that are missing. Among their many strands of work is to gather information about the individual cases, and send information into North Korea via radio and leaflets to communicate to Japanese abductees.

[20]   These insights are observations derived by the author during ten years of research and work in this area. For a more detailed discussion, please refer to Baek 2016.

[21]   Kretchun, Lee, and Tuohy 2017, 2.

increasing. The range of digital and radio content being smuggled into North Korea includes news, books, music, soap operas and other forms of entertainment, interviews with defectors and nondefectors, and stories about everyday life outside of North Korea. Storage devices via which the content is smuggled include USBs, micro SD cards, and hard drives. Smuggled media devices that can play content include laptops, note-tels, cell phones, radios, and MP4 players. Additionally, there are illegal phone calls made between South Korean-based defectors and their families remaining in North Korea, and North Korean citizens and Chinese-based residents.[22] The purposes of these phone calls are typically to share personal updates, conduct business, and send remittances between defectors and their families residing in North Korea.

The North Korean market demand for illicit foreign content is being met by both enterprising, profit-driven individuals and ideals-driven activists who live outside of North Korea. It is difficult to delineate between natural market activities and smuggling activities by activists that jointly push foreign media into North Korea. Market activities and smuggling activities are closely linked because smugglers who are tied to activists residing outside North Korea supply information goods to North Korean marketeers, who then sell the goods to their customers in North Korean street markets.

There are three broad networks of actors that comprise the North Korean information access landscape: the altruism-driven networks, the demand-driven networks, and the profit-driven networks. The three groups' different motivating interests for playing their role in pushing and pulling information into North Korea is precisely what makes their concerted efforts relatively stable. And the steady stream of information flow into North Korea is important because providing opportunities for people to have repeated exposure to foreign information is what deepens North Korean citizens' curiosity for even more information.

First, there are the altruism-driven networks.[23] These are the largely altruistic activists and advocates residing outside North Korea who raise funds, create content, fill storage devices, broadcast radio programs, and create distribution networks to supply the content to smugglers, who can in turn deliver the goods to North Korean marketeers for in-country distribution. All the NGOs previously discussed in this chapter fall into this first category. Next, there are the demand-driven networks – the North Korean citizen consumers of foreign

---

[22] Kim 2014, 24.
[23] I have previously referred to these networks as "compassion-driven" rather than "altruism-driven" (Baek 2016, xvii). However, I believe "altruism" – as a less subjective phenomenon – better describes the broader motive that encompasses other, more specific emotions like compassion.

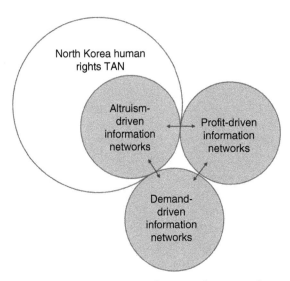

FIGURE 11.1 Relationship between North Korean human rights transnational advocacy networks and information networks

information. Despite the risk of severe punishment, curiosity to learn more about the world outside North Korea is only growing. Taking large risks to access foreign media is not a phenomenon that is restricted to elites or people residing near the China–North Korea border; almost every segment of society is consuming foreign media. Profit-driven networks comprise the third group of actors operating across the North Korean information access landscape. For these opportunistic individuals, the profits they make from delivering smuggled goods into North Korea outweigh the risks involved.

The different motives driving each specific, but still interlinked, information network – altruism/ideals, curiosity, and profits – ultimately align to create a relatively robust system to distribute information into and across North Korea. Maintaining a consistent flow of information into North Korea is crucial; repeat exposure to foreign information appears to have created a subtle, yet meaningful and irreversible change across North Korean society.

As Figure 11.1 indicates, there is a clear relationship between the human rights transnational advocacy network and the three interlinked information networks that send information into the country. The altruism-driven networks work with actors in the broader North Korean human rights transnational advocacy network and are driven by shared values and goals to improve the lives of North Koreans. The profit-driven networks are instrumental in enabling the altruism-networks/transnational advocacy network components to do their work, but they are, for the most part, not human rights advocates. They play a utilitarian role to make these networks function. Lastly, the demand-driven networks – the North Korean citizens – are the very reason why the overall transnational advocacy network exists. However, as information continues to flow into the country through various means, the North Korean government responds by developing its own mechanisms to monitor, censor, and deter the unwelcome information and media.[24]

THE EFFECTS AND IMPLICATIONS OF FOREIGN INFORMATION

What are the broader implications of an informed citizenry on the authoritarian regime of North Korea? From defector interviews, it can be extrapolated that the majority of citizens have consumed foreign media in large part due to defectors and other actors' efforts.[25] If large swaths of the population are repeatedly consuming foreign media and are questioning the veracity of the state's history and propaganda, what does that mean for the regime's control over its citizens, and for the future of North Korean human rights? How can more access to alternative sources of information improve the basic rights of North Korean citizens?

While there is no formula to predict how more information will improve North Korean human rights, there are mechanisms based on comparative historical contexts (such as the dissolution of the Soviet Union) and defector testimonies and surveys that can connect human rights with potential changes taking place inside North Korea. The following diagram is an attempt to organize how changes that have occurred (and have not yet occurred) resulting from information access may lead to improved human rights for North Koreans.

In Figure 11.2, the changes that have occurred as a result of information access are presented in bold, while the changes that have yet to take place are italicized. The box that squares "collective action" is emphasized to indicate that this is the immediate large-scale change that information campaigns are aimed at achieving as a causal step toward improved protections of human rights of North Koreans.

---

[24] For detailed research on North Korea's latest digital developments, including their signature system to block unsanctioned files from opening on North Korean devices, to further surveil and punish its citizens who consume foreign media, refer to Intermedia's latest report: Kretchun et al. 2017.

[25] See Do, Han, Hong, Kim, Lee, and Lim 2016, 208.

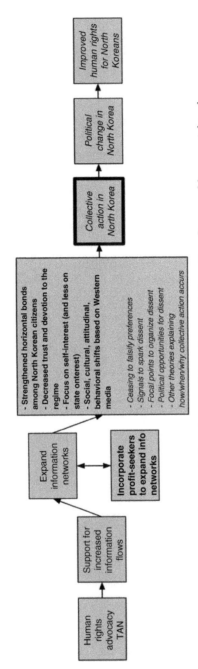

FIGURE 11.2 Mechanisms linking human rights advocacy, information flows, and human rights change

260

Several existing theories address the question of how and when collective action is triggered and mobilization unfolds. The select theoretical explanations which follow below help us begin to make sense of the unexpected nature of collective action and revolutions. That is, these theories can help guide thinking about the impact that information-access actors might have on the prospects of collective action in North Korea.

One model conceives of action that appears to have high costs attached to it as a form of signaling, which political leaders rely upon when trying to determine whether or not they should change the political status quo. The individuals who take the costly political action in pursuit of changing the status quo send signals both to other members of society and to political leaders.[26] This model assumes a scenario in which leaders are "office motivated" and wish to make policy that benefits the majority.[27] In North Korea, we know that at least some political elites have desired change: this has been demonstrated by high-level defections such as Hwang Jang Yop (1997) and Thae Yong Ho (2016).[28] However, the costs of action are extremely high (both actual and perceived political resistance is brutally repressed), and the likelihood of signals being sufficiently strong in a country with such severe restrictions on public information exchange is very low. Costly action thus remains an impediment in such a system, meaning that political leaders who might want to bring about change are not provided the incentives to do so. There is quite simply no meaningful political signaling taking place, especially not in the political capital of Pyongyang.

Another model suggests that focal points and their timing are what determine whether collective action will occur and escalate. Even if there were sufficient numbers of people in a society who harbor grievances and are convinced of taking a particular action, they might hesitate to act because there is no guarantee that others will join in such politically risky action.[29] But if there are focal points in society – such as fraudulent elections – that aggrieve much of a given population at the same time, individuals might feel assured that others will join in a given action. This way, focal points help to resolve the collective action problem of assurance barriers. Arguably, there has not been a focal point in North Korea meaningful enough to create the conditions for people who want to take action against the government to do so.[30]

---

[26] Lohmann 1993.   [27] Lohmann 1993, 320.   [28] Cotton 1998; Foster-Carter 2016.
[29] Tucker 2007, 541.
[30] It might be argued that the famine that occurred across North Korea in the mid-1990s could have served as such a focal point. However, as Fahy argues in her ethnographic study based on the oral testimonies of North Koreans now living outside the country, there was no space for collective action. Instead, resistance took on an individual form, and tended to be focused on

A different strand of theory argues that people will mobilize and protest if they recognize and are able to take advantage of an open political opportunity.[31] Perhaps collective action has been absent in impoverished North Korea because people are preoccupied with economic survival and consequently lack the capacity to think about, much less self-organize, dis-senting activities against the state. As Fahy argues, during the famine, an individual's decision to take action usually took the form of defection: "The individual act of leaving the North, while not personally identified as political or resisting authority, was the only way of generating the possibility for positive change in an individual's life trajectory. These revolts happened internally, and the risks and benefits were often those of the individual alone."[32] It is apparent that in North Korea there have not been any political opportunities conducive to collective action. Likely, the risk of state retaliation outweighs the potential benefits of action, even among those with sufficient access to information to incite them toward action.

The concept of preference falsification suggests that a revolution may occur when sufficient numbers of people in a society stop falsifying their preferences.[33] In an authoritarian state, the cost of speaking out against the state is very risky and, as a result, most people do not reveal their true opinions. Among a group of people who do not speak out are always a minority of individuals who harbor dissenting beliefs. Accordingly, when a critical mass publicly declares their true preferences, collective action may take place, and a revolution may occur. According to Kuran, "because preference falsification afflicts politics in every society, major revolutions are likely to come again and again as a surprise."[34]

North Koreans are prohibited from exhibiting their true preferences if those preferences are not politically acceptable. For example, all citizens must bow to statues of Kim Il Sung and Kim Jong Il because of the severe consequences of not showing respect to the leaders. The nation has been built on controlling its citizens' thoughts and actions so as to be completely loyal to the state. Thus, even if there are people whose actual private preferences deviate from the preferences they display in public, they are isolated, and usually unaware whether there are others that share their views. That is, North Korean people whose private preferences misalign with their public preference generally remain isolated because the cost of sharing such private preferences and having those opinions leaked to the authorities is too high.[35]

the task of surviving the famine rather than challenging the state apparatus. "Avoiding hunger in North Korea," Fahy (2015, 131) argues, "was a complex operation."
[31] Tarrow 1998; Kitschelt 1986.   [32] Fahy 2015, 130.   [33] Kuran 1991.   [34] Kuran 1991, 47.
[35] Baek 2016, 177, 194.

Conducting in-country surveys of people's true preferences and falsified preferences is not feasible. Therefore, the next best way to gain insight into the nature of the gap between public and private preferences among North Korean citizens is to interview defectors, as defectors can serve as a proxy – albeit an imperfect proxy – for North Korean citizens. It is common for North Koreans to bow to larger-than-life statues of Kim Il Sung and Kim Jong Il, attend mandatory self-criticism sessions, and participate in political activities while secretly harboring critical views toward the state. Defectors often state that despite their true feelings about the regime, such as not believing in the nation's ability to provide for all, they almost always displayed public political preferences that aligned with the expectations of the state. Conceptualized, this is a classic case of people falsifying their preferences due to the risk of stating their true preferences in public. When individuals hold views that do not correlate with publicly acceptable norms but do not wish to engage in risky political or social acts of defiance, they must choose to suppress or falsify their preferences.[36] As people consume unauthorized information and media, learn more about the outside world, and continue to question their government, the gap between public and private preferences will only grow.

Arguably, the absence of meaningful signals, focal points, and political opportunities, and the prevalence of preference falsification across North Korea, partially explains the lack of collective action in the country. However, increased access to foreign information could conceivably create conditions that are conducive to the sort of triggering signals, focal points, and political opportunities that these models show as leading to collective action.

We know that increased information access, whereby individuals in North Korea learn more about the outside world, has provided citizens with an increased number of reference points, and their absolute grievances have evolved into relative grievances. Drawing comparisons between their lives and the lives of those in other countries only magnifies the grievances that North Koreans harbor.[37] The more foreign information that actors send into North Korea, the more compounded people's relative grievances and critical opinions toward the state will become. Living in extreme poverty while believing that the North Korean government has the population's best interests at heart is different from living at the same level of extreme poverty and knowing that the North Korea is one of the poorest countries on the planet.

A rise in social trust and strong horizontal bonds among groups of people in any authoritarian country poses a direct threat to the central government

---

[36] This is explored in more detail in Kuran 1991.
[37] An interview with Jeong Gwang Il helped shape this insight. See Baek 2016, 168.

because social bonds lay down the groundwork for possible collective action in the future. Activists from across the political spectrum who seek to infiltrate North Korean borders with information share an assumption that the trust between close North Korean friends that enables sharing of illicit films could be repurposed for discussing sensitive political views in private. Such trust scaled up to broad swaths of the population creates a necessary – but not sufficient – condition for collective action. Aside from anecdotes of frustrated business owners arguing with local North Korean authorities, there is a dearth of publicly available evidence of citizen-led collective action taken against the North Korean government.[38] But there is evidence that social trust among citizens is growing. The growth of social trust is a historical precursor for collective action.[39]

As horizontal bonds strengthen across North Korean society, people may conceivably start sharing more about their private political preferences with each other. The more people reveal their private preferences to each other, the more emboldened people may become to take some type of action to change the status quo. While the author is not predicting a "Pyongyang Square" to take place anytime soon, she argues that the process of laying the groundwork for collective action has been underway in North Korea for some time, partly due to people's access to foreign media.

These collective action theories can help explain the possible implications that information-access actors may have, in the future, for collective action as a step toward improving the human rights of North Koreans. But there have also been observable changes in North Korea due to the efforts of information networks that are tangible signs of potential larger change.

MICRO CHANGES DUE TO FOREIGN INFORMATION
CONSUMPTION IN NORTH KOREA

North Korea's society and economy are experiencing an information revolution in slow motion, and much of the North Korean population, especially the millennials (or *jangmadang* generation),[40] are undergoing social, cultural,

---

[38]   I would like to caveat this sentence by recognizing that there have been known instances of resistance by military men, political camp prisoners, and students. These instances have been compiled on an influential North Korean human rights blog. See Stanton 2007.

[39]   Kramer, Brewer, and Hanna 1996.

[40]   *Jangmadang* are unofficial street markets. North Korean millennials comprise the age group of North Koreans born during or after the 1990s. Unlike children prior to the famine who took their ration cards to the local public distribution system and stood in line to receive their allocated food stuffs, children today ask their parents for cash to buy food and other items they need from these markets that are run by citizens. Attitudes toward the state will, of course, vary

attitudinal, and behavioral changes that could be linked to people's exposure to foreign media.

Despite the series of sanctions imposed on North Korea and the legally sealed China–North Korea border, trade between North Koreans and Chinese has powered the North Korean formal and informal markets.[41] Through this trading activity, North Koreans speak with Chinese traders and organically exchange information with them. In addition to human-to-human information exchange, North Koreans purchase foreign goods that inevitably make for comparisons between North Korean-made goods and higher-quality merchandise from other countries.[42]

The qualitative interviews that the author conducted for a larger book project that describes and analyzes the information underground in North Korea suggests that repeatedly consuming foreign information and media has a meaningful impact on North Korean consumers.[43] While defectors comprise an unrepresentative segment of the overall population, they are more accessible to researchers than North Korean citizens living within the country's borders. Defectors' interviews and testimonies are the closest proxies to the stories and experiences of citizens residing in North Korea. Therefore, the burden is on researchers to carefully and methodically extrapolate insights from such surveys and interviews of defectors and to try to generalize findings to the overall population. Based on this type of available data, it is possible to observe micro-changes taking place in-country that can be causally linked to foreign information and media.

by individual, but there are generalizable observations that can be made across generation and class.

[41] Depending on the source, there is an estimated range of 404–750 formal and informal markets across the country: Korea Development Institute estimates there to be 404 formalized markets in North Korea; Curtis Melvin counted 406 formal markets according to Google Earth satellite imagery as of November 2015; South Korean analyst Lim Eul-Chul of the Institute for Far Eastern Studies at Kyungnam University estimates 750 formal and informal markets across the country.

[42] For more information on the process and effects of grassroots marketization, refer to Haggard and Noland 2011.

[43] See Baek 2016. Because the government will never grant permission, it is not possible to conduct verifiable, statistically significant in-country surveys to track social and cultural changes taking place, and link them to foreign information consumption. However, large-N interviews conducted by South Korean think-tanks and government agencies as well as by the US Broadcasting Board of Governors surveys reveal a robust correlation between repeat consumers of foreign media, and carrying positive attitudes toward the outside world and skepticism toward the North Korean government, its indoctrination, and propaganda. Examples of such large-N surveys include InterMedia's two reports (Kretchun and Kim 2012; Kretchun et al. 2017), UN Human Rights Council (2014), and the Korea Institute for National Unification's annual white papers on human rights in North Korea.

Particularly since the 1990s and the famine, which brought with it markets and the infiltration of foreign information, peoples' experiences have started to contradict state propaganda. There is growing evidence, for example, that younger people in particular may be starting to question much of what they hear via state radio, television, and newspapers, and from school officials.[44] This lack of devotion to the state presents a clear challenge to the authoritarian government; it must either adapt its narrative and policies to meaningfully capture the younger citizens' loyalty or continue to lose credibility and support among the millennials, whose influence – over time – will naturally eclipse that of the older generations. If it does not adapt to the times, Kim's government risks experiencing unpredictable and dramatic changes that it may not be able to control.

The soft power of foreign media is having an extraordinary effect on the minds of consumers across North Korea, especially among younger people. The *jangmadang* generation has grown up depending primarily on markets and having unprecedented levels of access to foreign media.[45] As a result, a significant portion of the population is adopting social and cultural behaviors that reflect the foreign content of what they have viewed or listened to. Behaviors include using South Korean slang spoken in South Korean television shows, using clothing and hair fashion trends to imitate foreign actors and actresses, and adopting social and courtship practices that are more Western in nature.[46] While such behaviors may seem innocuous, if they are widespread they reflect a fundamental shift in how North Korean citizens now view South Korea, the United States, and other nonsocialist countries. While movie watchers may not view the United States and South Korea as friendly allies, it is likely that they no longer categorically perceive these countries to be the hostile imperialist and the puppet state, respectively, that North Korea portrays them to be. Rather, for young people, the trends and people from these historically adversarial states seem to be increasingly seen as worth imitating.

Another distinct observable difference between North Koreans today and citizens from two or three decades prior is that many people today appear to prioritize their self-interests over their loyalty to the state. One way this observation manifests itself is in people's resolve to watch and listen to foreign media. While cognizant that information crimes are severely punished, some citizens repeatedly break the law and engage in "Western decadent culture" to feed their appetite for news and media.

---

[44] Baek 2016, 185.
[45] See, for example, Baek 2016, 186; Lee and Swartz 2015. For a detailed account of the "jangmadang generation," see the LiNK documentary (Liberty in North Korea n.d.).
[46] Tudor and Pearson 2015, 134, 141.

Watching foreign media is not always a solitary act. North Koreans have devised rotational lending schemes among trusted friends and neighbors to circulate people's forbidden soap operas and movies.[47] Moreover, there has been a rise in interpersonal communication within North Korea and outside the country through both legal and illicit cell phones to conduct business, trade information about prices, and to keep in touch with family members who have defected. Trust among people enables parties to conduct business and transfer money, gain customers, and maintain good reputations to entice repeat business. In a society where a banking system does not exist for most of the population, people's business operations depend on trust and word of mouth. The increase in information-sharing through foreign media lending networks and alternative means of communication among North Koreans reveals rising social trust and stronger horizontal bonds among citizens than before.[48] In a country notorious for having political "snitches" in the *inminban* unit ("people's group"), and even within family units, this rise in trust among close friends and family is a novel social phenomenon that has broader social implications beyond sharing media and entertainment.[49]

CONCLUSION

The North Korean human rights transnational advocacy network encompasses many actors that actively support information flows and expanded information networks. There are significant observable social, cultural, behavioral, and attitudinal shifts in North Korea that can be attributed to consumption of foreign information. Such changes are arguably irreversible and are helping in gradually shifting social structures in North Korea. As small and nonpolitical in nature as the changes are, they do underscore that North Korean society is capable of change. Additionally, despite the widespread belief that Kim Jong Un has been cracking down on citizens consuming foreign information, his deterrent measures do not seem to adequately prevent people from taking risks to learn more about the outside world.[50]

---

[47] Baek 2016, 182.   [48] See Baek 2016, 222–3.

[49] *Inminban* is a neighborhood-based people's group, each comprising 20 to 40 families. Every citizen is assigned to an inminban, which is usually run by a middle-aged female resident. Its purpose is to surveil and monitor citizens, and also execute collective projects. For further descriptions, refer to Lankov 2013, 40–1.

[50] Kretchun, Lee, and Tuohy, 2017, 16. Baek (2016, 62) refers to dialogue with defector Gwang Seong, who discusses how even executions were not sufficient deterrents for people to commit "information crimes."

Ultimately, however, these micro-changes spurred by foreign information consumption were not a result of information campaigns changing the regime's behavior toward better protecting its citizens' rights. These changes were a result of actors directly targeting citizens, rather than trying to pressure the Kim leadership to adopt human rights norms. What can we learn from this?

The transnational advocacy network literature assumes the existence of a civil society in the norm-violating country that can then ally with outside actors to put pressure on the norm-violating government to change its behavior. This is most commonly conceptualized as a boomerang model of influence, as originally conceived by Keck and Sikkink.[51] The transnational advocacy network literature does not account for outliers such as North Korea, where there is absolutely no civil society. In this literature, human rights outcomes are usually focused on changes in state practice, but observable changes in North Korea point to information actors bypassing the North Korean regime to target citizens directly.[52]

In North Korea's case, the boomerang model of influence cannot materialize due to the absence of organized domestic groups to ally with international actors. However, what *has* happened is that North Korean defectors have allied with international actors to pressure the North Korean government to change its behavior and better protect its citizens' rights. Since many of these activists perceive that international efforts to *substantively* change the North Korean government's domestic behavior have failed, they have resorted to targeting citizens directly in the hope of improving human rights.

The strategy of directly targeting citizens in pursuit of change is based on the inherent belief that the Kim regime will never substantively improve human rights for its citizens, for fear of its own survival.[53] The assumption is that, if the Kim regime meaningfully expands the protection of some human rights (for example, the freedom of association, expression, and movement), sections of the population will certainly exercise these newly protected rights by expressing their grievances and demanding change and accountability. Acts of dissent and collective action may soon follow, and some form of political reform or even some kind of regime change may occur.

---

[51] Keck and Sikkink 1998.
[52] For more on this, see Chubb and Yeo (Chapter 1 of this volume).
[53] Separate interviews with human rights activists affirmed this assumption. Author's interview with Henry Song (North America director for No Chain), by telephone, July 12, 2017; Author's interview with Suzanne Scholte (Director of North Korea Freedom Coalition), by telephone, July 13, 2017.

Arguably, the best way to effect change in North Korea is a twinned approach of pressuring the regime to change and sending information for North Korean citizens' consumption, and this is what has been taking place. Governments have been pressuring the North Korean regime through formal channels to better protect its citizens' rights, and the human rights advocacy network has been working through informal channels to transmit information into the country. Increasingly, however, the information-access actors are losing hope that the regime will meaningfully change its behavior, and thus they put even more faith in pursuing better human rights outcomes directly, encouraging the development of an independent civil society within North Korea, with enhanced information initiatives.

REFERENCES

Baek, Jieun. 2016. *North Korea's Hidden Revolution: How the Information Underground is Transforming a Closed Society*. New Haven: Yale University Press.

Choe, Sang-Hun. 2016. A "Balloon Warrior" Subverts North Korea, Thousands of Leaflets at a Time. *The New York Times*. October 14. www.nytimes.com/2016/10/15/world/asia/south-north-korea-balloon-drop.html.

Citizens' Alliance for North Korea Human Rights. 2009. *The Criminal Law of the Democratic People's Republic of Korea*. Seoul: Citizens' Alliance for North Korean Human Rights.

Cotton, James. 1998. The Rajin-Sonbong FTZ Experiment: North Korea in Pursuit of New International Linkages. In *North Korean Foreign Relations in the Post-Cold War Era*, edited by Samuel S. Kim, 212–34. Oxford: Oxford University Press.

Defense Forum Foundation. 2017. Working for Regime Change in North Korea through Broadcasting and Other Means. *Defense Forum Foundation Congressional Defense and Foreign Policy Forum*. April 28. defenseforumfoundation.net/images/stories2017/DFF-042817-transcription.pdf.

Do, Kyung-Ok, Han Dong-Ho, Hong Min, Kim Soo-Am, and Lee Keum-Soon. 2015. *White Paper on Human Rights in North Korea 2015*. Seoul: Korea Institute for National Unification.

Do, Kyung-Ok, Han Dong-Ho, Hong Min, Kim Soo-Am, Lee Keum-Soon, and Lim Ye-Jun. 2016. *White Paper on Human Rights in North Korea 2016*. Seoul: Korea Institute for National Unification.

Fahy, Sandra. 2015. *Marching through Suffering: Loss and Survival in North Korea*. New York: Columbia University Press.

Foster-Carter, Aidan. 2016. South Korea-North Korea Relations: A Toxic Nuclear Tocsin. *Comparative Connections* 18 (2), Sept. 2016: 81–92.

Haggard, Stephen, and Marcus Noland. 2007. *Famine in North Korea: Markets, Aid, and Reform*. New York: Columbia University Press.

Haggard, Stephen, and Marcus Noland. 2009. *Famine in North Korea: Markets, Aid, and Reform*. New York: Columbia University Press.

Haggard, Stephen, and Marcus Noland. 2011. *Witness to Transformation: Refugee Insights into North Korea*. Washington DC: Peterson Institute for International Economics.

Kang, Chol Hwan, and Pierre Rigoulot. 2001. *The Aquariums of Pyongyang: Ten Years in a North Korean Gulag*. Translated by Yair Reiner. New York: Basic Books.

Keck, Margaret E., and Kathryn Sikkink. 1998. *Activists Beyond Borders: Advocacy Networks in International Politics*. Ithaca: Cornell University Press.

Kim, Yongho. 2014. Cell Phones in North Korea: Has North Korea Entered the Telecommunications Revolution? *A US–Korea Institute & Voice of America Report*. Washington DC: US-Korea Institute at SAIS.

Kitschelt, Herbert. 1986. Political Opportunity Structures and Political Protest: Anti-Nuclear Movements in Four Democracies. *British Journal of Political Science* 16 (1): 57–85.

Kramer, Roderick M., Marilynn B. Brewer, and Benjamin A. Hanna. 1996. Collective Trust and Collective Action: The Decision to Trust as a Social Decision. In *Trust in Organizations: Frontiers of Theory and Research*, edited by Kramer Roderick and Tom Tyler, 357–89. Thousand Oaks: Sage Publications.

Kretchun, Nat, and Jane Kim. 2012. *A Quiet Opening: North Koreans in a Changing Media Environment*. Washington DC: InterMedia.

Kretchun, Nat, Catherine Lee, and Seamus Tuohy. 2017. *Compromised Connectivity: Information Dynamics Between the State and Society in a Digitizing North Korea*. Washington DC: InterMedia.

Kuran, Timur. 1991. Now Out of Never: The Element of Surprise in the East European Revolution of 1989. *World Politics* 44 (1) 7–48.

Lankov, Andrei. 2013. *The Real North Korea: Life and Politics in the Failed Stalinist Utopia*. Oxford: Oxford University Press.

Lee, Jihae, and George Swartz. 2015. "Jangmadang Generation" at the Core of Change in NK. *Daily NK*. July 6.

Liberty in North Korea. n.d. The Jangmadang Generation. libertyinnorthkorea.org/ja ngmadang-generation/.

Lohmann, Susanne. 1994. The Dynamics of Informational Cascades: The Monday Demonstrations in Leipzig, East Germany, 1989–1991. *World Politics* 47: 42–101.

Lohmann, Susanne. 1998. A Signaling Model of Informative and Manipulative Political Action. *The American Political Science Review* 87 (2): 319–33.

North Korea Strategy Center. n.d. NKSC at a glance: NKSC's history. http://nksc.us /about-nksc/#history.

Polity IV. 2014. Authority Trends, 1948–2013: North Korea. *Center for Systemic Peace*. systemicpeace.org/polity/prk2.htm.

Reporters Without Borders. 2017. World Press Freedom Index. rsf.org/en/ranking.

Stanton, Joshua. 2007. Can They Do It? A Brief History of Resistance to the North Korean Regime. *One Free Korea*. March 6. freekorea.us/2007/03/06/can-they-do-it-a-brief-history-of-resistance-to-the-north-korean-regime/.

Tarrow, Sidney G. 1986. *Power in Movement: Social Movements and Contentious Politics*. Cambridge: Cambridge University Press.

Tarrow, Sidney G. 1998. *Power in Movement: Social Movements and Contentious Politics*. 2nd edn. Cambridge: Cambridge University Press.

Tucker, Joshua. 2007. Enough! Electoral Fraud, Collective Action Problems, and post-Communist Colored Revolutions. *Perspectives on Politics* 5 (3) 535–51.

Tudor, Daniel, and James Pearson. 2015. *North Korea Confidential: Private Markets, Fashion Trends, Prison Camps, Dissenters and Defectors*. Singapore: Tuttle Publishing.

UN Human Rights Council. 2014. *Report of the Commission of Inquiry on Human Rights in the Democratic People's Republic of Korea*. A/HRC/25/63. February 7.

12

Conclusion
The Contentious Terrain of North Korean Human Rights Activism

Andrew Yeo and Danielle Chubb

The chapters collected in this volume provide insights into the ways activists in various contexts have pursued the issue of North Korean human rights. The stories that emerge reveal a contentious terrain, where relations between activists and groups are defined by the different ideas they bring to the table, in terms of how to bring about real change for the North Korean people. The volume, therefore, brings the discursive frames that surround activists and their networks into the spotlight. By identifying and unpacking the ideas – as reflected in discourse – that drive activism, we shed light on the wide variety of debates taking place within the civil society sphere and the larger transnational advocacy network. Taken together, these expositions provide rare insights into the long and often difficult path activists have trodden in their quest to shed light on the human rights abuses taking place inside North Korea, and to advocate for better outcomes. The complex interactions within and between civil society and state actors in the North Korean human rights network have shaped public conceptions of how North Korean human rights are viewed today. We learn, crucially, about why certain rights conceptions have become more dominant than others, as well as points of convergence and divergence within debates over North Korean human rights.

In Chapter 1, we argued that activists' interpretations of their normative commitments, reflected in their discursive frames, carry consequences for advocacy movements and their subsequent outcomes. In the case of North Korean human rights, the outcomes pursued by activists are diverse and range from bringing about human-rights-compliant behavior in the repressive state to provoking regime change or collapse. As such, the chapters in this volume explore the varieties of discursive frames that activists deploy and the relationship between such discursive frames, transnational mobilization, and human rights advocacy outcomes. This concluding chapter will offer some reflections on the themes that have emerged in this volume, articulate observations on the value of empirically driven research into transnational activism, and consider the implications of the volume's findings for scholarship and policy.

The report from the UN COI on North Korean human rights puts the responsibility for post-COI action squarely in the hands of the DPRK, as well as a broad collection of outside actors including China, South Korea (and the South Korean people), civil society, and the "international community" as a whole. The recommendations put forward by the Commission's report are wide-ranging, including the referral of North Korean leadership to the ICC, the fostering of inter-Korean dialogue, and the promotion of people-to-people dialogue. Most poignantly, the COI report implored the UN Human Rights Council (UNHRC) to "ensure that the conclusions and recommendations of the Commission do not pass from the active attention of the international community. Where so much suffering has occurred and is still occurring, action is the shared responsibility of the entire international community."[1]

Our project began with the simple proposition that if we wish to understand the obstacles and opportunities facing the international community as it seeks to act on the report's various recommendations, we should first look at the evolution of North Korean human rights discourse, at both the domestic and transnational levels. The points of convergence and contention that have characterized discourse and activism in these spaces are reflected in the COI report, and a greater understanding of how state and nonstate actors have navigated this terrain provides a distinct and comprehensive reading of where the international community stands with respect to the North Korean human rights issue.

Three major themes emerge from this volume. First, particular interpretations of human rights dominate the network's agenda, thus reflecting the values and motivations of the actors involved within it. Second, the chapters reveal the important role that state-based actors have played within advocacy networks across a variety of domestic and regional contexts. Finally, we find that while a strong advocacy network clearly exists (corroborated by the similar patterns and parallels revealed across the chapters), actors within the network have proven themselves remarkably adaptive. The network is simultaneously

---

[1] UN Human Rights Council 2014, sect. V.94(f).

cohesive and fractured, and deliberately so. In the paragraphs that follow, we briefly consider each of these themes in turn.

Defining the Discursive Terrain: The Politicization of North Korean Human Rights

Human right advocates in this space have been engaged in long-running conversations about the types of approaches needed to bring about human rights change in North Korea, and which actors are best equipped to bring about such change. Conversations taking place in South Korea, the United States, Japan, and Europe, for example, take on their own distinctive discursive and normative forms, which then feed into the transnational sphere. At the same time, the evolving discursive terrain at the transnational level is reflected back into domestic debates, with actors continually responding to the changing shape of North Korean human rights discourse. A thematic focus of many chapters in this volume has been the question of how actors understand and interpret the North Korean human rights debate.

In South Korea, for example, debates over North Korean human rights have been dominated by conservative voices, as illustrated by Reidhead in Chapter 2. However, in part due to resistance from progressive South Korean lawmakers who were reticent to take a public stand on the North Korean human rights issue out of concern that it would jeopardize inter-Korean engagement opportunities, South Korea's National Assembly could not pass its own domestic legislation on North Korean human rights. This began to change with the establishment of the COI, which, alongside the growing transnational movement supporting the COI's findings, helped shift the tenor of human rights discourse in South Korea. Where North Korean human rights were once seen as an issue dominated by radical, anticommunist conservatives, the COI and the international profile and legitimacy the UNHRC provided pushed North Korean human rights into the South Korean conservative mainstream. As Goedde notes in Chapter 7, the COI report increased pressure on the South Korean government to pass a North Korean human rights bill which had been stalled in the National Assembly for more than a decade.

Although the COI report helped push North Korean human rights out of the shadows and placed it on the agenda of the international community, there is no doubt that debate on North Korean human rights – certainly, debate that is audible to the political mainstream – is politicized, and often framed through the lens of an isolationist, political-change paradigm. In South Korea, arguments around economic, social, and cultural rights are often disconnected from the broader human rights debate and tend to form part of a progressive, rather than conservative, agenda. The evolution of discourse in the United States, while forming a longer trajectory (as explicated by Yeo in Chapter 3) has also seen a great deal of interaction between conservative political forces and the civil society sphere. In the US context, discourse over North Korean human rights was shaped by Cold War–era debates suffused with anticommunist ideology. The conservative paradigm that tends to dominate discourse over North Korean human rights in both South Korea and the US has thus evolved within a broader political context. In Japan, too, discourse around North Korean human rights is linked inextricably with a localized, political agenda. Arrington's conceptualization of North Korean human rights discourse as "multivalent" highlights the interaction between the emotive abductions issue and the broader human rights narrative that has taken root. In Japan, different networks and organizations have come together and deployed distinctive conceptions of North Korean human rights.

Shifting attention to Europe, Narayan in Chapter 5 suggests that the conversation on North Korean human rights appears more diversified. Narayan points to the idea of "critical engagement" where human rights advocates have worked with states to shape a foreign policy outlook which seeks to maintain a constructive relationship with the North Korean government while at the same time introducing human rights issues into the dialogue. Of course, drawing North Korea into a dialogue about their own human rights situation is at the core of a UN-focused strategy. As Hosaniak demonstrates in Chapter 6, transnational coalitions have used diplomatic tools to introduce ideas of accountability into North Korean human rights discourse and advocacy. In Europe and at the UN, therefore, activists draw on ideas around dialogue and consultation, which coalesces with the EU's broader foreign policy framework.[2] Here, discursive frames employed by activists are less affected by local political ideologies than they might be in South Korea, the United States, and Japan, and this has proven to have direct consequences for strategies. Rather than seeking to isolate North Korea, activists seek to engage, or to at least place pressure on, the regime within the UN institutional framework.

Network Composition: The Role of the State

A second theme, and one closely connected to the above, is the important activist role that state actors play within the broader network. Their role has

[2] Keukeleire and MacNaughtan 2008, 165–7.

carried significant implications for the North Korean human rights movement's discursive and strategic evolution. Reidhead's observations of the trajectory of human rights discourse in South Korea leads him to the conclusion that the human rights debate has been entirely co-opted by political entities and linked to partisan ideas about how to induce change in North Korea. Yeo similarly sees a significant role for the state in the US context, arguing that state actors and discourse provided a preexisting discursive structure dating back to Cold War–era ideas around democracy promotion and civil and political rights. In both these cases, the insertion of (neo)conservative elements into the movement, while elevating the profile of the issue, also closed off network membership to activists and organizations not willing to associate themselves with what they saw as an increasingly politicized – and political – right-wing agenda. There is nothing natural about the association of the North Korean human rights issue with conservative ideology, and to understand how this has come about, the role of state structures and agents has proven to be important.

In Japan, the framing of the abductions issue as part of the broader story of North Korean human rights has taken place with a high level of coordination between state and nonstate actors. While a range of different categories of activists have all worked to shape the discourse on North Korean human rights, the strong involvement of the state in the abductions issue has influenced the trajectory of the domestic movement. Arrington describes the politics behind the signing of the 2006 North Korean Abductions and Human Rights Act, which consolidated the abductions issue as part of a broader human rights narrative. In Europe, while the issues at stake are very different from the Japanese context, here too activists work within a sphere that is already dominated by state institutions. EU dialogue with the DPRK tends to dominate the framework around which activism is formed in the EU. Here, the narrative is considerably less politicized than it is in Japan, South Korea, and the United States – most likely, as Narayan observes, because of the physical separation of the EU from the Northeast Asian region and its geopolitics. European nonstate actors, as noted earlier, thus work within a formal institutional template that has allowed direct interaction between state actors and the DPRK. We further explore the policy implications of this state-nonstate actor interaction in the final section of this chapter.

Fractured but Effective: The Benefits of Adaptive Activism

Finally, at the center of all these political debates lies the core question of which strategies will work best to draw North Korea into the fold of human rights-respecting states. We argued in Chapter 1 that current models of human rights change, which revolve around transnational engagement with domestic actors, must be expanded to take into account mechanisms for change applied by actors within the North Korean human rights movement. As Baek (Chapter 11) discusses in detail, some activists have turned their attention to strategies directly targeted at North Korean citizens. We label this approach "subversive" for its tendency to bypass state structures altogether and breach the North Korean government's information blockade.

At the heart of this subversive action is the motivating belief that change is impossible within the current political context and that the only way forward is to challenge the legitimacy of the North Korean regime by activating the consciousness of the North Korean people. Distinct from actors applying these sorts of direct mechanisms for change are activists that choose to work through the more well-worn pathways of state-centered diplomacy. As Goedde illustrates in Chapter 7, without local partners able to bring about change "from below," some activists have focused their attention on bringing change from "above." To do this, they must bring the state into the conversation, and it is in this context that legal mechanisms have become a key tool for activists. This approach differs substantially from that of activists promoting subversive change. Not only do these network actors work within the state-centric UN framework, their reliance on transnational legal mechanisms produces a top-down style of advocacy, contrasted with the bottom-up focus of those groups trying to plant the seeds of a grassroots movement.

As Goedde (Chapter 7), Chubb (Chapter 8), and Fahy (Chapter 10) all note, these twin approaches to the issue of North Korean human rights – pursuing change through top-down legal mechanisms and bottom-up information campaigns coupled with disruptive sanctions tactics – have worked to the advantage of the network. Actors have proven themselves adaptive insofar as they have leveraged off the success of each other. Actors advocating direct action actively participated in the COI information collection and cite the report as evidence of the legitimacy of their broader claims for change. Actors that prefer to work within UN structures have benefited directly from the profile of the dominant voices of the campaign – most of which align with the "direct action" side of the movement – in terms of raising awareness on North Korean human rights among the broader international community.

The North Korean human rights movement has also been notable for the role defector voices have played in providing important evidentiary weight to the movement's core claims. The very use of the term "defectors" is a political act, and one adopted deliberately by the self-styled "defector-activists."[3] Song, in Chapter 9, notes that defector narratives are shaped by a range of factors related to experiences following defection, which in turn shape the individual identities of defectors. There is no doubt, she argues, that the transnational agenda has conversely been shaped by the identity formation of these defectors, which coexists in a complex environment with human rights narratives. Without these defector voices – as complicated and at times controversial as they might be – the North Korean human rights movement would look very different today.

The evidence-based research undertaken by our contributors has provided a rich and varied understanding of how the North Korean human rights activist movement operates, the intranetwork dynamics at play, and the types of strategies adopted by actors in various parts of the movement. Their research provides nuance and depth to scholarly work that has previously approached the issue of North Korean human rights activism and policy from a normative perspective. This latter body of work tends to draw direct links between the motivations of actors interested in security issues on the Korean peninsula, and the human rights agenda of such actors. As we discuss in the next section, while the security–human rights linkage is certainly an important part of this story, it falls short in providing a comprehensive understanding of the actors and issues at play.

HEGEMONY, IMPERIALISM, AND SCHOLARLY DEBATES ON
NORTH KOREAN HUMAN RIGHTS

In our preface, and in Chubb's contribution in Chapter 8, we acknowledged a two-part special issue on North Korean human rights in the journal *Critical Asian Studies (CAS)*, guest edited by Christine Hong and Hazel Smith.[4] This special issue is perhaps one of the first major academic projects devoted to the topic of North Korean human rights published in English, and certainly one of the first to challenge the dominant framing of North Korean human rights.[5] On the one hand, the CAS special issue provides a useful corrective to the overwhelming focus on political rights (that is: torture, political prisons, arbitrary arrest, execution, and so on) by including articles which

---

3   As Hosaniak notes, this term does not belong to official UN terminology, where North Koreans testifying about human rights abuses are more commonly referred to as victims.
4   Hong 2013. While Hong is the sole author of the introductory article, the journal lists both Hong and Smith as guest editors.
5   Other scholars have written about North Korean human rights, including critical perspectives, but usually as part of a larger study on North Korean politics and society or as a shorter stand-alone piece. Lankov 2013; Moon 2008; Smith 2014; Feffer 2004.

address the right to health,[6] human security,[7] and humanitarian and development assistance.[8] On the other hand, we believe that the effort in the special issue's framing introductory chapter to link the North Korean human rights movement to a wider imperialist agenda[9] misconstrues the more complex dynamics of the advocacy network and the different domestic and transnational contexts in which North Korean human rights discourse has emerged. Because Hong's focus on narrative resonates with our own examination of human rights discourse (and also because it precedes our work), we find it useful to engage with this perspective and advance what we believe to be a more balanced and comprehensive understanding of North Korean human rights activism.

In the CAS special issue's introductory article, Hong seeks to expose the imperialist regime-change agenda underpinning the North Korean human rights enterprise. As Hong argues, the dominant framing of NKHR is "relatively presentist in its assignment of blame and politically harnessed to a regime-change agenda."[10] Hong continues that this agenda allows the human rights advocate to "assume a moralizing, implicitly violent posture towards a 'regime' commonsensically understood to be 'evil,'" and thus to militarize the human rights agenda.[11] Our research, to some degree, corroborates the findings and claims made in the CAS special issue. Reidhead's analysis of the shift in human rights discourse in South Korea from a humanitarian framing to one of political rights is consistent with arguments made by several contributors to the CAS special issue.[12] Yeo's study on the significant role state actors play in shaping human rights discourse in US foreign policy, and the alignment between security and human rights in the framing of North Korea within US policy and activist communities, also supports what Smith identifies as "the unconscious adoption of a securitized perspective through which knowledge about North Korea is filtered."[13] Despite these commonalities, however, we respectfully disagree with Hong's depiction of the North Korean human rights advocacy movement, and the heavy emphasis on US hegemony as the key culprit driving North Korean human rights discourse and advocacy.

Earlier, Chubb noted that Hong failed to take into account the diversity of actors working on North Korean human rights and the complexity of the strategies deployed within the broader network. Here, it is worth recalling in full Hong's characterization of the North Korean human rights movement:

---

[6] Shin and Choi 2013.   [7] Liem 2014.   [8] Bae and Moon 2014; Moon 2014.
[9] Hong 2013.   [10] Hong 2013, 511.   [11] Hong 2013, 511, 516.
[12] Moon 2014. See also Bae and Moon 2014 in the same issue.   [13] Smith 2014, 127.

> The North Korean human rights project ... has allowed a spectrum of
> political actors – US soft-power institutions, thinly renovated Cold War
> defense organizations, hawks of both neoconservative and liberal varieties,
> conservative evangelicals, anticommunist Koreans in South Korea and the
> diaspora, and North Korean defectors – to join together in common cause ...
> The past decade has been witness to the consolidation of a US funded
> transnational advocacy, propaganda and intelligence network under the
> elastic banner of North Korean human rights.[14]

We concur with Hong that many of the voices speaking on the North Korean
human rights issue engage in a binary representation of tyranny and freedom,
and that these voices are often the loudest and may even constitute the public
face of the movement. Such findings were supported by several of our contributors and corroborated by the hyperlink analysis of NGOs provided in
Chapter 8. However, neoconservative and liberal hawks, evangelicals, and
anticommunist South Koreans who might represent the hardline faction of
the transnational movement do not constitute the totality of human rights
activism. Nor do such binary categorizations underpin the language of the UN
COI report, which we take as our standard for evaluating North Korean
human rights discourse. Hong's assertion that human rights "advocates figure,
in the framework of North Korean human rights, as beneficiaries of future
violence"[15] derives from what we see to be at best an incomplete understanding of the network's discourse, goals, strategies, and ideas. As we argued in this
volume, activists are in fact nimble and demonstrate a remarkable ability to
negotiate a contested normative frame.

The brand of North Korean human rights advocacy articulated in the
CAS introductory piece (which is certainly not reflective of all the articles
in the special issue) is in part due to what we see as a selective reading of
North Korean human rights. The dominant human rights framing Hong
portrays resembles arguments most prevalent in the United States in the
early 2000s, when regime change rhetoric resonated with several leading
voices within US-based advocacy networks. Yet, this framing is not indicative of the broader discussion on North Korean human rights which has, in
the years since, taken place elsewhere – in Europe or in Japan, or at the UN
or EU.

If at one point the dominant narrative of North Korean human rights
revolved around regime change, today this is no longer the case, or at least it
exists in conjunction with other narratives (that is, the accountability
narrative). Our inquiry into the evolution of North Korean human rights

---

[14] Hong 2013, 511, 518.   [15] Hong 2013, 522.

discourse, and its relationship to the rise of a transnational advocacy movement, therefore assumes a more fluid understanding of narrative (and, by
extension, discourse). Narratives and discourse are not static, despite the
(re)production and recycling of evidence generated by North Korean defector testimonies, NGO reports, official government statements, and news
media accounts.[16] Even when such discourses are embedded in deep-seated
historical, institutional, and geopolitical structures, as Hong and Smith
suggest, actors carry the potential to shift existing narratives as they interact
with others. This is particularly true as new actors join the transnational
advocacy fold. Issues of credibility notwithstanding,[17] North Korean defector-activists have given the transnational advocacy network a new voice
since the early 2000s. A selection of NGOs, including some funded by the
National Endowment for Democracy, do continue to talk about regime
change. But many others do not, instead focusing their energies on social
and economic issues, regime accountability, and the application of international law to prod the North Korean regime to comply with international
norms and laws.

FROM SCHOLARLY DEBATES TO POLICY IMPLICATIONS

Putting aside important theoretical aims and scholarly debates, this project
was foremost intended to provide activists, policymakers, students, and scholars a better understanding of the evolution of North Korean human rights
advocacy. Much of this chapter has recapped various scholarly debates, ranging from new insights on transnational advocacy networks drawn from the
case of North Korean human rights to a critique of critical perspectives on
North Korea and the need for presenting evidence and facts from different
points of view. Moving forward, the research and findings from this volume
offer guidance and recommended courses of action for policymakers and
activists.

[16] Statements made by heads of government, key policymakers (including special representatives
assigned to address North Korean human rights policy such as South Korea's Minister of
Unification or the US State Department's Special Envoy for North Korean Human Rights)
and parliamentary leaders present an "official" discourse on North Korean human rights.
As an analysis of the US State Department's annual human rights report on North Korea
indicates, this language is often derived from reports produced by NGOs. Much of the
knowledge on North Korean human rights flows in a circular direction with NGOs and
government agencies citing the other's work, reifying an "official" narrative of NKHR.

[17] The case of Shin Donghyuk, who fabricated parts of his story which was then published by
Washington Post reporter Blaine Harden, is often cited here. See Chapter 9 in this volume by
Song, and also Song 2015.

Developing the Two-Pronged Strategy

We identified two different mechanisms for change in North Korean human rights: A legal/institutional approach which uses international law, sanctions, diplomacy, and other political measures to pressure and persuade the regime to comply with international human rights standards; and a more subversive, "hands-on" approach which attempts to work directly on the ground in North Korea by sending information into the country, or aiding defectors/refugees out of the country (and out of China, where they carry no legal standing).

Our research has shown that the two approaches have in fact complemented each other and should continue to be cultivated by state and nonstate actors in tandem. Critics may argue that a two-pronged approach sends mixed signals to North Korea. For instance, is the human rights advocacy network, and the international community more broadly, prodding the regime to adopt reforms to eventually enter the fold of international society? Or, on the contrary, does the advocacy network seek to undermine the regime, orchestrating its eventual demise? Human rights advocates, whether policymakers or grassroots activists, will remain divided on this point. However, given the slow and often nonlinear pace of human rights change, for the time being, both approaches, as top-down and bottom-up strategies, can be implemented without necessarily undermining the other's long-term goal. If the regime begins to implement serious rights reforms – for instance, adopting domestic measures to improve the political and economic well-being of its citizens – then it may behoove activists to curtail more subversive tactics to encourage the regime to move ahead with political reforms. Information warfare may, in fact, be less relevant at this stage if the regime relaxes barriers to information. Conversely, if the North Korean regime remains unwilling to address gross human rights violations, despite legal repercussions, then a continuation or upward dialing of the information campaign and other "bottom up" approaches to bring about change at the individual and societal levels becomes warranted.

Adapting Human Rights Language to Account for the North Korean Context

Despite the North Korean regime being a signatory to the relevant UN conventions, our research shows that when engaging with North Korean officials, the language of human rights has an inflammatory effect, often shutting down dialogue precisely when it is most important to open channels of communication. UN and other state-level policy officials may find it helpful to be mindful of this point, and to make efforts to adjust the discourse adopted in conversations with North Korean officials. This is not to say that human rights standards should be compromised, or even that the language of human rights should be jettisoned. Rather, as Goedde articulates at length, human rights are more likely to be diffused when they resonate with local norms and understandings.

This recommendation around localization and contextualization has implications for the two-pronged strategy described above. Information campaigns are more likely to be successful if they are able to adapt to the cultural context of the target population. This has certainly been the experience of North Korean defector radio stations. When radio broadcasts feature former North Koreans who are able to communicate in the appropriate vernacular and adopt a familiar style and cadence of talking via the medium of radio, they are more likely to resonate with local audiences. Likewise, information packets that frame human rights issues in relatable terms, or even draw directly on North Korea's own laws and regulations to highlight the rights already available to disenfranchised communities, are more likely to resonate with those populations that are at highest risk in terms of human rights protection.

Adding a Third-Pronged Engagement Strategy

The localization of human rights language also has relevance when considering the adoption of a more expansive interpretation of human rights. North Korea may be more responsive to the pursuit of rights objectives if it is addressed more fulsomely through a more diverse set of discourses. Several of our contributors took note of the marginalization of economic and social issues in North Korean human rights advocacy; discourse on North Korea has evolved in such a way that humanitarian concerns are often seen as distinct from human rights objectives. Moreover, groups and actors focused on meeting the humanitarian needs of North Koreans are often associated with the "engagement" camp, whose mission, to some human rights activists, is perceived as antithetical to the human rights agenda.[18] The gap between the human rights and the humanitarian assistance communities is also reinforced by discourse from within the engagement camp; some remain hostile to the human rights approach, assuming that its intent is to destroy rather than build up the North Korean state.

---

[18] Yeo 2014.

Important professional and logistical boundaries certainly exist which justify treating humanitarian assistance as distinct from human rights. In particular, the delivery of food aid or medical supplies requires some degree of access into North Korea and interaction with North Korean counterparts. Denouncing the regime for human rights abuses would not endear UN or NGO workers to DPRK officials, making it difficult (if not dangerous) for them to conduct humanitarian or development operations. This is a trade-off that is familiar to the humanitarian community, where actors continually seek to strike a balance that is compliant and ethical.[19]

The gap between human rights and humanitarian/development assistance communities has narrowed in recent years, in no small part due to the COI's explicit mention of "the right to food and related aspects of the right to life."[20] However, more work needs to be done to remind policymakers and the public that meeting the economic needs of North Koreans, even via people-to-people engagement initiatives, is equally valid and important in the fight for human rights as outlined in the COI.

Roberta Cohen, co-chair emeritus of the Committee for Human Rights in North Korea (HRNK), has presented one of the strongest cases for linking human rights and humanitarian approaches within a comprehensive human rights framework. For instance, she recommends that the UN apply its "Human Rights Up Front" (HRuF) framework to North Korea. As an initiative from the UN Secretary-General, HRuF calls on the UN to take measures which would elevate human rights across the entire UN system, including organizations and agencies which address problems related to development, peace, and security.[21] HRuF's application to the DPRK would mean that UN organizations, particularly humanitarian and development agencies working inside North Korea, would "agree to take steps to monitor and promote human rights."[22] The HRuF approach has also been endorsed by the COI and the UN Special Rapporteur on Human Rights in the DPRK.[23] As Cohen argues, by making reference to human rights in the UN's Strategic Framework for the DPRK, "humanitarian organizations would then have an entry point for

---

[19] See, for example, Schloms 2003.

[20] UN Human Rights Council 2014, 10; 16. The COI report stated that the DPRK must "[e]nsure that citizens can enjoy the right to food and other economic and social rights without discrimination ... promote agricultural, economic and financial policies based on democratic participation, good governance and non-discrimination; and legalize and support free market activities, internal and external trade and other independent economic conduct that provide citizens with a livelihood."

[21] For more on HRuF see the UN Secretary General webpage: www.un.org/sg/en/content/ban-ki -moon/human-rights-front-initiative.

[22] Cohen 2015, 16.   [23] UN General Assembly 2014, para. 24.

raising with North Korean authorities the human rights principles the DPRK itself accepted at the UN's Universal Periodic Review in 2014."[24] These principles might include nondiscrimination in food distribution, access to the most vulnerable population, and gender equality.[25] Other recommendations pairing political/civil with economic/social rights include granting access to healthcare in political prisons. In practice, this could mean providing aid workers access to administer tuberculosis vaccinations within the prison population.

Policy shifts as described above can help bridge the human rights and humanitarian divide. However, activists themselves must also begin to frame, or at least acknowledge, humanitarian engagement as a legitimate means of addressing human rights, including the right to food, shelter, and employment. While humanitarian groups may resist such linkages, in our discussions with NGO workers, we find that it is possible to build greenhouses, administer medication, or deliver food aid while still remaining fully cognizant of potential human rights abuses and quietly raising such concerns when opportune or warranted.[26] For the hardline human rights activists who remain critical of any form of engagement with North Koreans, two points are worth considering. First, if the goal of human rights is to free the oppressed from bondage (whether political or economic in nature, as the two are closely linked) and improve the lives of ordinary people, then many humanitarian and development engagement initiatives help achieve that goal, albeit on a small, localized scale.

Second, if bringing information about the outside world to North Koreans is a goal of human rights groups, then direct interaction between North Koreans and foreigners, particularly those from North America and Europe, may function as another channel of information. Americans involved in development, humanitarian, and/or business ventures in North Korea have commented on how their interactions with North Koreans have helped dispel existing myths about the "evil, ruthless American" which North Koreans are taught to believe the moment they begin school. Aside from perhaps defector surveys or anecdotal evidence, there is no way to measure if North Korean attitudes toward foreigners and foreign countries meaningfully shift (and if such shifts actually persist) over time as they repeatedly interact with the same foreign individuals for several years. But, if radio broadcasts are sufficient in prompting some North Koreans to question their government (or at least the message

---

[24] Cohen 2015, 16.   [25] Cohen 2015, 16.
[26] Yeo is a member of the National Committee on North Korea whose membership includes many individuals pursuing engagement-oriented operations in North Korea. See Yeo 2017.

their government has been sending them), it would not be unreasonable to argue that people-to-people engagement might leave a positive, lasting impact on North Koreans' attitudes toward the outside world (and perhaps conversely a negative view of their own leadership).[27] In short, engagement strategies should not be shunned, but instead embraced by the advocacy network.

Exercising Caution to Avoid Conflating Human Rights with the Security Narrative

At the time of writing (late 2017), the security situation on the Korean peninsula has shifted from bad to worse. North Korea not only tested its first intercontinental ballistic missile with the potential range to hit major US cities, it also conducted its sixth nuclear test in September 2017. In the meantime, Washington and Pyongyang have been caught in a precarious spiral of escalatory rhetoric as each North Korean missile and nuclear test is met with additional calls for tighter sanctions against North Korea and isolation of the regime, and, by extension, the North Korean people. Unfortunately, the attention on the nuclear problem has once again cast a shadow over human rights issues.

As argued in our volume, a dominant narrative of North Korean human rights, particularly in the United States, is one which securitizes the human rights issue. From a strategic messaging standpoint, it makes perfect sense for human rights advocates to frame (or "frame align," in academic parlance) their issue as a broader security problem.[28] First, North Korea's nuclear program and its abuse of human rights are linked, however loosely, in that both actions are a manifestation of the regime's totalitarian nature. The regime maintains its legitimacy in part by creating a highly militarized state, justified by a narrative of the constant threat of war from the United States. The development of nuclear weapons feeds into this narrative, with resources for the military prioritized over the rest of the population. At the same time, the regime demands complete loyalty and authority to the Kim family, restricting freedoms and civil liberties to perpetuate both internal and external security. In short, if human rights and security are two sides of the same coin, then one can easily frame human rights as a security problem, and vice versa.

Second, most governments see North Korea as primarily a security problem. As such, human rights activists can leverage ongoing nuclear concerns to draw

---

[27] See Kretchun and Kim 2012 for data on foreign media exposure and North Korea's positive impression of the outside world.

[28] "Security" here refers to international (or traditional) security rather than human security.

greater attention to the "evil" nature of the regime and its horrific abuses.[29] The first George W. Bush administration (2000–4) effectively portrayed North Korea in such terms: not only is North Korea a nuclear proliferator, but it has the audacity to starve the masses and throw its people into the gulags.[30] Conversely, human rights advocates remind those in the national security establishment that human rights (and related sanctions) serve as an additional pressure point to bend the regime toward compliance with international norms. The role played by human rights activist and blogger Joshua Stanton in the drafting of the 2016 North Korea Sanctions and Policy Enhancement Act[31] – which followed North Korea's fourth nuclear test and places sanctions on North Korean entities found to be, among other things, engaging in proliferation activities or complicit in human rights abuses – is one example of how this interaction has taken form in Washington DC.[32] In this way, the security community has used human rights as an additional point to justify isolation and sanctions against North Korea. It is no secret that the issue of North Korean human rights has attracted significant policy attention in part because of North Korea's status as a nuclear proliferating state.

There may be merit in linking human rights with security issues.[33] However, we recommend that human rights advocates in the policy and activist communities exercise caution in pushing the human rights–security nexus too far. One past consequence (particularly in the early 2000s) of the security–human rights nexus framing, as noted earlier, has been the dominance of conservative voices calling for regime change. While regime change may very well have been (and still remains) the end goal of some activists in the network, the association between North Korean human rights and regime change has had the unintended consequence of stigmatizing the issue as a conservative agenda. Although organizations dedicated to North Korean human rights, such as HRNK, have always approached the issue as a nonpartisan one, in practice activists from the political left, particularly in South Korea and the United States, remained peripheral in the advocacy network. This subsequently sidelined engagement voices early in the human rights movement – voices which should have been viewed as complementary to the larger objective of bringing human rights change. In turn, all forms of engagement, including people-to-people exchanges, were conflated with nuclear and diplomatic engagement.

---

[29] Conversely, the security community has used human rights as an additional point to justify isolation and sanctions against North Korea.
[30] Bush 2011, 422–3.
[31] North Korea Sanctions and Policy Enhancement Act of 2016, H.R. 757, 114th Congress.
[32] Joshua Stanton runs the blog *One Free Korea*. See freekorea.us.
[33] See Cha and Gallucci 2016.

Many in the human rights and humanitarian engagement camp today recognize the important work of other groups in facilitating change in North Korea, even if engagement groups still remain somewhat peripheral in the overarching North Korean human rights advocacy network. Nevertheless, the rapid advancement of North Korean nuclear and missile technology, and the dramatic escalation of tensions between the United States and North Korea, make it tempting to once again tag human rights onto security issues to prevent human rights from being completely subsumed by the nuclear problem. We do not deny the linkages between security and human rights, and to some extent they should be addressed in tandem. However, the international community now recognizes North Korean human rights as a grave issue, and the need to advance human rights in the DPRK can and should be articulated as an important issue in and of itself.

CONCLUSION

We simultaneously know so much and so little about North Korea. For two decades, human rights activists have collected, documented, and analyzed all available information to provide a persuasive outline of the restrictions and abuses experienced by everyday North Koreans. At the same time, we also know that ordinary North Koreans go about living their lives, experiencing human drama, tragedy, love, loss, and fulfillment as others do everywhere else in the world.[34]

Yet, despite all these insights, the humanity of North Koreans is often forgotten. When world leaders raise the possibility of military options against North Korea, where are the voices advocating the plight of the North Korean people? They are either missing or marginalized as the security of the Korean peninsula tends to be framed in military and not human terms.[35] It is in this context that the work of North Korean human rights activists takes on its highest importance. The chapters in this volume provide empirically grounded, contemporary accounts of the debates, ideas, strategies, successes, and failures of the North Korean human rights movement. We have tried to make sense of the wide array of actors working on this issue, by examining their discourses and interrogating the nature of their relationships. Like all activist arenas, the North Korean human rights movement is one where a range of actors – none of them particularly powerful – vie for recognition, funding, and influence. It is an imperfect human rights space, and one from which everyday North Korean citizens are absent, with advocates all claiming to best represent

---

[34]   Demick 2012.   [35]   Smith 2005.

them. Yet as imperfect as this space is, it is the only place where the plight of the local North Korean people is given any serious consideration at all. For these reasons, an understanding of the evolution of North Korean human rights advocacy and discourse will continue to remain relevant as we and the international community anticipate the day the North Korean people are able to realize the promise of human rights and determine their own future.

REFERENCES

Bae, Jong-Yun, and Chung-in Moon. 2014. South Korea's Engagement Policy. *Critical Asian Studies* 46 (1): 15–38.
Baek, Jieun. 2016. *North Korea's Hidden Revolution: How the Information Underground Is Transforming a Closed Society.* New Haven & London: Yale University Press.
Bush, George W. 2011. *Decision Points.* New York: Crown.
Cha, Victor, and Robert L. Galluci. 2016. *Toward a New Policy and Strategy for North Korea.* Dallas: George W. Bush Institute
Cohen, Roberta. 2015. Human Rights and Humanitarian Planning for Crisis in North Korea. *International Journal of Korean Studies* 29 (2): 1–25.
Demick, Barbara. 2012. *Nothing to Envy: Love, Life and Death in North Korea.* Sydney: Fourth Estate.
Feffer, John. 2004. The Forgotten Lessons of Helsinki: Human Rights and US–North Korean Relations. *World Policy Journal* 21 (3): 31–9.
Haggard, Stephan 2014. Cohen, Lee and Hong on Human Rights in North Korea. *North Korea Witness to Transformation blog.* January 29. piie.com/blogs/north-korea-witness-transformation/cohen-lee-and-hong-human-rights-north-korea.
Hong, Christine. 2013. The Mirror of North Korean Human Rights. *Critical Asian Studies* 45 (4): 561–92.
Keukeleire, Stephan, and Jennifer MacNaughtan. 2008. *The Foreign Policy of the European Union.* New York: Palgrave Macmillan.
Kretchun, Nat, and Jane Kim. 2012. *A Quiet Opening: North Koreans in a Changing Media Environment.* Washington DC: InterMedia.
Lankov, Andrei. 2013. *The Real North Korea: Life and Politics in the Failed Stalinist Utopia.* New York: Oxford University Press.
Liem, Paul. 2014. Peace as a North Korean Human Right. *Critical Asian Studies* 46 (1): 113–26.
Moon, Katherine. 2008. Beyond Demonization: A New Strategy for Human Rights in North Korea. *Current History* 107: 263–8.
Moon, Kyungyon. 2014. South Korean Civil Society Organizations, Human Rights Norms, and North Korea. *Critical Asian Studies* 46 (1): 65–89.
Schloms, Michael. 2003. The European NGO Experience in North Korea. In *Paved with Good Intentions: The NGO Experience in North Korea,* edited by Scott Snyder and L. Gordon Flake. Westport: Praeger.
Shin, Sanghyuk S., and Ricky Y. Choi. 2013. Misdiagnosis and Misrepresentations: Application of the Right-to-Health Framework in North Korea. *Critical Asian Studies* 45 (4): 593–614.

Smith, Hazel. 2005. *Hungry for Peace: International Security, Humanitarian Assistance, and Social Change in North Korea*. Washington DC: United States Institute of Peace.

Smith, Hazel. 2014. Crimes Against Humanity? *Critical Asian Studies* 46 (1): 127–143.

Song, Jay. 2015. Twenty Years' Evolution of North Korean Migration, 1994–2014: A Human Security Perspective. *Asia & the Pacific Policy Studies* 2 (2): 399–415.

UN General Assembly. 2014. Report of the UN Special Rapporteur on Human Rights in the DPRK. A/69/33701. October 24.

UN Human Rights Council. 2014. *Report of the Commission of Inquiry on Human Rights in the Democratic People's Republic of Korea*. A/HRC/25/63. February 7.

Yeo, Andrew. 2014. Alleviating Misery: The Politics of North Korean Human Rights in US Foreign Policy. *North Korean Review* 10 (2): 71–87.

Yeo, Andrew. 2017. Evaluating the Scope of People-to-People Engagement in North Korea, 1995–2012. *Asian Perspective* 41 (2): 309–39.

Index

abduction escapees. *See dappokusha*
abductions activism, Japan and
  for abducted Japanese citizens, 88, 91–3
    AFVKN, 95
    COMJAN, 95–96, 256
    NARKN, 95
  for abducted South Koreans, 89
  COI and, 103–6
    NGOs' roles in, 105
  contextual scope of, 85–7, 88–92
  dappokusha and, 87, 91
  framing of, 102–3, 276
  by Japanese Koreans, 98–99
  Kim Jong Il role in, 87, 88
  media coverage of, 88–9
  NGOs
    COI and, 105
    in North Korea-related networks, 95–97,
      98, 94
  under NKAHRA
    activist networks under, 99–103
    DPJ role in, 99–101
  North Korean defectors and, 90–1, 98–99
  North Korea-related networks, 93–99
    cleavages within, 97–98
    Japanese organizations, 95, 96–97
    through NGOs, 95–97, 98, 94
  public concern over, among Japanese
    citizens, 86, 88–9
  as victim-centered, 95
Abe Shinzō, 104
Abrams, Elliot, 71
access to information. *See* information access
accountability, in human rights, 105, 144–8, 172
Activists Beyond Borders (Keck and Sikkink),
  5, 62

advocacy. *See also* human rights advocacy
  networks; transnational advocacy
  networks
  domestic, 3–8
  of human rights, accountability in, 105,
    144–8
AFVKN. *See* Association of Families
  Kidnapped by North Korea
Ahn Myung Chol, 218
AI. *See* Amnesty International
All Party Parliamentary Group (APPG),
  110, 193
altruism-driven networks, 258–9
  for information access, 257
Amnesty International (AI), 16, 110, 133.
  See also Lameda, Ali
  ICNK and, 116
An Myong Hun, 235
analytics methods. *See* methodology
APPG. *See* All Party Parliamentary Group
The Aquariums of Pyongyang (Kang Chol
  Hwan), 76, 252
Armstrong, Oscar, 72–3
art production, collaborative networks in,
  32–3
Association of Families Kidnapped by North
  Korea (AFVKN), 95
authoritarianism, transnational legal
  mobilization under, 156
"axis-of-evil," 77

Biden, Joe, 68
Biserko, Sonja, 158
boomerang model, xxi–xxii, 5–6, 19–20, 21,
  242, 268
Brownback, Sam, 68